CRM at the Speed of Light:
Capturing and Keeping Customers in Internet Real Time, Second Edition

Paul Greenberg

Tata McGraw-Hill Publishing Company Limited
NEW DELHI

McGraw-Hill Offices

New Delhi New York St Louis San Francisco Auckland Bogotá Caracas
Kuala Lumpur Lisbon London Madrid Mexico City Milan Montreal
San Juan Santiago Singapore Sydney Tokyo Toronto

Tata McGraw-Hill

CRM .at the Speed of Light: Capturing and Keeping Customers in Internet Real Time, Second Edition

Tata McGraw-Hill Edition 2003

RZXYCRXDRQZBX

Reprinted in India by arrangement with The McGraw-Hill Companies Inc., New York

Sales territories: India, Nepal, Bangladesh, Sri Lanka and Bhutan

ISBN 0-07-053250-8

Published by Tata McGraw-Hill Publishing Company Limited, 7 West Patel Nagar, New Delhi 110 008, and printed at Sai Printo Pack Pvt. Ltd., Delhi 110 020

I never change the dedications to my books
because I never change the ones I love the most.

To my magnificent, loving parents, Chet and Helen Greenberg,
who I think about every day and who just make me thankful for my life.
Thank you, Mom and Dad.

To my wonderful brother, Bob Greenberg,
who has always inspired me to think outside the box and be better,
and to his family: his fantastic wife, Freyda, anyone's role model,
and my extraordinary niece Sara, who is an awesome young person.

And finally, to the one I set my life's clock by every day,
my eternal love and anchor, my wife Yvonne.

I use superlatives because they are superlative.

Contents

Foreword

There is no doubt now that the "relationship revolution" spawned by the rise of interactivity and computer technology is for real. The revolution has come of age, to the point where companies in every industry around the world are spending billions of dollars annually on new technologies and services. They have two goals in mind: building competitive advantage and maximizing the business benefits of customer relationships.

There's also no doubt that a large percentage (analysts and others report 50 to 80 percent) of programs aimed at building business through customer relationships fails. So the top priority at every enterprise contemplating the purchase of CRM software, the adoption of customer-based strategies, or competitive advantage based on building the value of the customer base is to understand why some initiatives fail to deliver ROI and others are successful. And how to be in the successful category.

The real questions to be answered, then, are:

▸ What do we need to do to build our business by growing the value of our customer base? What new capabilities and tools do we need to make that happen?

▸ How can we be sure our company will get our money's worth on what we're spending to build customer relationships and equity?

▸ How can I measure how much these benefits are really worth in order to make better managerial decisions and demonstrate sound business judgment?

It isn't possible to measure the return on investment in CRM applications and strategies the same way other types of investment spending are evaluated. The overall goal of any relationship-oriented strategy is to increase the overall value of the customer base—the sum total of customer lifetime values—but most firms can't yet estimate lifetime values in any systematic way. Instead, most measure proxy variables and "interim" events, such as purchase frequency, raw revenue, increases in cross-selling and up-selling, or improvements in customer retention or satisfaction. They measure click-throughs, complaints and inquiries, and the estimated or the obvious cost reductions that come from streamlining business processes necessary to treat different customers differently.

Even with growing sophistication in Lifetime Value modeling, there simply is no *easy* way to measure the ROI on customer-based business initiatives, despite the enormous funds companies are investing in these initiatives today. ROI is one of the single biggest issues we encounter with our consulting clients—across industries and around the world— and it is almost always one of the first questions asked of us at our speaking engagements all over the globe:

"How do we make the business case internally for adopting CRM strategies?"

"How should we measure the ROI on these strategies?"

"How do we make sure we succeed where others have failed?"

Our goal is to work with clients and business decision makers on how to establish the right vision, the best strategies for that vision, and how to incorporate the necessary cultural, organizational, and metrics changes to get the maximum return on the investment made in customer relationships. What Paul Greenberg does here in *CRM at the Speed of Light* (Second Edition) is to help companies know where to turn for help as they decide what to do. He doesn't pull any punches (he even made *us* wince a few times), but his goal is not to flatter. It's to provide a handbook of what to do to build the necessary capabilities, and how to choose the partners that will lead to successful customer-based ROI.

DON PEPPERS AND MARTHA ROGERS, PH.D.

February 2002

Acknowledgments

This is the fun part of the book because I get to thank people who I either love or care about or am grateful to. They also like seeing their names in a book. So this is a classic win-win situation. Cool.

It is strange who you think about during the time you write a book. You think about those who are directly helping you with the book through participation in some way or by simply being helpful and around. You also think about those who love you and who may have been involved directly or may have been a warm and fuzzy thought that helped you through writer's block or just through a rough patch of some sort. All of them are critical to you in some way, especially if you are of the mushy sort, like me. With that said, I'm going to start with those I love and thank them. This is not going to be exhaustive because I hate awards shows. I will start with the best of all—those I care about and love universally and forever.

That means my permanent, ongoing thanks and love to my mom, Helen Greenberg, my dad, Chet Greenberg, my brother, Bob Greenberg, my sister-in-law, Freyda Greenberg, my niece, Sara Greenberg, and to the one human being on this planet and in this universe I can't live without: my wife, Yvonne. I've been with her for more than 20 years of marriage and three years of prior courtship and my love keeps growing and evolving. I can't imagine a day without her.

I also have a special friend who has been around me for 32 years who I want to acknowledge. She is always with me when I write or, for that matter, when I walk or breathe. She didn't deal directly with the book. She deals directly with me, which is a much preferred state. She knew me when and she knows me now, and that is a testament to why I want to say how much I care about her. She is Liz Giese, a part of my life since we were both in college so many years ago. I mean, I was in college so many years ago. She was there just a couple of years ago, I swear. She has a heart of gold that is 24-karat and is my spiritual sister, if not by blood.

Now for those who participated in the book either through direct input or support.

First, from my company, Live Wire, I want to say thanks to some wonderful colleagues and friends, Nachi and Dipu Junankar. Nachi is the president of the company and has always backed me to the hilt as a businessman and friend. Dipu is his beloved and for good reason. She is just a great person and friend to me. To my colleagues, Pat Moore, Chris Miller, Oleg Ivanov, and Cheryl DesRoches, I say thanks for being there, my very dear friends.

Other friends I can't forget:

Scott Fletcher: This guy is one of the good ones. He's been a friend and collaborator for five years, and every moment of friendship and business advice has been invaluable and fun.

Paul McCauley: Even though I met him through the world of CRM, he is a balm to the spirit and a salve to the soul. He thinks outside the box, which is refreshing in a world that doesn't usually like that.

I'd also like to say thanks to the many people at the vendor companies and the service providers who worked diligently to set up interviews, provide me with demonstrations of their products, and get me the literature I needed and the analysts' reports, among other things. Most of them are just simply nice people to work with. They are a vast army. Space precludes me from individually thanking, but thanks to all of you.

There are several I would like to mention especially for the work they did that went beyond the company.

First, I'd like to single out a few of them. Special mention to:

Bruce Culbert: KPMG Consulting is very lucky to have this man running their CRM practice. His insights, compassion, and writing ability simply stand out. He is someone I'm glad I've gotten to know.

Scott McIntyre: Another KPMGer who handles their public sector. A good man, an evangelist for the cause, and a scholar and lover of books. We think alike. What a future (and present) this guy has!

The folks at SAS: Angela Lipscomb, Randy Betancourt, and Jeff LeSueur. They are amazing people. I know now why SAS does as well as it does. These folks are the reasons. They stood out with their timely cooperation and just utter decency.

Michael Chuchmuch: This man is an enthusiast par excellence and a creative and innovative thinker at Unisys. I met him via email and it just keeps going. His synapses crackle with energy.

Paul Steep: He does the analysis of Pivotal in this book. Read it. He is smart. An insightful analyst and good person. Yorkton Securities is lucky to have him.

Martha Rogers: She is a special person. Down to earth and brilliant; a kind, good person who also happens to know just about all there is to know on the customer experience. An inspiration to me.

Bob Thompson: Aside from being the chieftain at PRM, he is a great guy and a real pleasure to work with. One of the good ones.

Roger Siboni, CEO, E.piphany, and Brooke Savage, CEO, Pragmatech: For taking time out of their obviously busy lives to add something to this edition of this book. To those who did it in the first edition, too.

Now to the rest:

Thanks also to Don Peppers, Peppers & Rogers, Robb Eklund (PeopleSoft), Mickey Brazeal, Jamie Murphy, Laura King (PeopleSoft), Steve Olyha (CSC), Steve Pratt (Deloitte Consulting), Dick Fredrickson (Unisys), Peggy Kennelly (IBM Global Services), Juan Dominguez (IBM Global Services), Michael Park (SAP), Jim Dever (SAP), Jeff Pulver (E.piphany), Stacey McCarthy (Blanc & Otus for E.piphany), Bud Michael (KANA), Vicki Amon-Higa (KANA), Beth Likens (Onyx), Joe Greenspan (SalesLogix), Kevin Myers (SalesLogix), Donna Roveto (Salesnet), Diane Robinson (Unica), John Gill (ChannelWave), Laurent Philonenko (Genesys), Steve Ewaldz (Genesys), Gerhard Friedrich (RWD), Deborah Leff (Pragmatech), and finally to a very special friend and colleague, Kerry Glance of Searchcrm.com. They all helped put together what I needed to make this edition work. If I've inadvertently left anyone out whom I should have thanked, I'm sorry, and thank you.

Now on to Roger Stewart, Tana Diminyatz, Laurie Stewart, Lunaea Weatherstone, Sachi Guzman, and Jeff Wilson. They are also known as The McGraw-Hill Gang—they fit the profile. They are the ones who kick me around, tell me what to do and—when I step out of line—where to go. I couldn't be associated with better people. Roger has been my acquiring editor for both editions and also a friend and confidant. What confidence I have in my publisher comes from my confidence and trust in Roger. Tana was my AC (that stands for acquisitions coordinator, in publishing lingo) and she is a delight—an excellent coordinator with amazing follow-through and a scintillating personality. A winner and true professional. Laurie was my project manager and Lunaea was my copyeditor for both editions. My respect for them knows little boundary. They make me literate and readable. They leave my multiple bad jokes on the cutting room floor. They are editors extraordinaire and I count on them. I've been around a while in publishing now, and they are the best I've ever worked with or run across. Thank you.

Introduction

Life sure is a funny thing. Not ha-ha funny, but odd. When I wrote the first edition of this book about 18 months ago, CRM was an immature system with technology that was creating a panacea buzz around the corporate world. It would solve IT problems; it would solve revenue problems; it would solve personal problems (solved a couple of mine actually); it would solve everything that ailed a company, a salesperson, or a customer.

It didn't.

Not only didn't it, but by the time the book was off and selling (mid-2001), CRM was being subjected to the same sniping assault that ERP had been hit with in 1999, even though revenues continued. Word on the street was there was no immediate ROI, no way of determining what the ROI metrics were, a 55 to 75 percent failure rate, and low customer satisfaction with the vendors. It was so expensive that no one could afford an enterprise-wide implementation. After all, they had run out of money doing that with ERP.

The recession was declared to have started in March 2001, and what began to matter was not CRM particularly, but instead just surviving in business. But CRM was seen as a possible aid to that survival. The old adage "you have to spend money to make money," was still a consideration, if not a fact. Then September 11 hit, and it all didn't matter. And for a while this meant *all*.

But, after Thanksgiving, it started mattering again, though only in word and not in deed. The economy wasn't getting better. Money wasn't being spent, just hoarded, if it existed. People were interested, but they were just waiting until the New Year—mostly to purge themselves of the real fears, paranoia, feelings of despair, and any other layers of emotional trauma that we all felt because of September 11 and the down economy.

But New Year's Day, January 2002, could have almost been called New Life's Day, because a renewed sense of hope and promise began to generally permeate the population. Economic indicators began to rise, the stock market began a roller coaster that ultimately was up, and companies began spending money again. The differences? Caution, but still this sort of feeling that things would be okay even with the world irretrievably changed. Layoffs were continuing, there were still some bad signs, but 2001 was *over*! 2002 was a refreshing of the human spirit. It wasn't perfect, but it sure was better than 2001.

What the heck does this all mean to a CRM book? Well, it means CRM "things" and personal "things." Though I'm human, I'm not going to bother you with the personal too much. But the CRM…

CRM began mattering a good deal again in 2002. But not the CRM we knew and picked on. A new CRM, a dramatically slimmed-down version of the original. At least, in the eyes of the customers, it was that. What was that buff CRM version?

This was a CRM that was much more mature. It lost its swagger, its acne, and much of the baby fat. It was apparently pretty functional. ROI measurements had at least become a possibility. Customer Lifetime Value was also a value of CRM that mattered to the potential user. While enterprise-level CRM implementations were on the outs, curing the pain was in. That meant point solutions to solve problems became something that companies were willing to consider.

The middle of 2001 saw the edges of another change that was of little interest to a user, but very significant to the people who stared at the guts of CRM. That would be pure Internet architectures. All of a sudden the vendors were pushing their purity hard. These Internet architectures had been around in some fashion since 1999, but 2001 was their year to emerge. Something like a compressed-time version of Carlos Santana's re-emergence in 2000. He had been around 30 years before he was recognized again; it took CRM Internet architecture two years.

The landscape had changed dramatically, too. Siebel was still dominant, but losing some market share to PeopleSoft, SAP (who had burst on the scene as a major player in late 2001), and Oracle, despite its own troubles. Smaller players went out of business or were acquired by the larger vendors, leaving fewer boutique applications and less confusing choices. A CRM add-ons market began to evolve. ASPs lost their sex appeal and aged pretty poorly on the whole.

This was a good thing for everyone, because while the choices were fewer, it still could hardly be called a monopoly of anyone. Buffoonery disguised as software left the room. Elvis the King stayed.

Additionally, even with the renewed interest in CRM, there remained a glacé of suspicion. While CRM was in its honeymoon stages, everyone who ever talked to a customer declared themselves a CRM god. Most of them had as much credibility as a WWF wrestler. There were thousands of marketers jumping on a bandwagon that had three great tires and a bad wheel. Some of these dubious sorts still exist. But now, with the market maturing, there are also some actual CRM gurus who are doing well and rightfully so.

Corporate budgetary concerns remain strong in mid-2002, though things are certainly better than 2001. CRM is still expensive and still a little cloudy on its benefits, but when it works, it works great and remains worth the risk of investment. One reason for this cautious optimism on my part is that we've had another year of experience with it since the first book came out, and that year was good for identifying lots of things that weren't clear before. For example, we do have some metrics and ROI that we can identify. The Balanced Scorecard is increasingly integral to CRM. Customer Lifetime Value (CLV) is now a well-accepted part of CRM thinking and strategies. Analytic CRM has matured and has even been embedded in so-called operational CRM, dating the old "operational-collaborative-analytic" definition of CRM a bit.

Returns have been sighted. There are hundreds of case studies that prove various CRM value. There are identifiable weaknesses as opposed to dramatically emotional but vague fears about CRM. It's the difference between a creepy feeling of an unknown presence in the dark and a known evil. If the evil is known, it can be erased. But that creepy presence is scary because you can't do anything to it and you don't know what it can do to you. For example, we now know that the major reason for CRM failures (not the only one, though) is users don't use it, so there are lots of evangelists (me among them) who are pushing for intimate user involvement in the entire CRM selection process. "Build it and they will come" isn't true in the CRM universe. Build it, show them why the building is good for them, and then they will come.

Now, the Book...

Much to my great satisfaction, the first edition of this book has done remarkably well. It's been published in five languages (English, Portuguese, Japanese, Chinese, and Korean) and is due in Italian later in 2002. It has been read in at least 23 countries that I can identify through emails I've received from readers. It is used in courses on CRM all over the world. The ASEAN edition of *CIO* magazine placed it among the twelve "Most Influential Business Books you will ever read...contain the seeds of classical business wisdom..." The first edition of this book has sold extremely well and I'm not only gratified, but I realize that this makes my update for this book imperative.

Why? Things simply have changed too much not to update it. I've also refined my knowledge of CRM a lot and have solicited lots of suggestions from the readers of the book that I realized I needed to incorporate.

Because of that, I've added a number of new chapters to the book— a chapter on the small and midsized business market, a chapter on CRM strategy, a chapter on the key individual service providers, and so on. I've also updated and upgraded about 260 or so of the 360 pages of the first edition, with new information, changing trends, new products, new and old companies, shifted concepts, and much more. This is another book entirely—about 100 pages longer and very much rewritten. The tone is less tentative and a bit more opinionated, but always backed up by well-researched knowledge. There are areas I cover that no other book on CRM takes on.

Please note, even in the sections on the specific vendors and service providers, there is important general instructive material that is valuable. Knowing the different methodologies, practices, and cultures of the companies should give you a feel for the way that any company or culture works and the variations on those themes.

I hope that you'll also note the wonderful foreword by Martha Rogers and Don Peppers to this second edition. I'm a believer in the one-to-one business relationships that they have been the strongest proponent of for a decade. Ordinarily I don't support any system that isn't personalized, so to speak. But that is the beauty of their practice. It is personalized but still universal. Their foreword to this book is an honor.

I've done something a little different with this edition. Each chapter on each subtopic in CRM, such as partner relationship management or analytics, highlights one firm in a lot of detail. This is the company I think represents the best of its class and also is representative of a full-function version of the subset. The chapters where that approach doesn't apply are pretty obvious. The purpose of the highlighting is to show readers how these applications are put together and what they cover. Are they the right ones for your company? That depends. You may be comfortable with something else.

There's one other thing. An appendix that listed noteworthy websites, academic institutions, and magazines had to be cut from the book due to space reasons. However, if you'd like a copy of the appendix in Adobe Acrobat PDF format free of charge, email me at the address that follows.

I think this edition, thanks to the input of the readers of the first edition, covers pretty much what the story is with CRM. The book, I trust, is going to be useful to you when you read it. Once again, let me know if and where I fall down. Don't be afraid to rip into me. I can handle it. I'm tough, but I can always be better.

So here's the new take, folks. Once again, my email and cellphone. Note the changes to both. Even they've changed over the year. What hasn't changed is my strong support of CRM and the New York Yankees. Email me at: paul-greenberg3@comcast.net or pgreenberg@livewire.net. Phone me at (757) 342-6769. Remember the rules: CRM talk or Yankees talk. Either one is just fine. So is anything else.

1

What Is CRM, Really?

Most of the readers of this book, while perhaps not all that familiar with Customer Relationship Management (CRM), are familiar with the Frank Capra classic Christmas movie, *It's a Wonderful Life*. It is the story of George Bailey, played by Jimmy Stewart, a banker's son who takes over the family Building and Loan business, even though he has a restless soul and wants to see the world. What is commonly remembered about the movie is the timeless terrific theme that we all make an important difference as individuals. However, there is a CRM sub-theme that I'm sure Frank Capra wasn't particularly thinking about when he made the movie. It not only reflects the American social consciousness of the 1930s and 1940s, but it is also an important reflection of precisely what the twenty-first century economy is going through.

If you remember, Henry F. Potter (played by Lionel Barrymore and no relation to Harry) was the town's miserly, nasty, always-dressed-in-black banker. His life's mission was to make money for his bank and to squeeze that money from the townspeople whom he saw as "rabble." As a result of his success, he was "the richest man in town." George Bailey, as the head of Bailey Building and Loan, on the other hand, saw that because the townspeople were his customers, his responsibility was to serve them with the best possible personal customer service. Mr. Potter followed the strict rules of the bank. If the rabble wanted to borrow money, they did it on the bank's terms or not at all. George Bailey lent the hardworking townspeople the money at reasonable, flexible rates during what seemed to be the depression years because that's the service they needed. He was a participant in their lives, even though, in the strictest sense, they were his customers. But they were also his neighbors. He gave personalized service to each of the townspeople and made it a point to actually know them. If he were not there, the townspeople would be forced to deal with the bank-centric Mr. Potter, who engendered a cynical customer versus company business policy due to the heartlessness of the company. It was no coincidence that when George Bailey was removed from the equation in the more famous sequences of the movie, the town's name went from Bedford Falls to Pottersville and became a heartless, cold, adversarial place. The final scene of the movie shows the townspeople coming to George Bailey's rescue by providing him with money to restore missing funds that Mr. Potter falsely accused him of stealing, with each of the donors citing a time when George Bailey had rescued them from some difficulty. Heartwarming, indeed.

Putting it simply, who would you want to bank with—George Bailey or Henry F. Potter?

Let's fast-forward to the twenty-first century. There is a commercial on television for lendingtree.com that shows a couple sitting at a table with a banker. The banker says something to the effect of "Are you interested?" The couple says, "Can't you lower the rates a little?" The banker responds, somewhat insistently, "This is a good package." The couple, unexpectedly, laughs and says, "Sorry to have taken up your time. Next!" Another banker comes in and sits down as a voiceover explains how bankers will bid for the privilege of lending you money at lendingtree.com. The customer controls the interaction between the borrower and the lender, something entirely new to traditional commercial lending hierarchies. Customer-focused, customer-controlled interactivity via the Web.

But Customer Relationship Management (CRM) seems to be a relative newcomer that appeared on the business radar no more than perhaps four years ago, as enterprise resource planning (ERP) began its 1998 spin out of control. Even though CRM had been around arguably since the 1980s, the buzz for it began seriously in 1999. CRM then begat electronic Customer Relationship Management (eCRM), which popped out as something of importance from the Web-enabled egg of its CRM mother in late 1999. By 2001, eCRM had already grown up and was nearly indistinguishable from mother CRM. In fact, there was no longer any reason for the difference in designation as web-based (as opposed to web-enabled) CRM started showing up for the dance, looking better and even more elegant than anyone else.

How is all of this any different from the "George Bailey principle" of customer loyalty and retention? Or is it any different?

What Is a Customer?

While retaining customer loyalty has been a sales principle since the beginning of time (even Adam needed to retain Eve's loyalty despite immense pressure from his competitor, the Snake), CRM is actually a tremendous step forward in creating a system that can provide a means for retaining individual loyalty in a world of nearly 6 billion souls. In order to understand CRM, we have to look at the changing nature of the customer, because customers aren't what they used to be.

While "the customer is king" has been a mantra since the 1940s, its content has changed fundamentally over the past decade. It's interesting to begin with what is defined as a customer.

When I worked with IBM back in the early 1990s, I remember being a bit puzzled by a designation their departments used with each other. When department 1 did work for department 2, it charged department 2 fees and expenses. Department 1 staff members specifically referred to this process as charging internal "customers." At the time, I was surprised, thinking, "How could customers be employees of the same company even if they work for different departments? Aren't they fellow employees, friends, and such?" Nope. They were (and are) customers—even if they are fellow employees and friends. It seems to be nitpicking and perhaps just for bookkeeping, but they are customers. Why? Because you are providing a service to them for a fee of some sort. Additionally, a department has the right to get bids on the services from both internal departments and outside consulting firms. You could be competing within and without!

This led me to investigate what exactly the concept of "the customer" was becoming. At that time, I distinguished between what is now called the business-to-consumer (B2C) "customer" and the business-to-business (B2B) "client." Department stores had customers. IBM had clients. Or so I thought.

After a substantial number of discussions with my colleagues and friends who were also in the business world, I came to the conclusion that the distinction between traditional customers (people who were sold your products outside the realm of the store) and internal customers (a department or division or team or employee) was becoming murky. In fact, all of them were customers that were being sold to. IBM even had the bookkeeping to deal with it. It may have been going on for years. I didn't know. I just knew that my definition of customer had changed.

But even over the past couple of years, the definition of the customer has evolved from my murky past analysis as the CRM market has matured. For example, it is now *de rigueur* to define the customer as (1) your paying client, (2) your employee, (3) your supplier/vendor, and (4) your partner. What this means is that the historic customer (the individual or group that paid you for your goods and services) has become the contemporary customer (the individual or group with whom you exchange value). This makes the way that customers are handled far more complex—as if the world weren't complex enough.

You're a company. You have paying clients. They give you money. You give them products and/or services. That's Customer #1. You have employees. You give them a paycheck and benefits and bonuses and they give you (hopefully) productive work in return. That's Customer #2. You have suppliers. They give you products and/or services. You give them money. (Sigh.) Customer #3. You have channel partners. They give you leads, sales, added value services. You give them the same and/or percentages of a sale they help make. Customer #4. If we discover life on other planets or strike up relationships with the animal kingdom, there may be a Customer #5, but for now these four will suffice. *The individual or group with whom you exchange value.* Voilá— the contemporary customer.

How Do We Define CRM? Let Me Count the Ways...

A decade later, I began to write this book with the idea that it would be strictly about eCRM, which in my naïve way, I thought was *very* different from CRM. It wasn't and isn't. I plugged into the debates that are constantly being fought over what exactly CRM is. There is a standard industry rote response that says what it isn't: it isn't a technology. As you will see, that's true, but not strictly. I also heard that it was a "customer-facing" system. That it is a strategy and/or a set of business processes. A methodology. It is all of the above or whichever you choose. The Knowledge Capital Group defines CRM as a subset of something they call enterprise relationship management (ERM), which involves customers, suppliers, partners, and employees. See all the above customer definitions. They've developed a number of (useful) new terms such as "sphere of expertise" and "channels of execution" to help define it. Ultimately though, while there is a growing class of applications that would truly fit the ERM definition, even their definition still fits the superset: CRM.

In 2002, the buzz remains loud in this debate, though the market has matured. It occurred to me that what better way to try to define CRM than to get some of the significant names in the industry to tell me. So that's what you are going to see in this chapter. These are the people in the CRM industry who make it the blockbuster industry it is.

The Heavyweights Define CRM

These folks (listed below in alphabetical order) were chosen because of their influence in the CRM world and because they represent a variety of CRM opinions that matter in the information technology world. They include:

- ▶ The CEO of a company that owns a CRM product that handles large enterprise activity
- ▶ The president of a company who has extraordinary expertise in the midmarket realm of CRM
- ▶ The CEO of a company that has a portal-based CRM product
- ▶ The president of a company that specializes in partner relationship management (PRM) consulting
- ▶ The CEO of a company that has a pioneer web-based CRM product
- ▶ The president of a company that produces a product providing a value-added part to the CRM puzzle
- ▶ The president of a company that specializes in CRM management consulting

These people characterize a wide variety of industry leaders. The definitions of CRM that follow each biography of the individual are written in their own words. Check them out—they're good.

Craig Conway, President and CEO, PeopleSoft, Inc.

Craig Conway joined PeopleSoft in 1999 as president and chief operating officer, and was promoted to chief executive officer in September 1999. He oversees all PeopleSoft business operations, including sales, marketing, professional service, customer support, development, finance, and administration.

Mr. Conway was president and chief executive for OneTouch Systems, a leader in the field of interactive broadcast networks. Previously, he served as president and chief executive for TGV Software, Inc., an early developer of IP network protocols and applications for corporate intranets and the Internet. Mr. Conway also spent eight years at Oracle Corporation as executive vice-president in a variety of roles, including marketing, sales, and operations.

DEFINITION

Every time a customer approaches your business, they arrive with an expectation. It may be a service need or a new product interest, but in every case, they have an expectation that accompanies their interest in your business. What happens next will form an experience that shapes their behavior. A good experience may increase their loyalty and tendency to purchase again. A poor experience may transfer their business to your competitor. The ability to recognize this process and to actively manage it forms the basis for Customer Relationship Management, or CRM.

The ability to ensure that the enterprise will act with unity of purpose to ensure experiences that exceed every expectation is a monumental task. Customers interacting with employees, employees collaborating with suppliers—every interaction is an opportunity to manage a relationship. Only recently has technology advanced to support interactions with any role through any channel, to any touch point across the extended enterprise. Building this requires applications that can seamlessly support business processes as they span the enterprise, deliver information, empowerment, and insight to all individuals, wherever they are, and continually monitor, measure, and improve the process.

We are on the verge of the most significant transformation in the business landscape since mainframe applications migrated to the desktop a decade ago. The Internet blends computing and communications into a platform-independent, globally accessible, and universally usable medium. To date, the Internet's impact on business has been substantial, creating new channels for commerce, driving new market models, and enabling collaborative business-to-supplier relationships. This change is only the tip of the iceberg. The most significant benefit for business will be leveraging the Internet to support the very fabric of the enterprise. Delivering pure Internet applications directly to browsers will empower a global workforce to know, to do, to measure, and to improve their jobs in support of a common, customer-oriented strategy. This is the promise of CRM.

We experience CRM ourselves every day. Dining at a favorite restaurant or taking your car in for service is an interaction with a business that leaves you with an experience. If you recall pleasant or unpleasant memories of these experiences, think about how those feelings affect your propensity to return to those businesses again. Have you enjoyed special treatment as a regular customer at some establishments? Have you complained about poor service and vowed never to go back? Your experiences shape your buying patterns, significantly influencing your lifetime value as a customer.

Loyal, repeat customers can form a significant competitive advantage for a business in many ways. Truly loyal customers form a market share base that is unassailable to the competition. The cost of sales for existing customers is far less than the cost of generating market awareness, acquiring new customers, and establishing a business relationship with them. None of this should be particularly surprising. Savvy business managers have always catered to their most valued customers because they understand the importance it holds for their business.

The issue is not whether CRM is important for business, but how best to apply it. CRM can be a personal undertaking of small business owners and merchants who do a majority of their trade face to face, and on a scale permitting them to know and understand their customers, their business, and their partners personally. Good CRM becomes much more challenging to maintain as business scales up, and as technological and behavioral trends put distance and anonymity between the business manager and their customers.

As businesses scale up, it becomes impossible for one person to know and personally manage relationships with all of the business's valued customers. Initially, large enterprises attempted to address this by implementing distribution channels and an organizational hierarchy modeled after the military chain of command. By such a structured approach, business managers were still able to personally manage the few relationships for which they were directly responsible. At every level of the organization, people were able to personally optimize the business process and priorities for their "customers," and consistency was implemented via the top-down organizational structure.

Traditional businesses are now moving toward more direct interaction with their end consumers, and Internet-based businesses are experiencing growth rates that were unimaginable just a few years ago. These trends make it impossible for individuals to personally and consistently manage all business relationships across the enterprise. In addition, they are unlikely to conduct their interactions in alignment with an overall enterprise strategy. The sheer one-to-many employee-to-customer ratio may make it impossible for a single person to manage, let alone support, the growing number of ways in which a customer can and will attempt to interact with a business.

What's even more problematic is ensuring consistent behavior among all of the people in your enterprise. This becomes apparent when viewed from the customer's perspective. The customer's interactions with your business are now handled by a variety of employees in different roles and situations. Not only are the people involved different, with different skills, backgrounds, and motivations, they often have no knowledge of the other interactions the customer has had. What's worse is that they may also be unaware of a global strategy or desired service level for handling the particular customer. You may not have visibility and knowledge of inconsistent experiences being created for your customers, but your customers are acutely aware, and will behave with correspondingly inconsistent results.

One of the most dramatic influences on business today is being driven by technology. Technology is driving change at an unprecedented pace. One change that is significantly altering the traditional business landscape is how technology empowers consumers, who are now beginning to enjoy the upper hand in their relationships with businesses. The shift of power creates opportunities for smart businesses to increase their market share and competitive advantage, and also presents the potential for disaster on a far greater scale for businesses that choose to ignore the issue.

Technology has empowered consumers with the ability to conduct business with a variety of alternatives to the traditional face-to-face contact. In addition, it has given consumers access to far more information and choice than they have ever enjoyed before. This increased awareness, combined with increasing demands on personal time, creates consumers that are informed and impatient. Meeting their increased expectations is essential, perhaps critical.

Consumer-to-business interaction started at the distance of a handshake. It began to move farther apart with the invention of the phone. Once thought to be an invention of dubious value, the telephone is now the most significant customer interaction channel for most businesses. Almost all businesses today have a primary telephone contact number, and in many cases it leads to a sophisticated call center, with advanced skill set routing, escalation, and tracking systems that optimize the ability to deal with the customer. Growing in significance are the e-business channels: email, Web, and wireless. Growing consumer familiarity and comfort with these technologies is driving their growth as a medium for business interactions, creating additional challenges for businesses trying to maintain good CRM in the face of this increasing complexity.

Online commerce is maturing rapidly, shaped by changes in technology, consumer behavior, and innovation in business models. Even in its early stages, some fundamental consumer behaviors have emerged. The easy, immediate access to a wealth of information afforded by the Internet makes it very convenient for comparison shopping. Consumers can get much more information about the products that interest them in a much shorter amount of time. They can also identify a greater variety of businesses from which they could potentially get what they want. The informed consumer is much less likely to settle for an inferior product, price, or service, and consequently, has greater expectations. The Internet's immediacy and the growing demands on people's personal time are reducing their threshold of impatience. Customers are not as content to wait in line and are placing greater value on time. The buying pattern of browse by Internet, order by phone, and ship overnight satisfies the consumer's desire to get the best deal and ensures that the purchase transaction is correctly handled and that the wait to receive the benefit is minimized.

The problem for businesses arises from the reduction in personal contact they have with the customer. They may not even be aware of a potential customer traversing their website to comparison shop, and thus miss the opportunity to assess the prospect's value and attempt a corresponding level of service and sales. The order, if received, is handled by an anonymous agent in a call center, or perhaps automatically by the website. The order gets transferred to a fulfillment system optimized for efficiency and cost reduction, not for ensuring consistent customer experiences.

All is fine when there are no glitches, but the test of CRM comes when the customer calls wondering where the product is. Can your business identify the customers, treat them according to the service level they deserve, find their order no matter if it was placed by mail, phone, fax, email, or Web, and track it through the supply chain? If "find the customer's order" gives you images of disconnected processes and employees shrugging and saying "I don't know" as a manual fox-hunt spreads across several departments, buildings, individuals, and computer systems, then you have a serious CRM problem. Your customers couldn't care less about the struggles your organization endures—they just expect their needs to be met.

Another significant change businesses are experiencing is the waning ability to rely on traditional forms of differentiation for competitive advantage. Customers used to endure poor CRM because a business offered a significantly better product, happened to be geographically convenient, or could offer better pricing. These competitive advantages are being eroded by the changes technology is creating in the business landscape.

The oldest form of competitive advantage is location. Economic theory maintains that in the absence of other factors, customers prefer to travel the shortest distance to tender a transaction with a business. Businesses use this advantage with the local customers who won't bother to look further to meet their needs. This advantage is dissolving with the growth of the Internet and global express shipping. Now customers are much more aware of equivalent or better business opportunities on a global basis, and can receive fulfillment of their transactions with overnight shipping. The "best deal" may not be with the business across the street, but with the business across the ocean. Internet distance is measured by mouse clicks, and this virtual proximity is eliminating geographical advantage for business.

Size is the next traditional competitive advantage to suffer in the new economy. The advantage of size manifests itself in awareness, and in pricing advantages that result from economies of scale. Bigger companies have been able to leverage better pricing. Again the new, electronically linked economy is eroding this advantage. New online marketplaces aggregate supply and demand, enabling businesses of all sizes to benefit from economies of scale. The dynamic, interconnected Web of business-to-business e-commerce enables collaboration on supply, fulfillment, and even production, eliminating the need for a business to build and own it all themselves. Aggressive investment, often significantly in advance of any hope of profitability, enables new market entrants to pose competitive challenges to established business, both in terms of awareness, and more disturbingly, in terms of unprofitable business models permitting them to compete on price, at least temporarily.

Awareness and presence are also becoming easier to generate, regardless of size. Skillful use of the Internet can create the impression that a business is much larger than it physically is. Again the reach of the Internet, coupled with global logistics, allows even a small company in a single location to pose a competitive threat to a larger business with a larger geographic footprint.

Perhaps the most startling transformation is the shift away from product-driven differentiation to service-based differentiation. As product cycles continue to be driven shorter, the lifespan of any individual product advantage declines. This is particularly evident in the technology sector, but almost any product you can imagine is being driven toward commoditization. Consider a highly sophisticated, expensive, complex piece of machinery—the jet engine. Would an aircraft manufacturer select an engine supplier on the basis of a 10 percent improvement in power or fuel economy? What if that improvement came at the cost of decreased reliability or quality? Not a chance. In fact, the value of the supplier-to-business relationship—reliable delivery, service, support, and flexibility—may weigh significantly more than the individual product characteristics in driving purchase decisions.

In the face of all of these dramatic changes, relationships continue to maintain their value in determining customer behavior. As other traditional forms of competitive differentiation erode, relationships are growing in importance in determining whether businesses succeed or fail. In fact, they are one of the few remaining areas where a business can proactively manage and control their destiny. A business can't control the pace of technology, it can't control the economy, it certainly can't control its competitors, but it can control the way it manages interactions with its customers.

Given that the process of transforming expectation to experience is inevitable, what's available to assist businesses in implementing good CRM? Early CRM products were focused on automation and cost savings. These centered on a single isolated department or business function, such as support or sales. The effectiveness of these "islands of automation" was limited, as their reach did not extend past the department. As CRM products evolved into "suites," they linked the traditional customer-interfacing roles of marketing, sales, and support within a single system. The two major shortfalls of front-office suites are their limited effectiveness across the enterprise and the need to measure, analyze, and optimize the system on an ongoing basis.

CRM suites are more effective than a collection of disparate, isolated systems, but in reality the "island of automation" is just bigger than it was before. For CRM to be truly effective, it must integrate with and support the business processes that create customer experiences. These business processes span the enterprise, involving back-office functions like accounting, purchasing, production, and logistics in addition to the traditional front-office functions of marketing, sales, and support. Customers expecting the same great treatment they received from marketing and sales may be in for an unpleasant surprise when they connect with the call center to resolve a billing mistake. If the agent has no ability to access the billing system, customers may need to wait while internal process and communication find, verify, and fix the problem. They may just get transferred to the accounting department and an individual who has no idea who the customer is, how important he is, or how he needs to be treated. If the customer tries to use the Web to solve this problem, he may be out of luck if the website can't link to billing history and order status. If your most valued customer calls your toll-free number requesting a change in billing information for an order he placed via your website 30 minutes ago, can your enterprise guarantee he gets what he needs? For CRM to be truly effective, it must be integrated with the business processes spanning your enterprise.

Good CRM must be able to help people throughout the enterprise make smarter decisions faster. Workflow or process without the ability to measure, analyze, and improve its effectiveness simply perpetuates a problem. Similarly, gaining true insight into the value of customers is based on the ability to analyze complete information, which also spans the enterprise. For example, assessing customer value might be based on how much he or she has purchased. This is an inaccurate indication of value when you consider that the same customer may not be a candidate for any near-term purchases, and there may be others who are on the verge of purchasing significant amounts. This still doesn't give a truly accurate reflection of value until you factor in the associated costs of serving the customers. Often, marquee customers have customized support arrangements or service level agreements, making them much more costly to serve than other customers. Now we must truly have an accurate representation of customer value and how best to implement good CRM, right? Not if we also consider their current satisfaction level. Good CRM might focus more energy on the unhappiest high-value customer in an effort to retain them than the high-value customers who are already very happy and at less risk of abandonment.

Good CRM must also be accessible to every person in your enterprise who is involved in processes that shape customer experiences. It doesn't help to have a wonderful system that nobody uses. Technologies such as wireless PDAs and cellphones enable your mobile workforce to access your CRM system from virtually anywhere they need to be. Technologies such as pure Internet applications enable everyone in your enterprise—even your suppliers and partners—to access your system with just a browser and the right authorization. This type of pervasive access to CRM ensures that everybody who can influence customer experiences has the right information about the customers, their value, and their needs, and is empowered to ensure a positive experience for all customers.

I believe successful CRM must be integrated, insightful, and pervasive. Integrated CRM allows your entire enterprise to align around the common goal of exceeding the expectations of your customers. Insightful CRM enables you to truly understand which customers your efforts should focus on, and how to continually optimize your enterprise to meet their needs. Pervasive CRM applies technologies such as pure Internet applications to enable everyone who makes your enterprise work—your customers, your employees, and your suppliers—to easily access applications and analysis, wherever they may be. Together, these abilities will foster a successful CRM program that transforms expectations into great experiences, forming the foundation of competitive advantage, growth, and profitability.

Scott Fletcher, Vice-President, i2

Scott Fletcher joined i2 in 2001 as vice-president. Mr. Fletcher was vice-president of worldwide services for Annuncio Software, a leader in the field of e-marketing platforms, and then president of epipeline, a vertical CRM product company. Previously, he served as vice-president of PeopleSoft's Professional Services Group, a world leader providing e-business applications.

DEFINITION

The hype surrounding Customer Relationship Management has been pervasive within the business, technology, media, and academic communities since early 1997. Because of this hype, and the numerous constituents that contribute to it, there are as many definitions and interpretations of CRM as there are self-purported CRM gurus. Much like the hype surrounding Business Process Reengineering (BPR) and Total Quality Management (TQM) in the late 1980s and early 1990s, there is a tremendous value proposition hidden beneath all this. Businesses must move beyond the hype, though, to best position their enterprises to be successful CRM practitioners.

At its core, CRM is an enterprise-wide mindset, mantra, and set of business processes and policies that are designed to acquire, retain, and service customers. Broadly speaking, CRM includes the customer-facing business processes of marketing, sales, and customer service. CRM is not a technology, though. Technology is a CRM enabler. So why has CRM become so pervasive recently? Hasn't the primary goal of business always been to acquire, retain, and service customers? Why is CRM such a "novel" concept?

The answer to these questions is that advances in technology serve as the primary catalyst to the CRM bonanza. The rise of the Internet as a means to transact business, increasing and affordable bandwidth, and advances in computing power are all driving CRM. These technology advances greatly empower customers and position them to more easily access information on products, services, and competitors. In short, customers are in control more than ever before. For innovative and proactive companies that readily embrace this new customer-powered paradigm, the situation is great. By adopting customer-centric business processes and leveraging technology, these companies better serve their customers by developing improved products and services and delivering personalized service. For laggard companies, though, the customer-empowered new world order is nightmarish.

Fortunately, the confluence of technology advances, empowered customers, and an increasing competitive environment has given rise to a variety of technology-based CRM offerings to help businesses that are now catching the CRM wave. These CRM offerings consist primarily of sales force automation (SFA), marketing automation, customer service, and, to a certain extent, partner relationship management (PRM) software. These packages serve primarily to automate the various customer touch points within an enterprise. Whether automating an email marketing campaign, allowing a sales representative to configure and price a product on the fly, or allowing a customer to update his billing address via the Web, these offerings serve primarily to automate processes. While this automation does enrich the customer experience and allows an enterprise to better serve customers, it is not enough. To best acquire, retain, and service customers, enterprises must intimately know their customers. Enterprises must possess extensive knowledge of customer buying patterns, channel preferences, and historical contact information. This requires collecting and analyzing data to provide a comprehensive, cohesive, and centralized view of a customer.

The need and importance of this global customer view explains the rise in data-warehousing and business intelligence software vendors. By tapping into the wealth of data collected by the SFA, marketing automation, customer service, and PRM applications with business intelligence tools, companies are better positioned to execute their CRM strategies and serve customers. Thus, the CRM technology landscape today consists primarily of sales, marketing, and customer service software vendors coupled with data-warehousing and business intelligence vendors.

So what does this mean in the real world? What business interactions are examples of effective CRM? Effective CRM is allowing a customer to update her account information online and enabling your customer care, sales, and marketing organizations to have instantaneous access to that information. Effective CRM is providing a personalized online shopping experience to a customer by analyzing her past online and offline interactions and delivering product and service recommendations based on that data. Effective CRM is having the ability to determine which customers are most profitable, determining what drives that profit, and ensuring that customer-specific business processes and practices maintain or increase that customer profitability. Effective CRM is also having the ability to know which customers are not profitable, why they are not profitable, and being able to change tactics to ensure future profitability. In short, CRM is about knowing your customers. It's about creating and growing relationships with your customers. It's about remembering customer preferences and forging long-term relationships with them by delivering exceptional service and product offerings tailored to them.

Brent Frei, President and CEO, Onyx Software

Brent Frei is president, CEO, and co-founder of Onyx Software, a global supplier of customer relationship management software that is known for its ease of customization, integration with other systems, and implementation, as well as its flexibility and scalability. Since the company's inception in 1994, Onyx has grown exponentially. In 1999, Onyx Software was named a Deloitte & Touche "Fast 500" company, and the tenth fastest-growing high-tech company in America, with a 21,051 percent revenue growth rate from 1994 to 1999. In 2001, the company was once again named to the "Fast 500," and ranked nineteenth on the Washington Stage Technology Fast 50. Under Mr. Frei's leadership, the company has won several prestigious awards for fostering an outstanding corporate culture. The company has established offices throughout the United States, in Australia, France, Germany, Hong Kong, Singapore, and the United Kingdom, as well as an impressive network of software, hardware, services, and distribution partnerships worldwide. Onyx's award-winning software has been licensed to more than 800 global customers in a variety of industries, including financial services, high technology, health care, manufacturing, and telecommunications. The company became publicly traded on NASDAQ under the symbol ONXS in February 1999.

As a leader, Mr. Frei has been recognized as a "Pioneer in Technology" by the Smithsonian Institute and was recently among an exclusive handful of global CEOs selected to represent the technology industry at the Technology Pioneers' session of the 2000 World Economic Forum in Davos, Switzerland. In June 2000, Mr. Frei was the sole recipient of Dartmouth College's Thayer School of Engineering Fletcher Award for lifetime achievement.

Mr. Frei has been a contributor to numerous publications, and is a co-author of an upcoming book titled, *Firing Up the Customer: Aligning Brand, Strategy, and Technology to Deliver the Extraordinary Customer Experience.*

Prior to co-founding Onyx, Mr. Frei was a programmer analyst with Microsoft Corporation, where he was the primary architect of an integrated, international Customer Relationship Management system still in use today for sales, marketing, customer service, and product support by Microsoft's international subsidiaries. Before his tenure at Microsoft, Mr. Frei received patents for several of his cellular system designs as a mechanical engineer at Motorola. He received a Bachelor of Engineering degree from Dartmouth's Thayer School of Engineering and his A.B. in Engineering Sciences from Dartmouth College.

DEFINITION

What is CRM? It is a comprehensive set of processes and technologies for managing the relationships with potential and current customers and business partners across marketing, sales, and service regardless of the communication channel (see Figure 1-1). The goal of CRM is to optimize customer and partner satisfaction, revenue, and business efficiency by building the strongest possible relationships at an organizational level. Successful CRM requires a holistic approach to every relationship with the entire organization sharing and contributing to that view.

But before companies can implement a CRM system or even begin to assess the validity of a CRM system to address their needs, some very fundamental truths must first be underscored and communicated.

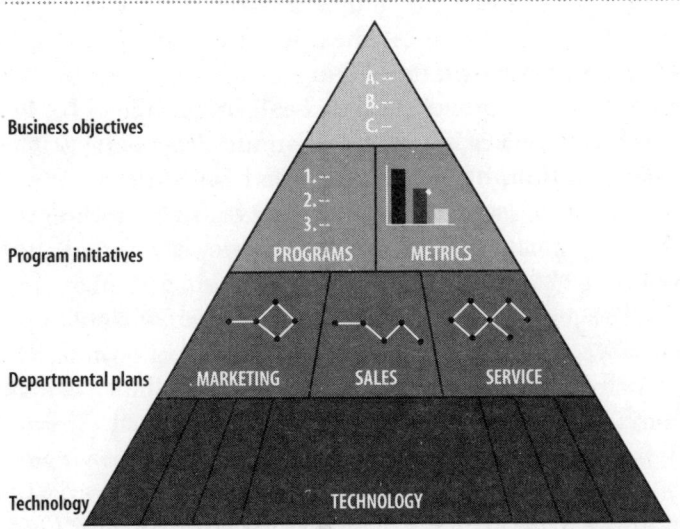

Figure 1-1: Onyx view of building a business that will use CRM (Copyright 2000, Onyx Software. All rights reserved.)

Business objectives outlining two- to five-year strategic goals should be clearly defined. These can include revenue, market share, and margin goals. They might also dictate corporate style such as "be a customer-centric company" or "differentiate on service levels." These should then drive the next level of business fundamentals: program initiatives.

Program initiatives are typically one to one and a half years in scope. They are the near-term game plans intended to move the company another step toward the long-term objectives of the company. They take the form of directives such as "build out the direct sales force in a vertical market," "focus on expansion within the customer base," and "improve customer satisfaction by five points." These initiatives are then associated with specific measurements that will be the clear indications of successful forward progress. Underlying these program initiatives are the specific departmental plans.

Departmental plans are the processes and behavior that form the fabric of everyday work within the organization. Examples include deploying an automated email response system, enabling customer self-help on a website, or streamlining the call center processes to answer customer inquiries in shorter time frames. There are often dozens of major processes within a department and many that cross departments. Organizations range in ability or desire to coordinate and integrate these process pieces. The three layers of business operations are then supported by technology.

Technology is used to automate and enable some or all of the business processes and initiatives. Organizations use either many separate best-of-breed solutions or larger, integrated platform solutions to achieve the goals of technology-enabled business. The technology strategy is generally a reflection of the coordination, or lack thereof, of the organization.

Organizations tend to execute their technology strategies in one of four stages, which are indicative of how coordinated the organization is from top to bottom and side to side, and how effectively and efficiently it is executing. The stages can be classified as (1) functional, (2) departmental, (3) partial CRM, and (4) CRM. The future of CRM is at least one stage beyond these, to an inter-networked business model we call a Business Relationship Network. A company that operates as a Stage One, or functional, organization is characterized by the compartmentalization or granularity of its independently managed business processes. This is typical of Fortune 500 companies that have extremely large operational infrastructures. Intra-team coordination and cooperation is challenging, and inter-departmental coordination and cooperation is nearly impossible. Process and the technology to support it are executed in very granular pieces. Examples of this would be sales forecasting, automated email response, and Web self-help as standalone technical solutions.

Return on investment in this model is typically only possible in very large companies where economies of scale make it feasible. This is one of the reasons very large organizations become increasingly inefficient as they expand. The technology deployed in this environment usually provides benefits only into the bottom layer of the operational structure, helping to manage the departmental plans. Since the technology tends to be fragmented and only benefits the specific departmental processes, large data warehouse and large integration and synchronization projects are common. These become the technologies necessary to serve the top two layers of the operational structure.

A company that operates as a Stage Two, or departmental, organization is characterized by intra-departmental synchronization by implementing coordinated processes and deploying technology across an entire department. Cross-departmental process and technology is sparse. Typical examples of structures on this level are sales force automation, call centers, and channel management. This is possible in companies of all sizes.

Return on investment in this model is typically two to five times the initial and ongoing investment. The technology deployed in this environment usually provides benefits through the bottom layer and into the middle layer of the operational structure, helping to make an entire department more efficient and effective. Rarely does this structure account for a dramatic increase in customer loyalty or revenue because the company does not treat the customer holistically. This type of organizational structure might allow an individual or a single department to serve a client better, but it does not create an affinity for the company at large.

A company that operates as a Stage Three, or partial CRM, organization builds upon previous processes, still honing intra-departmental synchronization with coordinated processes and departmental technology. This level, however, does benefit from cross-departmental process and technology coordination characterized, for example, by sales and marketing sharing a customer database or synching up strategies. In this model, multiple master customer databases still exist. This model is increasingly possible as you go down in company size. Return on investment in this model is typically four to seven times the initial and ongoing investment. The technology deployed in this environment generally provides benefits through the bottom layer and into the middle layer of the operational structure, helping to make several arms of the business more efficient and effective.

A company that operates as a Stage Four, or full CRM, organization has achieved a single master customer database upon which the whole organization coordinates process and strategy. This model is very difficult for large organizations to follow as it requires significant operational coordination and process.

Return on investment in this model is typically five to ten times that of the initial and ongoing investment. The technology deployed in this environment typically provides benefits through all layers of the operational structure, helping to make all arms of the business more efficient and effective. Technologies such as data warehouses are less common and less necessary in this model.

This level is characterized by:

► A single, universally shared customer instance and data

► Coordinated departmental strategies and processes

► Closed loop reporting and real-time analytics

► Internet-based and traditional processes woven together into a single CRM mosaic

Only by creating this environment within a business can you begin to develop and nurture customer fidelity to the entire business rather than just the individual serving the client. Businesses that have deployed Stage Four CRM operating systems across the entire organization have seen far greater revenue growth, margins, customer satisfaction, and customer loyalty than businesses deploying partial CRM systems.

As an illustrative example, consider the customer relationship in the home building industry. An individual architect who provides an exceptionally high level of service will stand above those who don't. He or she will create a level of customer satisfaction that will generate substantially more referrals than his or her peers. However, that referral stream is for the individual architect alone who will quickly become overbooked with clients. If, however, that service level and satisfaction can be extended across the architect's entire firm and the client feels that the whole firm is working for him, then the relationship moves from an individual to an organizational relationship, and now the firm will get the referrals even if the individual architect is unavailable.

This is the difference between organizational effectiveness, which creates a competitive advantage for the business, as opposed to individual effectiveness. This difference presents itself in almost every industry. Ever been in a company where a salesperson takes his customers with him when he leaves the company? This happens because the relationships didn't extend from the individual to the company. Stage Four CRM prevents this by creating competitive advantage at the company level in addition to the individual.

The future of CRM is to extend this relationship strength another step further—beyond Stage Four and into other parts of the customer's relationship (service) network.

Let's say the architecture firm does a lot of work with a specific general contractor. If the general contractor and the architect interact with the customer only within their own silos and don't communicate with each other on the customer's behalf, the customer will quickly get frustrated at the inefficiencies of repeating the same conversation over and over. And the customer's satisfaction with both parties will go down very quickly even if they are both providing high levels of service independently. If, on the other hand, the architect and contractor share the right information at the right time every time, the customer will feel everyone is working together to best serve him or her, and satisfaction with both parties will be even higher than that generated by the parties independently.

This relationship network continues from the contractor to the subcontractors, interior designers, landscapers, and the like. Almost every industry operates in some likeness to the home building industry, with customer information passing from one entity to another, and collaboration among entities being desired, if not required. In the mortgage industry, the mortgage broker works with the realtor, wholesale lender, underwriter, escrow agent, title agent, and appraiser, among others. In the enterprise software industry, the software company works with the management consulting firm, systems integrator, hardware company, database vendor, and other software partners. In the sports industry, the franchise owner works with the league, arena, concessions vendors, merchandisers, and opposing franchises.

Within every industry there is a network of people and organizations that need to work together to better serve each individual customer. This is the future of CRM. Businesses that can serve the customer seamlessly across the broadest network will be those with the highest margins, most loyal customers, strongest partnerships, and greatest revenue acceleration.

So how does a company go about creating a relationship network for its customers?

To create relationship networks, companies must develop Stage Four CRM for each customer-focused business unit, and extend that system to other customer units and organizations within the customer's entire relationship network. Full CRM is the building block for relationship networks and is required to participate in this world of distributed Customer Relationship Management, which we call the Business Relationship Network. The goal is to extend the full CRM approach beyond the traditional four walls of the organization to other people and entities within the particular relationship network of every customer. Businesses that can serve the customer seamlessly across the broadest relationship network will be the market leaders in their respective industries and will create significant barriers to entry for companies not in the network.

Peter Keen, Chairman, Keen Innovations

Peter Keen is the founder and chairman of Keen Innovations (formerly the International Center for Information Technologies). He has served on the faculties of Harvard, MIT, and Stanford, with visiting positions at Wharton, Oxford, Fordham, the London Business School, Stockholm University, the Technical University of Delft, and Duke University. In 1994, he was profiled by *Forbes* magazine as the "consultant from Paradise." In 1988, he was named by *Information Week* as one of the top ten consultants in the information technology field.

His research, writing, education, and public speaking all focus on helping firms make a management difference in their deployment of information technology as a business resource and on bridging the gap in understanding, language, and planning between business decisions and technology choices. When all leading firms in an industry have access to the same technology, the competitive edge comes from fusing people, process, and technology. The management challenge is for business managers to lead IT, without having to know the details of the technology, but understanding and enacting the key decisions about policy, infrastructures, and funding that enable their technical professionals to design, implement, and operate the platform. That integrated platform is an essential base for business innovation in just about every industry today and vital for coordinating operations in a global environment.

A prolific writer, Peter Keen is the author of many books that have strongly influenced the business-technology dialogue, starting with *Decision Support Systems* (1978), which introduced the concept of IT as a support to managerial judgment, *Competing in Time: Using Telecommunications for Competitive Advantage* (1986), the first book to anticipate the immense impact of telecommunications on the basics of business, and *Shaping the Future: Business Design Through Information*

Technology (1991), a book addressed to senior executives that has been translated into many European and Asian languages. *The Process Edge: Creating Value Where It Counts* (1997) looks at business processes as invisible financial assets and liabilities to be managed as a portfolio of capital investments targeted at increasing shareholder value. His most recent books all address the management side of electronic commerce and the Internet economy. *The eProcess Edge* (2000) focuses on sourcing process capabilities and *From .com to .profit* (2000) zeros in on the value imperatives that drive effective business models. Earlier books are *Trust by Design, Business Internets and Intranets,* and *On-Line Profits.* Most recently, he wrote *The Freedom Economy: Gaining the mCommerce Edge in the Era of the Wireless Internet* (2001).

He has worked as a consultant on a long-term basis as an adviser to top managers in helping them fuse business choices and technology decisions. Examples of companies with which Mr. Keen has worked in this mode include British Airways, British Telecom, Citibank, Glaxo, IBM, MCI Communications, Royal Bank of Canada, Cemex (Mexico), Sweden Post, Unilever, World Bank, IATA, CTC (Chile), HP, and many others. His work with these companies has generally included the development and delivery of senior management education programs for action (rather than just "awareness") as a lever for taking charge of change and making IT part of everyday planning and management thinking. He is on the advisory boards and boards of directors of several Internet companies, including e-Credit, WebIQ, and Celosis.

DEFINITION

I wish we could get rid of the term CRM, but it's established and there's no point in trying to change it and add yet another piece of jargon to the IT vocabulary. I'd prefer CREE—customer relationship experience enhancement—instead of Customer Relationship Management. My objection to CRM comes from a "here we go again" feeling. You don't "manage" customers; you enhance their relationships with your company. The information you collect and how you use it should be targeted at the customer experience, from the customer perspective.

IT people largely think in terms of structure and control and leave out the reality of the human as human. We first had "user involvement"—turning colleagues, clients, and collaborators into an abstraction. Then we had office "automation" and "reengineering"—"Hi, we're the BPR brigade and we're here to reengineer you." CRM largely began as "data-warehousing," as if information about customers and their interactions with the company are just boxes of records stored in the attic. In the CRM arena, there's now plenty of talk about "sales force automation." That's an interesting view of what sales representatives do and why.

CRM—I'll stay with the term—runs the danger of becoming a way to view customers from a distance as a statistical database of information that can be used to segment markets, target promotions, identify niches, and customize and personalize websites. All these are valuable, but they look at the customer from the company's viewpoint and they ignore many elements of the customer experience. Here are my three tests of a company's real, as opposed to well-intentioned but merely espoused, commitment to enhancing the customer relationship:

▶ Has your company put in place the combination of software, processes, and accountability mechanisms to ensure that every customer email gets an answer from a qualified source within 12 to 36 hours? That source may be an automated service, but when the customer has a "problem" it's more often a crisis that requires human judgment. If your firm is like well over half the companies surveyed on this topic, the email disappears into the electronic ether. So much for "relationship."

▶ Are personalized financing options a core part of your CRM database and data warehouses? No? But the core of any commercial relationship is financing.

▶ Is 25 percent of executive bonus compensation based on some metric of customer relationship satisfaction? If not, then clearly the customer relationship is secondary to meeting budgets, filling quotas, and the like.

With this as background, here is my personal definition of CRM as I hope it will be:

Customer Relationship Management is the commitment of the company to place the customer experience at the center of its priorities and to ensure that incentive systems, processes, and information resources leverage the relationship by enhancing the experience.

In terms of technology, CRM is the design, communication, and use of information to ensure that customers grow more and more in confidence, trust, and sense of personal value in their relationship with the company.

Ronni T. Marshak, Senior Vice-President, Patricia Seybold Group

Ronni T. Marshak is a senior vice-president and principal consultant/ analyst with the Patricia Seybold Group. She is a principal consultant in the firm's Customers.com consulting practice, which specializes in jump-starting, improving, and/or salvaging business-to-business and e-business initiatives. This parallels the winning formula outlined in Patricia Seybold's best-selling book, *Customers.com*, by identifying how to "make it easy for customers to do business with you."

Ms. Marshak served as editor and co-author of *Customers.com*. The book is a *Business Week, Wall Street Journal, USA Today*, BN.com, and Amazon.com best seller.

Ms. Marshak is also the customer value practice leader in the firm's Customers.com Strategic Planning Service. This practice area focuses on developing and implementing strategies for being in a positive and profitable relationship with customers. She has consulted for such vendors as IBM, Microsoft, Lotus, Digital, and Hewlett Packard, as well as user organizations such as the International Monetary Fund, Blue Cross/Blue Shield, the American Cancer Society, and the Commonwealth of Massachusetts. Her research has appeared in such publications as *Fortune, Network World*, and *Computerworld*.

Ms. Marshak is the author of *Word Processing Packages for the IBM PC* and co-author of *Integrated Desktop Environments and Database Software for the IBM PC: The Desktop Generation*, both published by McGraw-Hill as part of the Seybold Series on Professional Computing. She has appeared as a speaker at such industry events as AIIM, Group-Ware '9x, the Workflow Conference, Comdex, Windows-OS/2 Conferences, UnixExpo, Unisys Open Forum, and the Office Automation Conference.

Ms. Marshak holds a Bachelor's degree from the University of Massachusetts and an M.Ed. from Northeastern University.

DEFINITION

CRM has become the new buzzword of e-business. And it seems that there are almost as many definitions for CRM as there are vendors promoting products for getting closer to customers.

We propose that establishing and managing customer relationships is first and foremost a strategic endeavor, not a technology category. Just as your company established goals, strategies, plans, and objectives, you need to determine how your customer relationships are being served at each step.

Technology fits only at the tactical level—as the tools with which you implement your plans to support your strategies.

On the technology side, we have identified two different types of technologies that support your customer relationship strategy (CRS): CRM, the customer-facing, interaction systems, such as support, campaign management, and sales force automation; and Customer Intelligence (CI), which provides tools to capture, store, process, access, organize, and analyze/model customer data. The results of this analysis are typically put into action via the CRM systems.

Remember the old commercial, "It's a breath mint." "No, it's a candy mint." "Why, it's two, two, two mints in one!" (Or for "Saturday Night Live" fans, "It's a floor wax." "No, it's a dessert topping!") So goes the ongoing debate over Customer Relationship Management. Is CRM the customer-facing applications of customer service/support and sales, or is it the back-office applications of customer data interpretation?

I believe that this question misses a crucial point—that managing customer relationships—which is, after all, what CRM is all about—is not simply a group of applications, nor should we be focused on technology.

Establishing and maintaining long-term, mutually beneficial relationships with your customers is something that must be at the core of your organization's *raison d'etre*. Your executives must mandate it. Your employees must embrace it. It must become a core value of your company. You have to feel it in your gut!

That has nothing to do with technology.

So, here I am, espousing motherhood and apple pie. You all know that customers are vital to every business. You know that relationships with your customers are the key to your success. But with the advent of new and exciting technologies that focus on customer interactions and analyzing customer information, we've gotten caught up in the inner workings of CRM technologies. We are now able to perform customer-related processes over organizational boundaries in real time! We can be in constant touch with our customers. The technology is exciting (and confusing), and we are spending all our time trying to figure out which products to implement rather than determining how we want our customer relationships to look and feel. We've lost sight of the bigger picture—the strategic importance of our customer relationships.

Let's look at it another way. Every company's game plan includes what I call the "G-SPOT." (See Figure 1-2.) This stands for Goals, Strategies, Plans, Objectives, and Tactics. Here's how it breaks down for CRM:

Goals Every business has clearly defined goals. At the most basic level, these include things like profitability, worldwide recognition, and high stockholder value.

Strategies To achieve your goals, you establish strategies, such as designing innovative products, focusing on international markets, and establishing long-term relationships with customers.

Plans Executing strategies requires plans. For example, to design innovative products you might implement a plan of hiring top product engineers; to focus internationally you might develop a public relations plan that targets worldwide press; and to establish customer relationships you might determine to measure customer satisfaction and behavior and to invest in technology to support customer interactions.

Objectives These are the measurable goals of each plan, such as maintaining a 60 percent customer retention rate or lowering product return rates to less than 20 percent.

Tactics Tactics are how you achieve the objectives that are part of the plans to implement the strategies to achieve the goals (whew!). For example, you might establish a 24/7 call center or create a data warehouse that consolidates all customer information.

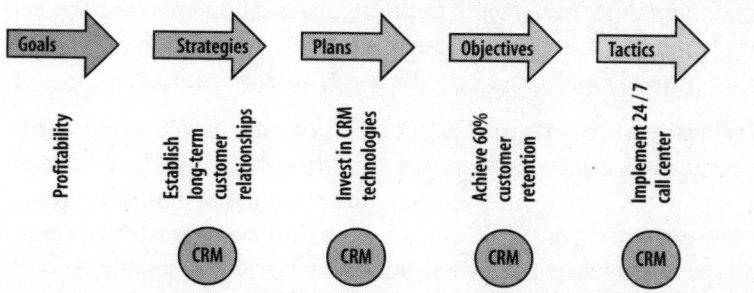

Figure 1-2: The CRM G-SPOT: In this example, the goal of profitability (which, of course, breaks down into many strategies) is supported by a CRM strategy and implemented using CRM tactics. (Copyright 2000, Patricia Seybold Group. All rights reserved.)

I'm sure you've noted that CRM topics and technologies fit in almost every area (see Figure 1-2). Customer relationships are, in themselves, a strategic concern. The plans lay out how to establish the relationships. The objectives indicate how to recognize (via measurements) successful customer relationships. And CRM technologies are implemented at a tactical level in support of the strategy.

Now that we've positioned technology in the strategic planning and implementation process, we can go back to the original question: Is CRM the customer-facing applications of customer service/support and sales, or is it the back-office applications of customer data interpretation?

Basically, we see two dimensions of CRM technology: customer-facing applications and company-facing applications.

Customer-facing applications are fundamentally those that customers actually experience. These might also be considered customer interaction applications, wherein customers interact with your employees, your website, and/or your systems.

The old standby CRM applications—the ones originally featured at all the CRM trade shows—fall primarily into the customer-facing category:

Sales force automation (SFA) Epitomized by Siebel Systems, SFA applications include such capabilities as lead tracking, opportunity management, contact management, and (more recently) aspects of partner relationship management.

Customer service and support Led, again, by Siebel (after its Scopus Technology acquisition) and PeopleSoft (which acquired Vantive), these customer-facing applications include areas such as call center management, online help facilities, internal helpdesk, and expert knowledge-based systems for problem resolution.

Marketing automation The automation of marketing functions encompasses a wide variety of capabilities, some of which are customer facing, such as automated email response systems, campaign management/execution tools, surveys and contest management, and the management and distribution of marketing materials (both hard copy and online) to sales personnel and partners.

Marketing automation, however, is the primary culprit in the confusion between customer-facing and company-facing applications.

While the execution of campaigns, the customer engagement capabilities (such as surveys and contests), and direct customer research (soliciting feedback from customers) all involve interacting with customers, the major portion of marketing responsibilities are actually handled within the organization. Thus, these should be called customer-facing. At the Patricia Seybold Group, we call these applications Customer Intelligence.

The Customer Intelligence (CI) process (described by Lynne Harvey in her July 13, 2000, report, "How to Provide Customer Intelligence," http://www.psgroup.com/) consists of four steps:

1. Gathering customer data

2. Analyzing that data

3. Formulating a strategy based on the analysis in order to recognize customer value

4. Taking action based on the strategy

There are six different categories of tools to achieve Customer Intelligence (as Ms. Harvey described in her August 10, 2000, report, "The Customer Intelligence Landscape," http://www.psgroup.com/). These are tools for:

▶ Gathering customer information

▶ Storing customer information

▶ Processing customer data

▶ Accessing customer information

▶ Organizing customer data

▶ Modeling and analyzing customer data

The line between customer-facing and company-facing applications is very blurry, however. This is because the customer-facing products are typically the solutions used to gather customer data (from call center databases, contact managers, and so on) and, similarly, the action taken as the fourth step of the CI process is usually delivered via customer-facing systems (offers in a campaign, new loyalty programs, and so on).

Further adding to the confusion is that vendors that offer solutions on both sides of the equation don't stop at the border! Sales systems, such as Siebel's, offer data capture, storage, and analysis. Analysis systems, such as E.piphany's, offer campaign management and execution.

The key difference is in the purpose of the two types of solutions. CI is an internal process for truly understanding who your customers are and what they want from you. The customer-facing applications, which I continue to call CRM, are all about being in touch with customers, getting their input into your databases, and giving them ways to interact with you so that these interactions (and behaviors) can be captured and analyzed.

There is truly a symbiotic relationship between Customer Intelligence and Customer Relationship Management. But it helps everyone when we can attach more granular labels to the different technology areas.

Thus, I propose that we reserve the acronym CRM for the front-end, customer-interaction systems. The company-facing analysis and strategizing should be called Customer Intelligence.

Both are implemented in support of a customer relationship strategy. And thus, heretical as it may seem, I propose that we call the strategic aspect (which is removed from all technology) CRS (see Figure 1-3).

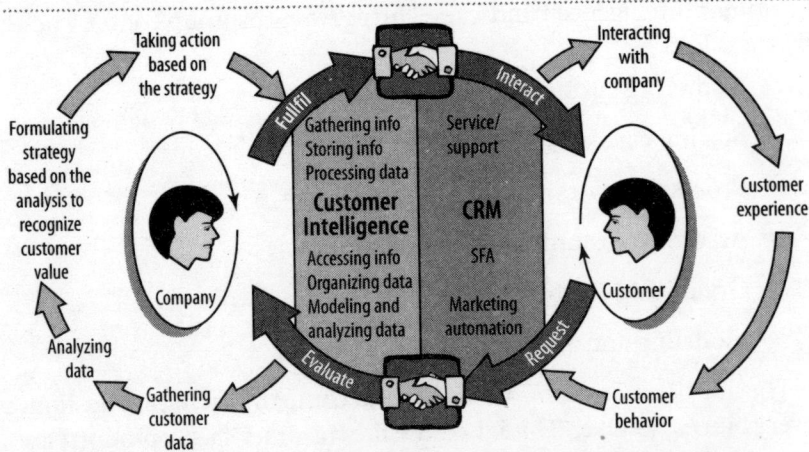

Figure 1-3: Your customer relationship strategy (CRS) is supported by two dimensions of technology: The Customer Intelligence products that act in support of the overall CI process (indicated with the arrows on the left) and the CRM products. (Copyright 2000, Patricia Seybold Group. All rights reserved.)

Where does eCRM fit in? I've heard dozens of definitions for how eCRM is different from regular old CRM, such as it is the Internet-based stuff; it is the automated stuff (no person is involved, such as automated email responses); it is the different customer touch points (website, phone center, email), and so on.

The term "eCRM" was first coined by people who were communicating with customers in new ways, typically referring to using the Web as the interaction point. But since then the term has expanded into irrelevance. Most, if not all, CRM solutions now have Web-based components (or will soon have them). And using the Internet has become a standard way of doing business, not something new and innovative.

Marketeers still use eCRM as a PR play. I find it an arbitrary distinction. If a CRM product doesn't provide some or all of the many eCRM functions, it won't be around for long.

In spite of my emphatic insistence that we clearly differentiate CRS, CRM, and CI, the definition of CRM will continue to encompass just about every technology or strategic initiative that even mentions the word *customer*. Vendors will continue to position products that are clearly in the Customer Intelligence space as CRM for a couple of reasons. First, as mentioned, CRM technology is often the beginning and end point for the CI process. Second, CRM, as a concept, is hot! Customers and the press are paying attention.

If you take away only one message from this perspective, it's that your relationships with your customers need to start at the strategy level. You must establish and be committed to a comprehensive customer relationship strategy. The CRM and CI technologies are there to be implemented in support of the strategy. Remember, when you implement a sound strategy, you can achieve your corporate goals.

Brooke M. Savage, President, Pragmatech Software, Inc.

Brooke Savage is president and co-founder of Pragmatech Software, Inc. The company develops packaged sales effectiveness tools specializing in proposal automation, RFP response, presentation automation, and sales content publishing systems. Mr. Savage has been in the software industry since 1975. Earlier in his career, Mr. Savage programmed financial planning software for CIGNA Corporation. He later joined the General Electric Company in New York City as software development manager, financial systems. In 1983 he moved to Ross Systems, an early supplier of packaged applications software and rose to become vice-president, marketing. He then joined CODA, Incorporated, a start-up subsidiary of the English software company the CODA Group, Ltd., as vice-president, marketing. He became group vice-president and was appointed to the Board of Directors in 1992. In 1993, Mr. Savage was on the four-person executive team that took CODA public on the London Stock Exchange and that same year he founded Pragmatech.

Definition

I was recently "CRMed" as a customer of a large bank credit card service with which I have happily been running consistent balances for many years. The service representative left a message on my phone machine indicating that "your account needs updating immediately." On returning the call I was told that I had been selected to receive the ubiquitous "low fee" Platinum card upgrade and that they would be pleased to consolidate all my other credit card balances for me as well. I politely declined, commenting that I was very happy with the relationship as it stood and enjoyed the services provided by my current Gold card, but might consider a change in the future. One might have thought that the objective of the bank had been achieved. The customer was contacted, actually returned the call, communicated satisfaction with the relationship, and held out the promise of potential additional business in the future.

But of course this pleasant ending was not to be. The sales rep continued to press, next highlighting the exact outstanding balances I had on competing "exorbitant interest" credit cards while mentioning that my home mortgage balance was so low I could easily add an option for a home equity line of credit as well. Frankly, I was stunned at the level of detail available to the rep. When asked, he revealed that they had pulled my full credit report prior to the call. He was insistent that they had a right to do so because they were a bank. Privacy may be dead, but fortunately a good pair of scissors is still very effective at severing relationships with overly intrusive credit card companies. Thus ended a carefully "managed" customer relationship of more than ten years. CRM run amok?

Surely it's clear by now that we have sufficient software and hardware resources from many reputable providers. Most companies can procure a technical CRM solution that ostensibly meets the needs of their business. Systems can now collect massive volumes of data on customers, prospects, and influencers, analyzing these groups in almost any way imaginable for an unlimited number of uses. Part of the ambiguity in defining CRM, and hence measuring its success as a category, may lie in the expectations that both customers and sellers bring to the table rather than in any underlying technical or functional deficiency.

The bank wants more of my business. They know who I am, and that I have already been a long-standing customer. From the credit report, they know exactly how much I can give them, if properly motivated, and have correlated that to my past business with them. They've identified me, qualified me, and quantified my business potential. Good CRM systems work on their end! Their failure was not in their system, per se, but in their sales methodology; a crucial distinction. I was a happy customer, but became a very unhappy *sales prospect* when I felt my personal information was being used outside the bounds of the existing relationship.

One of the great promises of CRM was that it would expand revenues from existing clients. While difficult to quantify, the underlying work to support effective sales processes, now that we have these systems, demands additional attention. The basics of selling have not changed: establishing trust, defining the value proposition, articulating benefits, handling objections, and closing the sale. Perhaps one of the disappointments attributed to CRM implementations could be overcome by focusing on fundamental selling strategies that no system will ever replace. Ultimately, we need to create more nuanced and subtle implementations that don't leave buyers feeling "CRMed."

Roger Siboni, President and CEO, E.piphany

Prior to joining E.piphany, Mr. Siboni was deputy chairman and chief operating officer of KPMG Peat Marwick, LLP, a member firm of KPMG International, the $9 billion, 85,000-person worldwide accounting and consulting organization. As COO of KPMG, he was centrally involved in driving the firm's rapid growth, including growing its consulting practice by 100 percent over the last two years and its high technology practice by 250 percent over the previous four years. Before that, he was the managing partner of the firm's information and communications practice. During his twenty-year tenure at KPMG, Mr. Siboni helped grow numerous technology startups into major public companies as he led KPMG efforts to serve clients worldwide in the fields of semiconductors, software, computers and peripherals, telecommunications, cable television, broadcasting, entertainment, publishing, and advertising. Mr. Siboni serves on the boards of Brience, Inc., Cadence Design Systems, Inc., Corio, Inc., FileNet Inc., and is the chair of the Walter A. Haas School of Business at the University of California at Berkeley. He is a graduate of the University of California at Berkeley.

DEFINITION

Simply stated, CRM is about getting, keeping, and growing customers. However, the term CRM been defined many different ways, resulting in customers feeling confused and over-sold.

In the past, CRM has been defined by legacy systems designed to automate processes and transactions. These systems created departmental silos where marketing interactions were managed separately from sales interactions and service interactions. Although companies were able to gain short-term efficiencies in operations, they were unable to gain a single view of their customer, resulting in a poor customer experience.

The definition of CRM has changed. Today, CRM refers to an enterprise transformation that places the customer at the center of all activity. The departmental silos of marketing, sales, and service must disappear. In this new organization, every channel leverages marketing, sales, and service capabilities to engage the customer with a dynamically personalized and compelling experience. The technology allows for companies to use each interaction as a basis to gain knowledge about customer preferences and enhance the level of service so that each interaction builds into a more meaningful relationship.

The new era of CRM characterizes brains over brawn. At E.piphany, we call it *Smart* CRM. *Smart* CRM has challenged the traditional CRM vendors by redefining the space around a differentiated CRM solution that is based on an intelligent, open architecture that operates across multiple channels in real time. *Smart* CRM provides the flexibility to be custom configured to meet the needs of the organization's business processes at the department or individual level. *Smart* CRM is driven by an embedded recognition of the customer followed by immediate, real-time action to meet the needs of the customer. *Smart* CRM embraces a pure Web architecture that leverages existing investments, delivers rapid ROI, a low total cost of ownership, and a higher adoption rate.

The benefits that *Smart* CRM delivers over traditional CRM are clear to any business user or CIO.

The leading companies will move quickly to implement *Smart* CRM to lock in customer value, and then they will hold on to those customers through understanding their preferences and being relevant to their lives. The laggards will find themselves left behind where wallet share has already been determined.

Michael Simpson, President, 5ᵗʰ Line, Inc.

With more than 14 years of experience in the software industry, Michael Simpson has often been recognized as a leading marketing and industry strategist. He is currently the president of 5th Line, Inc., a management consulting firm. Prior to this he was chief marketing officer for Interact Commerce Corporation. Mr. Simpson contributed to their position as the leading mid-market CRM provider and helped further the growth of the best-selling contact manager, ACT!

Before joining Interact Commerce Corporation, Mr. Simpson worked for Novell, Inc., where he last served as director of strategic market planning. He joined Novell in 1992 and is widely credited with engineering the core positioning and marketing strategy for their directory services business that helped power a turnaround at Novell, the world's fifth-largest software company. Before Novell, he was general manager of a network integration and consulting firm.

Mr. Simpson has been a guest speaker on industry direction in more than 20 countries and has appeared in the global business and industry press, including *US News & World Report*, the *Washington Post*, CNN, and CNBC.

DEFINITION

What is CRM? Well, I guess the answer to that is usually determined by the person you are asking, and what he or she gets out of having a customer relationship managed. Therefore, it is important to look at it from the perspective of the different participants. We'll get to that in due time, but we first must lay some groundwork to measure those perspectives.

Most people and businesses look at CRM as a combination of software and business process to accomplish a particular set of goals, usually centered on growing top-line revenue. The component milestones, or methods, around the base revenue objectives are often disputed. And, in fact, I would argue they morph a bit along the edges for each company even after initial implementation depending on the current condition of the business. But there should be some absolutes that are fundamental constants.

There are the obvious basics that may or may not be necessary to mention, but I'm doing it anyway. First of all, CRM should not be totally self-serving in its individual methods of implementation, meaning it needs to assist your customer, but it had better benefit the top and bottom lines of the company as its ultimate goal. After all, you're not in business to implement cool technology—you're in it to make money, plain and simple. What smart companies understand—well, actually, any company that has survived its own business or market's initial growth period and subsequent reality—is that your level of understanding and effort toward your customers' experience in dealing with you versus your competitors is the primary determining factor of future revenues. And, of course, your ability to retain customers is a major determining factor in what your bottom line looks like because the cost of acquiring new customers is exponentially greater than selling to existing ones.

So, the elements of CRM that need to be understood must start with what the essence of a relationship is. A lot of people are fond of saying that relationships are based on trust, but frankly, that's a crock. Certainly, positive and mutually "enjoyable" relationships are based on trust as a major factor, but that is not required for a relationship to be mutually beneficial, thus justified, and even relatively solid. If you strip away all the hype around how to "do" relationships, you are left with one simple concept. The real essence of a relationship is simply a memory of past interactions.

Think about it. Once you have an interaction with an individual, bi-directionally, you carry that memory into your next interaction. But you don't start over from scratch each time unless maybe it's your 103-year-old grandmother you're talking about—you build on those past interactions. How you constantly recall and apply past interactions to present ones defines the quality of your relationships. I know this sounds like a bunch of philosophical mumbo-jumbo, but understanding this foundational truth is paramount to building a filter for every effort you make in the world of CRM.

When you have a relationship with an individual, you would be pretty frustrated if every time you spoke to that person he or she had no recollection of your previous conversation. If every time you were forced to start from scratch, you would, in short order, realize that your relationship wasn't going anywhere, was too frustrating and time consuming with very little return, and you would avoid that person completely. In fact, you would likely even be angry enough to let others know about your negative experience with that person.

Well, when you have a relationship with one of your customers, you may think about the individual as a component of their overall account; but that is rarely the case from your customer's perspective. Whether you sell through partners or direct sales, if the salespeople represent themselves as you, your customers will think they have a relationship with *your* company because they have a relationship with a representative. Whether that customer is truly an individual, or an individual in a business that's a customer, the customer thinks of your company as a single entity. Freud might have been comfortable dividing people into their ids, egos, and superegos, but most of us consider ourselves to be single entities. And that's how customers view our companies, too. That goes for your websites as well.

This highlights one of the greatest objectives of CRM: to create a consistent customer experience. Your relationship with a customer should be thought of as an ongoing conversation without end. Regardless of who your customers talk to, whether your accounts receivables person, customer service rep, salesperson, or in receiving a call from telemarketing, a direct marketing letter, or even returning to your website, they expect that you have some collective consciousness. Fail to demonstrate that collective consciousness and they'll believe you just don't appreciate them or their business. The result is that your relationship is vulnerable to the next price war or marketing program from a competitor. You could be just a click away from starting over with that customer, but doing it from the doghouse, a disadvantage a competitor who, has no history with your customer, is free from. That's right, the history of your relationship with your customer could very well be the thing that makes you vulnerable if you don't take it seriously.

So how do you create this collective consciousness? Well, CRM is obviously the solution, but although software is a necessary component, there is more to it than that. Getting people to use the software is the key—and that requires some business process, a clear understanding of the value it provides the individuals, some pretty serious efforts in internal evangelism, and clear, measurable returns.

You must build an infrastructure that links a history of your customer interactions together in a common data source. Yes, you can connect your customer-facing sales teams, support, marketing, back office, and Web presences so that you can get everybody sharing a common understanding of that customer. And you should mold the solution to the way your people and your customers work—not the other way around. Whether wireless, Web, remote, or in the office, they need to be completely informed to be effective.

CRM is about creating a consistent customer history so you can create a consistent customer experience. This enables accountability and team-based assistance in managing that customer. It enables potential and existing customers to feel cared for, deepening their loyalty, resulting in increased sales.

When you think about what CRM is for you, think about what every participant in that management process needs to be successful—including your customer.

Robert Thompson, President, Front Line Solutions, Inc.

Robert Thompson is founder and president of Front Line Solutions, Inc., an independent CRM consulting and research firm specializing in the emerging field of partner relationship management (PRM). Through his groundbreaking research in PRM requirements and best practices, he has earned a reputation as the industry's leading PRM consultant.

In January 2000, Mr. Thompson founded CRMGuru.com (http://www.crmguru.com/), which has become the largest and fastest-growing CRM portal, with more than 100,000 members worldwide. CRMGuru.com unites a worldwide community of business managers who want to learn about CRM and exchange ideas and perspectives with others.

Mr. Thompson is frequently quoted in industry publications such as *InformationWeek*, *Computerworld*, and *CRN*, formerly *Computer Reseller News*, and speaks at numerous industry conferences. In 2000, he was the chairman of the first two PRM conferences in the United States and participated as chairman or keynote speaker at several conferences in 2001. Mr. Thompson writes a regular column for *VARBusiness* magazine, publishes the CRM e-newsletter *On the Front Line*, and is the moderator for CRM.Talk, the world's largest CRM email discussion list.

Throughout his career, Mr. Thompson has advised leading companies on the strategic use of information technology to solve business problems and gain a competitive advantage. Prior to starting his consulting firm in 1998, he had fifteen years of experience in the IT industry, including positions as business unit executive and IT strategy consultant at IBM, and as vice-president of a large value-added reseller.

Mr. Thompson is a board member of the Northern California chapter of the CRMA, a professional association dedicated to the CRM industry. He earned a Bachelor's degree and an M.B.A. from the University of California, Irvine.

Definition

CRM is a term that gained widespread recognition in the late 1990s. Market analysts say that billions of dollars will be spent on CRM solutions—software and services designed to help businesses more effectively manage customer relationships through all types of direct and indirect channels.

Yet even as the market for CRM technology expands, confusion reigns. The most common question asked at our CRM portal CRMGuru.com is simply: "What is CRM?"

A panel of CRM experts—the "gurus" working with CRMGuru.com—developed this answer:

> Customer Relationship Management (CRM) is a business strategy to select and manage customers to optimize long-term value. CRM requires a customer-centric business philosophy and culture to support effective marketing, sales, and service processes. CRM applications can enable effective Customer Relationship Management, provided that an enterprise has the right leadership, strategy, and culture.

So there it is, simple question and simple answer, right? Well, as many business executives and CRM project managers can attest, effective CRM is not all simple or easy. For starters, how exactly does a company create a "customer-centric business philosophy and culture"? Not with a software package, that's for sure.

As the pyramid diagram in Figure 1-4 shows, CRM must start with a business strategy, which drives changes in the organization and work processes, which are in turn enabled by information technology. The reverse does not work—a company cannot automate its way to a new business strategy. In fact, the majority of projects that focus on technology first, rather than business objectives, are destined for failure, according to extensive best practices research. However, a customer-centric business can reap significant benefits using CRM technology.

CRM as a business strategy is not a new idea. Savvy business executives have always understood that they should focus on customers with the best potential for sales and profits, and provide good service so they'll come back again and again. And technology is not required for effective CRM. Consider a successful small business. The business owner and the staff work hard to provide personal, high-quality service, building a loyal customer base over time. Computers are not necessarily required.

Why, then, has CRM become so popular? The bottom line: Power has shifted to customers due to the convergence of three powerful trends:

▸ ERP systems are no longer a source of competitive advantage for most companies. The back office is fully automated, now what?

▸ The cycle of innovation to production to obsolescence has accelerated, leading to an abundance of options for customers and a shrinking market window for vendors.

▸ The Internet has made it far easier for customers to decide which supplier to buy from and, if necessary, to switch to another vendor at the click of a mouse.

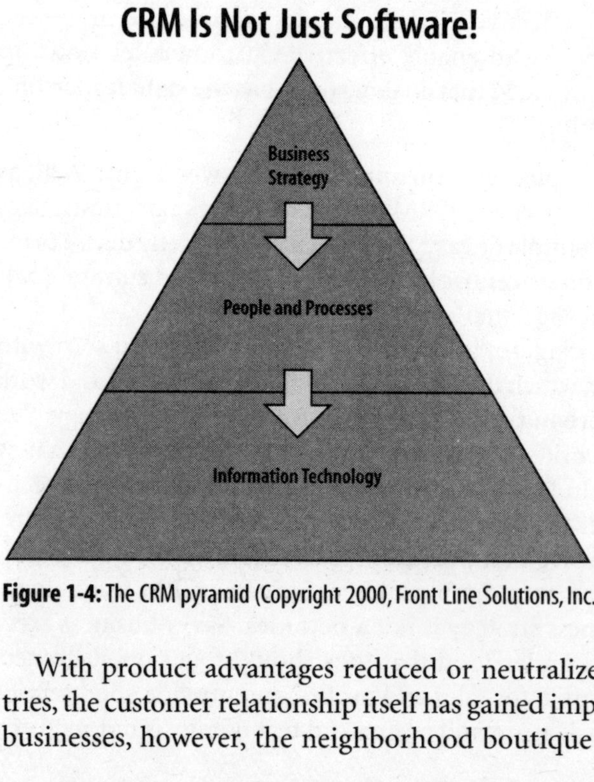

CRM Is Not Just Software!

Figure 1-4: The CRM pyramid (Copyright 2000, Front Line Solutions, Inc. All rights reserved.)

With product advantages reduced or neutralized in many industries, the customer relationship itself has gained importance. For larger businesses, however, the neighborhood boutique approach doesn't work. CRM technology provides a more systematic way of managing customer relationships on a larger scale.

CRM applications support marketing, sales, commerce, and service processes, as shown in the CRM Solutions Map in Figure 1-5.

Traditionally, enterprise employees have been the primary users of CRM applications. Then e-business or eCRM applications were introduced to allow enterprises to interact directly with customers via corporate websites, e-commerce storefronts, and self-service applications. Finally, starting in 1999, PRM applications hit the market, designed to support channel partners and other intermediaries between an enterprise and its end customers.

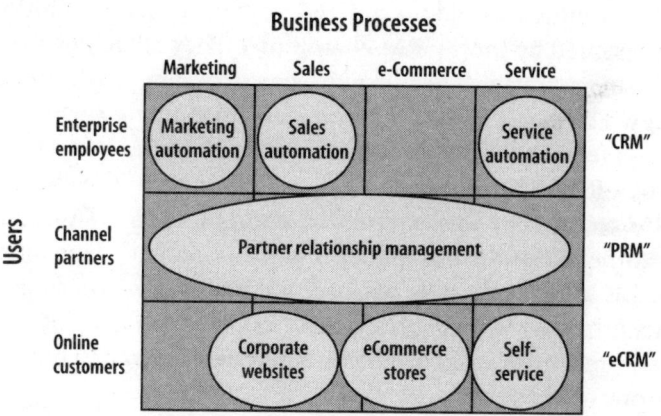

Figure 1-5: CRM Solutions Map (Copyright 2000 Front Line Solutions, Inc. All rights reserved.)

These applications support the following business processes involved in the customer relationship life cycle:

Marketing Targeting prospects and acquiring new customers through data mining, campaign management, and lead distribution.

Sales Closing business with effective selling processes, using proposal generators, configurators, knowledge management tools, contact managers, and forecasting aids.

E-commerce In the Internet age, selling processes should transfer seamlessly into purchasing transactions, done quickly, conveniently, and at the lowest cost.

Service Handling post-sales service and support issues with sophisticated call center applications or Web-based customer self-service products.

In summary, CRM is a disciplined business strategy to create and sustain long-term, profitable customer relationships. Successful CRM initiatives start with a business strategy and philosophy that aligns company activities around customer needs. CRM technology is a critical enabler of the processes required to turn strategy into business results.

What Is CRM Technology?

You can see the confluences and the differences in the general definition of CRM as presented by these CRM champions. They all define it as a disciplined business strategy. They acknowledge technology as the driver of the strategy. This book is about the car, and particularly, the driver. So with that agreement, we now have to take it a tad deeper. What is the technology of CRM? The industry standard definition of the components of CRM technology was expounded upon by the META Group in "The Customer Relationship Management Ecosystem." This interesting "delta," as META calls it, is available for free after registering on their website, http://www.metagroup.com/. In plainspeak, a delta is a substantial summary designed to get you interested enough to buy the report. This one could work.

Types of CRM Technology

In the accepted META Group-driven definition of CRM, there are three segments: operational, analytical, and collaborative. The technological architecture is spoke-to-spoke between the operational and analytical. Operational CRM is the customer-facing applications of CRM—the aforementioned sales force automation, enterprise marketing automation, and front-office suites that encompass all of this simultaneously. The analytic segment includes data marts or data warehouses such as customer repositories that are used by applications that apply algorithms to dissect the data and present it in a form that is useful to the user. The collaborative CRM reaches across customer touch points (all the different communication means that a customer might interact with, such as email, phone call, fax, website pages, and so on). It includes applications such as the partner relationship management

(PRM) software you will become familiar with as you move through this book.

While this definition is still a useful heuristic device for understanding CRM, it is beginning to evolve. One milestone in its evolution is the use of embedded analytics in the operational and collaborative CRM applications. Analytics become a real-time tool for understanding the transactions and the data that operational and collaborative CRM evoke. Thus, once again, the waters of CRM definitions get muddy. Just as we find that nice, clear, now-useable-for-crops "CRM-and-eCRM are no longer different" filtered H_2O, we find that upstream is becoming murky at the point we wanted to build our settlement. Operational, collaborative, and analytical CRM are beginning to mean something somewhat different in 2002 than they did in 2000 and 2001.

Operational CRM

This is the "ERP-like" segment of CRM. Typical business functions involving customer service, order management, invoice/billing, or sales and marketing automation and management are all part of this bandwidth on the spectrum. This is perhaps the primary use of CRM to date. One facet of operational CRM is the possibility of integrating with the financial and human resources functions of the enterprise resource planning (ERP) applications such as PeopleSoft and SAP. With this integration, end-to-end functionality from lead management to order tracking can be implemented, albeit not often seamlessly. In fact, CRM project failure rates, according to the oft-quoted studies done by the various analyst organizations, are purported to be between 55 and 75 percent. One reason for project failure, and sometimes the cause of problems even when the implementation is successful, is the inability to integrate with legacy systems.

Analytical CRM

Analytical CRM is the capture, storage, extraction, processing, interpretation, and reporting of customer data to a user. Companies such as MicroStrategy have developed applications that can capture this customer data from multiple sources and store it in a customer data repository and then use hundreds of algorithms to analyze/interpret the data as needed. The value of the application is not just in the algorithms and storage, but also in the ability to individually personalize the response using the data.

Collaborative CRM

This is almost an overlay. It is the communication center, the coordination network, that provides the neural paths to the customer and his suppliers. It could mean a portal, a partner relationship management (PRM) application, or a customer interaction center (CIC). It could mean communication channels such as the Web or email, voice applications, or snail mail. It could mean channel strategies. In other words, it is any CRM function that provides a point of interaction between the customer and the channel itself.

CRM Technology Components

Besides the types of CRM that are available for you to choose from, there are components that make it up. What is the difference? Imagine operational, analytical, and collaborative CRM as the car models. The components are the under-the-hood things—some with chrome, some encrusted with grease, but all under the hood.

CRM Engine

This would be the customer data repository. The data mart or data warehouse is where all data on the customer is captured and stored. This could include basic stuff such as name, address, phone number, and birth date. It could include more sophisticated information such as the number of times you accessed the Lands' End website (I *know* you did) and what you did on the pages you accessed, including the amount of time you lingered over that cashmere sweater. It could include the helpdesk support and purchase history with Lands' End.

Ultimately, the purpose is a single gathering point for all individual customer information so that a unified customer view can be created throughout all company departments that need to know the data stored in this CRM engine house.

This engine provides the personalization that most of the readers of this book are familiar with through Amazon.com. Tell me, readers, have you ever bought a book from Amazon.com? Have you ever bought a second book from Amazon.com? Have you ever bought a book from barnesandnoble.com?

I can almost *guarantee* that you've bought more than one book from Amazon.com and none from barnesandnoble.com. Yet the inventory is the same, the pricing nearly the same, and both are websites. I'm sure that you still love to wander the bricks and mortar part of Barnes and Noble. Yet you don't shop there online and you do at Amazon.com. Why is that?

Interestingly, I put these questions to an audience of 350 CIOs, VPs of IT, and the equivalent in June 2001 at the Computerworld Premier100 Conference in Palm Springs, California, the world's hottest (meaning: highest temperature, which to me = least desirable) resort town. After some backing and forthing, their answer was that it is a much warmer and fuzzier experience, more personal at Amazon.com than barnesandnoble.com. Amazon.com seems to know what I want. Barnesandnoble.com doesn't. It was that simple.

Under the hood, this means a much more substantial customer data repository and a much better extraction and analysis engine. This part isn't so simple, but what results!

Front-Office Solutions

These are the unified applications that run on top of the customer data warehouse (CDW). They could be sales force automation, marketing automation, or service and support and customer interaction applications. The important thing is that analytics, reports, and the easy instant access to this information are hallmarks of these solutions. In the client/server environment, and now the more revved Internet environment, they provide employees with the information they need to make informed choices on what to do next with a customer—whether it is a sales opportunity closing or solving a customer complaint.

The more specific applications provide an element of self-service for the customer. For example, when you log onto Amazon.com with your personal ID and password, you get specific recommendations that are based on those complex analytic algorithms, interpreting what it sees as your preferences in a pretty sophisticated way. Nary a human soul touched your file. It was all automated. The self-service is your ability to act on the recommendations (that is, to purchase them). In fact, when I queried those CIOs, et al, about how many of them had spoken to a human at the warm and fuzzy Amazon.com, the answer (out of 350 people) was one.

Both types of applications are essential to a complete CRM system.

Enterprise Application Integrations (EAIs) for CRM

These sit between the CRM back office and front office. They also sit between the newly installed CRM system and the been-around-forever enterprise legacy systems. They also allow CRM-to-CRM communications. "They" are pieces of code and connectors and bridges that as a body are called EAIs, formerly known as middleware. EAIs provide the messaging services and data mapping services that allow one system to communicate with disparate other systems, regardless of formatting. With the move of the Internet to the mainstream, it is hoped that the Extensible Markup Language (XML) will be the universal go-between, allowing one system to correspond with another. However, because of the current state of XML, with the evolution of vertical XMLs with different data descriptions particular to the vertical industry, XML universality is not quite there, though it continues to gain ground as the standard. The issue for EAI connectors has always been price, with connectors that would link Siebel to SAP amounting to a cost of tens and potentially even hundreds of thousands of dollars to purchase and configure. More recently, though, companies like Scribe Systems have been producing reasonably priced, very effective connectors and interfaces for multi-system interaction.

With their arrival in late 2001, Internet architectures (see Chapter 2) are reducing the need for these pieces of code. Through its HTML code heritage and its XML meta-tag superstructure, Internet architectures allow for integration without the middleware, APIs, or EAI code chunks. More on that later.

CRM in the Back Office

In the first edition of this book, I identified analytic tools as the "back office" of CRM. I'm not exactly recanting, but I'm changing that. There has been significant evolution in CRM over the past year plus since the book was written (note: I didn't say "since it was published"—the cycle is different). Analytics are becoming increasingly integrated from the beginning with the other elements of CRM. In fact, embedded analytics are now part of a few of the multifunctional CRM applications such as PeopleSoft CRM 8.0. So while the operations of the analytic algorithms are still occurring in the background, they have clear and distinct visibility (you can see for miles and miles) within the operational applications you are accessing in real time. That means if you need to see your clients' sales performance, you can see it as it occurs or at least as it is entered into the system. This is a significant advance in the real value of a CRM system for the users of that system.

Customer Life Cycle

What about the customer? What about the customer life cycle? Is the life cycle what the customer rides in order to get him back to good health? Not exactly. You are going to see references to this throughout the book and an entire appendix devoted to customer lifetime value (CLV). What the hell is all this about?

Pretty straightforward, really. It is far cheaper to retain existing customers than to acquire new customers. During periods of economic decline, this becomes a survival necessity, not just a value proposition. Therefore, presuming that this is the goal of most companies, whether prosperous or struggling, the next thing to determine is the value of the customer to your company. A customer who is consistently losing money for you, while he has been with you for 40 years, is not valuable to you directly, though there may be some value to you in the marketing. But how do you figure that out? The life cycle of the customer is the process the customer has been undergoing to be with you for all these years. This includes the customer's purchase history, perhaps how often she's taken advantage of special offers directed at her or her customer class. Depending on what you identify as important to your return on investment (ROI), it could also include your customers' marketing value to you and how much revenue that marketing value could be worth indirectly. To find out what is the expected revenue generated from a single customer over the anticipated lifetime of that customer's relationship with you is both the customer life cycle and the CLV.

Customer Interaction

Some of the value that technology brings to the table in CRM is through increased customer interaction that doesn't necessarily occur with a human being. It is convenience and the ability of the customers to get something they need without having to rely on a busy human being, or worse, a lazy human being. I would rather be able to act on a recommendation from the Amazon.com personalization machine than have a human being suggest what I should read—unless that human being was someone I already trusted. Big difference. The psychology of this automated interaction is interesting. If I see a recommendation to buy *CRM at the Speed of Light: Capturing and Keeping Customers in Internet Real Time*, and I'm interested in CRM, I'm going to give it a look and perhaps purchase this worthy title. If a salesperson recommends it to me, unless I asked him to recommend a good CRM title, I'm going to think he is telling me to buy something so he can get a commission. I'm always going to be a tad suspicious that he is pushing overstock (heaven forbid!) or a book that has his agenda behind it, not my interest. Oddly, if it is a book suggested by my reading habits, the very nature of the suggestion—impersonal, analytic— is going to make me more inclined to look. It's more my agenda, under my control. Yet, I haven't spoken to a single human throughout the transaction. Hmmm.

As you'll see in Chapter 9, what used to be helpdesks or customer service calls can often be taken care of on the Internet with the customers helping themselves to an answer. The early "interaction" was document fax back. Now it is far more sophisticated, with both service information instantly available to the customer service representative (operational) and service without service representatives, but with customer interaction available.

This interaction is a critical component of CRM—especially the online variety.

I think that we're ready to move on. CRM defined. Now on to eCRM.

2

Making the "e" in eCRM Vanish: The Newest Thing

A year ago, it was troublesome trying to figure out the differences between CRM and eCRM (besides the "e"). In discussions and writings, I often used them interchangeably. I was right—sort of. As we lope through 2002, no matter what you hear or see from the big bad wolves of marketing, there is *no* difference between eCRM and CRM. None at all.

What makes this contentious statement all the more definitive is that Web-enabled CRM is now the norm for the CRM industry. If you don't have CRM that can be run through a browser, you might as well be a small-market baseball franchise. You simply won't compete. It doesn't matter what you think or prefer to do. Read my lips: You-will-not-compete. However, note that I didn't say that Web-*based* CRM is now the norm. As we will see in this chapter and elsewhere, Web-based CRM is the cutting edge as 2002 rolls.

I don't exaggerate here at all. Begun by the creation of the "e" suites of E.piphany as a Java-based architecture in 1999 and the release of Onyx's OEP the same year, the final nail in the e-coffin was driven by the June 2001 release of PeopleSoft CRM 8.0 and the more recent release of Siebel 7.0 with its Smart Web architecture. Why? Their architectures are written from the ground up in Internet lingo such as Java, JavaScript, HTML, or DHTML. Every tier is defined by its Internet code purity. It is only a matter of time before the other vendors wise up.

CRM and eCRM: What's Different? Anything?

It used to be that the difference between CRM and eCRM was that eCRM was Web-enabled, self-service applications while CRM tended to be client/server based. Then eCRM was seen as CRM that had a portal or a browser-based entry point. The debate raged; the discussions were emotional and ultimately not all that important. There were myriad issues, questions, approaches, technologies, and architectures that were different from client/server-based CRM. Some of them were general issues related to the Internet. Others were general issues related to the creation of applications for the Internet. The third group was related to eCRM directly and its actual value to business.

Take a look at a "headline" from 2001:

> "How is CRM different from e-CRM, and do CRM packages have functionality to make them e-CRM packages?" (SearchCRM.com, April 26, 2001)

The answer that Paul Sweeny gave (correctly) was that the distinction between the two was beginning to blur.

After the so-called dot-com bomb exploded, the recognition of the real value of the Internet as a communications channel became mainstream knowledge. This had an overt effect on the CRM versus eCRM debate. eCRM was a channel, not a separate technology. Companies like consulting firm Breakaway Solutions among many others were using CRM and eCRM interchangeably in their presentations, just like I did in the first edition of this book. But it was rightfully seen that the "e" was an added dimension—a powerful, flexible channel that customers could use to interact with companies. Please note that, in this second edition, eCRM, except for this chapter, has now been folded into the CRM franchise. It is a post dot-com-bust merger of terms that has been added to the dictionary of twenty-first century business. It's a better addition than "junk bond," "negative equity," or "coredump," isn't it?

But by mid- and late-2001, to "e" or not to "e" was still a question. As the differences became increasingly unclear, frightening warps began to appear as vendors and others began to rework how they viewed this terms merger. For example, an article in one CRM-focused publication printed a table from a CRM software company that claims one of the differences between traditional CRM and eCRM is that traditional CRM is "company-centric!" Given what is clear about CRM already, traditional or otherwise, my only response to this can be: What a fraud! This was concocted by a vendor who wanted to justify and pseudo-differentiate their "eCRM" suite. It goes on to state that there are more differences between this traditional CRM and eCRM, such as the fact that sales force automation and enterprise marketing automation are not integrated in traditional CRM as they are in eCRM. They also stated that with traditional CRM, customer data was used for history review and in eCRM it was used for personalization, up-selling, and cross-selling. Yikes! Defile CRM just so their "eCRM" suite was "differentiated." Their eCRM is what CRM was by that time and is now. This self-serving piece is a good example of how absurd things got when the differences were no longer really there. This was May 2001. The time for the terms merger was fast approaching.

The drive toward this merger of terms had technically begun in 1999, with the previously mentioned release of Onyx OEP (Onyx Enterprise Portal) 1.0 and E.piphany's E.4 suite. But these releases didn't mean that Internet architecture had national corporate acceptance into either the hearts or minds of the business world. While, even at this writing, you can still find occasional attempts at differentiating CRM and eCRM in the world of techno-speak, the pesky "e" is pretty much gone. With the June 2001 release of PeopleSoft's CRM 8.0 (and the release a year earlier of the same Internet architecture for People-Soft's ERP applications) and the later release of Siebel's 7.0 Smart Web architecture, the coup was almost complete. CRM is the champion. The "e" is outré. The reason? To be twenty-first-century CRM or use it, you need to either have or use a browser-based application.

What's Wrong with the Old Way?

Can't we just do things the old way (client/server CRM being the "old way")? Nah. The use of the Internet as a main business artery is why there is a CRM continually evolving as we write. As the U.S. population becomes increasingly comfortable using the Internet *securely*, it is increasingly likely that more of the standard business transactions that are done on the phone or even in person will be done via the Internet. The initial and continuing popular trust of online business activity is coming through America's favorite pastime—shopping. This is reflected in a Roper/AOL Cyberstudy conducted in early 2000 about online purchasing habits. It showed an increase from 31 percent of the Internet community purchasing something online in 1998 to 42 percent of the same group purchasing semi-regularly online in 1999. The increases were due to more women getting involved. In 1998, 24 percent of the purchasers were women; in 1999, women comprised 37 percent of the total. This same behavior is expected to drive the percentages even higher this year because studies done in mid-2000 indicate that, for the first time, Internet users are primarily women (52 percent). In fact, by 2004, according to the Forrester Group, the business-to-consumer (B2C) market is estimated to be $184 billion.

This is nothing by comparison to the potential for the business-to-business (B2B) market. Prior to the dot-com bomb, the estimates for the B2B markets were wildly optimistic. The B2C $184 billion is dwarfed by Forrester's estimate of $2.7 trillion in B2B —and they were the pessimists. The Gartner Group for the same time period estimated $7.3 trillion. However, since the collapse of the Internet companies and in the wake of the events of September 11, 2001, the market forecasts were tempered, though not as dramatically as you might think. For example, in October 2001, IDC issued a report on the state of the global IT market and forecast a spending of $1.3 trillion over the five quarters beginning in fourth quarter 2001, on information technology–related expenditures alone! This after everything had already hit.

Estimates notwithstanding, what is significant is that the evolution of secured trust in engaging in commercial activity online is increasing dramatically. What does this mean for CRM? How does translating to the Web mean something either better or at least significantly different for a business?

The Web Experience

As hokey as it may sound, there *is* a "Web experience." It is a complex set of relationships between the Web surfer and the people (either anonymous or known) at the other end of the Internet line, with the Internet being the channel the parties use to communicate with each other. The relationships between the parties and the *interactions* between them are very different from other forms of interaction. For example, how often have you decided to email a friend rather than call him? The thought behind it is that it is easier to email than call. Is that the reason? Let's take a quick peek. You're emailing him a four-paragraph note on something that happened to you at work. You'd, of course, like his comments on it. You then feel compelled to comment on his comments. *Ad infinitum*. The total time was about ten minutes of typing and sending the email. If no response is necessary, five minutes max. A phone call, especially if he was on speed dial, was probably two minutes, or five minutes total with responses. But doing it the email way stripped out the other things that go on in phone conversations (including nuance and tone), could be composed at your leisure (meaning no particular block of time was roped off to do it), sent at your leisure, and responded to and from at your (and your correspondent's) leisure. Additionally, there were no distractions in the discussion. The subject matter written was the subject matter referenced. No more, no less. The interaction was there without the interaction being actually there. No baggage, no emotion, and no complicated thought process. It was what it was—and it didn't save you a bit of time. It just seemed that way because you had more individual control over the process.

That reflects what is both good and peculiar about the Web experience. Why peculiar? It is a social interaction done in isolation that creates as many problems as it solves. There is never actually a substitute for human interaction, but there is also no way an individual human can cover all bases all the time with a customer. For example, if you are a salesperson making a call to a customer site and meeting with the executive vice-president of a company, it would be helpful to know that the EVP had emailed to the site with a customer service question to a different division a week before. He had also spent time studying the Web pages that were concerned with your expenses-tracking software and your ERP financial package. Additionally, he watched a demo and downloaded a white paper on the integration of CRM and the back office. All this information related to the EVP's Web experience was captured by the various site tools and centralized in a customer repository. It was analyzed through various analytic algorithms that were then compiled into a report you access using your laptop or Palm, depending on what eCRM software you use. By the time you reach the EVP's office, you are armed and ready (with the information, that is). The website he logged into promoted your products very well. He was able to identify your financial package as the one he wanted. He also enjoyed the look and feel of the website and the sophistication of the demonstrations. This gave him more subliminal faith in your product's sophistication, your company's professionalism, and thus your ability to deliver your application successfully.

The EVP's transactions are a small segment of the Web experience. What is the purpose of the Web experience in the CRM world? It is to identify a customer, derive the value of the customer, and interact with the customer. This is so, whether it is a single individual who buys more frequently than other individuals or a corporation that is doing more business (or less) with you than any other customer. Its odd nature makes innovation necessary to make the identification, derivation, and interaction happen to the benefit of your customer and your company.

CRM's value (the pre-terms-merger eCRM) comes from giving a customer that "total experience" on the Web. Traditional client/server

CRM channels can't do that because they are based on applications that may not be amenable to giving the customer direct access to interfaces and functionality. Ordinarily, CRM provides a set of tools that, while possibly Web-enabled, aren't designed from the ground up for the Web. They have been intended more for the corporate department or the individual employee to do his customer-related intelligence, marketing, and service more effectively. In the past—until Onyx, E.piphany, and later, PeopleSoft—there hadn't been a ground-up creation or redevelopment so that all functions, external and internal, are entirely Web based. For example, personalization tools are more appropriate to Web customer experiences than they are to client/server-based internal corporate processes (see Chapter 8 for a detailed discussion of personalization). However, even this Web-enabled or Web-based "experience" doesn't guarantee that eCRM is entirely wonderful. Brent Frei, president and CEO of Onyx Software, provides this caution:

> eCRM is a term that some people have used to describe the customer-facing Internet portion of CRM. The term usually implies capabilities like self-service knowledge bases, automated email response, personalization of Web content, online product bundling and pricing, and so on. eCRM gives Internet users the ability to interact with the business through their preferred communication channel, and it allows the business to offset expensive customer service agents with technology. So the value is largely one of improved customer satisfaction and reduced cost through improved efficiency.

> Today, you do your firm and your customers a disservice to make a distinction between eCRM and whatever else is left over. Customers define your firm and your brand based on your people, processes, and offers. If they get one experience through your website, another when they call on the phone, another when some salesperson calls who has no idea they're a customer, another when they walk through your door, and still another when you send out a marketing piece offering something they already own, you have a problem. If the customer's interactions through one channel are not seamlessly integrated with those taking place through all the others, it's just a question of time before the customer becomes frustrated and vulnerable to offers from firms that can get it right. The one piece of advice I'd offer on eCRM is to stop making the distinction, and start thinking about delivering a seamless customer experience everywhere you touch the customer.

The Features of CRM Architecture

The technology of the "e" has probably been the most debated facet of the eCRM versus CRM debate. That debate is over, though there are many who may argue with me about that. The Internet is now the communications engine of choice for most IT. It is also the architecture of choice for CRM, despite the fact that Internet architecture is still cutting-edge. It is only a matter of time before it becomes the complete Henkel knife set.

The Machinery: Rebuilt Engine or New Engine?

Some CRM companies have Web-enabled their existing application and called it "Internet ready." Others have redesigned it from the bottom up so that it is a Web application, rather than a client/server application that can be viewed on the Web. These are fundamental architectural differences. Mere accessibility from a browser does not give CRM applications Internet architecture. For the technology to fulfill its true promise of making the desired customer activity possible, the invisible technical details really do matter. For example, do you want to have an application that is optimized for Internet activity—meaning it uses HTML; is accessible from your desktop, your Palm, or your laptop; can be accessed securely using Internet security protocols; is reachable via TCP/IP; and so on? Or would you rather have something that works from a more standard client/server architecture and can be accessed in a more kludgy fashion via a browser, but is only half as functional as the pure Internet-based application? (Pardon my biases here.)

Application servers drive the pure Internet CRM applications. The application servers that are often found in three-tier architectures are not created just for the Internet—client/server architecture is, in fact, why the three-tiered approach was fashioned. But n-tiered approaches are the best contemporary architecture for the Internet. The application servers provide preconstructed Web pages to a Web server that delivers them to the users through their Web browsers. This model preserves the fundamental value of the Internet as a communications medium—common, platform-independent access to data anytime, anywhere. There is no program or application code that needs to reside on the user's PC; therefore users gain immediate access to the application with the right URL and security authorization. It's just like using your Web browser to view any other Web page: Click the right link and you see the information.

However, that doesn't mean that all Internet architectures are alike (would thinking that be Web-ist?). Let's take a quick, very broad look (in Table 2-1) at some of the differences in how the CRM companies who have what they claim are Internet architectures are built, so that you can see that what I say is true.

Table 2-1: Comparative Look at CRM-Pure Internet Architectural Components

Company	Components of Internet Architecture
PeopleSoft	PowerHTML, JavaScript, XML, WML, WMLScript, HTTP, WAP
Oracle	HTML, Java, Oracle forms moving toward pure HTML
Siebel	DHTML, JavaScript, XML, Document Object Model (DOM), WML, WAP
E.piphany	C/C++, HTML, JavaScript, moving toward Java 2 Enterprise Edition (aka J2EE), has common metadata platform
Onyx	XML Integration Platform, n-tier, aimed at taking advantage of Microsoft.NET Web services
Pivotal	XML, Microsoft.NET focused
KANA	XML, J2EE, Enterprise Java Beans, COM and KANA Data Objects (KDO)

In Depth: PeopleSoft 8.0 CRM Internet Architecture

Let's take an in-depth look at the architecture of one of the vendors just mentioned—PeopleSoft 8.0 CRM.

Why Them? How I Chose the Examples in this Book

Explaining the criteria I used to choose PeopleSoft as an example will show you how I put this book together and how biases, whether to your liking or not, work. Politics never come into play in something like this, but biased neutrality does. To write this book, I have to have cooperation from the vendors, their customers (that is, senior management and users), CRM analysts, systems integrators, independent CRM consultants, vendor partners, and IT journalists, as well as rely on my own observations and independent research. I'm a highly opinionated guy, and like anyone else who writes, a lot of what I do and say is influenced by research from primary and secondary sources. It takes lots of time to make this work. I do a very careful analysis of what I get from those conversations, copious handwritten notes, clippings, Acrobat and MS Word files, search engine results, and many other paper and electronic sources. The results make for a book that reflects my

(Continued on next page)

WHY THEM? HOW I CHOSE THE EXAMPLES IN THIS BOOK (*continued*)

opinions on the CRM world. I try to stay fair in expressing these opinions, even the insulting ones, though I'm sure I fall off the edge now and then. But this huge amount of work goes into making even the seemingly simple choice as to what vendor I use for examples.

Now on to the specific reasons I chose PeopleSoft as my example:

1. *PeopleSoft has large market presence with active enterprise-level applications for the front and back office, making them a complete package and thus showing maximally how Internet architecture can be used. So does Oracle.*

2. *PeopleSoft has a history with this architecture. PeopleSoft implemented this architecture with their Human Resources and Financials packages (formerly known as ERP) two years ago, making it representative of what a mature Internet architecture should look like. (The other two-year-old architectures are E.piphany and Onyx.)*

3. *It is scalable (though so are several of the others mentioned, notably E.piphany and Siebel) and is thus available in all sizes—with caveats I won't outline here.*

4. *When I do multiple advanced Web searches with multiple tools on CRM Internet architecture, PeopleSoft CRM 8.0 is by far the most prevalent name that pops up, thus showing the value of good marketing and their ability to get their metatags placed well.*

5. *They were among the most cooperative in giving me the details I needed to get a thorough look at the architecture, though others were nearly as cooperative.*

6. *Outside analysts have called PeopleSoft's Internet architecture "best-in-class" and, hey, you readers deserve the best!*

What wasn't at issue was how the architecture was constructed because that varies widely from vendor to vendor, as Table 2-1 briefly shows.

That said, I chose PeopleSoft, which was the survivor when run through all these filters.

The PeopleSoft Internet architecture (see Figure 2-1) is built with totally new code in what PeopleSoft calls PowerHTML and works with standard Internet protocols and languages, such as HTTP and XML.

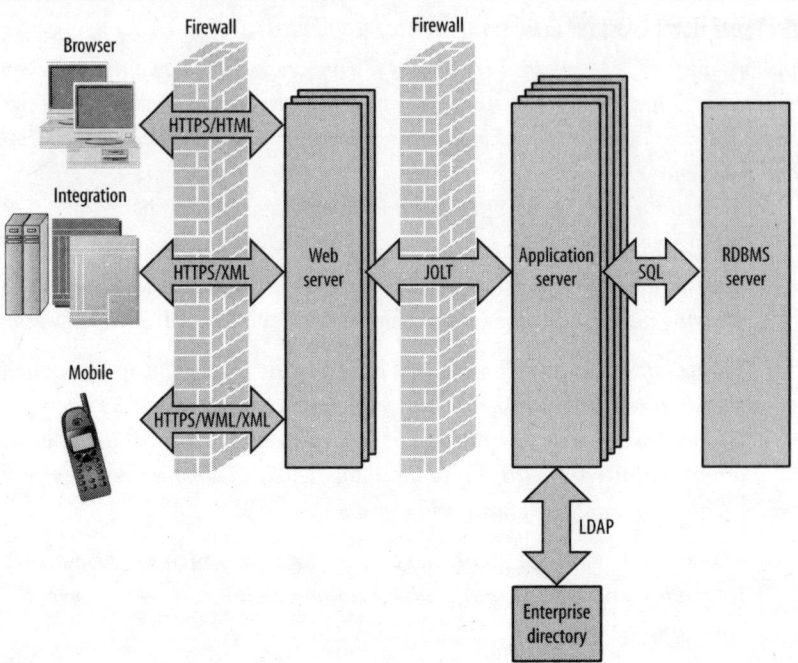

Figure 2-1: View of PeopleSoft CRM 8.0 Internet architecture

Their Internet applications can easily be accessed from a Web browser. The Internet applications user experience is maintained through the Web look, feel, and usage paradigm. It is not "Windows Millennium on the Web."

Here is where there is a key difference for IT managers. No client software is installed with pure Internet applications—the browser is the client. The software is installed on the server. It is called, ubiquitously, "zero code on the client." The architecture is a true multi-tier, server-centric model, featuring separation of presentation, business logic, and data management functionality. If you're not familiar with Internet-centric applications, think of what you assume about the loading of the application and interface when you open Microsoft Word 2000 or XP. I presume the answer is nothing at all. It's just a routine thing that you do—like walking. It just happens. There is nothing interesting or special about it. Think about that when you load Internet Explorer 6.0 to get onto the Web. You think about the fact that you are loading up your Internet connection. You are not thinking about how much code you are loading or what the total cost of ownership is. Those impure thoughts are left to the IT managers and the chief financial officers (CFOs). They are not part of the desktop. With Internet-centric applications, the browser is no different from the Word interface. It is just part of the desktop. No modem, no special anything. Something that's part of the landscape, not separate from it. This works particularly well when you have a broadband Internet connection such as a T1 or T3 line, cable modem, or DSL that allows you to be up and running on the Internet 24 hours a day, 7 days a week. With a CRM application built from scratch, it is as ubiquitous as the desktop is from wherever you are connected.

There is one other important point to the zero code on the client. If it is as transparent as you, the user, thinks it is, you shouldn't really care whether there is zero code on the client, unless it makes your productivity better and your job easier. The IT value is best left to the senior management financial gurus and the IT managers who need to explain total cost of ownership to the senior management financial gurus. You want it because you can access what you do wherever you access a machine—whether from the desktop or PDA or notebook, or, if you're just too cool, a wearable computer.

By contrast, CRM Web-accessible applications don't provide nearly the same level of business utility because they are not purely data driven. These systems rely on application code—applets or controls that must be downloaded and installed on users' systems to enable them to communicate with the CRM database. This can defeat platform independence and present logistical challenges to the anywhere/anytime promise afforded by the Internet. Requiring code to be installed on each user's system is invasive. It increases the challenge and cost to manage and maintain, and it may not even be feasible to do in all cases. If your vacationing sales director forgot to bring a laptop along (it's a vacation, after all), the sales director may not be able to convince the Internet café in the area to allow the download and installation of a specific applet needed to view the latest pipeline. Your partners, too, may not appreciate having to install "your system" on their system to work with you.

If it's important to you to be able to connect your employees with customers, partners, and suppliers, it's important to understand the limitations that "Windows Millennium on the Web" can impose on your business processes. Can you imagine having to install a special application on your PC to read a newspaper or trade stocks over the Web? Like any other purchase, *caveat emptor*.

INTERNET ARCHITECTURE AND ENTERPRISE INTEGRATION

Internet architectures have a very rocky road to navigate. Perhaps the company that is purchasing the CRM system has a long history of using SAP or has built its own internal system or has both client/server and mainframe systems at their multiple sites. How do you integrate all of that with the newfangled Internet architecture? Keep in mind that one of the knottiest problems that will likely occur is that the way the existing systems of the customer deal with data and legacy stores will be different from what the Internet architecture knows. That can be a disaster unless there is some way of dealing with the problem that the Internet architecture can provide. Perhaps the greatest strength of the PeopleSoft architecture is the elegant approach to integration it takes. Through what PeopleSoft calls its "Integration Broker" and a large number of open, available Enterprise Integration Points (EIPs), coupled with highly sophisticated portal technology, the ability to work with and access anything is pretty much the norm, though not without some headaches. In the CRM world, nothing is as it seems, nor is it perfect. The Integration Broker centralizes all transaction processing to allow whatever legacy or third-party activity that must go on to go on.

The idea of EIPs is central to all Internet architecture, even if it's not called that. They are open, standard, reusable pieces of code that provide developers with the preprogrammed means to communicate with external systems and other PeopleSoft systems. In SAP's world, they have been called BAPIs (Business Application Programmers Interfaces). In my world, they are called "I'm-so-glad-I'm-not-a-programmer."

PeopleSoft provides these EIPs through their Open Integration Framework (OIF). The OIF is a multi-featured framework that provides the foundation for the various interactions between systems. It consists of several parts:

Application messaging This is the publish/subscribe (push/pull) model of communications and synchronization between one system and another. It works with XML messages that the other system doesn't have to have knowledge of. When a specified business event occurs, the message is created and sent to any number of users who have subscribed to that message.

Business interlink Business interlinks are an internal version of what has been called middleware or Enterprise Application Integration (EAI). Through the use of C or C++ or Java or COM APIs in the other system—or, if that fails to excite, XML over HTTP—these business interlinks are plug-ins that identify the transaction, wrap themselves around the third-party API, and then allow data to pass to or from the third party. Very cool stuff. Saves you the trouble of buying EAI applications if it works well. The downside is that your APIs may not respond, though that is not likely.

Component interface API The components are the easily recognizable interfaces in the business world, such as a sales order, invoice, or form of some other sort. The interface is the ability of the architecture to recognize, through the API, the document in the other party's form and pass PeopleSoft data to that form. It can be done through the same languages and protocols as the Business interlink plus CORBA and EJB.

PeopleCode Java This is actually not as exciting as the other pieces of the OIF. There are PeopleCode-specific Java classes provided for the programmers who are heavily invested in Java. PeopleSoft 8 also packages BEA System's WebLogic Server, the leading Java 2 Enterprise Edition (J2EE) Web application server on the market, so you can implement the J2EE-compliant servlets, Java server pages (JSP), Enterprise JavaBeans (EJB), Java messaging services (JMS), and other platform services. It's not that this isn't useful—it is—but it is not all that distinct. It has lots of value to programmers, but not to the likely reader of this book.

File Layout Object and Application Engine When file-based processing is how PeopleSoft integrates with legacy systems, it uses the Application Engine for large-scale batch processes. The File Layout Object is a metadata representation of a flat file whose data is in either an XML format or delimited by columns or delimiting characters (such as CSV).

EDI Manager This is useful for those legacy systems that still use EDI, rather than XML (many would giggle right about here, but there actually are still a lot of companies that use EDI). The EDI Manager handles both the X.12 and the European-popular EDI-FACT standards for EDI. Trading partners can be set up. Outbound transaction mapping can be done through the Manager. When an incoming EDI transaction is recognized, it is translated to a PeopleSoft Business Document and processed. This is a surprisingly useful piece, given the current use of EDI.

Open Query This is a tool and an ODBC driver that allows third-party applications to communicate with PeopleSoft via ODBC. Simple.

This is a classic representation of a well-functioning (at least in principle) Internet architecture. It is mature, ready to work with third-party/legacy systems, and on the whole, sophisticated enough for any-sized enterprise.

The best way to understand how the various code pieces work is to look at two or three different EIPs and figure out what they do. The descriptions in Table 2-2 are straight from PeopleSoft. They represent specific types of activities that these EIPs can, in a pre-evolved way, carry out. They are how the Internet architecture can be read by systems that ordinarily are functioning in another world.

Table 2-2: Representative Enterprise Integration Points

EIP Name	Description
PRODUCT	Synchronizes product information with CRM or third-party external system. Affected information items include Product Item, Product UOM, Product Price by BU, Product Group, and Product Competitor.
SALES ORDER	Creates sales order header, line, and shipment information from an external system. This message loads sales order information into the order staging tables. This message can receive transactions from XML/EDI (850 transaction) messaging, CRM integration, or third-party external systems.
LOCATION TABLE	Synchronizes Location Table data between PeopleSoft's HRMS and ERP databases, and between PeopleSoft and third-party systems. Use the Location Table to establish physical locations within your organization, such as corporate headquarters, branch offices, remote sales offices, and so forth.

Ultimately, the difference between Internet architecture and the more classic form of Web-enablement is in:

Occupied real estate The pure Internet application usually rests on the server with the browser as a zero-code client. The Web-enabled client/server application needs downloaded applets and applications to the desktop to carry out a specific function.

The feel With the browser as the client, it is easy to feel that access anywhere and anytime is true because all functions are accessible transparently. When you load and unload applets each time you need a specific function, you feel less in control of your Internet CRM destiny. However, with the pure Internet architecture, you get access from your PC on the desktop or your notebook on the road— or if you are upset even by 6.5 pounds of baggage, your Compaq IPAQ 3835 in your Dockers mobile-pants pocket—without a single piece of client code, when it is done properly.

The backend code While CRM is considered a front-office technology, meaning that the applications are both available to the customer (customer-facing) and impact the customer, there is a backend to the front office. In other words, to put the "e" in eCRM (which, of course, we are removing after this chapter), the development tools for the Web have to be used for a proper Internet architecture. Tools that use HTML, Java, JavaScript, Enterprise Java Beans (EJB), Perl, CGI, or XML are the groundwork for the "webification" of CRM. With the emergence of the PDA market, you can add WAP and WML to that mix.

PeopleSoft 8.0 CRM Internet Architecture versus Siebel 7.0 Smart Web Architecture

At the end of 2001, the two most significant pure Internet architecture contenders were PeopleSoft and Siebel. They have re-engineered their applications and have rewritten their code to purify their Internetedness. (I made that word up.) Obviously, given that one of the Internet's greatest strengths is that the coding is pretty standardized, there can't be too much of a difference—or can there be? After all, isn't HTML just HTML, and JavaScript just JavaScript, and so on and so forth? Take a look at Table 2-3.

Table 2-3: PeopleSoft 8.0 CRM Internet Architecture versus Siebel 7.0 Smart Web Architecture

Subject	PeopleSoft CRM 8.0	Siebel 7.0 Smart Web
Protocols and languages	PowerHTML (XHTML/JavaScript), XML, WML, WMLScript, HTTP, WAP	DHTML, Java applets, JavaScript, XML, Document Object Model (DOM)
Client	No code on the client, zero footprint	No code on the client, zero footprint
Browser support	Internet Explorer, Netscape Navigator	Internet Explorer
Server(s)	Internet Application Server	Web Server as middleware
Portal technology	Most mature portal in CRM enterprise-level market	Plumtree adaptation of their Enterprise Class Gadget Framework, called the Siebel Systems Framework new portal technology (certification still pending, 2002)
Degree of interactivity	Medium to high	High
Buzz: Good and bad	Called best in class by AMR	Strong GUI tools; no compatibility with standard Web development tools (Dreamweaver, other IDE tools)

My conclusion? Pick your poison. What you need is what you need. The champion is the one that fits your CRM system.

CRM and Portals

So what are these portals? Before the Internet, enterprise portals were space-time continuum holes that Star Trek's flagship went through. With the emergence of the Internet, enterprise portals took on a whole different meaning. They became the gateways to entire Web-based communities and customer activity.

A *portal* is a gateway to an array of services or, optimally, a community. It is a centralized entry point, usually centered on a Web server that links multiple information and interactivity sources and allows a personalized view of any or all of the services according to the user who is entering. The personalization is accessible through a password and user ID. Each different user has a different view of the array of information, goods, and services available to them. This is an easygoing concept that maximizes the control of the viewer. Each person using the portal personalizes the view. Yet the collection of goods, services, and information is universal and available on multiple servers sitting behind the portal doors. This way, thousands of users can get what they need, with all things available to all people and with the workflow and security built in. Probably the best example of a portal-building product is Plumtree Software's Corporate Portal 4.0 tool, released at the end of 2000. Plumtree's tools allow the creation of interlinked portals combined with "gadgets"—portal add-ins in multiple locations, through the use of their Massively Parallel Processing Engine (MPPE). This adds superpower to portals by letting a portal user access multiple portals, increasing the selection of goods, services, information, and communities by magnitudes.

How would you deploy a portal? What benefit does it have to your company? Onyx's Brent Frei has some advice:

> A good CRM portal aggregates all relevant customer information within a single application or desktop in a format that is customized and personalized for the department or individual interacting with the data. An ideal portal doesn't just provide access to customer data, but becomes a knowledge base that is tailored to the needs of each different audience, culling together Web content, third-party applications, reference materials, detailed customer information— anything within or outside of the enterprise that customer-facing groups can utilize to enhance their understanding of a customer's experience and needs.

Several things are important for a highly successful CRM portal strategy:

- ▶ The system should be architected around the customer, instead of around specific job functions. By putting the customer at the application's core, no matter who is viewing, using, or sharing the information, companies are assured a seamless customer interaction process.

- ▶ Deploying a CRM portal solution only in one department or one business unit will not yield the same results as an enterprise-wide solution that gives every front-office employee access to the critical customer data and knowledge base.

- ▶ A thin-client or Web-based portal system saves millions of dollars in time, employee turnover, and other costs by greatly reducing system implementation and management time. While there is still a need for client/server technology, and Onyx still supports it, the future is on the Web where installations, upgrades, and expansions can be managed from one location, on one server, and all end users need to gain access is a Web browser.

- ▶ Different audiences require different views and different types of information, making it absolutely necessary to tailor content and structure to each. Onyx has broken these into three main buckets: customer, employee, and partner. These three main audiences can then be segmented further into departments, divisions, and job function—even down to the individual so that every person interacting with the CRM system is viewing only the relevant information, in the format that makes the most sense for the individual and with rules in place that make the most efficient use of the individual's time."

Onyx

Onyx, which specializes in the mid-market, but has some enterprise-level clients, has taken a creative and distinctive approach to building its CRM application suite. Portals are the centerpieces for all its CRM functionality, whether through a client/server platform or online. They are more advanced than the typical CRM application because Onyx provides multiple elements of Web-based self-service for customers, partners, and employees, all of whom could be called customers without much stretching. While they don't have the only available approach to portals, they do represent a distinctive, instructive approach.

Onyx Employee Portal

The Onyx Employee Portal is an enterprise-wide Web solution that combines CRM functionality with third-party applications and relevant Internet content. Its purpose is to maximize the efficiency of marketing, sales, and service teams, which it does very well.

There are several CRM functions that the Employee Portal provides:

- **Sales** can review an account's complete history, manage sales pipelines and opportunities, forecast deals, and review win/loss data.

- **Marketing** can create customer and prospect lists, conduct marketing campaigns, and manage leads via fax, email, or postal mail.

- **Customer service** can resolve service inquires as well as seamlessly manage service queues and monitor customer satisfaction.

- **Relevant Internet content** links to Internet sites that are integrated directly into the interface, giving employees instant access to company profiles, stock quotes, competitive research, maps, sales coaching, and such.

- **Third-party applications** integrate into a single interface so employees no longer have to open and close multiple applications to access the information they need.

Onyx Customer Portal

Onyx doesn't stop with employee portal access. The Customer Portal is a personalizable, Web-based product line application that markets to, sells to, and services prospects and customers across multiple channels. E-marketing capabilities enable companies to tailor their marketing efforts to the individual needs of distinct customer segments. Some of the functionality provided includes:

- **Online catalog** that helps customers thoroughly research products by accessing all the information they need.

- **Lead capture and profiling** that captures prospect information on your website and lets you leverage that information for followup.

- **Online surveys** gather preference information. This can be used for qualifying prospects.

- ▶ **Literature fulfillment** provides automatic fulfillment of prospect and customer literature requests by email, fax, or postal mail.

- ▶ **Email marketing** enables personalized, outbound email messages based on prospect profile information.

The Customer Portal also provides e-commerce capabilities to streamline a customer's buying experience and strengthen your company's sales effectiveness. These features include:

- ▶ **Online product configuration** enables customers to design and configure a product to meet their unique requirements.

- ▶ **Online order processing** makes information from online transactions available to sales and service employees for cross-selling, up-selling, and improved customer service.

Finally, and perhaps, most importantly for eCRM, the e-service capacity offers customers options for self-service and interaction using the most convenient channel. This is where the self-service features that are essential for proper eCRM become apparent:

- ▶ **Web self-help** empowers customers to solve problems themselves, 24/7, using an online knowledge base of solutions.

- ▶ **Online service** allows customers to submit and track service and support incidents over the Web.

- ▶ **Email management** automatically routes, prioritizes, and escalates inbound emails from customers.

- ▶ **Profile management** allows customers to update profile information themselves.

- ▶ **Product registration** enables customers to register products online, quickly and easily.

ONYX PARTNER PORTAL

Through its powerful portal applications, Onyx forgets no one. There are strong PRM elements embedded in the Partner Portal capabilities, including:

Collaborative selling Onyx collaborative selling capabilities enable partners to become virtual members of your sales team by providing the following functions:

- • **Lead entry** gathers detailed information from partners about new sales opportunities.

- **Lead distribution** assigns leads to partners, using rules-based routing and escalation.

- **Pipeline management** manages and monitors channel sales processes for improved planning and forecasting.

- **Online catalog** handles partner requests for self-service training.

Collaborative e-commerce Onyx collaborative e-commerce features are interesting. They aren't just aimed at alliance partners; they are aimed at channel partners. A channel partner sells your product or services and, in return, makes money and gets some serious discounts and extra help. They are often value-added resellers (VARs) because they can sell the product and, frequently, can provide specialized services to enhance the value of the product for the customer. The value to the vendor is that the channel can sell more than half the product sales in a given year with far less overhead than maintaining a sales force to do that. Note that several of the features that are available to the channel partners are also available in a slightly different format, but with the same technology, to the customers. With that, take a look:

- **Literature fulfillment** enables partners to order sales and marketing collateral from the Web.

- **Online product configuration** empowers partners to configure custom products for customers online.

- **Online order processing** allows partners to easily place orders with you over the Web.

Collaborative service Again, Onyx's collaborative service is an advanced use of eCRM online capabilities. This involves a version of employee or customer self-service: partner self-service. The features include:

- **Web self-help** allows partners to solve their customers' problems.

- **Online service** allows partners to submit and update customers' service incidents using the Web or email.

- **Customer surveys** allow partners to submit preference information on behalf of their customers.

- **Customer product registration and order history** enable partners to register products online and research order history on behalf of customers.

ONYX E-BUSINESS ENGINE

The Onyx e-Business Engine—the backbone of Onyx 2000—powers all of these portals. Four elements of the Onyx e-Business Engine work together to deliver scalable, enterprise-wide customer management:

- ▶ **e-Business data center** provides a single repository for all customer information, with enterprise-wide access. What is intriguing here is that the data center is accessible through the portals. This makes Onyx's product different from others on the market.

- ▶ **e-Business process technology** enables a consistent customer experience. It takes all CRM-related sectors, including marketing, sales, and service, and unifies the view of the customer. It does it through a workflow that consolidates all reporting functions, including the consolidated view of tasks, data, and events in all the sectors, and it routes appropriately so they can be managed or escalated if necessary.

- ▶ **e-Business integration framework** integrates Onyx with enterprise applications, including ERP applications, telephony systems, Internet content, and Web applications. An integration framework is vital to any eCRM application because if the application can't link to the legacy systems or future enterprise systems, the use value declines dramatically. Integration is the knottiest problem in the CRM world. It is elegantly solved here.

- ▶ **Universal interface framework** creates convenient, custom interfaces for your employees, partners, and customers, and combines multiple applications into one user interface. Again, this is a valuable feature because it provides individual views of the universal customer view. The ability to easily customize what you see when you log in with your Internet Explorer 5.5 is something with inestimable value. Why should you be looking at the marketing funds allocations for the class of customers labeled "young and restless" when you are the account manager for the Lockheed Martin account and you need the prospective sales figures for the quarter? It's nice to be able to look at whatever you need to and eliminate superfluous information and mouse clicks to get to the pertinent stuff.

The Partner Portal 3.0, released in April 2002, adds a permission-based security model to its foundation. This is a very important addition. One of the most fragile pieces of any PRM application is the possibility that sensitive information owned by one partner will accidentally fall into the hands of another partner. Not only does this model prevent that, but it prevents sales channel conflicts, handles secure lead distribution, and makes the partner profiles private matters. This is a smart move by Onyx, allowing partners to breathe a sigh of relief because their information is their information, not the entire program's.

CRM and eCRM Are Really Not Separate, Are They?

Have I said there is no difference between CRM and eCRM? I have? Okay, then. Just one more time and one more point. The Knowledge Capital Group, a group of analysts, in their year 2000 report, "KCG Marketview: CRM Redefined," called the "e" a "fatal distraction" in the following sentences:

> ...the danger is that companies will attempt to optimize the "e" channel—the Web channel—at the expense of all others. CRM, however, is inherently a multi-channel strategy. Customer relationships transcend the Internet.

Good point. CRM has progressed far enough for me to agree with KCG. But using the Internet for CRM is now a necessary strategy, not a market edge. The vendors who don't optimize their CRM applications for the Web are the vendors who will be out of business soon enough. Internet architecture gets you serious CRM twenty-first century style points and a reputation for the smarts now, but eventually will be the ho-hum architecture, ubiquitous and ever-ready for deployment. That will be a good thing.

The implications of this, technologically and practically, were addressed throughout this chapter. Without much further commentary, suffice it to say, the "e" is exorcised from eCRM. Welcome to the world of just plain CRM.

3

Sales Management Versus CRM

This is not a long chapter. It is here to do one thing—give you a brief definition of the difference between sales management and CRM. If you haven't figured out what CRM is after reading Chapters 1 and 2, then the apocalypse is upon us. This chapter is just a final mop-up so that we can get on to more substance in the book.

CRM Is Not Sales Management

Traditionally, sales management is what it sounds like—the things that you do to find sales opportunities and close them. That can include contact management, prospecting, lead qualification, opportunity management, and account management. If you are a sales manager, it also includes managing the sales process. That means forecasting and pipeline management (that is, the tracking of stages of deal closure and probabilities related to that). The facets I've just described resemble a subset of CRM called "sales force automation" (SFA), a topic I cover thoroughly in Chapter 6, so I won't go into it right now. Suffice it to say, this differs from CRM.

However, there are things that involve sales management that don't involve CRM, such as managing the other salespeople on your sales teams (for example, training salespeople in techniques to close deals) or developing a sales-oriented culture. CRM isn't part of the human resources issues involving salespeople. It doesn't concern itself with recruiting salespeople or creating mentoring programs for the younger salespeople. Though it does concern itself with the compensation of those salespeople, CRM primarily concentrates on tracking commissions and management by objectives (MBOs). In other words, CRM is concerned with the variable compensation that is directly or indirectly related to the sales deal and not, ordinarily, the recording, analyzing, setting, or identifying of fixed compensation, such as salaries.

There are distinct differences between sales management and CRM's sales force automation, too.

CRM is a business strategy with technology being a critical component. It involves the measurement of the lifetime value of a customer so that weight can be given to attention to each customer. CRM also encompasses analytical, operational, and collaborative functions. It involves not just sales, but also partnerships, marketing, and customer service. In other words, sales management pales by comparison when it comes to attempting to ensure that customers have a lifelong relationship with companies. Sales force automation is the subset of CRM that concerns itself with how the sales force is going to use technology to effect the job it does much better by managing opportunities, contacts, accounts, and the sales pipeline. In its classical definition, sales management concerns itself with maintenance and improvement of the part of the customer relationship that involves the singular sale itself. Customer acquisition and retention are secondary considerations to the sale. That is a narrow definition and I'm sure there are those who would dispute this one, but that's okay. That said, let's now move on.

Contact Management: Not Your Father's (or Mother's) CRM

Another easy source of confusion is CRM and contact management. I've often been asked a question something like this: "Doesn't ACT! do that?" (ACT! being one of the leading contact management software applications available today.) On occasion, my answer has been yes. But even then, the context is very different and the power is, too. It's the equivalent example of seeing a lion in your house and saying, "Oh, that's a nice kitty, isn't it?" ACT! and Goldmine up to version 4.0 were often assumed to be what was meant by CRM. They are not. They are contact managers. Goldmine, with the release of version 5.0 and a name change to Goldmine Front Office 2000, has made a transformation that brings them closer to being a sales force automation tool. In 2000, Goldmine became a division of Frontrange Solutions. They added a customer call center product called Heat and pushed into wireless CRM with the late 2000 announcement of Goldmine Everywhere

Server. This has brought them considerably closer to broad CRM functionality, removing them from the world of contact management. But as of 2002, they still hadn't, in my humble opinion, reached the level of CRM.

Contact managers are essentially only an evolutionary step up from personal information managers. Don't get me wrong: contact managers (especially ACT! 2000) have real value. Small businesses can often use them in lieu of CRM. They have many of the features that are defined by sales force automation packages, but they are not SFA. They are certainly not CRM. Table 3-1 points out a few of the differences between the two packages.

Table 3-1: Some Differences Between Contact Managers and CRM Applications

Contact Managers	CRM Applications
Functionality limited to contacts and some associated sales functions.	Functionality encompasses sales, marketing, customer service, and analytics.
Some sales processes embedded. No (or limited) customization possibilities.	Embedded best practices and sales processes that are also entirely customizable to fit.
Views limited to contact related with tabs such as notes/history, opportunities associated with the contact, and so on.	Views nearly unlimited and customizable to any degree of complexity.
Limited data synchronization, if any.	Data synchronization for both the desk-bound and the mobile sales professional.
No real integration with legacy systems. Primarily standalone.	Integration through native hooks or through powerful third-party tools.
Can be Web ready, but not often built for Web. Multiple users tend to be client/server based.	Frequently built from ground up for Web.
Not too scalable. Even the network versions are focused on the very small office. Not designed for more than a few handfuls of users.	Can be scaled to tens of thousands of users or down to fewer than ten.

Really, that's all there is to say about it. Sales management and CRM are different. Contact management and CRM are different. That is the end of the matter. On to CRM and its offshoots!

4

CRM Strategy: So Many Choices, So Little Time

Crm strategy is complex. Not because it involves strategy and not because it involves CRM, but because it involves both. Why would it be more complex than, say, an ERP strategy or a network strategy? Because it involves our contemporaneously defined customers. If you were developing an ERP strategy, while it would be *big* and it would be complicated, the level of complexity only begins to approach CRM. With ERP, you're basically involving the back office folks, the senior management, the IT department, and a smattering of others because they are the ones who will be involved in the system, be it finances, human resources, or manufacturing processes. You can even stretch the definition to include the supply chain, but that's it. With network architecture, other than some user surveys, you're really only involving the IT department because the user doesn't know much at all how the guts of an IT infrastructure work, nor do they care.

Frankly, a strategy for network architecture is pretty narrowband when it comes to ordinary humans. But CRM begins to reach all those customers who we defined in Chapter 1, so the elements are much more involved. Of course your senior management and users are involved, but your partners, vendors, and clients are also a direct consideration for involvement in the planning of how your strategy is going to work. If your CRM strategic objectives involve customer satisfaction, it probably pays to find out from the customers what satisfies them, doesn't it? Additionally, customer-facing processes dominate most organizations—sales, marketing, customer service, and even human resources and finances to some extent are among those examples. A technology-enabled CRM strategy to meet customer-focused objectives involves the majority of any organization's people and processes.

For example, a typical grand objective of a CRM strategy is to create a unified, 360-degree view of a customer that is cross departmental. That is the holy grail for successful CRM. Ideally, if a CRM strategy succeeds, the system in place will allow any department to see whatever the appropriate view of the customer is for them in order to tend to the customer's needs, wants, and desires. However, the holy grail is something that neither King Arthur nor Monty Python ever found—or found with enormous heartache (and heartburn)—so be forewarned. There are multiple pitfalls in the path of a successful CRM strategy.

Since the customer has already been tagged with a new definition, it behooves us to move on with a definition of strategy. This chapter will cover the overview and elements of CRM strategy, not the details. To some extent, there will be elements that overlap with implementation strategy, which is covered in Chapter 17. Bear with it. The planning stages of CRM are the most important, the most dangerous, and the most involving. They are every bit as daunting as the implementation. It will keep you busy beyond belief, and you can't leave out any strategic elements or you will join the many CRM shipwrecks that litter the enterprise version of the Sargasso Sea. The package you pick will be the package you fail with, unless you plan well.

The Grand Strategy

First and foremost, remember, as Shakespeare once didn't say, "know thy customer." When you are sure of the range of customers you are going to encompass, be they your paying clients, your vendors, your employees, or perhaps your partners, you can capture the view from Everest and look for the paths for the descent. The "grand strategy" is usually the starting point: what the major objectives and results should be from implementing CRM successfully. In short, they are:

Value proposition What does the company want to get out of the project?

Business case What are the benchmarks and key performance indicators (KPIs) that will be used to determine the success of that value proposition? What will be the return on investment (ROI)?

Value Proposition

The value proposition is the result you want from your CRM implementation. Do you want to increase the number of customers by x-fold or make sure that your customer retention rate goes up x percent to $x + 1$ percent? Do you want to reduce the time it takes to solve customer problems? Do you want a reduction in administrative work time so the sales team can go out and sell more often? Do you want to automate the processes that measure the effect of various marketing campaigns or be able to change those campaigns actively in real time? Do you want to establish the capacity to measure the lifetime value of the customer so you can decide how to spend your carefully managed available funds for sales and marketing? Do you want to establish a pipeline to your channel partners so their contributions to your revenue are increased to some determined level? Do you want to increase customer satisfaction by some number that also makes you happy? *Ad infinitum.*

All of the above represents possible objectives that CRM can bring to fruition—hopefully. There are too many others to mention in this limited space. They will vary from company to company. But the value proposition must be established concretely before anything else is done. This provides the ground upon which a foundation can be poured.

Business Case and Metrics

Next comes the creation of the business case that will show how CRM will support the successful execution of the goals and objectives. It is here that the formal studies for ROI and the establishment of key performance indicators—those measurements that identify the tangible and intangible goals success factors—are done.

What makes this difficult is that this is the place where you quantify what can be intangible goals. How are you going to quantify customer satisfaction? Are you successful if your customer hugs you when he or she sees you? If determining how you will spend your dollars more effectively on the more important customers is your business goal, how are you going to determine the measurements of what "important" is in your business model? If there are employee self-service objectives such as reducing the amount of administrative work that the sales force does, how are you going to:

- ► Determine the percentage reduction number that is going to make you happy?

- ► Determine how that number is to be reached?

- ► Determine how the newly liberated sales guy will be using that extra time?

For example, is a smile on the salesperson's face an effective measurement of successful liberation? I don't think so. But how do you quantify the subjective?

Luckily, it didn't take a brain surgeon, but it did take a doctor of the Ph.D. kind, to figure out a method (one of several existing) of doing this.

The Balanced Scorecard

Back in 1996, Dr. Robert Kaplan and David Norton co-authored what has become a landmark book called *The Balanced Scorecard* (HBS Press, 1996). This book established a strategic management system that took not only the tangible objectives (financial goals and internal business processes), but also the intangible (customer appearance, learning, and growth) and developed a method to quantify these into a coherent, balanced whole.

Each of the segments had a question attached:

Financial How should we appear to our shareholders to succeed financially?

Of course, this is the historical measurement of performance for businesses. They can be such measures as return on capital employed or operating income.

Customers How should our customers see us to achieve our vision?

This is normally segmented by business unit. Measures include market share, customer retention numbers, or customer satisfaction. For a more drilled-down example, let's look at what Robb Eklund, vice-president of Product Marketing for PeopleSoft's CRM products, has to say:

> Key performance indicators for customer satisfaction might include how quickly the customers pay their bills or how frequently they buy maintenance renewals. These can be indicators of how happy the customer really is.

Internal performance management In order to satisfy the above two, what should our business processes be?

What works for the company today and what will work for it tomorrow? Which processes have value and which don't? It's the management of the present and the future and discarding of the past that can provide the basis for future success. This needs to be a key part of the CRM planning process because major cultural change is going to happen, like it or not.

Learning and growth To achieve all of the above, how do we sustain our ability to grow and learn?

Since the market has shifted from demand-driven to customer-driven in the last five years or so, the company needs to shift accordingly, which is why CRM is implemented ordinarily. Indicators of success in this venue are employee satisfaction through retention measures, information systems performance, and the organization's calibration with employee incentives that are aligned with customer satisfaction.

The measurement of KPIs has been widely adopted, with or without the rest of the Balanced Scorecard, as the framework of measurement for tangible and intangible corporate goals and objectives.

As you can see, the possibilities that are touched upon in these simple questions are enormous. The consequences of success are potentially fantastic; the results of failure potentially devastating. That's why these questions have become a bonafide development in the last five years. In response, several CRM vendors have embedded the Balanced Scorecard into their application set, notably PeopleSoft and SAP. But remember, vendor application functionality and usability cannot be a factor at this stage of strategic planning, whether they incorporate the Balanced Scorecard or not. The vendors' importance comes considerably later.

What gives the Balanced Scorecard credibility, despite its initials, is not so much the questions that are clearly being asked here but more so the idea that intangibles are not only a viable "thing" to be measured, but also are mission-critical elements of any strategic planning. Once the four questions are answered, the idea is to align the enterprise with the answers so that there is no isolation between mission, vision, strategy, and departmental actions. Continuous feedback is part of the Balanced Scorecard's plan so that adjustments can go on in near real time throughout the planning and execution of the strategy.

A good idea? Gartner Group estimates that by the end of 2000 over 40 percent of the Fortune 1000 had incorporated Balanced Scorecard applications as part of their system for corporate strategic management and planning. META Group estimates 38 percent of all companies are using such a toolset. A good idea gone mainstream.

Does Understanding Mean Action?

Despite the penetration of this important tool into the business center, companies aren't packing the stores to buy Balanced Scorecard power drills. In fact, note the number I used to show how well accepted it was—40 percent. So more than half the Fortune 1000 isn't using it and may not be using any method at all to establish a CRM strategy. More than 62 percent of companies in general aren't using it, either.

Sadly, this shows that a lot of companies aren't putting together any formal criteria, and thus, almost guarantee CRM failure before they even select the package they are going to fail with. These formal criteria are an essential part of your CRM strategic planning because it is these measurements that will be used to determine the success or failure of the CRM rollout. A formal business case is critical. A recent study by AMR Group through the CRM Project found that 58 percent of the companies that were spending countless U.S. dollars on CRM implementations hadn't done a formal business case. Another small study done by IMT Strategies of 50 CRM heads at varying companies found that 90 percent were implementing CRM on faith, with no ROI or metrics planned! This is a deadly game to play when millions of dollars, countless jobs, and even corporate success or failure are on the line. Educated guesswork is not sufficient. Keep in mind, the previous statements are coming from a guy who dislikes formality in almost anything under most circumstances. Ask my wife about my aversion to suits and ties.

In "normal" economic periods, commonplace metrics for customer satisfaction levels and retention rates and reduced costs of services and/or sales are used. In good economies, customer acquisition and increased sales and revenue are often measured. In recessionary times, head count reduction becomes a factor in CRM strategic planning.

That grim statement made, onward to the rocky path of strategic reality.

Elements of Strategy

The grandest and highest levels of strategy are the mission/vision statement and the writing of the business case. But the down-and-dirty details are the next step and the next place for a misstep. There is so much detail to be planned and so much to monitor when the plan is being executed that it is actually necessary to plan how to monitor the plan. Whoa, isn't that a bit overdone? Unfortunately, especially in the larger enterprises, the answer is no. It is not only *not* overdone, it is a necessary and important body part of the CRM strategic plan. Once the objectives are set and the metrics for identifying the successful execution of those objectives are completed, the elements of the strategic plan have to be decided, and the successful, real-time monitoring of those elements and the resultant organizational change has to occur. Because CRM is a technology-enabled strategy that encompasses the breadth and depth of an enterprise, it involves creating a unified view of the customer that is accessible across multiple departments of a company through multiple communications media. Business processes may be changed, remain, be eliminated, or added. Corporate culture may be dramatically altered in unexpected ways. The CRM technology that is agreed upon has implications far beyond what package or packages or even what approach to the packages you select. Imagine what happens if you don't really understand what is going on as you plan. If you're in charge, it's not hard to figure out what will happen to you, given contemporary corporate accountability.

A Look at Strategic Planning from an Industry Leader

For the last ten years, KPMG Consulting has played a prominent role in strategic planning for CRM. The market is barely that old and has an acronym younger than even its existence. By that token, KPMG can be called a pioneer in the planning of CRM planning. In fact, they developed a Connect-to-Customer Solution that has evolved to a results-driven holistic approach for CRM. It is instructive to take a brief look at this real-world example so you can get some idea of how CRM strategy has a genuine practical application.

CRM Strategic Planning and Getting Real

KPMG Consulting looks at how the total enterprise gains value from the application of CRM, rather than just parochial departmental gain. They investigate and create what they call Relationship Equity, which converts customer intelligence into highly differentiated, personalized, and explicitly valued customer experiences that, if successful, will translate into sustainable revenue and direct profitability because of the improved knowledge of and use of customer behavior. Okay, sure. What does that mean, though?

For example, let's look at a health services company. Suppose that this health care provider receives a request from you for a brand name pharmaceutical product. This will trigger an action that compares your request against both your purchase history and available generic brand drugs of the same type as the brand name you requested. An email will be sent to your address with the suggested alternative generic drugs,

their prices, and the savings that purchasing the generic drugs will provide. In other words, you have gotten a differentiated (your drug
request and the generic drug alternates), personalized (the check
against your purchase history), and valued (savings on the cost of the
drugs by purchase of the generic version) customer experience via one
of many possible customer touch points. This is relationship equity à
la KPMG Consulting.

Making This into a Strategy

Bruce Culbert, senior vice-president and CRM Global Solutions Leader
for KPMG Consulting, says:

> Unfortunately, even after investing heavily in CRM initiatives, too
> many organizations are still struggling to define exactly what CRM
> is and to identify the ROI benefits it can provide. Organizations are
> often thrust into action by one or another market or corporate
> mandate, too many of which consider CRM as a project or a piece
> of software, rather than a strategy.

KPMG Consulting calls its enterprise-wide commitments and attitude Enterprise Value Creation (EVC) for CRM. To execute EVC,
KPMG Consulting has developed a set of diagnostic tools for enterprise
value that somewhat mirror Customer Lifetime Value, but for the
enterprise. These diagnostic tools provide greater visibility into their
customers by identifying and prioritizing the highest-impact opportunities based on what makes economic sense. Thus, the highest
weights are given the highest value-creating opportunities. It's done
by looking at the distributed value chain of an enterprise and identifying, coordinating, and integrating cost benefits that help clients meet
long-term goals and some more immediate short-term goals. Proprietary financial algorithms and diagnostic tools are applied to the customer's current "state of business" against a projected future "state of
business." What will show up as valuable in the strategic planning are
projected areas of greatest business performance improvement and
greatest points for optimization. This is done through incremental
value creation, which sets both the long-term direction for revenue
growth and enables the planning of short-term cost reduction and
operational efficiencies.

While this might seem to be awfully blue blood, the reality is that
metrics, KPIs, and tools for identifying and achieving those KPIs are

an essential part of CRM strategic planning. KPMG Consulting uses Value Chain Blueprints and Value Realization Roadmaps for CRM as the initial business designs and financial models that offer clients both a strategic and tactical view. These tools and methods were developed using both internal and external market research and financial metrics.

Mr. Culbert again:

> We always stress with our clients the importance of having the success criteria for a CRM project identified upfront, and an agreement on how we will measure the value over time. If our client does not see the importance of doing this, we get very nervous, as we know that this is the first sign of a potentially disastrous situation. We then work with our client to make sure each initiative has a clear value proposition, an acceptable ROI, and is consistent with the client's overall CRM strategy.

Stakeholding Committee

To make sure that the business processes are re-engineered with the corporate vision, benchmarks, and KPIs in mind, the formation of a team of stakeholders that will drive the CRM strategy, planning, and implementation from the point of vision to the final rollout of the applications is the first essential step. But there is a conundrum. Since CRM is ultimately an enterprise-wide project, it needs to be driven by senior management. Yet, since the primary reason for the high rate of CRM failure is that users simply don't use it, the users have to be as involved from the beginning of the project through to the end as senior management. "User-as-stakeholder" involvement might be considered a bit of a controversial position. It is not widely recommended yet, though it is gaining credence among the integrators, vendors, and analysts. I'll drive a stake (holder) in the ground here. It is not only valid, but critical to the success of any CRM project. Let's look at it.

Who are the users? They are the employees who are going to access the CRM applications chosen to effect the changes in the business processes. They are the customers who are paying the company for products and services. They are the partners who are working in tandem with the sales team of the company. If one of the stated objectives of the CRM strategy is to improve customer satisfaction, then it makes sense to involve those customers from the beginning in helping you architect the program for their satisfaction. It becomes almost a self-perpetuating, self-contained CRM strategy because the customers are happier when they are involved in planning a CRM strategy and business approach that is aimed at their own satisfaction.

The same goes for the employees who will be using the applications and the new system. The primary cause for the 55 to 75 percent CRM project failure rate that is espoused by many analysts is that the system is not used by the users. Thus, for the CRM strategy to be successful, it must include continuous input from key user representatives. The best group to serve would be the appropriate "natural leaders," those employees who are respected in their departments, not due to their titles, but to their deeds. These natural leaders can be a powerful stakeholding voice because they know what their departments need to make the system useful to their colleagues. They can be the evangelists back in the department when the implementation is complete and the training for the system is about to begin. Why? Because they are providing input on functionality and usability from their colleagues to the system in a way that their colleagues feel empowered from the beginning of the planning. What is the likelihood of the departments using the system effectively in this scenario as opposed to a senior management mandate dictating its use?

Senior management would thus play a different role than traditional senior management stakeholders. The elements of their role would be to make sure that

- ▶ There is a clear ROI defined for the project.

- ▶ The metrics and benchmarks are crystalline and sharp.

- ▶ The mission/vision remains corporate and doesn't fall to the level of any single interest group, either departmental or external.

On the other hand, senior management would not be the people who are primarily concerned with what functionality is usable and useful and what functionality isn't. Let's face it. They are never going to use the system. They are the guardians of its ROI and normally (unless there is a chief customer officer at the company) are not going to be dealing with the customers directly in any way. Their interests are essential to the project, but fundamentally different from the people who will use the system.

Executive Advisory Board
KPMG Consulting, in addition to the normal stakeholding committees, tries to gain even more stakeholder commitment by the establishment of an executive advisory board. This is aimed at getting the

continued buy-in and commitment from the executives of both internal and external stakeholders (the customer, the vendor, and the integrator, for example). An executive oversight committee should be established during the proposal and contracting phase of a large or important CRM engagement. That way the senior executives who are major stakeholders would have the opportunity to review and discuss the project's progress. If need be, they could make timely and strategic decisions to reinforce the vision and direction of the project. This takes the onus from the project teams, freeing them up to concentrate on delivering the actual goods.

A typical executive advisory board might consist of the sponsoring customer executive (usually the vice-president of CRM or the chief marketing officer [CMO] or vice-president of sales), a second non-sponsoring customer executive (CEO, CIO, COO), sales and development executives from the software vendor, and the appropriate global practice leaders from integrators. This board would meet for the first time 30 to 45 days after starting an initiative. Depending on the length of the project, this board would review the project every 30 to 90 days. As key stakeholders these executives are available and accessible for consultation during the engagement on:

- ▶ Typical items addressed by the advisory board
- ▶ Vision alignment and realignment
- ▶ Resolution of organizational and political issues
- ▶ Risk mitigation strategies

This forum also serves as an important element in the overall project communication plans and helps to keep all parties in sync with the priorities of this given initiative.

However, rest assured, this does *not* take the place of stakeholding committees that involve the users. This is another cog in the many-spoked wheel of CRM strategic planning.

Business Processes

Thorough examination of how the company does business is a prerequisite that needs to occur long before any vendor selection. There is a very strong tendency in the world of senior management to let CRM sexiness get in the way of a clear view of corporate business processes and methodology. CRM "coolness" can be incredibly hot to a senior executive who looks at the politics of success. CRM vendors' claims tease and tantalize, but often bear little relationship to what any company actually needs. All this good stuff is exciting and seems easy. On the other hand, taking a hard look at the business methods and rules of a company often is agonizing because, to accomplish the objectives set out in the value proposition, it becomes obvious that the existing system doesn't really work and the customers aren't really happy. That means major overhauls of how the company does business, time-honored or not, can be necessary. Sometimes this means tweaks and a few adjustments. But it can also mean eliminating those processes, practices, and rules that don't conform to the new mission or changing those that have some merit but aren't entirely appropriate. For example, if there are no incentives to involve the channel in selling for the company, then neither the channel manager nor the channel partners will be very effective. It may mean the creation of an entirely new channel program, the installation of a significant PRM application, and the revamping of channel partners to do the job. For example, Siebel, which was named by Forbes in 2001 as having one of the best software company partner programs, still had no qualms in axing most of their mid-market partners because of non-production. That is a significant purge. While perhaps not the answer, it is a look at what was a radical rebuilding of part of a highly touted channel program. These things might have to happen at times.

How do you know what programs and processes need to be changed or axed, kept or otherwise? If your KPIs and other objectives are in place, the changes are often suggested. It is the impact of those business process changes that has the dramatic and potentially surprising punch.

Once the assessment of business processes is complete, the next step is to be aware of what functionality is going to be necessary to successfully execute the changes. This has particular bearing later on the package selection process. Suffice it to say, if the analysis of the business has been thorough, the functionality needs will be clear.

When these steps are done, risk factors have to be assessed. By the way, this can be going on simultaneously with these other steps, too.

Evaluating Risk

CRM risk evaluation, viewed solely from an enterprise level or as a single factor, is a potentially disastrous mistake. CRM risk factors need to be segmented individually. When you are dealing with multiple modules or even a single module, the risks engendered can involve the culture, processes, technology, goals, and objectives. Some of these elements are immature, some mature. Some play a small part in the CRM planning, some a large part. Some interact with others. All of this has to be taken into account when evaluating risk. Some risk factors to consider are:

Lack of cross-functional planning Compartmentalizing things into individual stovepipes

No formal CRM business strategy Leading to arbitrary approaches and educated guesswork

Poor or no senior-level support Leading to lack of corporate vision and poor knowledge of financial factors

Poor or no user support Leading to lack of use of the final product

Blinding light of the vendor Leading to purchasing a vendor solution with no understanding of corporate objectives, goals, or vision for CRM

This list could go on extensively, but suffice it to say the risks are great and need to be identified and controlled prior to any implementation or vendor selection.

Corporate Culture and Change Management

Implementing a CRM strategy is a high-stress activity. Unfortunately, it places that stress on the workings of the company, not necessarily on the individuals doing the planning. Going to the gym is not the way to deal with the impact on your company's corporate life that CRM will have.

Most of the company is going to be impacted not just by the implementation and its execution, but also by the preparatory work for the strategy. It calls such fundamental questions into play as: How do we make our customers happy? How do we change our business model? With rare exceptions, the changes that are acceptable alter the company landscape vividly. Acknowledging and planning for this and the organizational effect is the single most complex part of creating a corporate CRM strategy. For example, the company has been focused on demand-based, company-based, or product-based business activity. The entire way the company and its employees think is embedded in its dusty past. Maybe your idea of customer service had historically been that you will take care of customer complaints within 72 hours. A change to make it a 24-hour response time will dramatically affect the corporate culture. More people have to be in for longer hours or you'll have to hire new and competent people to handle the more rapid turnaround. If you have a contact center, how you determine the numbers of personnel you need to staff that contact center at varying times of day, due to volume considerations, will be influenced.

Perhaps Excel has been your application of choice to track your sales pipeline or Outlook has been your contact manager. Senior management and sales managers realize that the company has grown sophisticated enough to need better tools for managing that pipeline or for reducing the sales team's administrative work. Yet, that doesn't really mean that much to the user. The user has been using Outlook and Excel just fine, thank you, and doesn't see that changing over to CRM is really going to make it any easier for him to do his work. It probably will make it harder. The idea that it's for their own good (and the corporate good) has to be transmitted by the CRM evangelists in the company. How?

Compensation incentives that show these loyal and productive folks that they can be more productive and that there is something in it for them sure can help here. To put them in place and to get the new CRM system up and running will change the old corporate culture and assign it to where the Roman Empire sits today—the dustbin of history. These changes, both positive and negative, have to be planned for. Managing the change as it occurs is of the essence. While the statements of the importance of change here may seem dramatic, they are actually true.

Change Management: Measuring the Comfort Zone

There is more than one kind of change management. The more familiar version is how to handle customer changes to the statement of work (SOW) during a project. That means that there is a well-established method of saying, "Okay, if you want to do this, it will cost you this much more, take that much longer, and affect the scope of the project. Are you still sure you want to, esteemed customer?" That is best left for either the implementation chapter or another book. The change management I'm going to highlight here is a well-constructed method of looking at the impact of change on an organization. Perhaps the best representative method is O^2—Opportunity Optimization. This is not a mix-up in the elemental composition of water. It is a well-established methodology owned by RWD Corporation and used by companies such as SAP as both a tool and a sales item to determine the impact that a change in a corporate culture will have on the organization of that company. It is both classic and innovative and worth a look.

WE'VE GOT ANSWERS? YOU'VE GOT QUESTIONS!

Organizational change management is a way for corporate leaders to gauge how the personnel of a company are taking to alterations in their corporate way of life. It is a real methodology, not a particularly touchy-feely exercise, as much as it could sound like one. What makes it interesting, though, is that while it is a true methodology, what it is tracking actually has a touchy-feely element embedded in it, so it is a human endeavor, not a cold capitalist corporate commercial abstraction.

O^2 works to answer a series of core questions:

► How can we quickly and efficiently gauge the organizational readiness for our change initiative?

► We're (doing the mission). How can we assess what impact this will have on our organization?

► We've just gone live with our new system. How can we test how well the organization will commit to its utilization and ensure the outcomes we expected?

► How can we ensure the communications process throughout our implementation is really effective, understood, and accepted?

► Will the solution we're implementing require us to change our organization culture, and what would we have to do?

► Is there a way of benchmarking and measuring our progress in implementing the organizational change aspects of our program in order to make the needed course corrections along the way?

► We need to assess, anticipate, and mitigate the organizational risks associated with our solution implementation program and get the key people to take ownership. How do we best do that?

Note that these questions operate in direct parallel to the overall CRM strategic planning methodology. They seem to overlap, but they don't really. For example, look at that last question. The fact that stakeholders and risk assessment are involved might seem to be enough to handle change. But what is interesting about good organizational change management is that it doesn't just identify the necessity of the task, but it specifies how to do it so that it can continuously assess organizational impact. The endgame is to align expectations with reality so that when reality does assert itself—and it always does—the stakeholders will not just be not shocked, but actually happy with the results.

Traditional organizational change techniques are often individually focused. That means that change is a matter of a smaller group (could be 10, could be 50) of stakeholders and focus groups who are worked with individually over several weeks, who then are polled for surveys. There are detailed assessments of findings published near the end of the cycle and action recommendations from the various change consultants on the job.

The O^2 methodology is designed to accelerate the process and is more dynamic than the traditional change management. The focus is to complete the entire process from preparation through summarization in roughly eight business days. The stakeholders involve a much wider group (could be 50, could be 150) and they meet all at once. The change readiness survey is already validated and there are immediate results from the meeting and an action-planning workshop over a two-day period. The detail is presented in the summarization stage (a couple of days at the end). There are defined metrics and targeted action plans based on the reality curve identified by the change consultants for the particular company—nothing generic.

Whatever methodology you use for organizational change management in your CRM planning, the one certainty is that you will need a change management program to monitor the success (or failure) of the cultural impact of the strategy.

Technology

Do you know what technological infrastructure and architecture already exists in the company? As in many companies, there has probably been a major investment in what are now legacy systems and, also potentially, third-party applications. Who among us wants to spend lots more money on IT infrastructure? Not so many since the dot-com bomb of 2001. Utilizing what you have is now very important in the CRM scheme of things. That also means that a technology survey is necessary to assess what platforms, applications, and hardware exist. Do you already have an enterprise resource planning (ERP) system in place? How easily can the CRM applications that you are thinking of implementing integrate with your existing technology infrastructure? For example, if you have an SAP Financials system in place, it might be easier or more cost effective to implement an SAP CRM solution simply because of the obvious integration points between them. There is the added benefit (particularly in SAP's case) of utilizing common data from the data store that your system uses. A complete technology survey and plan is paramount for any sort of CRM strategy. Know thy infrastructure.

Package Selection

Okay, you've decided on the value proposition, built the business case, assessed the business processes, identified the technologies, determined the risks, and looked at the cultural change that is likely to occur. Hopefully, your users were involved from the beginning or much of what I'm going to say now is moot. It's vendor time! Time to decide what is going to be implemented with what you need done, and who is going to do the implementation. Needless to say, if we lived in a perfect universe, this would be either obvious because of all the other work done so well to date, or the package picking would be done while you're completing your plan. But I'm sad to say, it isn't a perfect world and this is a particularly political part of the overall strategic planning. The politics of who likes what for whatever reasons now asserts itself. Even though it is only 24 percent of the cost of the implementation, it is about 70 percent of the aggravation and, hopefully not at your company, 90 percent of the maneuvering that will go on. Why? Careers are made and broken on these things. The wrong pick and despite all your other careful planning, your project is ruined. The right pick and the vice-presidency is awaiting you.

Prior to picking the package, the package strategy that overlaps with the implementation strategy has to be decided. Simply put, are you going to implement an enterprise-wide solution or a modular one with one or a few of the modules at a time? Are you going to implement a single package or best of breed in the areas that you identify as mission-critical for CRM? Are you concerned about the way the package integrates with what IT infrastructure you already have—or can it even integrate with it at all? All of these questions are vital and are directly affected by all the factors that have already gone into the strategy.

Don't leave out the economy here. For example, in a recessionary economy, since the value proposition tends toward customer retention and cost reduction, the approach that is often taken is modular. Find out where the bleeding is occurring in your processes and fix that with the implementation of particular modules of a CRM application. If your obvious weak points are in the production of your sales team, then sales force automation (SFA) might be the domain you want to look at. Within that context you can find modules for any facet of sales management you want. However, if your weakness is elsewhere, such as bad communication with your business partners, or you are pushing for the channel to sell about 25 percent more product than they have historically done because you let go 50 percent of your sales force, perhaps partner relationship management (PRM) is the way to go.

Once the strategy for package selection is decided, then a vendor review starts. That is a fairly obvious thing because by the time you get to the vendor selection, if you've correctly developed your CRM strategy, you will know what you need pretty clearly. There are a few salient points to be made nonetheless.

When you buy the application, you buy the vendor. This means the application isn't the only thing that must be evaluated. How good is the vendor at customer service? Do the vendor's account managers have a good relationship with the point people at the company? How financially stable is the vendor? How well do they understand the business model that the enterprise works with? What experience do they have in the particular industry? Is the vendor's CRM corporate culture customer-friendly, or is CRM just an application to them? These matter very much in the considerations that you have here. For example, what if the company CRM-appointed staff doesn't get along with the vendor's account managers? What will happen when you need something from the vendor, which is inevitable?

Most of the applications have similar functionality. Since human beings tend to give similar labels to similar things or the same labels to the same things, opportunity management features tend to be pretty standard stuff. The more pertinent question at this stage is how usable is that functionality? Can the users understand it right away (or with some training) as something important to their productivity that is not that difficult to grasp? How well the application executes the functionality is essential.

How well does the CRM architecture integrate with your existing systems? There is hardly a company that is implementing CRM that doesn't have information technology systems already in place that they've invested millions into. One aspect of package selection that is vital is how well that package fits those systems you are not replacing. If you are a mainframe-based company, does the architecture of the CRM system allow mainframe data to pass to the CRM application? Can it handle a very mobile workforce? Will it integrate with third-party systems that you bought last year? Can it gather data from multiple data warehouses or data marts? Must you have capabilities for remote synchronization or are you a one-office company? Will the hardware be sufficient for purely Web-based architecture? Most of the major CRM vendors have either or both Internet architectures, synchronization, integration "points" such as APIs (SAP calls them Business APIs [BAPIs]; PeopleSoft calls them Enterprise Integration Points [EIPs]), and toolkits that allow for customization. There is also Enterprise Application Integration (EAI) software that operates as "middleware"—passing data from one place to another in disparate systems. In any case, this is an important consideration in package selection.

While hardly the only considerations in the package selection stage, these are three critical considerations that the company stakeholders must be aware of while they are making their selections. There are many more, but that's what professionals who do this for a living are for. Engage them.

Implementation Strategy

Once the package selection is complete, the final step for the purposes of this chapter is the implementation strategy. Keep in mind that implementation services ordinarily cost about three times what the software licenses cost, so this is a critical phase. The initial questions to be asked (and these apply to all enterprise-level packages, not just CRM) are who is going to do it and how are they going to do it?

Some options are:

Internal The least viable choice. Very rarely is there an internal group of employees who have the experience and/or the time to actually implement a very CRM-complex system by themselves. The internal team should play an integral role in working with the vendor or consulting services implementation teams.

Vendor professional services This can be a good alternative and provides the customer with an experienced team with access to the latest information from the vendor. This can be very expensive, but you are pretty well guaranteed the knowledge of the product and have the resources of the vendor's entire enterprise as part of the package.

Integrators Whether large or boutique, this is often the best option for price and commitment. Look for a certified partner of the vendor you are using for the software. Be sure of their experience in implementing the CRM applications and customizing the applications in the industry that your company represents. This can be a huge plus. If you choose to go to a less experienced firm (everyone starts from somewhere), get a serious price break from the firm.

Implementation, the next step, is covered substantially in Chapter 17. Nonetheless, I would highly recommend that there is a clear statement of work as well as a well-established procedure and terms for changing what is described in the statement of work. This should all be agreed upon between parties before the implementation starts.

Summary

I've barely touched on the major elements of a CRM strategy. It may seem like a daunting task to put it together, and it is quite time consuming. But taking care to identify all the objectives, processes, cultural changes, technology biases, and so on will lead to a likelihood of success in the use of this new CRM system. That can lead to happy employees, happy customers, increased revenues, better use of those valuable dollars, and—ultimately—a successful company. That's what it's all about, isn't it?

5

Why Does Your Company Need CRM?

The costs of CRM in dollars, personnel, and time can be steep. CAP Gemini recently released a study that found that the average total investment in a CRM implementation is $3.1 million. The payback period is 28 months. The most significant cost may be in impact on staff, which is reflected in an 8 percent turnover increase in year one and 16 percent in year two. This is a heavy price to pay in an era of increasing labor shortages. Yet to retain customers who can get what they want cheaper, often via mouse click, is not easy. CRM implementations aim at solving this conundrum. But how do you convince the corporate officers and other stakeholders to do the deed?

In order to successfully persuade these internal targets to approve and support your CRM project, it is necessary to understand what the key internal metrics should be for the CRM implementation. While each company has a set of ideas and ways to measure those ideas to define its customer success story, ultimately, it falls to customer response. That means that the first measurement, whether the company is conscious of it or not, should be the increasingly popular customer lifecycle management (CLM).

Customer Lifecycle Management (CLM)

Customer lifecycle management, also called Customer Relationship Planning (CRP) by the Gartner Group, is mapping customer data to define customer behaviors so that the processes of a company are fully occupied in acquiring, selling to, and maintaining a long-term relationship with a customer. The "engagement" is long term, and modifications of the responses to changes in the behaviors are done in real time. Although CLM is inherently a strategic issue, most companies manage their customer relationships tactically, which means the transition to a system that centers on the customer and organizes processes, technologies, and channels around that customer may not be easy.

CLM defines the full spectrum of customer interaction. The META Group defines CLM as "engage, transact, fulfill, and service." The purpose of CLM is to envelop the customers so deeply in your corporate mesh that they are captured and retained forever, optimally. While the intricacies are sophisticated, the pieces of CLM are easy to define. They involve an optimized, intermingled conglomerate of methodology and process, technology, and tools that will add to customer lifetime value (CLV) or, minimally, help define CLV. When you become customer-centric, you can build a CRM strategy that encompasses the CRM ecosystem (described in the introduction and Chapter 1). CLV-measurement tools, analytic applications, and customer services provide a full lifecycle management system for your customers. Ultimately, they are captured and kept as long-term friends of the company. The tools are myriad for this and technologically can involve business intelligence tools, data warehouses, and customer-facing technologies via the Web.

Customer Lifetime Value (CLV)

CLV is not just another acronym. It is a measurement of what a customer is projected to be worth over a lifetime. CLV is also not a new concept—it is a staple of one of the earlier incarnations of CRM, database marketing, and has been calculated by direct marketers for years. Its importance has increased due to contemporary customers' freedom of choice. It is also due to the vicious competition to acquire those same customers. It is a measure that allows you to allocate a weighted version of your resources and focus on a specific customer depending on the projected CLV of that customer.

E-Acme.com spends $1 million on a series of email promotions sent to 100,000 qualified email addresses. The cost of their email list is $1,000 per thousand addresses. They pull the Forrester Group study-determined click-through rate of 5.5 percent on the emailing. This generates 5,500 sales at $69.95 for their Videocam package. Historically at this company, the CLV of customers acquired through email is a total dollar expenditure of $400 and a profit of $80 per customer. By dividing the $1 million by 5,500, the acquisition cost of each customer is $181.81. Those 5,500 Videocams at $69.95 each generated $384,725 in revenue immediately. A big loss: $615,275 on the cost of the campaign minus the revenue generated. However, each of these customers, due to the anticipated CLV, will generate $440,000 in profit on $2.2 million in revenues, thus turning an apparent loss into a big gain. The presumption is, of course, that these customers remain for their "lifetime," which is a given number of years determined by corporate metrics. The company's ability to understand and employ these CLV metrics creates a valuable tool in the successful management of their marketing actions.

Needless to say, this is a gross oversimplification. There are a substantial number of factors that will determine the final CLV for any group of customers for a specific company: actual customer retention rate, the average dollar value of an order per customer and the number of orders per customer per year, the costs of customer acquisition, other direct and indirect costs, profit per order, and net present value (NPV) considerations. The simplified example doesn't consider the fact that some groups of customers are more valuable than others.

One of the most complete CLV methodologies belongs to Mei Lin Fung, a managing director at Wainscott Capital, an early stage VC fund with offices in the Silicon Valley, New York, and Washington, DC. For example, in a paper that she wrote in 1998, Ms. Fung identifies how you can determine which leads become the most profitable customers:

Assuming you have a process in place: Measure cost of acquisition, selling cost, customer care cost, and revenue. Then calculate net profit for those you think are your most profitable customers. When you've looked at your top 5–10 most profitable customers, examine how you acquired them. We anticipate you might be surprised. Some of the most valuable lead generation activities occur by happenstance and not by design. Some are repeatable, some are not. Look at the repeatable ones and design programs to repeat them. Look at the happenstance and see what you can do more of, to be ready to respond to and take advantage of unanticipated opportunities. Profitability is dependent on good followup, not just at the prospect stage, but through the very latest encounter. *The price of profitability is eternal vigilance.*

Assuming you don't have a process in place, for example, a new sales channel like the Web, or a new business: Describe the most profitable customers that you would like to have. What will it take to find them and keep them? Define the acquisition, selling, and customer care process. Calculate the ROI on these "ideal case" customers. After checking that they really have the potential to be profitable, you now have defined a process for finding the most profitable leads.

The framework helps you see how to decide what to do next, based on your calculations. Here you are "staging the customer experience." Discordant effects not in harmony might annoy or frustrate the very people you are trying to build relationships with. Starting with the people you already are satisfying gives a sound basis for understanding what people like and come back for. Divide into the three sections: acquisition, selling, and customer care. Don't forget the impact of referrals. Prospects who never make a purchase themselves might make referrals that bring a steady stream of profits.

All of this lead generation is based on a sales pipeline plus an awareness factor that anticipates the level of sales needed to get to a goal. Then, based on historic data, it identifies the number of leads or opportunities needed in January, for example, to achieve objectives in May.

Thus, your customer relationships become qualified, rather than amorphous; your objectives clear, rather than vague. For more information and considerably more detail, please refer to the appendix, a primer on CLV by Ms. Fung.

Once the CLV is established, it is considerably easier to design programs that can escalate the customer-type's CLV. That can take the form of increased revenue from the customer through up-selling, building exit barriers so that the customers will remain a customer, and cross-selling to expand the customer's "revenue horizon."

Many analytic applications are designed to help identify the obvious and hidden factors that determine CLV. Knowing and using CLM and key CLV metrics are essential to successfully managing marketing efforts and resources. These metrics become critical when you are trying to justify and sell a CRM implementation in-house.

Convincing the Stakeholders

Most companies have internal procedures to evaluate proposals for large projects. Such a project could be a major internal IT project to improve the overall sales analysis and forecasting process or creation of a new factory or distribution facility. It also could be a decision to invest in a customer management project that promises long-term return. One step in securing approval for your project is to identify the potential decision makers for the project and convince them that the company needs to make your proposed investment. Frequently, the approval process for substantial projects involves several different functions—the CxOs within your enterprise. The rest of this chapter will take a look at the minds and eyes of two of the decision makers—the president/CEO and the CFO—with a more cursory look at the vice-president of sales. The idea? Letting you get a picture of how to sell this to these mission-critical decision makers.

President or CEO

This is probably the most difficult person to convince, aside from the CFO. The president is the strategic thinker, the person who is responsible for it all and, for the most part, the board of directors' fall-person if something goes wrong with revenue. So the metrics and projections, benefits and pitfalls of a CRM implementation are particularly sensitive to him or her. Since this is the person who has the relationship with the outside world, how the internal implementation "looks" is actually a very important consideration.

Scott Fletcher is vice-president of the southern region for supply chain management software king, i2. He has a considerable background in implementation planning and execution as the vice-president of technology services for PeopleSoft and EMA vendor Annuncio and, most importantly, as president of epipeline.

In an interview conducted in late 2000, Mr. Fletcher said:

CRM systems have great promise, but no system, CRM or SFA or ERP, is good unless it provides better information or improved business processes. Hopefully, both.

The drivers are business considerations, not technical.

The rule of thumb for an implementation of a packaged application is that it has 80 percent of what you want and needs 20 percent customization. Mr. Fletcher stated:

Many of the CRM packages are integrated with best practices, much as ERP was. If your proposal calls for too much customization, then you might want to revisit how you are dealing with your customers, or if it's an SFA implementation, how you're managing your sales force. I'd be looking to see if you need to change the customer processes or if you are simply choosing the wrong package.

The system should differentiate the company from its competitors. When push comes to shove, the top companies in a particular domain produce a similar enough product or provide contemporaneous enough services to be not all that distinguishable. In the IT world, product lifecycles are so short that your competitor's product can leapfrog over yours every six months. "The real differentiator is how you reach back to the customers," said Mr. Fletcher.

Internal Implementations Are Very Competitive

Mr. Fletcher emphasized the importance of the relationship to the vendor:

> If your main competitor is using vendor X, what impact would the system have if we used vendor X instead of another system?

There are a variety of vendor points to look for when you are getting ready to produce your dissertation to the corporate stakeholders:

> ▸ Is the relationship your competitor has with the vendor strategic? (In other words, is your competitor a key beta partner or does the competitor run the user community?)
>
> ▸ How does the competitor understand the technology?
>
> ▸ How much is the competitor's use of the technology written up in the press?
>
> ▸ Can you become a strategic partner of the vendor so you can implement key new features early, which then allows you to get to market earlier than your competition?

This may seem an unusual view of what is apparently an internal implementation, but the purpose of these systems is to provide the level of customer interaction that drives significant revenue so that you are number one in your domain. The CRM system is one of the key management systems for differentiation from your competition in the New Economy. Customer participation is the driver of success because in turn it provides the foundation for the revenue growth. That means features such as Web enablement are very important to the system. If your competition uses the same system and is a strategic partner, they will know how you work because they are using the same processes you are. The flip side is, of course, also true.

Mr. Fletcher continued:

> When I was president of epipeline, I put less emphasis on the cost of the project than I did on the payback for acquisition and retention of customers. I looked at Dell and how they handled their customer processes and then looked at Compaq and realized that Dell won hands down—and it showed. The one or two million that it might have cost for the project was not critical. Did the application

have features that are beneficial? Was the vision of the vendor similar to the vision of epipeline? These were factors that mattered to me. They were strategic because of the ROI that we would get if it succeeded and they were the things that I wanted to know.

A well-known ERP vendor, in its earlier, more carefree days, had an account management program where they assigned one account manager per 15 customers. When they were small, this worked well. They grew to a client base of thousands and this became unmanageable, so they went to a well-known CRM package. However, rather than take advantage of the excellent features of the package, they simply created a redundant system that tried to do what the account managers did rather than view the implementation of the new CRM system as a means to effect significant and important change throughout the company. It was a disaster. No one worked the system, and the account managers kept the information to themselves and never really updated the system. In other words, rather than an agent of change, the system became the equivalent of a dumb terminal.

Stated Mr. Fletcher:

For the CRM system to succeed, it has to be seen as an agent of change and integrated into the culture of the company so that it can transform the culture. The recognition of the CRM system as a change agent would be something I would be very alert to when a proposal comes to me. Several years ago, Paul Strassman wrote a book in which he took companies and correlated the size of their IT investments to their success. There was no correlation at all between expenditure and success. If you are proposing putting a CRM system into mirror current practices, then it won't make it past my door. Customization to the old is not good. The use of the system must be forward thinking. This could mean things like enabling the customer with the capacity to track his own call status and call logs, it could mean that training becomes Web enabled, it could mean the creation of customer communities, or a large number of [other] things.

In summary, said Mr. Fletcher:

The bottom line that you need to convince me of is how it gives us strategic competitive advantage and how it will help revenue generation. If all you are looking to do is use the CRM implementation to automate current practices, outsource that to an ASP or something like that. CRM is strategic, not back office.

CFO

How does the CFO think? Time, money, and "energy densities" (productive, efficient uses of time and money) are thoroughly intertwined in any project—both short and long term. Craig Thompson, a seasoned CFO, identifies what it takes to convince a CFO of the value of a CRM implementation. Mr. Thompson has seen the process from several viewpoints:

▶ As an external consultant with Accenture, creating justification analyses and helping senior management validate justification analyses

▶ As a CFO, reviewing investment proposals

▶ As a CFO, making proposals for key information systems

▶ As a general manager, sponsoring projects

Mr. Thompson says:

There are three questions that need to be answered to make the general business case. One: What is the sound reason for the investment? Two: How consistent is this CRM proposal with the longer-range corporate strategy? Three: Is the execution plan sound?

According to Mr. Thompson, the key point in considering CRM for most companies is probably not a question of *if*, but of *which* (technology) and *when* (to do it). CRM is the current electronic frontier. The ease of use and instant response available to your customer also can put a wealth of information in your hands immediately. Not only do you get data in electronic form, you get your customers to enter most of it for you, you get it instantly, and you get it in a structure that matches your product and customer identification structures. What a deal! Further, if you don't figure out how to grasp this data and effectively turn it around to better meet your customers' needs, don't worry—your competitors will show you how.

Why Invest?

For the CFO to give his stamp of approval, he needs to see a credible benefits statement. According to Mr. Thompson, benefits from a successful CRM project can come from two major areas. First, internal cost reductions from new efficiencies. For example, will the CRM system provide the capability for better inventory or manufacturing production scheduling? This often occurs as a result of improved customer demand information through faster order capture or customer requirement forecasts. Can it improve sales and support activity cost metrics by eliminating customer support tasks through Web-based customer self-help features?

However, cost reductions should only be a small part of the CRM justification.

Growth Is a Good Thing

As a key component of the marketing process, the CRM should provide clear advantages for customer retention (thereby improving CLV). It should also increase competitive position through ease of use, enhanced customer response times ("anytime, anywhere"), and other differentiation features. A company's "product" is not just the tangible service or product that is delivered, it includes the "wrapper" of how your customers interact with you and how satisfied they are with that interaction.

Accordingly, the second class of benefits—longer-run marketing effectiveness—should be the most compelling. The advantages provided by a successful CRM implementation should lead to a stronger competitive position and higher revenues. That could include:

▶ Enhanced customer retention by means such as electronic bonding, enhanced customer satisfaction, and so on. For example, once you have all of your customers' profile data and ordering history and have trained them through repetitive use, why would they ever want to leave you and start that process all over again? Your history of their interactions with you is a marvelous tool for you and them. Use it internally and present it back to them for their use. My local auto repair store has me as a customer forever because they know what they have done on my three cars for the past five years. I can't afford to leave them—do you think I want to manually track that data?

▶ Stronger marketing differentiation through "wrapper" characteristics such as ease of use, anytime-anywhere interfaces, and better channel support features (market electronically to end-users, but sell through your channels).

▶ New customer acquisition opportunities through electronic ordering/payment options. Leverage the automation available through the Net.

▸ Unique features that can be created out of your interactions that meet key needs of your customers or your channel's customers.

Mr. Thompson points out that the metrics used to identify these benefits vary from industry to industry, and among different business models within industries. He continues:

> However, companies should know which metrics are relevant to their success based on their business structure and should be using those metrics in day-to-day reporting and in their planning models by the time they are ready to propose a CRM implementation.

You need to look at the historical statistics and then quantify the degree and timing of improvements based on the functionality of the proposed system.

To a CFO or a CMO, a broad CRM application can be very effective for both direct and indirect customer channels simultaneously. One example Mr. Thompson mentions is how a major U.S. chip manufacturer used CRM to directly support end-users and keep their distribution channel happy:

> They put up a Web-based system for key end-user decision makers (PC board designers—not purchasing managers) that gave them anytime-anywhere access to chip specs and even samples for prototypes. However, the ultimate purchase of the chips used in the manufacturing production runs still came through the distributors, so that the direct and indirect channels were both serviced.

In fact, the high level of service provided to the decision point probably helped cement the final production orders. How should the proposer measure the proposed benefits? What are the metrics? Mr. Thompson makes it very clear what wins his support:

> The metrics have to be clear and specific. These can be things like revenue per customer, sales rep quota loading, reduction in complaints per customer, marketing efficiencies of varying sorts, pure sales numbers, or increased market share. But above all, they have to be credible, meaning reasonably quantified and specific. Guarantees of future results are not necessary or believable. We are looking for well-thought-out analysis that is consistent with the company's management process. All investments involve risk and uncertainty. We know that.

Executive Ownership

Another key factor to the CFO is clear executive ownership of the enhanced metrics. Are the relevant department heads whose performance is expected to improve in agreement and endorsing those improvements? Mr. Thompson answers:

> You need to demonstrate that this has been thought through, the right executives have bought in, the deliverables are owned by the appropriate people, and the promoters are clear on what the enhancements to our business will be with the successful CRM implementation. You tell me why this will help us. I assume that you've done your homework. Stand up for what you are going to deliver. Additionally, it's linked to the budgeting and planning systems. The expected benefits will be reflected in improved metrics on the next business plan cycle.

Strategic Consistency: Business and Technology

In an overlapping, CFO/COO hybrid vein, Mr. Thompson, who has served as general manager in several companies, identifies another key decision point. Is the proposed application consistent with the company's strategy in both business terms and IT infrastructure terms? Are you building platforms that move you in the right direction? A CRM system is not easy or quick to implement and certainly would be very difficult to change. Half the battle of implementing a key infrastructure system is getting the technology to work with the rest of the IT systems in place, but the other half can be even more daunting—institutionalizing it within the company. Institutionalization may include:

- ▶ Integrating the CRM system with management practices and philosophy. The metrics from the CRM system should become a part of the ongoing management reporting process.

- ▶ Day-to-day staff in the company should be familiar with how the system works, should direct their activities using data from the system, should immediately be aware of any deviations from norms, and should use the system and its data in wide-ranging ways.

The larger the company, the more time- and more energy-intensive the CRM implementation. However, there are huge benefits on the backend. Changing it would be a nightmare.

On the technology side, says Mr. Thompson, the CRM system should not be a data island. "The prevailing principle should be 'enter data once, use it often.'" Data consistency provides the foundation for the single customer view throughout the organization. On the technical side, there are several obvious "shoulds" that apply to most systems:

Strong, reliable vendor You don't want to spend three times as much as the system costs to implement it and then have the vendor wash out.

Standards-based open architecture This means that future changes to the architecture or expansion of the system are easily done, rather than having to deal with the nightmare of a new architecture or a different standard.

Open APIs or other integration hooks By using an open API, you can customize the basic code provided to your specifications.

Flexible reporting tools Reporting is the basis for so many corporate decisions that easy construction of reports with lots of options means smarter decisions and improves that "single customer view" considerably, by providing the same reporting information to different groups within different departments.

Mr. Thompson continues:

I would see a higher risk component if we are talking about implementing version 0.9 of a new CRM application. There would have to be very clear differentiating factors for doing so. We don't want to bet our business on a risky application. We have enough challenges modifying our practices to meet the system structure, training our people, training our customers, etc. Adding application risks on top of that simply increases the "failure risk." We are betting our marketing image and customer relationships. The implementation plan would have to recognize those risks and have appropriate pilots and checkpoints built in. The vendor that would reduce our risks has a stable application, a stable corporation, referenceable sites, and proven business application for his software.

Mr. Thompson would be unmoved by a proposal that sells technology "gee whiz" factors, cutting edge or not, rather than deliverable benefits and results. The expectation is that you are buying current technology. There is a time and place to implement technology, but the justification for doing so is still in the benefits to be obtained. You don't improve your company's share value with technology; you use it to drive successes that produce tangible value.

Execution Control

Mr. Thompson wants to see an execution plan that will deliver the expected benefits on schedule. To do this requires a crisp, clean, credible implementation plan. Risk points should be identified and managed. A lot of the considerations here are based on the quality of the implementation plan and the team's track record. There are specific elements that the budding CRM promoter needs to be alert to when his CFO questions him. The CFO is going to look to see if the execution plan:

- ▶ Is thought out and disciplined in its approach

- ▶ Has an adequately seasoned technical and functional team that can handle issues appropriately (and if not, what outside resources are required?)

- ▶ Has executive ownership

- ▶ Has adequate checkpoints and review points

- ▶ Has sufficient team membership to involve all key users

- ▶ Has a phased implementation approach

According to Mr. Thompson, a phased implementation plan with milestones that can get phased return value is much easier to accept than a "big bang" implementation approach.

Big bangs are not wrong. They are just more risky financially and operationally. Virtually all of the implementation costs are committed before any payback is seen and any success measured. That is high risk. It might be necessary sometimes, but requires a very experienced team, lots of overview, and very careful validation of each step. You only get one chance to succeed. Phased implementations allow learning curves to be looped back to the implementation team and small direction changes to be made early. Early success also builds acceptance throughout the company.

The CFO's decision-making is affected by the track record of the implementation team. If they've done it many times, the deal could be a rubber stamp. If it is the first time that they are implementing anything, much less something with the complexity of CRM, the risks are higher. Additional resources are committed (such as outside consultants who have "been there, done that") or the schedule and business justification have realistic provisions for schedule slippage and corrections.

This is no different for the overall company and its management. If the company has frequently implemented core applications, it already has change management experience, and the new system will be easier to implement. If the CRM system is the first major system, especially if it is the first major Web application, this will be a demanding project. Many existing paradigms are changed in Web-based applications. The management processes have to be crystal clear before the CFO will say yes, especially in this circumstance. States Mr. Thompson:

> A strong implementation plan generates a higher success probability. If you can make me comfortable that you can do this or have taken appropriate risk management steps, I'll be comfortable with the risk.

Mr. Thompson further cautions that the credibility of the implementation plan and the inherent risks identified in that plan affect the phasing expectations. Factors that create higher risk are things like limited company experience in larger projects, limited individual history, limited funding, and political risks. In these cases, smaller phases are suggested—"microbursts, rather than big bangs." Build success patterns and confidence increases. If you practice bursts of clean execution and the implementation strategy looks like it will be successful, the CFO—and, in fact, all the executive stakeholders—will buy in a lot more confidently.

In summary, Mr. Thompson says:

> As a CFO, I'm looking for a clear reason to do this implementation, a well-defined measurable set of expectations, and a consistency with the company's overall business and technology strategies and value propositions. I will expect to see the appropriate metrics associated with that in the proposal and the deliverables in the implementation plan. With that and the other less tangible factors clear to me, I'm far more comfortable in the success of this CRM value proposition for the company. Recognize that I am a backer of key projects. Not doing a CRM project because of a poor justification could be the biggest failure of all. A company needs to move forward, or be left behind in the "also ran" category. Tools like CRM are essential parts of that progress. I want to do this, just do the homework to educate the management team and we will back you, risks and all.

Mr. Thompson has been involved in the implementation of numerous IT applications and company management platforms in several companies. He served as a consultant in a leading IT consulting firm, an implementation team leader, a sponsoring executive, and an executive on the approval team. He has an extensive management background in the IT and telecommunications industries. He can be reached at mail@craig-thompson.com.

Vice-President, Sales

The VP of sales is easier to convince. If it impacts the bottom line with increased sales and more revenue per salesperson, plus cost savings, the vice-president of sales is a happy camper. However, there are going to be concerns that this VP has, among them ramp-up time for each salesperson to learn the system, which takes away from the time they are selling (as does pretty much everything but selling). They have to see the long-term benefit because of the potential short-term difficulties.

The Sales Cycle

At Live Wire (my company), we've ascertained that roughly 24 percent of the salesperson's time is spent on any particular client sale, with only 5 percent in front of the client. Roughly 35 percent of the time, the salesperson is involved in administrative work of some sort, ranging from deal sheets to updating the client files, to surfing the Net for intelligence and opportunity. That means roughly one third of the time, the salesperson is doing paperwork and not prospecting or mining, so to speak. Lot of gold lost here. CRM will reduce this administrative time significantly, allowing increased customer contact, opportunity mining, or whatever else the salesperson can do to develop more sales.

Reduction in Ramp-up Time

In sales there is a period that is called "ramp up" by many sales organizations. This is the time needed by a new salesperson, either rookie or experienced, to learn the company processes, corporate style, how to deal with clients that are handed off to her from the previous salesperson, and products or services offered, as well as time to master the collateral material and understand the compensation structure. Depending on the level of experience, this often can take several months. Most companies write off the ramp-up period as one with little performance results. CRM implementations, since they embed much of the information such as business rules, methodology, easily accessible client information, and pipeline forecasting, reduce ramp-up time considerably. The newly hired salesperson has easy access to what he or she needs, rather than chasing down managers or other salespeople or endless database mining. There are a few things, including getting to know the clients personally, that cannot be fully resolved by the CRM applications.

Customer Incident Solution Time

If your CRM implementation involves automated customer service such as call centers, there is a significant time reduction per incident or transaction due to a variety of time savers. (See Chapter 11 on call centers.) These could include automated self-service, Voice Over Internet Protocol (VOIP), easily available customer information, or information on past incidences with a client onscreen. It could mean time efficiencies because there is a single accessible customer view regardless of what department is looking at the customer records. This eliminates redundancies and information "translation" problems.

Manager Involvement

The managers are the trackers—the ones who are watching the sales pipeline, tweaking the sales forecasts, and often determining the qualifications of a sales opportunity. With CRM, the qualification process is quicker and, because there is more customer or potential client information available, more effective.

Costs

Prior to Live Wire's SalesLogix implementation, we initially looked at the potential return with the following parameters:

▶ Normalized cost of sales. For us, this meant the cost of sales in 1999. This included basic cost of the salesperson's salary and cost of the recruiter's salary, multiplied by the anticipated labor time in mining, qualifying, chasing and closing the opportunity, travel, phone bills, and a myriad of other cost factors, and then multiplied by the anticipated rate of change of costs in 2000—the latter, a very small percentage increase.

▶ Expected hourly rate per consultant on a time and materials project, or the expected average hourly rate for a consultant on a fixed price contract with unpaid hours built in. This was multiplied by the expected paid hours. We also took the costs of the consultant into account, such as travel, accommodations, food, local transportation, phone bills, and other incidentals. Our gross margins were gleaned from this final number.

For a business such as ours, due to its intensely competitive and time-sensitive nature, any reduction in administrative time meant increases *hourly* in dollars. So time reduction and energy-dense time efficiencies were our main objective. Cost savings, except for the fact that we were self-funded, was less of a concern.

However, as we moved through the internal trail of implementation planning, we began to realize that there were a significant number of other costs involved. The implementation cost was obvious, but also there was a dislocation cost while the system was living a dual existence with our legacy Outlook address books and the other contact managers used by the staff. There was anticipated downtime while the data mapping and translation was going on. There were anticipated (and sadly, unanticipated) system crashes as we found out what SalesLogix worked well with and not so well with (on the whole, not bad at all). There was the ramp-up time for the software and use of the software on the Web. If our salespeople used ACT! 2000, data mapping was no problem because the founder of SalesLogix was also the co-creator of ACT! so that the translators were built into SalesLogix. But if they used the robust Daytimer 2000, there was an ASCII flat file that had to be created, and that didn't work nearly as well. In other words, there were hidden costs that we had to allow for in this implementation.

Another cost that we anticipated was that there was significant customization that had to go on. For financial relief, we did it in a phased way. First, we put up the basic plain-vanilla, out-of-the-box system. We used it while our MIS department began a well-planned months-long customization features inclusion. That helped keep our costs spread and manageable.

One cost we didn't anticipate was a very good salesperson who decided that he didn't like the system. The time spent in working with this valuable employee was a significant budgetary drain, but ultimately worth it. Cultural dislocation and even sheer cussedness can take a real toll on the company implementing CRM. Remember that statistically, 8 to 16 percent of employees leave within two years when CRM is implemented.

Each of these is either an anticipated or unanticipated cost that could lead to serious cost overruns. So how can you measure revenue gains to mitigate the cost and persuade (or dissuade) the CFO to approve the implementation?

Most Important: The User

This is the hardest person to convince and the least consulted. The normal failure rate for CRM projects quoted by the CRM analysts such as Gartner or Forrester Research is a scary 55 to 75 percent. Most of that is due to the simple truth that once implemented, whether on time or on budget or not, the users never use it.

It was pointed out in Chapter 4 that users are an essential part of the stakeholders' teams. But what does a user look for in the system? What convinces these difficult, correct-in-their-crankiness people that CRM has value to them?

It isn't the amount of code on a client PC. They have a hard drive. It isn't a lower total cost of ownership. It isn't an increase in the company's profitability or the ability to measure the value of an individual customer over a lifetime. It isn't the smiles of a customer except in a metaphysical sort of way.

What impresses users is something that can make the users' job easier and that they don't have to do much with what is under the hood. If you have a drag-and-drop interface and the user is PC-savvy enough to use it, then there is value. If you have tools that let the users do their job better, then it is beneficial. For example, a marketing professional could plan a fairly complex marketing campaign by plugging in elements of that campaign onscreen through dragging these pre-existing elements to a tree or something similar. The salespeople can see their pipeline graphically, easily understand the potential rate of success or failure overall, and calculate the commissions in a number of what-if scenarios.

User needs are the simplest to identify, yet the user may be the most difficult to convince. Even if the above needs are fulfilled, if the application does the work slowly, if the user has to reboot due to buggy code, or if there are missing elements the user thinks he needs, the narrow border between CRM success and failure is crossed.

The users will drop the Excel spreadsheets and the Word documents when they find that they can feel better about the work they are doing because they have a system that lets them do it better.

ROI

The downturn of 2001 and the additional fears due to September 11 made ROI a big CRM issue. Normally, the simplest ROI for a CRM implementation (or any implementation, for that matter) is the impact on the bottom line. How many more sales closings per salesperson will it create due to timesaving? A single time and materials deal for Live Wire is about $100 per hour for four months (total revenue value). In those four months, the consultant is expected to work around 640 hours. That means around $64,000. Multiply by 3 to annualize the revenues and you get roughly $192,000 per salesperson per year with a single additional closing per period. If we have five salespeople, that means roughly a million dollars to our bottom line. However, it means a few other things as well. First, this is the average value of a deal, not the actual value of a deal. Could be more, could be less. Second, this isn't the margin. Third, this assumes seasoned, ramped-up salespeople from January 1. Fourth, this isn't a net value that presumes any ending of deals or fall-offs for any reason. Fifth, the costs of the project are upfront while this (speculative) value is gained over the year. For a self-funded company, up-front costs are the biggest possible problem, since cash flow is always an issue. Sixth, the savings are anticipated, not real—until they are real. Finally, the quality of the deal has to be taken into account to see the actual value.

However, a "real" ROI for a CRM implementation is far more complex and impacts a variety of departments and divisions, much as ERP did in its heyday. It also is subjective, and what is appropriate for one company is not even on the radar of another. For example, the META Group did a study in early 2001 of 800 businesses that are doing CRM implementations. Nearly two-thirds of them were doing CRM to improve the company's workflow. META Group rightfully concluded that this was very shortsighted since the ultimate goal of CRM is to keep buyers loyal, not to make the company more cost effective. But those two-thirds were measuring their ROI on how well the workflow worked. Peculiar, but still an ROI metric because the company using it wants it to be. Is this a real CRM ROI? Debatable. But lots of companies seem to think so.

The other difficulty in determining ROI is that there are an incredible number of ways of doing it. ROI to me isn't ROI to you and we probably calculate it differently. Some calculations are entirely ad hoc.

However, there are some general calculations that make sense when ROI is based on customer satisfaction and customer value. Jay Curry, chairman of the Customer Marketing Institute (http://www.cus-tomermarketing.com/) and a smart CRM strategic consultant, has a series of calculations that he recommended in the CRM-Select forum. Without going into the details, he segments the customer base into four segments: the top (1 percent), the big (4 percent), the medium (15 percent), and the small (80 percent). The designations are based on the revenue produced by customers. The calculations he makes are based on deriving operational profit and dividing that by CRM costs to get an ROI calculation. This is a useful bottom line approach to find-ing out which customers you want to spend time with and will derive some ROI benefit from.

Let's look at some examples of ROI—how analytic applications within the CRM implementation might affect the departments directly affected by the implementation: sales and marketing.

It is now 28 months since the CRM implementation, and the sales reps are up and running on the SFA component of the applications. They can access sales data wirelessly via the Web on their PDAs. The benefits that evolved are quicker response times to opportunity, reduced administrative time, shared best practices, more accurate fore-casting for the sales pipeline, and better deal tracking and problem solving. The resulting ROI is more deals per salesperson due to a shorter sales time, better risk management, less administrative time, and shorter closing time. Of course, that means more deals per year and more revenue.

In marketing, due to the marketing performance analysis and cam-paign management software, all senior marketing executives are able to track the success rate of any particular campaign, with multiple opportunities to slice and dice the data in infinite varieties to see who, what, when, where, and how a campaign is successful. The metrics for success in marketing ROI identify the more profitable customers (CLV), more revenue derived from more highly focused types of campaigns, improved cost savings, and improved product/services profitability.

Ultimately, as in all good ROI, customer acquisition and long-term customer retention leading to increased revenue is the bottom-line best answer to the effectiveness of a CRM implementation. When you are convincing your president, CEO, VP of sales, or CFO, the meas-ures that could make your business great are the measures that need to be justified to implement CRM.

Now that you've been so convincing, on to the implementation and who is going to provide it.

6

Sales Force Automation: Good Products Aren't Enough

It used to be, back in the good old days, selling a product to a customer was enough to ensure success—if it was a good product. Now while a good product is still necessary, it isn't enough to guarantee the sale. There are dozens of similar good products competing for markets that have worldwide scope and localized distribution needs. With the accession of the Internet to the mainstream, small and large companies compete to do business in the same marketplaces. It is no coincidence that customer retention has become one of the primary focuses of contemporary sales and marketing. It is easy to be lured away by Cathay's riches when the distance between you and Cathay is just a website away. No longer is Marco Polo necessary to bring back silk, gold, and gems. Get on the Web, order bullion and brocades, and get them via FedEx the next day by 2:30 P.M.

Suddenly sales process command and control, and tracking customers and potential customers, are high-powered necessities. For every Dell, there is a Hewlett Packard, Compaq, Gateway, and Micron lurking. For every Macy's, there is a Nordstrom selling the same merchandise at pretty much the same price. For each time you see a commercial for IBM, there is another one from Microsoft. What's a company to do?

Sales force automation (SFA), a candidate for father of CRM, is the answer to the salesperson's prayers. SFA is designed to help salespeople acquire and retain customers, reduce administrative time, provide robust (the industry's favorite word) account management, and, basically, make salesperson activities something that earns them and their companies money.

Acquiring Customers Means Keeping Them

If there is anything that can blanch a sales manager's skin, it is the fear of losing customers. The process involved in getting a new customer is not only costly in pure financial terms, but it is also a psychic drain on sales teams. Retaining that same customer is far less costly and much more a matter of relationships, not products.

The cost of a Web commerce customer acquisition in pure dollar terms is often seen to be roughly 1.5 to 2.5 times the value of an average sale. For example, the online Gap retailer might spend between $100–$120 to acquire a customer, who will then spend $75 on a clothing sale. What's the value? If he or she does it twice, the Web retailer's acquisition becomes profitable. Then the value of retention becomes obvious.

Shop.org, in a study released in late 2000 and followed up in mid-2001, based on survey responses from 66 North American online retailers, showed that customer acquisition costs continue to decline from a high of $71 during Q4 1999, to $45 in Q1 2000, to $18 in Q1 2001. Not a bad reduction at all. More interesting than that is the breakdown between the different ways that retailers do business. Look at Table 6-1, developed from studies done by Boston Consulting Group and McKinsey Consultants.

Table 6-1: Customer Acquisition Costs According to Channel

Type of Business	Cost per Customer
Internet-only retailers	$82–$95
All online retailers	$32
Brick and mortar retailers	$31
Catalog retailers	$11
Multichannel retailers	$30

What makes the results in the table particularly interesting (as interesting as anything like this gets) is that multichannel retailers, those often called "click and mortar," have acquisition costs that are among the best of the lot, except for catalog retailers, whose cost is the mailing list and the production of their catalogs. This is in keeping with current Internet wisdom because it makes the Web nothing more than another communications channel. It shows that an effective mix of these channels is truly the cost-effective path for use of the Internet, rather than the Fantasyland version of the Web as a democratized leveler, a do-all/cost-nothing approach to business.

Shop.org thinks this cost effectiveness is due, in part, to a shift away from relatively expensive television advertising to online advertising and marketing. I would say, rather than the shop.org reasoning, the use of more effective approaches through targeted marketing online and multiple channels has decreased the costs of customer acquisition dramatically.

With the economic downturn of March 2001 and the additional layer of discomfort and fear triggered by the September 11, 2001 events, customer retention became a number one priority, far surpassing customer acquisition. Prior to this, oddly, customer acquisition was a far greater initiative. For example, the online pure-play "e-tailer" (such as barnesandnoble.com) spent 76 percent of their revenues on acquiring customers and 3 percent on retaining them. While this may or may not have been a wise decision in prosperous times, in down times it is not too smart. According to a study published by *The Industry Standard* magazine in November 2000, it is *five times* more costly to acquire customers than to keep them, which makes it very expensive to acquire customers. But keep in mind that customers are customers whether you are acquiring or retaining them. In down times, it pays to retain because, conversely, it is one-fifth as expensive to keep those customers. So acquisition or retention, as Billy Joel croons, "All you need is looks and a whole lotta money, but it's still rock and roll to me." A customer is a customer if he or she exchanges value with you, folks. Choose what you want to do.

Compounding the problem is that it is so much easier to switch from one product to another these days. A mouse-click or two and a delete check box or three and you have switched merchants. The cost of customer switching is very, very low to the customer. It is compounded by the increasing similarity between products. There are some differences that can be outlined between ordering this book from amazon.com or from a brick-and-mortar Barnes and Noble bookstore. But what's the difference between ordering from amazon.com or barnesandnoble.com? Actually, this question will be answered more than rhetorically in Chapter 8. But for now, let's leave it as a rhetorical question. For the customer, there is very little obvious difference at all, but for the user, well...

Sales Force Automation: The Purpose

What is expected of successful sales force automation? Not just the standard increases in revenue and margin. With the success of the "intangibles measurement" methodology represented by the Balanced Scorecard, there are means for quantifying measurements of customer satisfaction and sales force effectiveness that complement increases in the bottom line, as tangible as those increases are.

Increased Revenue

Needless to say, this is the *ne plus ultra* result of SFA: improvement in the bottom line. But a gross increase is not a sufficient answer for SFA success. Just as important are the increases in revenue per salesperson and in the gross profits per year. If you have an increase of 100 percent in sales revenues but your cost of sales has increased, or it came strictly as a result of your increased sales force, your SFA implementation failed.

Reduction in Cost of Sales

In bad times, sadly, reduction becomes an important word. The reduction you don't want to run across goes by the acronym of RIF. That stands for *reduction in force*—meaning fewer employees, which, of course, potentially means you. Not a good thing. In fact, in really bad economic periods such as the recession that began in March 2001, RIF is often one of the more distasteful justifications of CRM budgets.

Happily, in this case, we're talking about a reduction in the amount of time that is used by salespeople in coordination of their efforts, continuous and repetitive data entry, and often unsuccessful attempts to extract and interpret data without the tools to do so. Studies have been done that show that sales time to fulfill administrative functions is almost half of a salesperson's activity. By reducing the time engaged in these administrative or other non-sales–related efforts, the cost of sales is reduced. This is one of the most successful results of sales force automation. Those same studies have shown an improvement of between 12 and 26 percent in reducing administrative time for salespeople.

Customer Retention Due to Company, Not Product or Service

If your customers are happy, they stay with you, even if they are paying a bit more. Myer-Emco, a very successful custom home theater and consumer electronics equipment installer, puts a large amount of time into making sure their customers get excellent service. They probably are 10 to 15 percent more expensive than comparable retail equipment dealers in the Washington, D.C., metro area. However, they have a loyal clientele willing to pay the extra cost, simply because the level of personal service is so effective. It's not about the money; it's about the relationship with the company and, often, the relationship with particular salespeople within the company.

SFA's benefit is to provide you with a view of the customer that allows that great salesperson or awesome company to understand the value of the individual customer through customer history and communications with the company. While never a substitution for personal interactions (what is?), SFA can provide the intelligence and view to better plan how to actually do good things for your clients.

Sales Force Increasing Mobility

The Internet wasn't exactly the panacea that we all hoped it was going to become. But one of the best results of the Web as it entered the mainstream was the proliferation of the wireless world. Look at the millions of Palm OS–based PDAs from Palm and Handspring sold. Look at the increasing popularity of the Pocket PC 2001 and 2002 devices that are outselling the Palm because of their mini-desktop functionality and the sexiness of the Compaq iPAQ. Aether Technologies grew from 70 employees to more than 800 in a year, went public, started an acquisition binge and then, after all this, in late 2000, announced proudly that they had their first customer! Convergence of PDAs and cellphones is becoming a "thing to do," with Samsung announcing a color Palm OS cellphone and Handspring regularly selling out its cellphone plug-in module. Wearable computers such as those produced by Xybernaut are not just the stuff of science fiction anymore. They are being used by field service teams as they are reduced in size to the point of almost fully functional desktop-level computers that you can wear on your belt.

Not only that, the sales force is out of the office more often than ever—meeting customers, moving through airports, and prospecting for leads on Broadway with their PDAs. This is making mobility a competitive issue, requiring effective competitive mobile tools, such as the Internet and the handhelds. Most CRM companies have established wireless components for sales, such as SalesLogix, PeopleSoft, and Siebel (more later in this chapter), or the wireless access to the various SFA.com portals.

Easily Available Customer Information with Single View

Multiple departments may have an interest in viewing the status of a customer account or opportunity. For example, the sales department wants to see the status of opportunities. The accounting department wants to see the state of invoicing and billing for the same accounts. The marketing department wants to see reports on varying degrees of success or failure of their campaigns with individual accounts.

Within each department are individuals with different roles who each have their own agendas for what passes through their crosshairs. The vice-president of sales wants to see all the activity of all salespeople in his department, including their contact lists and opportunities. He also wants to get a sales pipeline report to refine his sales forecasts for the coming quarter. The account manager doesn't need that much information. He wants a national view of all of the sales activity around the accounts he owns (for example, all the sales meetings and reports related to IBM or 3COM or whoever the customer happens to be at any given moment). The sales manager wants to see opportunity progress, but not all the contact lists of each salesperson. Each salesperson wants to manage the customer accounts he owns. Each of them has the individual view that allows them to see all the data they need to—that is, have the permissions to see—but at the same time, there is a universal view of all the data available to all departments at all times.

The Biggest Barrier to Successful SFA

Salespeople must use it, not merely acquiesce to it or grumble about the learning curve. We also want to stress the theme "Process + Technology = Successful CRM/SFA," as automating haphazardly or ineffective selling or business processes only makes them go faster. You can only get the most out of your CRM investment by automating predictable, measurable, and repeatable selling behaviors—making *how* you sell as important as *what* you sell. For example, SalesLogix has partnered with Solution Selling to bring best-of-breed selling software together with best-of-breed selling methodology. This marriage of process and technology signals the next step in the evolution of CRM/SFA software. It provides organizations with best practices for selling, and the technology and training to effectively automate them.

Kevin Myers, vice-president of product marketing and business development, for SalesLogix sees it this way:

Salespeople have to see it as a tool to help them, not as a tool for "big brother" to make them accountable. If they don't enter the customer contact information and properly track their sales through the predetermined corporate sales process as Solutions Selling and others suggest, the data that management is using will be inaccurate and essentially useless. Therefore, usability and a short learning curve should be paramount to the software selection process. The real *quid pro quo* for salespeople is that it must help them be more effective personally, do their job better, and make them more money. It is also critical to roll out quickly to show a return on investment as fast as possible. Salespeople are skeptics and individualists. Because they will always look for excuses to not use any corporate-mandated solution, they must feel part of the process and find that the process has something to offer *them*, not just the organization at the 50,000-foot level.

Sales force automation emerged to allow individuals to not only manage their contacts, but also to allow businesses to manage their accounts. The difference is that in a business, the relationship is owned by the company, not the individual. The larger the organization, and the larger the customer account, the more people are required to be involved with each sale. Sales force automation originated for three primary beneficiaries: the individual salesperson, his or her sales team, and the management. Of course, the customer ultimately benefited because of better service during and after the initial sales process, but just like the bottom line is for most business decisions, the initial purpose of SFA was somewhat self-serving for the company implementing it. One of those purposes was raw efficiency, by enabling sales teams to work better together. If more than one person is involved in an account, such as telesales helping the major account representative to generate business in remote offices after you get a corporate contract, it is critical that everyone understands the history and future plans for the account. Theoretically, each future interaction is incrementally more effective than the last because of the organizational learning that has taken place.

In an ideal world, businesses would be able to continue a successful relationship with a customer regardless of who is on the account. Of course, that's impractical, but it becomes more likely if there is a shared knowledge of the past interactions with that customer. A shoebox or file folder with a bunch of business cards and notes is like crashing, clearing the wreckage, and starting over from scratch. But an online shared history of an account that includes not only all contacts, but also all promises, conversations, negotiations, and meetings is more like refueling in midair.

The business transaction history is as important as the human relationship, so for larger organizations, contact management software doesn't go far enough—especially where there is management accountability or team selling involved.

Sales Force Automation: Functionality

At its roots, SFA has the same fundamental features, regardless of the vendor. The differences between vendors are nominal, though there are some differences that are worth looking at. The treatment of the core features tends to vary only in the depth provided and the look and feel of the interface and the transparency to the user. Accessing feature A from feature B might differ from application to application, but feature A and feature B are both extant on all SFA applications. Some of the additional features or modules added to some of the vendors' suites are a bit of a stretch, others are interesting functional additions, and a few are genuinely useful and unique. But, at the core, the features provided are lead management, contact management, account management, opportunity management, sales pipeline management, sales forecast tools, quotations and orders, a toolkit for customizing the application, and an engine for data synchronization. The list that follows is a pretty complete representative feature set for sales force automation. There are core features such as contact management and prospect management that are essential and will be covered generically below. Other features are more peripheral. There are some specialized features such as a sales assistant for newbies to the sales game, some fairly cool features such as voice recognition, and even a few that don't really make much sense at all for SFA such as e-procurement, which may or may not belong but some vendor thought it did. The following list is a compilation of multiple SFA applications from the leading vendors:

Contact management See "Contact Management" section later in this chapter.

Opportunity (or prospect) management See "Opportunity Management" section later in this chapter.

Account management See "Account Management" section later in this chapter.

Proposal management This feature is not found full-bodied in too many vendor modules. However, it should be because it's an extremely important part of the sales process. When implemented, it is a way of coordinating and tracking extant proposals. It normally has a workflow that is determined by who is responsible for what part of the proposal. Additionally, it can control the effective completion of the proposal by guiding the stages of evolution of the parts of the proposal.

Quote generation A simple tool that generates quotes for customers. Usually, it uses information on pricing in the product catalog that is available with the SFA application and has been customized for individual company offerings.

Order tracking This feature tracks the status of the invoice and the product delivery. This is normally tied into the back-office financial functions.

Sales forecasting See "Sales Forecasting" section later in this chapter.

Pipeline analysis See "Pipeline Management" section later in this chapter.

Sales quota management This is normally for sales managers. It allows them to see how the individual salesperson is doing relative to their quotas within some defined time segment.

Commission management This is a tool that calculates the commissions for salespeople. While it seems simple, it isn't. Salespeople can often share opportunities, which complicates the calculation of the commissions. Additionally, depending on the company, the sales team very well might have some private arrangements going, which are normally okay with all but the stiffest rules-driven companies. These arrangements are known to the managers and have to be programmed into the application so accurate commission checks can be cut. This is a very important feature of SFA and far more complicated than it seems.

Territory management This is another important feature that solves a complex problem. It is not particularly complicated until there is a change in the territory. That can mean a new person takes over an existing territory or a territory can be "redistricted" and redivided among existing salespeople geographically. For instance,

Mid-Atlantic and Southeast territories might be carved out of what was a Southern region, or accounts could be moved from one territory to another. Think about how complicated this is, especially if the accounts have history and the salespeople have been there awhile. This is usually a very dicey proposition since there are many salespeople who truly believe in Robert Ardrey's territorial imperative: "What's mine is mine and what's yours is mine!" Redividing territory becomes a very political issue that has to be managed carefully. It's hard to blame the redistricted because they often lose lucrative accounts in the interests of corporate "neatness." That means lost income to them—not a good thing. PeopleSoft CRM 8.0 actually has a slick way of dealing with this by using a tree metaphor to make the changes so that with just minimum tweaking, the trickiest territorial changes can be made with the click of a button.

Other SFA applications:

Incentive compensation system This is a functional godsend, and there are standalones devoted to this, not just SFA modules. This particular feature allows vice-presidents of sales (or their designated equivalent) to design compensation plans and to track them. It is an application unto itself, often requested and not often found. Siebel and Oracle have it, among others. It is often a big ticket item.

Competitive information system This is often tied into multiple sources so that, as a salesperson, you could do the research online and internally to find what you must. There are some external programs that are not tied to CRM that search among multiple sources well (see DTSearch for a fairly inexpensive super-powered standalone option of this type), but there are some serious advantages to being able to integrate Internet searching with server and desktop searches. This way, you can scan Dun and Bradstreet's database and your company's historic databases to find out about your competition's offerings and history with you, and work with reports that provide you a neatly tied package (at least in the perfect world we like to envision in CRM).

Telesales campaign management Oracle and Siebel do this one fairly well. This feature helps inside sales managers design telemarketing campaigns. Thus, they have an organized, sophisticated way to track how well the telemarketers are doing at irritating you around dinnertime.

Sales assistant This feature is for the newbies. With constraints, methodology, and best practices built into the SFA system approached through step-by-step wizards, beginners will learn the sales process of the company they work for. PeopleSoft and Siebel both have excellent "sales assistants."

Expense reporting This feature ties expense reporting into both accounting and CRM systems. This is an enterprise application feature that integrates back and front office functionality. PeopleSoft is perhaps the best at this.

Learning management system/content delivery tool This feature provides a means for newer employees to understand the sales process and experienced employees to request and receive appropriate sales information and tools ranging from brochures to competitive information. It is more of an engine than a blatantly obvious feature.

Marketing encyclopedia This is a centralized repository for all the marketing materials so all salespeople have access to appropriate materials for their customers.

Partner management capabilities This really doesn't belong in an SFA application, but some limited functionality is usually there so that indirect sales opportunities that are either farmed to partners or brought by partners can be tracked. If this is very important to you, because the channel might be responsible for most of your sales, then a partner relationship management (PRM) application is probably smarter (see Chapter 9 for PRM in detail).

Integration with service, marketing, and Internet applications This is where it hooks into the other CRM pieces through common architecture (see Chapter 2) or through the creation of little pieces of code called application programming interfaces (APIs). SAP has what they call BAPIs (business application programming interfaces)—predeveloped "hooks" to integrate with either third-party systems or their own back-office systems.

Mobile applications for field sales force See "Sales Force Automation" section later in this chapter.

Custom sales process and methodologies This is built-in best practices and known methodologies, such as SalesLogix embedding Solutions Selling into their application. The value is that companies have the benefits of using well-established and consistently popular sales methodologies. The downside is that often these methodologies are simply not appropriate to the needs of a company's sales team because of its particular composition. So if the methodology is used, it's used for its own sake, rather than its value.

Consistent sales methodology framework This is the framework for the preceding feature.

SFA-centric workflow This is a sales-specific workflow that ties permissions and roles to either specific people or titles. For example, a sales manager might need to approve an opportunity that is entered into the system by a salesperson because of the resource cost of that opportunity. A flag on that opportunity would then notify the sales manager of the need to approve it before it can be officially registered into the sales pipeline.

Customer needs assessment Using templates and a comprehensive set of questions and interviews, the salesperson is able to work with the customers to determine what they are specifically looking for. This means that the functionality has to include the ability of the salesperson to understand the customer's business processes.

Custom product configuration This function allows the salesperson to provide a customer-specific set of products that meet their actual needs. It will ordinarily draw on multiple products and variable amounts and prices for products so that the individual customer has an individual order based on the needs assessment done by the salesperson.

Sales order creation from quotes This generates the actual order for the customer and the back office based on the quotes that were developed from the price and product configurations designed via the needs assessment. Very much a hipbone connected to the thighbone kind of sequential chain.

Email I don't think I need to tell you what this is. If I do, please return the book either to the bookstore or to its rightful owner.

Track and query website inquiries This is useful for what the sales world calls "prospect mining." That means finding a potential sales opportunity by tracking who is on your website for how long and what reason and where they went after visiting you.

E-procurement I'm not sure why this is included as a feature in an SFA package. I know the justification (someone is purchasing something), but the reality is that this is not part of the sales pipeline but a different back-office function altogether. Companies like Ariba make a living on this, and SAP identifies this as part of the supply chain. So there is a disconnect here, but it is included in a couple of packages—or at least trumpeted as part of the package.

Automated customer billing This is an integration point. It means that the back office can generate the customer invoice automatically from the information that the sales rep has entered into the customer records. It all stems from the processes mentioned earlier.

Other SFA features/functions:

Software distribution to mobile users This is more of an infrastructural feature that makes simplified distribution of code to multiple users in multiple locations much easier for system administrators.

Quote pricing engine Simply put, this is the feature that draws from customer records, product catalogs, needs assessment, and customized product configurations and generates a quote to the customer.

Smartscripts These are customizable scripts for telesales or newbies or to maintain some sort of monolithic sales organizational "integrity." While I'm not a fan of scripts, the ability to create and deploy them enterprise-wide is a feature of most SFA applications, even if, in my view, it's a dubious one. Find your own personality.

eBriefings This is a feature that allows the creation and deployment of specific discussions—on intelligence or otherwise—according to defined workflow.

Voice recognition This is a cool but not really very advanced feature. Right now it means not much more than making calendar entries of varying sorts such as appointments and getting your current customer data via interactive voice recognition (IVR) over the phone. Someday this will get beyond bells and whistles and go to the symphonic. Not yet, though. However, there are technologies out there that can make it much more than it is.

All that said, let's take a detailed look at some of the more critical parts of this CRM subset.

Contact Management

As you saw in Chapter 3, contact management is a basic sales tool; it has entire applications devoted to it. ACT! has had millions of devotees over the years. Contact management as a module takes on an added degree of complexity when it is integrated into an SFA package, primarily because it has to be linked to all the other modules incorporated. So, for example, when you see Paul Greenberg's name and the company Live Wire, Inc., depending on the specific application you are using, you are hyperlinked to the account management module by clicking on the name Live Wire, Inc. Or click the specific one-line Paul Greenberg activity description and be transported to the activity section where you can get details of his specific activity with your sales team.

Otherwise, contact management covers the basics: name, address, phone numbers, company, title, personal and business information; activity related to the individual; attachments related to the individual; and level of the decision maker. Some applications, such as Siebel Sales, are able to take this contact information and create organization charts for salespeople so they can see whom they have to deal with at what level of the customer's hierarchy—a useful feature, indeed. The most sophisticated versions will include contact behavior characteristics so that each behavior can be associated with templated next steps—valuable for rookie salespeople.

Account Management

This standard feature allows the salesperson or sales manager to handle individual corporate accounts. (See Figure 6-1.) Each account has multiple links to other information, beyond the corporate name or address, including the contacts by corporation and the proposed opportunities by corporation. Fundamentally, it is another view of the customer and potential data that is designed to work with sales departments that have account managers or that want corporate information. It can include either general or highly detailed views of an enterprise.

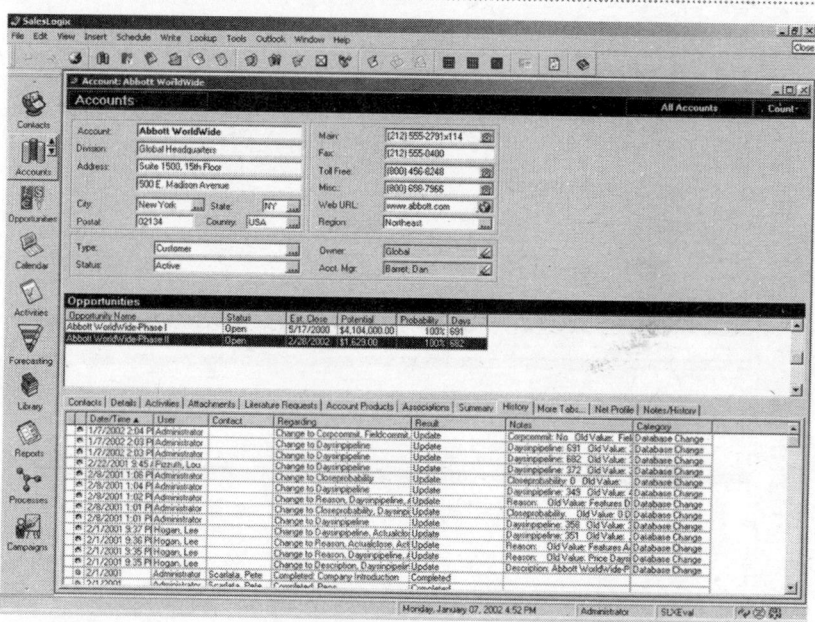

Figure 6-1: SalesLogix Accounts management screen. Typical of account management functionality. (Copyright 2002, Interact Commerce Corporation. All rights reserved.)

Opportunity Management

This is often seen as the most essential of the SFA modules. With no drama intended, it is here that deals can be won or lost. The facets that opportunity management covers include the specific opportunity, the company it belongs to, the salesperson or team that is working it, the assignment of revenue credits if there is a sales team, the potential for the closing of this particular opportunity, the final results of this opportunity, the stage of the sales process this opportunity is in, and the potential closing date (sadly, a dynamic function) for the opportunity. (See Figure 6-2.) Additionally, competitive information is included here: who is specifically competing for the opportunity against your company and how big a threat they represent. Even more interesting, in the better SFA packages, a competitive product matrix can be brought up to see how well your product stacks up against the competition's product equivalent. This can give the salesperson a valuable selling point.

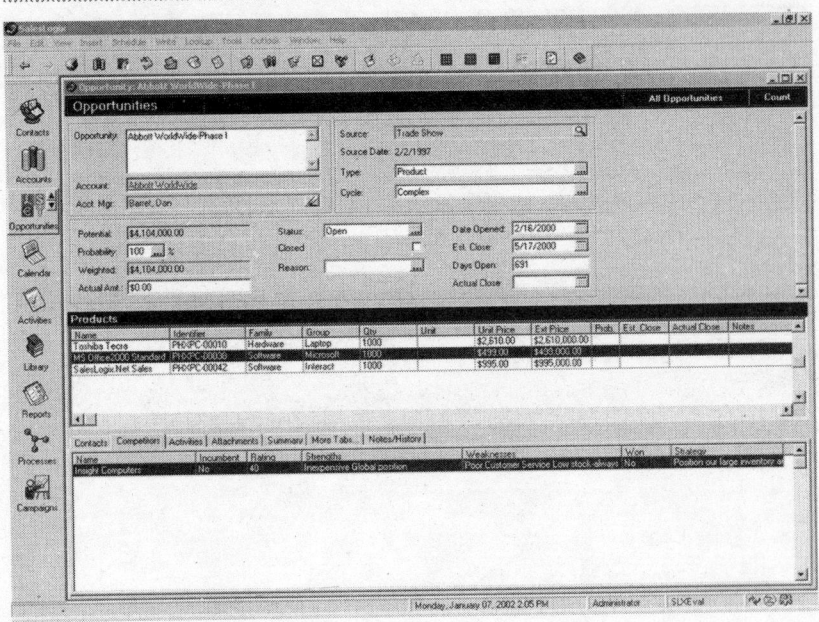

Figure 6-2: Opportunity management is probably the most important function in SFA. (Copyright 2002, Interact Commerce Corporation. All rights reserved.)

If the product is really sophisticated, it can provide information on what the weights of different issues are to the customer—for instance, how much price/cost weighs in against functionality, ease of use, availability, maintenance services, or whatever other criteria you want to compare. This provides a decided sales edge. If the salesperson knows that price is less important than availability and rapid delivery, he or she can make the immediate delivery of the goods more important than the price in discussions with the client.

Lead Management

If your company buys leads and qualifies them, there has to be some way to weigh prospective value. Lead management functionality can be seen as a subset of opportunity management, though I'm sure there are those who don't see it that way. A qualified lead becomes an opportunity. With SFA packages that have strong lead management features, the salesperson can import leads from multiple sources and, using criteria established through the sales process, weigh the potential of these leads to become opportunities.

Pipeline Management

The "sales pipeline" is a peculiar term for the execution of the established sales process. Each company has its criteria for what constitutes its sales process, but opening and closing tend to be the process bookends. For example, one company could set up salesperson objectives that are weighed by the steps of the sales process. One typical sales process sequence could be the one outlined in Figure 6-3, which shows the SalesLogix visual process generator. The pipeline process reflected in the largest SFA packages may be similar to that in Figure 6-4, a PeopleSoft CRM 8.0 pipeline.

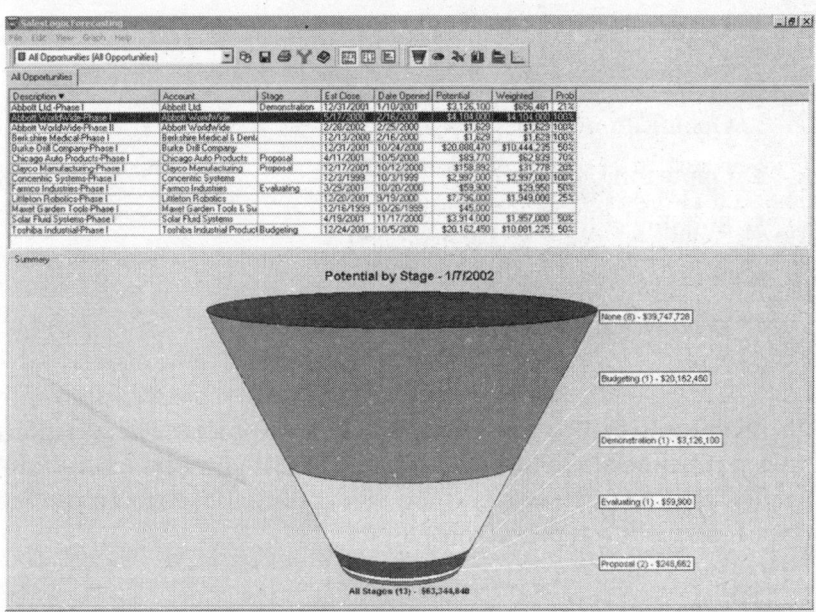

Figure 6-3: Pipeline management à la SalesLogix (Copyright 2002, Interact Commerce Corporation. All rights reserved.)

Opportunities

Use Sort to reorder the list of Opportunities. Use Filter to narrow the list of Opportunities.

Personalize Columns   Sort by [Customer   ] ▲ ▼

Filter: My Opps & My Staff's Opps & My Team's Opps

Opportunities						Find | View All First ◀ 1-8 of 20 ▶ Last		
Customer	Customer Role	Opportunity	Status	Sales User	Sales Stage	Est. Revenue	Est. Close Date	
📖 Bickers,Colin	Consumer	Credit Consolidation - C. Bickers	Open	Farley,Ed	04-Develop Proposal for Customer	☎ 22,000.00	▶ 01/31/2002	USD
📖 Clark,Carol H	Consumer	Clark Family Accounts	Open	Hunter,Jim	03-Close Sale	75,000.00	12/25/2001	USD
📖 Coolidge,Hunter	Consumer	Coolidge Life Insurance	Open	Hunter,Jim	02-Qualify Customer	☎ 5,500.00	▶ 02/15/2002	USD
📖 Fast Grandma's Restaurants	Company	Leasing Terms of Condition	Open	Hunter,Jim	03-Develop Solution	800,000.00	02/22/2002	USD
📖 Gilbert Architects	Company	Gilbert Architects 401K	Open	Farley,Ed	02-Generate Customer Proposal	100,000.00	◀ 12/20/2001	USD
📖 Hierarchical Inc	Company	New Fiscal Evaluation	Open	Bergeron,Jeff	03-Develop Solution	▼ 880,000.00	02/13/2002	USD
📖 Jordan Enterprises	Company	Jordan 401K Plan	Open	Farley,Ed	04-Develop Proposal for	100,000.00	◀ 12/15/2001	USD

Figure 6-4: For larger implementations, PeopleSoft CRM Sales 8.0 (Copyright 2002 PeopleSoft, Inc. All rights reserved.)

A sales process sequence different from those in Figures 6-3 and 6-4, but also typical, could be:

1. Prospecting

2. Potential lead

3. Qualification

4. Opportunity

5. Building vision

6. Short list

7. Negotiation

8. Closed: won or lost

In other words, every company has its own sales process. The variations may not be infinite, but they are extensive. If you can successfully embed your sales process into the SFA application, you can use the application as it was meant to be used.

Sales Forecasting

Part of pipeline management is getting the forecasts from sales and then managing the sales activities to those forecasts. Let's face it: If your salesperson is expected to do $2.5 million in business and does 40 percent of that, you (and he) have a serious problem. If that is due to poor forecasting tools that add to the problem, the SFA also has a problem. However, most SFA programs have adequate sales forecasting tools—fairly sophisticated spreadsheet-like tools for forecast fundamentals. But most sales forecasts are still nothing more than good guesses, regardless of how many algorithms you stuff in a program. The value of the tools lies in the management of the guesses in near-real time.

Quotations and Orders

Most good SFA packages have automated generation of quotations and orders. However, what goes into customizing the system to be able to automate that order/quote generation is not a small matter. Product catalogs—whether they cover physical inventory or services offered—have to be created. All the services, products, and combinations of services and/or products have to be entered into a catalog, given an appropriate SKU or other identifying number, and associated with a base price. Then a pricing schedule that allows for special discounts, volume discounts, timed discounts, and such has to be created based on some criteria. For example, your salesperson might be selling 10,000 units of tubing to a valuable customer who you know is being courted by another tubing company. The normal pricing schedule, the North American one, sets a discount of 5 percent for 10,000 units or more of SKU#122222, 1-inch copper tubing. To prepare a quote that would be good for this customer, another pricing schedule for valued customers can be added to this quote, offering an additional 2 percent discount so that a 7 percent total discount is offered. Imagine what goes into creating all that. This is what a good quotation and order generation system in SFA can do.

Sales Force Automation: The Technology

What makes SFA powerful is not just the functionality, but also the combination of the functionality and the flexibility of the technology. The two make SFA useful to both the professional on the road and the manager back at headquarters. It allows each of them to analyze data, stay on top of opportunities, embed best practices for future salespeople, and do it with a desktop or a PDA.

One of the most significant technologies is data synchronization. I'm going to give you a sense of its power so you can understand a bit about what's under the SFA's hood.

Data Synchronization

Data synchronization is the process of updating information among unconnected computers—laptop, mobile, or desktop. Each synchronized system gets data that conforms with the data on any other disparate system. Salespeople in the field can maintain a subset of the master database and update their local data while others are working with the same data simultaneously. Synchronization also allows corporate managers and sales teams to share information created by field salespeople, such as meeting notes, schedules, and forecasts.

Important recent sales trends related to mobility and wireless data make synchronization even more important:

▶ Salespeople are spending more time out of the office with customers and prospects. Many salespeople are telecommuting—working out of their homes rather than in corporate branch offices.

▶ Salespeople operate as members of sales teams as products become more complex and technical, so the need to share information grows.

▶ Entire sales and marketing organizations are using computer-based customer, sales, and project information to sell more effectively. Field salespeople can leverage this information to close sales faster, and managers can access information input in the field.

This means that for SFA, data synchronization becomes a most essential piece of technology.

The Data Synchronization Process

Data synchronization takes up a fair amount of network infrastructure bandwidth. It actively involves a lot of what comprises the corporate information system. To take a look at the technical steps in data synchronization from a lay standpoint, we are going to examine SalesLogix data synchronization, which is one of the most sophisticated CRM data synchronization processes on the millennial market.

How Does It Work?

Field salespeople with laptop computers need to download a pertinent subset of data, manipulate and update the data, and reconcile their changes with the new information from the host database. The typical process of synchronizing data between remote and host systems requires several basic steps, as illustrated in Figure 6-5.

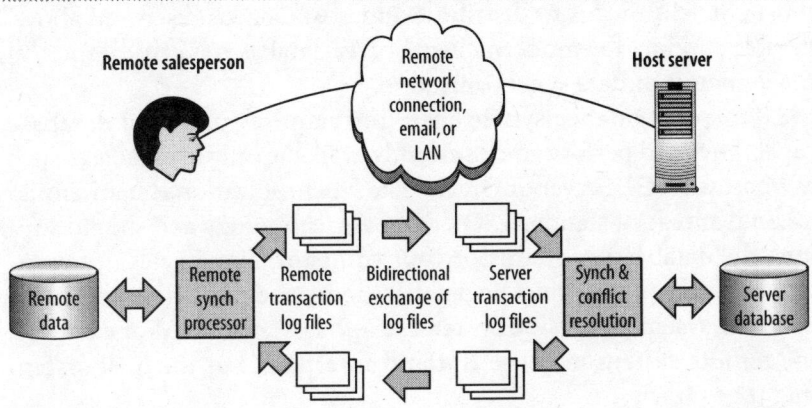

Figure 6-5: SalesLogix data synchronization requires a bidirectional exchange of data between host systems and remote users. The server system should support multiple remote connections at the same time. (Copyright 1999, Interact Commerce Corporation. All rights reserved. Reprinted with permission of Interact Commerce Corporation.)

Remote databases are created for mobile salespeople and branch offices. Each database is a relevant *subset* of the corporate database. For example, the information on a field salesperson's laptop need only pertain to his particular accounts.

The synchronization system tracks changes pertinent to the particular salesperson to both the remote databases and the host database. Remote salespeople can connect to the home office using low bandwidth modems or wide area network (WAN) connections. Salespeople or managers who are at a desk can connect via their local area network (LAN). During the connection, log files are exchanged that contain new information to be updated in the respective databases. After the connection is completed, new data is applied to each database so that each database has up-to-date information. It is estimated by the Gartner Group that by using the localized version of data synchronization, where, in effect, only updates are being done, 50 percent of the communications costs will be saved.

Flexibility and Performance

A synchronization system should be capable of supporting large-scale field implementations with potentially hundreds of users, even if your remote sales force is currently small. Some synchronization systems perform fine in small test environments but become impractical in real-world situations, especially for large groups. Besides using the most efficient means to distribute and post data, as discussed above, flexible support for modern client/server databases is critical to meet the demands of data synchronization.

High-performance synchronization requires powerful database capabilities and performance currently available only in databases such as Microsoft SQL Server or Oracle. The synchronization system should take advantage of standard SQL database technology and should support the database standards of your company. Nonetheless, the synchronization engine must be database independent to allow different database systems to reside on remote and host systems. For example, the remote system may use Borland InterBase, but the host system might be Oracle.

Reporting Tools

The importance of reporting is often underestimated. However, lack of or poor reporting can lead to bad strategic or tactical decisions, redundant work efforts, and missed opportunities. As large companies open more offices and as small companies allow more telecommuting, the need for tight communication becomes paramount. Good reporting tools as part of the technology of SFA (and CRM) are essential.

Many of the reporting tools embedded in SFA applications are third-party tools. The most popular is Seagate's Crystal Reports, which has 160 original equipment manufacturer (OEM) deals. These deals embed the software into other software that is marketed with Crystal Reports as its reporting tools.

Reporting is the creation of customized onscreen or printed views that provide the viewer/reader with information specifically in the form they want and with the content they want. Crystal Reports has a strong report-processing engine that is newly Web optimized. The essential technical factor is the use of dynamic data sources to generate reports by passing the report as it is generating to the client's browser page by page, not report by report. Even more interesting in Crystal Reports 8.0 is the use of Dynamic HTML (DHTML) so the reports can be seen on your screen in real time. Additionally, there is an option that allows the report to be generated in Java, if you are a Java-centric company. For those applications that need an embedded report viewer in Java, there is a Java Bean option to do that. The report engine supports all the major relational and flat-file databases.

What makes this so valuable is that the engine pulls information from multiple sources, including your financial applications, your customer data repository, and your SFA application, and can put together reports on an ad hoc basis that can be dynamically altered. For example, you can view the sales figures for the year, quarter, or month, by customer, salesperson, or profitability—all by simple drag-and-drop operations. It saves money, makes analysis easier, and can be critical for decision making.

So there is significant functionality and significant technology embedded in SFA applications. Who are the market leaders in SFA? What makes them different from one another? Well, that leads me to…

Who's Best in the Land?

The leading segment of the CRM market has had the oddest metamorphosis from 2000 to 2002. CRM consolidated in every segment and new players emerged as older ones were bought or failed. SFA moved into a weird space that is virtually no space of its own at all. There are very few SFA-specific players of consequence left in the marketplace. The major multifunction players such as Siebel, PeopleSoft, SAP, and Oracle have functionally complete SFA modules for their CRM packages. SalesLogix is one company that has gone through several changes the other way. First their corporate name changed from SalesLogix to Interact Commerce Corporation (IACT). Then IACT was acquired by Sage. Then it took back the name SalesLogix. While that churned, SalesLogix evolved from what was an SFA application to a much more multifunctional CRM suite that has an SFA application at its core.

Ultimately, this was one market that almost "overmatured." SFA doesn't really have any standouts that are standalone. The only real standouts in the marketplace that are strictly SFA anymore are the online services such as Salesforce.com, which has succeeded against the odds where most of its online ilk have failed. More on them later.

Even here, there is a merging and a muddling to a large extent. With the release of PeopleSoft CRM 8.0 and Siebel 7.0, the architectural differences between the online-only services and the multifunction CRM suites' SFA modules have been reduced to the size of a pinhead. However, a difference remains. The SFA.com online services are still just that: services provided through a Web interface. The Internet architectures of the SFA modules for Siebel and PeopleSoft are architectures that are still application-based and have open standards.

All in all, this market, as of 2002, is peculiar in that it is no longer really much of a market aside from the multifunctional suites themselves. Let's take a look at the state of the SFA state.

Siebel Sales 7.0

In October 2001, Siebel System released Siebel 7.0, a complete revamp of Siebel 2000 and an application that is several functional and architectural steps above Siebel 2000. This, coupled with their usual hectic acquisition pace, addressed several serious weaknesses (though not in areas beyond architecture and functionality) that had been targeted by the analysts in 2000–2001. Siebel Sales, in particular, got a major overhaul and is now perhaps the most fully functional SFA module on the market (this is not a comment on usability in any way, just functionality). Siebel addresses several problems that salespeople were having, ranging from a difficult user interface to more than 100 out-of-the-box sales reports so that customization time is reduced. Those were taken care of. They added incentive compensation planning and calculation so that salespeople can not only calculate what they are getting in commissions, but also estimate commissions across any potential deal in the pipeline.

There are three applications for Siebel Sales that might be called new: the general Siebel Sales 7.0 module, Siebel Mobile Sales, and Siebel Incentive Management. These three form a comprehensive integrated set of modules with an incredibly large—though not all that confusing—array of features geared to very large enterprises that have intricate sales programs, processes, and politics. Now let's look at the guts of Siebel's SFA application.

Integrated Sales Strategy

Siebel Sales subscribes to several selling methods that they have integrated into Siebel Sales 7.0. The ones that they specifically mention are Target Account Selling, the Enterprise Selling Process, and Strategic Selling. It's useful here to check out what these different methods are since they are integral to SFA and seem to excite the vendors a great deal. I've always had a hard time subscribing to any one theory of sales simply because each of us who has ever sold does it on the basis of the quality and sustained belief in the product and the nature of our personalities. But it is instructive to look at the different methodologies that are embedded in Siebel 7.0 so the differences are apparent. They are:

> **Target Account Selling** At its highest level, Target Account Selling (TAS) analyzes common behavioral patterns that are common across accounts and then assesses your personal strengths and weaknesses to see how you can respond to those consistent behavioral elements. Theoretically, this increases the chances you have against your competition.

For example, it attempts to identify who in the potential customer's influencer circles is favorable toward you and who favors the competition. Once TAS identifies those individuals for both sides, and places them in their respective decision-making hierarchies, it works on strategies for influencing the influencers. The strategies take you and the prospective customer's decision-makers' personalities into account when the strategy is being developed. TAS is a sales methodology for analyzing customer organizations, business opportunities, and competitive intelligence.

Enterprise Selling Process This is a strictly Siebel Systems–created methodology that they integrate into their software. It seems to be the least sophisticated of the three mentioned here. Enterprise Selling Process (ESP) is aimed at large strategic accounts, just as Siebel's product is. This homegrown process includes tools such as Account Maps that summarize where and what a sales team sells and includes the status of the team's relationship with key executives, business partners, and account marketing activity. Other features include Account Plans, which seem to be similar in nature to Strategic Selling Account Plans, and an Account Scorecard, which tracks the progress of the sales plan and is used by the account team leader and the sales manager. The Account Scorecard identifies and uses metrics for tracking the success of the Account Plan. In combination with a series of initial training workshops and some "reinforcement" workshops (another marketing name for follow-up workshops), it provides a fairly comprehensive classic sales process methodology.

Strategic Selling Developed by management consulting firm Miller-Heiman, this is less "personal" and more "strategic" than TAS. It places heavy emphasis on pre-investigating the prospect, the competition's relationship to the prospect, and the prospect's organizational hierarchies long before the first call is made and proactively before each subsequent call is made. It uses a method of determining the four "buying influences" that seem to be present in each sale—two that are predisposed toward sales and two that aren't. It is a positioning methodology, positioning yourself before the sale so that you come into the sale stronger than your competition (interesting if they're also using this method!), and during the sales process by positioning yourself with the actual decision-makers and not just the posturers. It helps you identify "coaches" who will work with you at the prospect, and who know the territory. It has templates for creating strategies and action plans with timetables. Most interestingly, it distinguishes between personal wins and business results. Smart move here, because what satisfies you in the sales world isn't necessarily going to get your company revenues. Do a good turn for a potential customer and that doesn't necessarily guarantee a closed contract, just a good feeling.

This provides a good look at sales methodologies that companies spend zillions of dollars for so their salespeople can sell. Now you can get these methods embedded in a multimillion-dollar piece of software. Lucky you. Don't get me wrong. They do have some value if your sales organization (not necessarily you) can buy into the methodology. But each person has a different style and method of living, and thus, behaving. Some are great, some are good, some are mediocre, and some are garbage. To use these methodologies as a uniform approach could be helpful in the mediocre or garbage division, but whether their value is appropriate to your institution is something you have to take extreme care with. They can be as damaging as they can be helpful.

Forecasting and Business Planning

The sales strategy components mentioned above play a significant role in the Siebel Sales 7.0 business planning process. Included is the hooks that Siebel Sales has to competitive intelligence services external to the internal sales organization. However, the other shoe for the move forward is the revved-up forecasting capabilities that are built into Siebel Sales 7.0. Their forecasting tools are now able to track real-time changes in the business across product, channel, or geography among other venues. Additionally, the forecasting core includes recurring revenue forecasting and a serious set of tools for forecasting across channels or programs (such as sales indirectly from marketing campaigns).

Pipeline and channel analyses measure performance and profitability, lead quality, and sales progress. There are metrics for forecasting shortages, pitfalls, and sales crises—in real time or by snapshot over time. Their claim is that their forecasting tools can measure "revenues, upside, downside, cost, margin, or product quantities over time" right from the start. Siebel incorporates an Executive Information System into the Siebel Sales 7.0 product that can do sales pipeline analysis, competitive analysis, activity analysis, and quota achievement analysis. Not only that, the EIS can deliver the information with summary indicators and KPIs shown in high relief. (Siebel's marketing machine calls this Smart Reports.) It can return the data in more than 100 predefined graphical modes. This is all tightly integrated to the Siebel Data Warehouse.

Opportunity Management

This is a classic example of "if it ain't broke, don't fix it." Siebel made modest changes in their opportunity management capabilities. In fact, most were general changes that they made across the application, such as a more robust calendar and improved mobile versions for all mobile/wireless platforms. As with any opportunity management, it provides a complete picture of an opportunity, its history, milestones, and the key decision makers. What is useful (but again, not different in function from any other opportunity management) is the availability of information on quotes, proposals, presentations, to-dos, history of success or failure, competitive information, lead sources, products involved, level of interest, progress of the prospect, and bottlenecks to be solved. It is the place where the potential revenue that is used in the sales management forecasting sits. Options such as proposal and presentation generation and expensing are also available. But, as options, they cost extra, so determine what you want and get only what you need.

Territory Management

Territory management is a workflow-enabled process that automatically routes opportunities, accounts, contacts, or activities to the team members that are defined by the business rules provided in Siebel workflow for the territory. The rules assignments can be based on a wide range of criteria, including geography, industry, product focus, or whatever else you decide is a good criterion. There are workshops associated with the management process for territories, by geography or vertical market. In line with their trademarked ESP sales methodology, they provide their Siebel Sales customers with templates for a Discovery Guide so that key business information can be captured to determine best-fit offerings and value for customers. They have a tool called Territory Plan that is designed to determine predictable revenue streams in key markets and can assign appropriate resources to see that these forecasts are met. There is also a Territory Map designed for specific geographic or vertical segments. Siebel Sales Assistant, a sales coaching tool that is used across the entire Sales suite, is used here to provide a consistent methodology across the entire company, presenting a single face to the customer. It is both a teaching tool and a constraining factor.

Account Management

Siebel Account Management does pretty much what all account management tools do. It provides a complete history of targeted accounts and the interactions of the sales teams with those targeted accounts. It provides product and services delivery. Where it differs a little bit—at least what it claims—is that it has a strong focus in "long-term supply-oriented sales processes including those typically found in the consumer goods industry, the chemical and energy industries, the communications and utility industries, and the financial services industry." This claim is not made by any other vendor with an SFA product.

Again, ESP is part of the process and perhaps plays its most essential role with its focus on executing account plans and developing key account relationships.

Knowledge Management

This has never been Siebel's strong suit. With Siebel Sales 7.0 they have provided an upgraded capability with eBriefing and eContent, which allow the creation of accessible personalized briefings for the sales team member. On the other side, it can create an enterprise-wide briefing that is easily deployed.

Interactive Selling

The components of a sell-side SFA suite are sales configuration, electronic catalogs, and content management, areas where Siebel has not been strong. Historically, they have tended to ally with, for example, a content management provider like Vignette, in order to make sure that content management tools are available. With the release of Siebel Sales 7.0, several analysts feel that Siebel addressed concerns in at least one area critical to face-to-face selling and sales configuration. They have added a stronger pricing configurator, integrated with Onlink's object modeling, that allows them to generate multi-line item quotes a lot easier. They continue to work on the sales configuration functions and are addressing the other interactive selling deficiencies that exist as we wait for newer versions by the end of 2002.

Siebel Mobile Sales 7.0

Siebel Mobile Sales 7.0 is good. Their wireless disconnected solutions now range from laptop controls to Palm devices to the Pocket PC 2002, and from Windows CE devices to cellphones and RIM Blackberry devices. The only mobile device that is not entirely standard is the Palm device, which separates data from Siebel's calendar functions from the data with the Palm's calendar. Otherwise, there is apparently seamless data synchronization and integration. There is a wireless messaging capability built in allowing critical alerts and updates to be pushed to the devices through SMS (Short Messaging Service), email, and other communications standards. It even uses interactive voice technologies to do some of the cooler things related to account management and calendar management.

Even systems administrators have something for them here. You can easily deploy the software to all devices after a single configuration.

Siebel Incentive Compensation

The Siebel Incentive Compensation module offers basic sales compensation management, processing, and reporting capabilities. This is a good upgrade since it barely existed in Siebel 2000, but still isn't on par with Oracle's Incentive Compensation.

Siebel Sales 7.0: Summary

With its increased functionality and upgraded capabilities, combined with the Smart Web architecture, Siebel is a strong choice, though an expensive one, for large enterprises. It's worth looking at if you have the bucks to burn.

PeopleSoft CRM 8.0

When PeopleSoft purchased Vantive and its second-place 6 percent CRM market share in 1999, there were a number of pundits who questioned the purchase, wondering what PeopleSoft thought they were doing entering the CRM world. With the release of PeopleSoft CRM 8.0 in June 2001, it's now apparent they knew exactly what they were doing. Much of Vantive's CRM Fortune 1000–level functionality is fully integrated into the PeopleSoft 8.0 product suite, which has been rearchitected from the ground up and additional functionality not present in Vantive built in. The expertise of the former Vantive employees was instrumental in building this brand new PeopleSoft CRM 8.0 product.

According to PeopleSoft, the new CRM suite, as of the end of 2001, had dozens of customers and wide interest. This seems to be the case, as the rise of PeopleSoft CRM has placed PeopleSoft on a par with Siebel according to an October 2000 *Computerworld* article that calls People-Soft one of the largest CRM vendors—a successful reinvention of the former ERP company. (See Chapter 14 for much more on PeopleSoft.)

There are five areas that distinguish PeopleSoft CRM 8.0 Sales from the rest of the pack: their sales portal, their integration between front and back office, their real-time embedded analytics, their use of knowledge management tools, and their territory management functionality. This unique feature set is part of the 2001 edition of PeopleSoft CRM 8.0 Sales. There's a cornucopia of singular features in PeopleSoft's offering that are designed to expand or enhance the more standard management tools that are general to all SFA products. The features reflected in the CRM corporate sales portal shown in Figure 6-6 give you an idea of its strength.

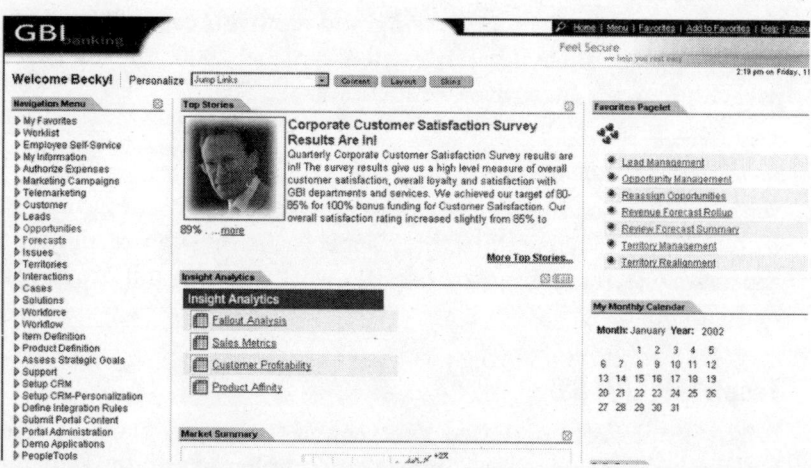

Figure 6-6: The powerful PeopleSoft CRM 8.0 Sales view from the portal entrance (Copyright 2001, PeopleSoft, Inc. All rights reserved.)

What Kind of Portal Is This?

PeopleSoft provides a highly customized and customizable portal for its Sales application that is based on its Employee portal. What makes it all so interesting is that PeopleSoft CRM 8.0 is working with an architecture that is already Internet-based and J2EE (Java 2.0 Enterprise Edition) compliant. The portal and all the power behind its door are accessible from multiple media. Want to enter the portal from your Palm? Go ahead. Your notebook needs a portal visit? Do it. Is your desktop aching to find out what your sales pipeline looks like? Click on that browser, enter the password, and you can access incredible amounts of personalized sales information. PeopleSoft's offering in this domain is particularly strong—probably the strongest of all CRM applications.

PeopleSoft Integration Management

The power of integrating the back and front office cannot be underestimated. The integration of any disparate software is difficult enough. Having to integrate a multimillion-dollar ERP implementation and a multimillion-dollar CRM implementation is often nearly impossible and has brought many a company and its system integrator to their knees, begging for mercy. To have integration from the get-go is a time-saver and a money saver. Connectors exist not only for PeopleSoft, but also for other back-office third-party applications like SAP, to provide easy integration.

But PeopleSoft CRM 8.0 has taken it two steps further with their CRM Sales applications and across the whole suite. One step, which I mentioned in Chapter 2, is the creation of multiple pre-coded Enterprise Integration Points (EIPs). More germane is CRM Interaction Management (IM), which integrates the sales, marketing, support, supply chain, financial, and human resources systems in any enterprise so that all customers can be managed at all levels of the sales cycle and well beyond that. For example, you could easily link sales forecasting to demand planning. Visiting a customer who needs to know when and how much product can be delivered for how much? Through the Integration Management framework, a salesperson can provide all the data and generate the quote based on current and future levels of inventory.

In fact, because of the integration ease, unlike most SFA packages, PeopleSoft CRM 8.0 Sales adds functions such as enrollment and literature fulfillment. You can sign your customers up for a training class and enter them into the rolls of the company—another tie to the back office that, while looking like PeopleSoft's Student Administration functionality, originally came from the Vantive side.

Knowledge Management

Equally impressive are the knowledge management tools built into PeopleSoft Sales. Probably the most eye-popping is the Marketing Encyclopedia. The Marketing Encyclopedia provides a repository in the form of a single database that stores product literature, competitive analyses, industry news, sales case histories, and pretty much any sales-related intelligence. What makes this even more fun is that push technologies built into the system can notify sales representatives—by pager or email—when new information that is useful to the particular salesperson is available, such as an updated analyst report on a competitor. You can get hot news immediately as it emerges on the website.

Knowledge management doesn't stop there. There is a Capture Insight Tool that will collect critical information and, using the native workflow built into the package, route it appropriately through the sales organization. This workflow engine is powerful, even automating the distribution of leads to partners based on predesigned criteria for those leads. It can also take prequalified leads that come from marketing campaigns and route them to the appropriate field or inside salespeople or teams. This is what workflow is for. Very few SFA products have this strength. In fact, these workflow properties rival the workflow engine of Lotus Notes, the workflow head of state.

A customer data warehouse, something that is not endemic to sales or CRM applications, is a native part of PeopleSoft CRM Sales. Through the List Import Wizard, you can import sales contacts and leads, including purchased leads or leads in other external formats to the system.

With the knowledge management and workflow components being so strong, the tools that are designed to use the knowledge effectively are equally powerful. There is actually a best-practices selling tool that prompts the salesperson to ask the right questions and complete the right tasks at each stage of the sales process. This is a rules-based tool that has the characteristics of the best parts of PeopleSoft's enterprise resource planning.

Embedding the Analytics

There is a major upgrade in the way that analytics are both realized and reported in PeopleSoft CRM 8.0 Sales (and throughout). The graphs and real-time results of ongoing algorithms are embedded directly as appropriate and personalized to the individual salesperson through the portal. If you are a sales manager and have configured your portal to show you how each salesperson is doing in some graphic format, when you enter the portal, voilà! The visualized data will be staring at you as you stare at it. It will change as the entries to opportunity management screens change. Take a look at Figure 6-7.

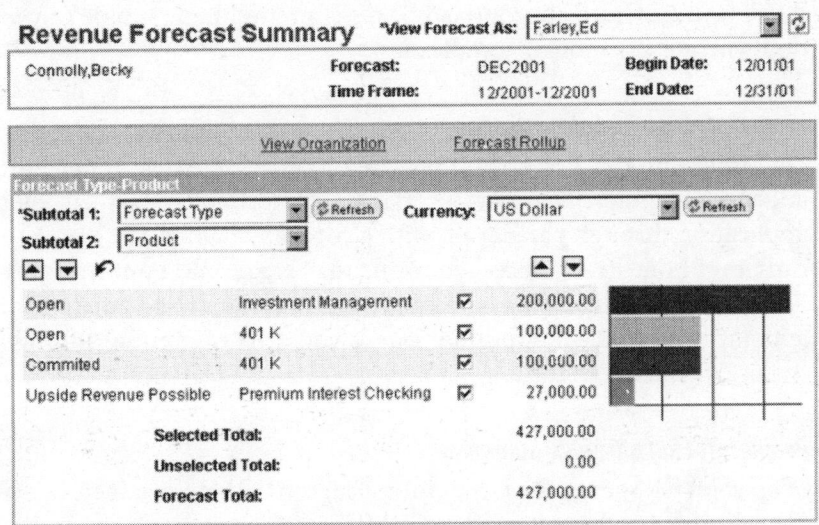

Figure 6-7: A real-time view of PeopleSoft embedded analytics for sales

The foundations of these analytics are the PeopleSoft Insight (formerly known as workbenches) products. The PeopleSoft workbenches were always a major addition to PeopleSoft, providing analytics to the PeopleSoft installation through what is called enterprise performance management (EPM). The analytic Insight applications for CRM 8.0 Sales are personalized and Internet based. They are specific to individual roles, functions, and vertical industries. For CRM 8.0 Sales, there is Sales Effectiveness Insight, which can measure individual sales efforts and their impact. Most importantly, there is Customer Profitability Insight, which can identify what weight to give to which customers—a leg up on the calculation of customer lifetime value (see the appendix). These are heavy-duty tools. And imagine—browser based, Internet-architected. This is very good stuff.

Territory Management

While their contact, account, and opportunity management is as good as any out there, PeopleSoft shines in territory management. PeopleSoft

Territory Management makes a difficult function easy. It organizes each territory in any direction you want and then shows it as a tree within the sales manager's portal. You can transfer the accounts of John Smith to Tom Jones, except for two that John will keep while he assumes the accounts of Pat Higgins. With a simple drag and drop from one to the other, all information across the applications that are associated with it will be transferred appropriately. This is a refreshingly simple way to deal with an enormously complex task.

PeopleSoft CRM 8.0 Sales Telephony

One final fun, but not critical feature of CRM 8.0 Sales. PeopleSoft added a Computer Telephony Interface (CTI) technology to their Sales application through partnering with a company named JustTalk. You can now phone in and access your calendar, email, and opportunities. But even more interesting, you can make calendar entries and set up appointments that will appear in your calendar via your phone through the use of voice recognition.

PeopleSoft CRM 8.0 Sales: Summary

PeopleSoft CRM 8.0 Sales is the cutting edge in CRM technology. Functionally, it does what most other CRM SFA applications do. It handles contact, account, and opportunity management, lead generation, sales pipelines, and all the commensurate functional subsets. It has strong mobile features. In addition to the differentiators above, PeopleSoft has added new functions such as a product configurator and strong scripting capabilities that are highlighted by the ability to generate multilingual scripts on the fly. But it does all this SFA differently and with a bit more ease than most of the other sales-oriented applications out there.

On the whole, it does what an SFA module has to and does it well no matter what other applications you're running, PeopleSoft or not. A most democratic, very advanced CRM.

Oracle

Oracle is worth mentioning, but not because its CRM sales component is that fantastic. It's not. Oddly, its Oracle Sales Online Web service has more functionality than its current product incarnation. If you look at the Oracle sales offerings they are not the usual. Besides

Oracle Sales Online (see the "SFA.com" section later in this chapter), they have:

Oracle TeleSales Integrated with call center telemarketers and Oracle Telephony Manager.

Oracle iStore Tools for designing and managing Internet storefronts to sell products and services.

Oracle Field Sales for Mobile Devices A wireless product to handle customers, opportunities, products, prices, and quotes for Windows CE, Palm OS, cellphones, and Windows-based laptops.

Oracle Sales Intelligence Real-time data viewed across the enterprise in report formats that cover analytic areas such as performance and effectiveness, revenue management, products, channels, and pipelines.

Not much so far. But they have what has been called by many analysts one of the best sales configuration programs on the market, if not the best. All difficulties they may have had when they rearchitected Selling-Point, a product purchased from Concentra, are now gone. Oracle Configurator can work across Oracle Sales Online, Oracle Telesales, and Oracle iStore to provide guided selling, requirements-based product selection, and a strong validation tool to handle as complex a product and pricing configuration as you want. Their Order Capture tool is likewise a gem. It can execute order capture requests that extend beyond ordinary products and services configurations and include events, seminars, service level agreements, renewals, and collateral requests.

Oracle: Summary

Oracle has outstanding configurator and order capture products. But that alone is hardly SFA, and the rest of their offering is kind of quirky, with the exception of Oracle Sales Online (covered later in this chapter).

Interact Commerce Corporation (SalesLogix, Sage LLC)

This company is a marvel. Founded in 1996 as SalesLogix Corporation by Pat Sullivan, Interact Commerce Corporation (IACT) jumped to the head of the midmarket pack because of their excellent application suite, SalesLogix. Not one to rest on their laurels, Interact reacquired ACT!, a Pat Sullivan co-creation. Staying one step ahead of the technology curve, they developed a highly sophisticated data synchronization engine that both overcame the slowness of MAPI data synchronization and at the same time set the stage for the now popular wireless data synchronization at a transfer rate that was useful, not irritating. From both a functionality and technological standpoint, this product is the real deal.

They are one of the Sandbox Playmates and will be covered in even more multifunctional and multidimensional detail in Chapter 14.

My small company chose to use the SalesLogix SFA suite after an extremely careful and arduous selection process. The selection process criteria and how SalesLogix passed the test are presented here because it will hopefully show what you should be thinking about if you're a midmarket company considering an SFA or CRM implementation. (Of course, there is always the caveat that your company is different from my company.) It also will highlight some of the stronger features of SalesLogix. They include:

Pedigree Pat Sullivan, named one of the top ten influential people in the history of CRM by *CRM* magazine, founded Interact Commerce Corporation, now known as SalesLogix. He also was the co-creator of ACT!, the number-one contact manager in the world. The proven track record of ACT! indicated one thing clearly: Pat Sullivan, when he developed SalesLogix, knew the needs of salespeople and had a complete understanding of the technology that would meet these requirements.

Vertical market expertise I was able to identify roughly 45 specific vertical markets that SalesLogix had penetrated, including the very difficult legal profession. This means the product is adaptable and customizable.

Toolkit It has the most flexible toolkit on the market. One of the most impressive and useful tools is the visual SalesLogix Architect tool (see Figure 6-8), which allows you to graphically develop sales processes. It can take an existing process and create the flowcharts for that process. You can modify the process directly on the screen. It actually resembles a CASE tool for the masses. It is a truly powerful addition to a great toolbox.

Web-enabled SalesLogix uses a Web client to allow individual access to the complete functionality of the client/server product via the Internet without losing a beat.

Wireless capabilities SalesLogix is enabled for both PDA and Web phone. SalesLogix for Web phones and SalesLogix Wireless for Palm-powered handhelds are their current wireless applications.

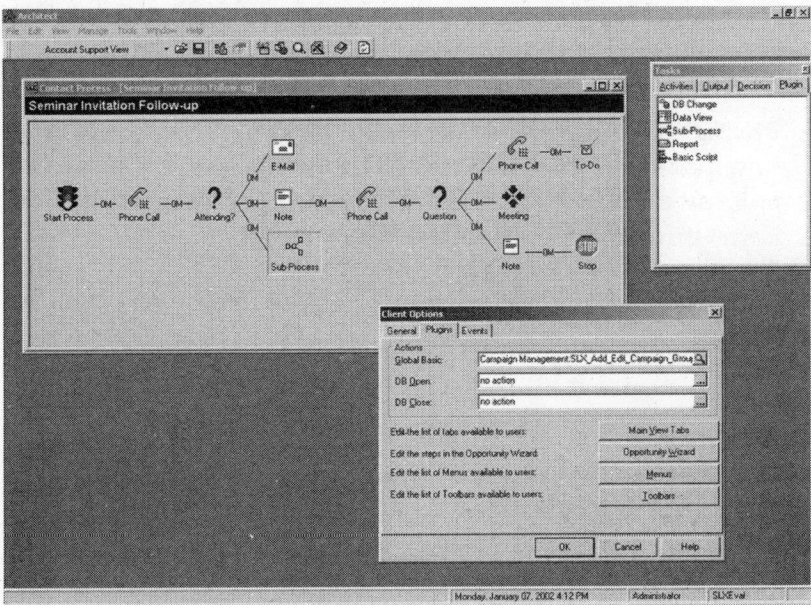

Figure 6-8: The SalesLogix Architect in action, building a contact process (Copyright 2001, Interact Commerce Corporation. All rights reserved.)

Corporate culture SalesLogix has an intensely relaxed corporate culture. I went straight to their headquarters and, unlike a number of the other vendors, found them accessible to the top, so that I was able to meet with their corporate chieftains like Pat Sullivan, CEO and founder, and Mike Muhney, the executive vice-president of SalesLogix at the time. The staff made it clear that partners were a welcome addition to the SalesLogix family.

Functionality SalesLogix is a full-featured application that has lead, account, contact, opportunity, and pipeline management, and quotations, charts, and multiple reporting capabilities. Reporting has recently been enriched with a partnership with Seagate Software. Crystal Reports 8.0 is being included in SalesLogix for increased reporting capabilities. SalesLogix is structured to scale to the small business and midmarket.

Technology They have the most advanced data synchronization capacity in the industry. The databases it uses are commonplace, including Oracle, Microsoft SQL Server 7.0, and Borland's Interbase engine. The interface is easy to handle. The only difficulties we had were somewhat quirky relations with Windows NT 4.0 Service Pack 6. Otherwise, it was an utterly clean installation/implementation.

Pricing The pricing is actually reasonable. I won't specify this here, since pricing in the eCRM and CRM worlds is very volatile. The unit cost to us was well within the scope of our budget. It had the lowest price of all of the vendors we examined.

Implementation/configuration time The implementation time for a typical SalesLogix implementation is on the outside around three months, far shorter than the much larger and longer Siebel implementation. This represents major increases in potential productivity and cost savings. Ours was shorter than most.

Knowledge of the midmarket SalesLogix has unparalleled knowledge of the small and medium business (SMB) market, with more than 3,500 customer implementations since 1998. They are the undisputed market leaders in this domain—most likely because they are the only company exclusively focused on this space.

Channel The SalesLogix channel strategy is superlative, leading to around 80 percent of all SalesLogix sales being conducted by SalesLogix partners/resellers. This is comforting to me because it shows the faith the channel puts into the product. There are dozens of technology partners, including Live Wire, which has led to a very large community of producers of additional functionality. This way, I don't have to build the back-office connectivity for SalesLogix. I can buy it from Scribe, a company that produces the connectivity, or from any of their many OEMs, such as Sage, Macola, or Made2Manage. I don't need to produce a PRM module. That's done by Elantix, a SalesLogix partner. It made me rest easy to know I can get what I want at a reasonable price and don't have to build it.

SalesLogix: Summary

SalesLogix makes sense for the small and medium-sized companies who want sales teams working as a strategic body in the company. It is sophisticated, provides plenty of functionality, and achieved a high level of customer satisfaction in a survey done by CRMGuru and Hi-Yield Marketing, among others. It is one of the very few surveys ever done on CRM vendors and customer satisfaction. SalesLogix understands that they are not going to be a large enterprise CRM vendor and are the best of breed in their marketplace.

SFA.com

Despite the low entry cost of some of the SFA products, small companies that have no venture capital, angel funding, or significant revenue streams still might have a hard time affording SFA. Enter the SFA.com world. SFA.coms are Web service centers that provide interactive professional sales tools and services to companies that are too ill-financed to afford the full-figured SFA applications and to small companies that are geographically scattered with a highly mobile workforce that lives on the Net. These online subscription-based SFA service centers provide a range of services from free to inexpensive. Their reasonable expectation is that your use of their services will grow with your company. For a small price, they will cover:

- ► Calendaring and scheduling

- ► Contact management

- ► Lead generation (for example, free leads with premium memberships)

- ► Task management

- ► Pipeline management (some)

- ► Forecasting tools (very limited)

- ► Reporting tools (small number of customized templates)

- ► Customization based on corporate business processes

- ► Integration of legacy system data

- ► Data synchronization with your favorite PDA (such as Palm or wireless Web phones)

- ► Company briefings (for example, data on private and public companies)

- ► Competitor briefings

- ► Free consultations with technical support

- ► Online education (such as articles by leading sales experts)

- ► Moderated discussion forums with experts for your company or multiple companies

- ► International weather, airport reports, and news feeds

- ► Collaborative private Web meeting rooms

In other words, these are highly functional online SFA applications for pennies per month. There is an upside to working with these SFA.coms: The service level is solid. Your MIS department has no worries except perhaps some customization and legacy data woes. The downside is your security concerns, which are more often just concerns rather than real risks. Scalability is also a serious downside, since the few remaining SFA subscription services are not able to handle large enterprises, with the exception of perhaps Salesnet. Oddly, the most significant weakness of these sites is that the sites are purely SFA. They do not integrate well (or in some cases, at all) with marketing applications, customer service applications, and the like, though as they mature, significant APIs have been developed to attack this problem. With the exception of the claims of Salesforce.com, they cannot provide a full-service CRM solution. Salesforce.com says their Enterprise Edition will compete with the full-bodied versions of CRM but that's a claim they make and haven't proven yet. Even so, despite occasional marketing pretensions, SFA.com companies are not realistically an intranet; they are hosted Web solutions.

There are three significant online sales presences, each with a unique model and a separate purpose. While they have a good deal of value to small businesses, many of them have a tenuous hold, as a dot-com market that isn't profitable is looked upon as happily as an invasion of locusts. In fact, by the end of 2000, Siebel had repurchased Sales.com and brought it into their e-business suite. Interact.com, the SalesLogix-based online SFA presence, had morphed twice, changing its model from a Web-based services model to a Web-integrated part of SalesLogix and ACT! to non-existence. Happily, the online SFA services that understand their own mission and business model are solid business propositions and one of the better places to be if your only need is sales force automation. But there aren't many of those available. Some of those available are Salesnet and Salesforce.com along with UpShot. I'm going to look at the first two.

Salesnet

This is without a doubt the most dynamic and interesting of the online SFA subscription services. They have a clear business model, a well-defined market, a customer-friendly strategy, and a highly functional product that could compete and even beat standalone SFA applications if there were any out there. They were founded in 1997 by Richard

Perkett and Jonathan Tang, two former Adams Media employees. One of the more interesting aspects of this SFA site is that before the principals actually started the company, they did research! They interviewed hundreds of sales professionals to find out about sales methodology and sales technique. This led them to the conclusion that an ASP model probably best served those professionals. What makes this appealing is that they consulted the users, not the CFOs, prior to the creation of the business model they implemented. A great start.

By 2000, the great start had become a great start-up and had added Mike Doyle as their CEO and chairman. That year, they made a couple of decisions. First, they decided that rather than be all CRM things to all people, they would be the best-in-class SFA application. That was smart move number one. Do what you do best and you will succeed. Second, they began to focus on the enterprise sales market. Rather than the five- or six-seat company, they chose the 20 to 5000+ user company, the mid-sized and larger enterprise—the one that plays in the $100 million and up space. Once they realized that this is where they wanted to sit, they never stood up again. Second good decision.

Salesnet has a unique sales process methodology that is strongly focused on making sure the customer is taken care of at every step. Not only is the sales process that the customer uses customizable to the needs of the individual company, but, in something I have yet to see anywhere else in the online world, Salesnet provides what they call "business solutions consultants" to help identify and characterize the company best practices in sales so that they can be embedded in Salesnet's native applications. In fact, Salesnet has a significant number of interesting features that deserve mention:

Process Builder This is where the best practices that the business solutions consultants help you uncover are embedded. This is a patent-pending tool that lets the sales teams actually track the steps of their selling process, as is shown in Figure 6-9. It is entirely flexible and allows modifications and new customizations at any time. Basically, it builds in the business rules designed to establish the enterprise-wide approach to sales. I'm not sure if this is unique, but I will say that features like this aren't found in anything but the normally very high-end large enterprise CRM applications like PeopleSoft and Siebel.

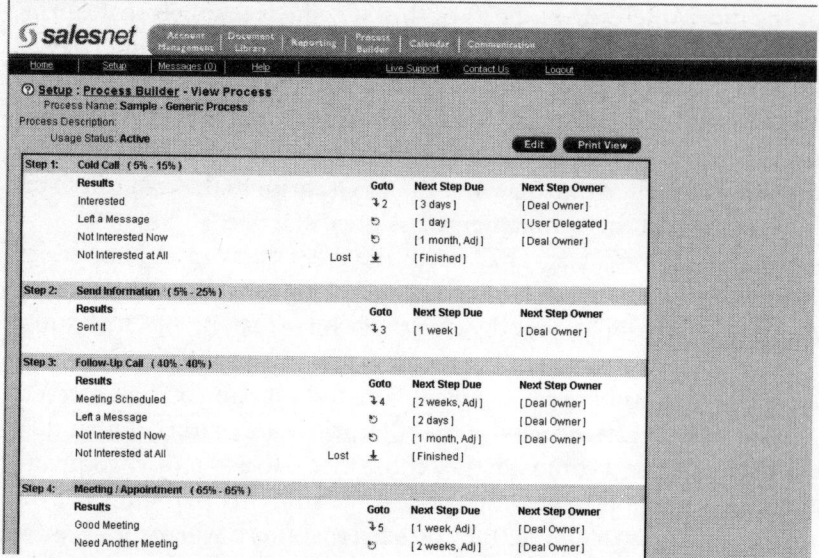

Figure 6-9: Salesnet's Process Builder. Best practices in action. (Printed by express permission of Salesnet, 2002.)

Report Writer This is the most flexible report tool in the SFA.com world, with yearly, quarterly, and even monthly reporting capabilities. What makes this particularly striking is the fact that these timed reporting capabilities can deal with the ghosts of Fiscal Present, Fiscal Past, and Fiscal Future. The reports can be drawn from multiple data points across accounts, deals, or contacts. A very nimble tool.

Company-defined fields Another major plus that is rarely seen outside the big boys. Companies can actually customize data fields, rather than deal with only plain vanilla templates that are fixed and unalterable. These can be either text or calculated fields with company-embedded formulas.

Salesnet Wireless This is a very smart part of the package. The Salesnet wireless capability handles 32 PDAs (as of early 2002) and WAP-enabled cellphones galore. That means Palm VIIX or Handspring Visor or HP Jornada 567 or Compaq IPAQ 3870. It means RIM Blackberry 857. It means PDAs that have been rumored but never actually seen by humankind. Bigfoot PDAs. In other words, this is a complete wireless solution and a major initiative given the current direction of sales forces around the world.

Communication Manager   A rather lofty title for something that is practical and actually not lofty at all. This is tight Microsoft Word integration, allowing for export and mail merges that work and don't say, "Dear Mr. User-defined."

External data capture   This means customizable HTML forms that can capture leads from websites, intranets, email, call center activity, marketing databases, and a host of other sources. It has a workflow that actually notifies the appropriate Salesnet user of the incoming new prospect and begins the sales process automatically.

Strong integration   Salesnet has extremely tight integration with Microsoft products, being a player in the Microsoft.net initiative. For other applications and platforms, they have built hooks via APIs to make the integration easier, though with no promises of seamlessness.

Excellent support   Not only do they have the business process consultants, but they have live chat for real-time problem solving, help pages, phone support, and Web support that is comprehensive and 24/7. In fact, they take complaints so seriously that every one they get is personally looked at by the CTO of the company and appropriately directed. Now, *that* is a CTO.

This is slick stuff that, with their vision and solid model, has positioned Salesnet as what I would call the premier online SFA. They have actual implementations of between 650–1,000 seats to their name, which are gigantic numbers of users by online standards. One other good sign, according to chairman and CEO Mike Doyle: "In the last six months (mid- to end-2001), we sold more seats to current customers than through new customer acquisitions. The confidence level in our product grows as the customers use it. We even found through various surveys of our customers that if you use it, the sales pipeline is twice what the non-user has. What made us focus this way was our target market. We are aimed at results-oriented sales leaders, those who take responsibility for the bottom line of their company. We know that they have to be up and running quickly and have to have substantial tools to do the job they have. As an example, we got a major company that had 650 sales reps across about ten different countries up and running and trained in six weeks. It took us 15 man-years to develop this product, but it has been worth it."

I agree.

Their website: http://www.salesnet.com/.

Salesforce.com

Salesforce.com is the granddaddy of the SFA subscriber services. In the latter part of 2000, it added deep pockets to its Dockers when IBM joined the fray and became a partner with them. The partnership not only added money, but also adds a variety of services through IBM's WebConnections service package. Shared Internet access and business-class email for up to 100 employees, secure remote access, firewall security, website blocking, 24/7 technical support, and an Internet connection via analog, ISDN, or DSL are all new additions. Its engine functions significantly more like a Web-integrated, client/server version of Siebel or SalesLogix than its pure-Web portal siblings.

Until early 2002, Salesforce.com provided small businesses with SFA applications for a small price. It did it reasonably well, but with clumsy reporting tools and notable lacks in tools such as forecasting. There are other small oddities. For example, when you click to produce a print-able version of a report, you get an Excel file. When you click to get a report that can be imported to a spreadsheet, you get a comma delimited ASCII text file. Sadly, there are many of these small quirks that make their applications less than ideal, but they are still generally usable. Its SFA fundamentals are available in rudimentary form: contact, account, opportunity management, calendaring, some not-too-strong sales pipeline analysis, and some weak forecasting and reporting tools.

Sounds like there is a need to strengthen their offering, doesn't it? Yet, rather than being the best of breed they could be if they worked harder, they decided they can take on Siebel, PeopleSoft, SAP, and Oracle by releasing first (in early 2002) an Enterprise Edition that went beyond SFA to adding Enterprise Marketing Automation (EMA) and Support to CRM. Then, in late February 2002, they decided they were going to become an Enterprise Application and deal with the back office too, announcing Salesforce.com E-Business Suite, a limited foray into the world of ERP. That is extremely presumptuous, given that they haven't even gotten the SMB-sized sales force automation application right yet. It's worrisome when companies forget their mission and let their funding be their guide, rather than their users.

Their website: http://www.salesforce.com/.

Oracle Sales Online

This is a strong offering that actually has both solid standalone functionality and an ulterior motive. Note their following comment on what they can do: "Oracle Sales Online enables salespeople to create configured quotes using the latest inventory, price list, and discount information through integration with Oracle Order Management and Oracle Configurator." The latter two, Order Management and Configurator, are not part of Oracle Sales Online at all, thus providing a revenue stream that is not part of Oracle Sales Online. With the optional additions integrated, this can be a very strong offering. Note this sentence quoted after the one quoted above: "Oracle Sales Online delivers customer, opportunity, and product information and allows salespeople to create configured quotes using the latest inventory, price list, and discount information through integration with Oracle Order Management and Oracle Configurator." Something tells me that they're anxious to sell Oracle Order Management and Oracle Configurator.

There is a lot to this SFA.com. It is the Web version of a nearly completely featured sales force automation application. Oracle's original strategy was to offer all the basic SFA modules free online. The idea was that delighted customers would purchase the other Oracle CRM applications, or at least, other SFA-related applications such as Oracle Configurator that can be used with the ERP applications, too. Additionally, there would be some fee-based services that were attached to the site so that Oracle could derive some revenue directly from the site. Some of the fee-based services were to include:

- Incentive and compensation management
- Travel and expense management
- Time and expense reporting

Other SFA modules, such as sales force compensation, are not free and can be add-ins to Oraclesalesonline.com. Among the online application's most advanced features are basic sales forecasting and some pipeline analysis tools. Additionally, unlike the other SFA.coms, it has the facility, though limited, to do partner/salesperson revenue splitting and revenue crediting to highlight its substantial feature set.

Started in August 2000, by October 2000 it had 6,000 companies using it and it remains successful through 2001 and into 2002, and quite a few of them were not small companies at all. For example, companies such as Knight Ridder Publications, India's billion-dollar enterprise Tata Technologies, Rational Software, Oregon Steel Mills, and

VTEL Communications were all using the free service—not the market it seemed to be aimed at, but certainly a market that it hit.

Deals with Hoover's Online were completed at the same time to provide services for corporate information and competitive intelligence. Oracle planned to be online with all its CRM by mid-2001. This hasn't happened. They have Oracle Support Online but it stops there.

Their website: http://www.oraclesalesonline.com/.

The SFA Return on Investment (ROI)

There is a pre-ROI benchmark that gains a faddish kind of following when a hot stock market becomes shaky. It is called "path to profitability." The prevailing wisdom of the concept works like this: ROI doesn't matter in the present because you are currently investing what you have to in getting to a point where you become profitable. *Then* you will be looking at ROI, but until then, the investment is in building the road, not traversing it. Most analysts say this is hooey. These analysts say that while you can ignore ROI in the short term if you must, it is always lurking and waiting to get you if you turn your back to it at any time. Be mindful of ROI at all times, whether your metrics are short or long term. ROI matters.

Sales organizations work with fairly straightforward benchmarks for ROI. How many sales ultimately occurred due to the investment in SFA? That is the ROI's bottom line. But it is not the interim lines of ROI. There are a large number of factors at play in SFA ROI. Some depend on what sales processes you set up. For example, if you are a company devoted to telesales, an increase in the number of successful calls per day per salesperson would be more important than an account manager who is looking more for successes with a longer sales cycle and higher revenue per success. Another metric could be the success of the sales forecast—the closer to 100 percent accuracy, the better. Other metrics could be lowering administrative time, decreasing cost, increasing the win rate, or decreasing the time from process step 1 to process step final. The measurement of ROI is a matter of corporate taste. Chapter 12 covers CRM ROI in depth.

SFA on the Move: The Economy's Mobile Sales Force

You're a salesperson on the road with your cellphone, your PDA, and your wireless modem, and you're young and hip and wow! Good life.

How productive is all this cool stuff, though? What can it do that will at least emulate some of the features of the desktop system or the SFA application? How can it work on your phone?

Most of the SFA applications, such as SalesLogix for Web phones, Siebel Wireless, or PeopleSoft's wireless capabilities, do the same basic things. They provide calendar, contact, and account information on the phone or PDA. The types of services you'll be able to get on your Web-enabled cellphone are essentially directory services—names and phone numbers, street and email addresses. Then you make a call or send an email from the phone. This will become part of a viewable history by contact or account. To-do reminders and all those other features you have come to expect in a comprehensive calendar on your desktop will be available on the phone. Actually, what makes this very attractive, if not sexy, is not the features, which are the standard features you can get in SFA applications when it comes to the phone. What *is* sexy is that you don't have to download this information from anywhere or carry out the functions, such as email, elsewhere. It's all on your handheld PocketPC or Palm or in your cellphone; it's self-contained. Synchronization is not necessary. You can be cool, young, and mobile and not tied down to anything but the four winds and your customers—with information at your disposal that only the desk jockeys had access to previously.

The under-the-hood features are very strong. Installation is a point and click administrative task. The wireless SFA phone features are registered through a Web URL, the phone is enabled, the data is downloaded to the phone along with the appropriate applications, and you're ready to go.

Security is also quite good. For example, SalesLogix for Web phones deploys a three-stage security model, similar to the other wireless SFA services, though not identical:

1. Transmission and identification of unique phone ID.

2. Secure data transmission using industry-proven protocols.

3. Password-protected and security-profile-driven access to SalesLogix server data.

What we have here is a revolution in SFA that has moved from traditional sales management functionality to a client/server-based CRM philosophy/architecture/technology and now a wireless, Web-based mobile SFA. Not bad for something that is both old as eons and new as muons.

7

Enterprise Marketing Automation:
New Kids on the Old Block

Companies market. That is, they sell themselves. This is a simple fact of business life. In small companies, the level of marketing that goes on can be as simple as a printed brochure and a website. Even the smallest companies are creating static websites that operate as online brochures for their wares. As companies move up the size scale and the marketing budget scale, campaigns use direct mail, email, promotions, interactive voice response, newsletters, contests, events, and other customer "touch points." Indirect marketing campaigns, such as advertising in the print media or on TV and radio, reach traditional mass markets. Then there is "branding": working with agencies to establish name recognition through public relations, media, and advertising.

The estimated total spending on advertising in the United States has been at about an average of $187 billion a year from 1995 to date, including television, radio, newspapers, magazines, outdoor billboards, telephone directories, direct mail, and the new frontier of Web advertising. That figure is growing at about 7 percent per year. However, traditional methods of advertising (such as media ads) are getting more expensive and more competitive, but yielding less return. Historically, the return has been minimal with the conventional service bureaus only being able to engage in limited campaigns and produce subjective metrics that may or may not be accurate. The data collection is sketchy, the turnaround is slow, and much of the analysis and the follow-on marketing campaign modifications are ad hoc. Dollar spending does not guarantee brand recognition. In 1999, eBay spent $5.5 million on advertising and achieved number one brand position with 22 percent of the consumers who were polled. Ameritrade spent 20 times that number and achieved 1 percent top-of-brand recognition. Admittedly, this is an extreme example because eBay's competition is minimal and Ameritrade's is substantial. Achieving 22 percent if you're the only one is not a great achievement. But, still, take note of the point.

Enterprise marketing automation (EMA) starts to change all that.

Marketing in what is now the not-so-New Economy is neither traditional nor is it "new." It is transitional. It still involves the identification and capture of potential long-term and profitable customers who are appropriate to your business. It is still about the competitive seizure of mindshare and market share within targeted socio-economic segments. It is still promotions and advertising and snail-mail pieces and other direct and indirect means of reaching prospects and customers. It is still a high-ticket item that may, at times, leave a questionable return on investment. It is still a bit of a crapshoot. What *is* new about marketing in the not-so-New Economy is enterprise marketing automation—also known as e-marketing—using Web-based applications and the Internet to improve the effectiveness of traditional marketing and to create new methods of marketing and campaign management using the Web and information technology to craft finely tuned successful efforts.

Unfortunately, certain marketing truths seem to never change. How many times have you wanted to do bodily harm over the phone with telemarketers bombarding you during business hours, dinner hours, and recreation time? I received four phone calls in one day from a bank I happen to have a credit card with. How often have you gotten frustrated at the pop-up window advertising something you have no need or desire for? The new fashion is pop-under windows, pioneered by X-10, that show up under your browser and appear to you when you close the browser. How often have you been swamped by spam—that particularly grating, unsolicited email that seems to be as endless as the viruses produced by 15-year-old hackers? It gets worse when the spammers use programs that change the source subject line each time they send the spam, thus defeating many of the filters on the market.

There actually is a name for this kind of marketing—one that seems obvious. It is called *interruption marketing*. Interruption marketing worked well in the television era when you had four or five major channels with more than 200 million people watching shows, and commercials timed to be pretty much roughly at the same time and the same breaks during each network's programming. "Now for a commercial message" was not considered a problem, and the ads held your attention. If you are over 45, it's easy to finish the jingle, "Winston tastes good…" even though the Winston commercials haven't aired for more than 30 years. Even now, on a bad night, a popular TV show like "Friends" will capture 24 or 25 million viewers, and a bad show like… well, a bad show can be considered a flop and still capture 9 million viewers. But this is the era of the Internet. By the end of 2001, there were 141 million Internet users who spent $34.1 billion online in the United States alone, with 112 million unique visitors to online news media websites in February 2002 alone. "Nightline" would love to have even a tiny percentage of that projected audience. Those numbers dwarf anything you see with TV. It's a whole new ballgame. The choices per user are endless, and the competitive level between like sites is fierce. Even with the dot.com bomb, have you noticed a reduction in the amount of spam you get in email or websites that are trying to get your attention? It's hard to halve infinity.

The Core Belief: Embedded Permission Marketing

Seth Godin, Yahoo!'s vice-president of direct marketing, claims that the average consumer sees 1 million marketing messages a year—which is roughly 2,800 per day. Think about that. An assault on your senses for items that you most likely ignore or minimally respond to with great irritation. The irritation comes from the lack of control you have over this visceral mugging by muggers who want to not only steal your money but also bury you under junk after the theft. At least, that's how it feels.

How would you respond if you were wooed by someone who meant something to you and with something that could be of value—and it was your decision whether the wooing started and whether it became a courtship? This is *permission* marketing as defined by Mr. Godin in his book *Permission Marketing*. Permission marketing asks for your permission to "speak" with you about its product and, at the same time, provides consideration for your acquiescence every step of the way. Mr. Godin identifies it as "dating your customers" and defines it as a five-step process:

1. Offer the prospect an incentive to volunteer to receive your email or other marketing media.

2. Using the attention offered by the prospect, offer a curriculum over time, teaching the consumer about your product or service.

3. Reinforce the incentive to guarantee that the prospect maintains the permission.

4. Offer additional incentives to get even more permission from the consumer.

5. Over time, leverage the permission to change consumer behavior toward profits.

This is a courtship, pure and simple. By the end of the initial cycle, the prospective customer, having been through the five steps, will know your product, your company, and you. He or she will be amenable to becoming an actual customer who will remain loyal because you didn't try to go "all the way" within the first five minutes of the first "date."

Enterprise Marketing Automation (EMA) enhances the courtship through an intoxicating aphrodisiac mixture of email, e-fax, the Web, the telephone, and other technology tools. It intensifies the experience for the prospective customer when personalized or segmented customer preferences are determined by use of analytical tools. These tools define customer segments that are appropriate to your business and can help evaluate the successes and failures of e-marketing campaigns in near real time so that significant adjustments to the incentives and direction can be made quickly. All the trials and tribulations of the courtship are monitored and adjusted continuously. Enterprise marketing automation philosophically propagates permission marketing, though I can't say that it is solely devoted to you. With that introduction, I present to you…

Enterprise Marketing Automation (EMA): The Market

EMA has undergone fairly dramatic changes over the last year. It first showed its unwrinkled brow in 1998 with about $100 million in sales and has since grown to what is expected to be a more than $2 billion market by the end of 2002 according to the META Group. The analyst community is divided about EMA's maturity and even its ability to ultimately stand on its own. The Aberdeen Group and Forrester Research think that EMA and sales force automation (SFA) must converge. The conjoint offering must then be integrated into customer support and call centers to succeed. In other words, a fully integrated, complete CRM packaged offering is EMA's real chance for success. The META Group also estimates that 60 percent of the Global 2000 will use the Internet-based EMA rather than the client/server structured database marketing by the year 2002. The Gartner Group sees this progression also, but at a slower pace. As mid-2002 approached, Gartner's cautions seemed to be considerably more accurate than the META Group's 60 percent. The proliferation of serious niche players (discussed later in this chapter) indicates that it is capable of standing on its own as what is now become a mature application.

Why the significant upsurge by year-end 2002? In an article in *CRM* magazine, Tom Gormley, a senior analyst at Forrester Research, states that while business-to-business (B2B) e-commerce is currently the rage and is expected to carry transactions worth $5.7 trillion by 2003, it is in the business-to-consumer (B2C) market that the need for e-marketing arises. EMA has the analytic engines that are necessary to identify and personalize campaigns with millions of stored customer data records to slice and dice.

One extant problem with EMA is its high cost. The typical cost of a full-blown EMA implementation is in the vicinity of $600,000 to $1 million, which is a lot for such a small part of the enterprise. While few EMA vendors were around prior to 1998 and most had fewer than a dozen customers as of 2000, the year 2001, despite the economic problems, changed the EMA market landscape as it gained credence in the marketplace. No vendor has a truly end-to-end suite, though several such as E.piphany and Unica are approaching that. It still is generally one of the more expensive components of CRM and thus has the *caveat emptor* warning attached to any purchase of the software. With the right vendor and the right thought applied, the results can be spectacular.

Components of Enterprise Marketing Automation

Why is there any advantage to automating processes that are by nature attempting intimacy with an audience? How personal can you get with the results of millions of customer records? Oddly enough, with the aid and comfort of the software and the Web, you can get very personal. The key here is not what the software can do for you, but what you can do to the software. It provides simple, user-friendly customization that says, "We can give you what you want with a few simple commands. You merely have to spend the few minutes clicking and checking several options."

EMA is the technology of end-to-end marketing. Its core component is campaign management—the end-to-end organization and execution of a marketing thrust. The "e" component of campaign management is the provision of a single view of the customer to the entire enterprise and those with responsibility for that customer, which are all available with a browser. Most e-marketing toolsets, like those of Siebel or Unica, are focused on a suite of products that provide the following:

- Customer intelligence
- Extraction and analysis of the intelligence

▸ Campaign definition and planning based on that data analysis

▸ Campaign launch

▸ Campaign monitoring tools that handle lead generation

▸ Response management

▸ Workflow so that there is a uniform customer view across the enterprise

When used in the near real-time environment of EMA and response management, refinements are related to the individual customer, rather than the ad hoc response analysis of service bureaus. In more sophisticated systems, such as those of RightPoint, data mining and analysis are done from multiple sources. Several companies such as SAS are currently evolving from the purely analytic side to become more of an EMA set of applications.

Marketing Campaigns

What kind of marketing campaigns can the e-marketing applications run? Surprisingly, though they don't often function as smoothly as you might want them, they can cover a lot of ground. Embedded in most of the e-marketing software from many of the major players such as Siebel, Unica, Chordiant, and Annuncio is the process identified by the permission marketing mantra, "opt-in, opt-out."

Opt-In, Opt-Out

How many times have you gone to a website and entered a contest, downloaded a free book or white paper, or played a game? When you fill out an online form at this website with your vital statistics, often at the bottom of the form there are checkboxes that ask you whether you would like to receive further information or an email update on the product. This is opting-in. There is also an opt-out variation—the checkbox is already checked and you have to uncheck it to opt out of the newsletter update or further information. When you get email from this company, you feel that it was fine to receive this mail because you allowed it to arrive at your desktop. It was solicited and accepted. That's what "opt-in, opt-out" is. *La Forza del Destino*—control over your destiny, minus the grandeur of Verdi's opera, of course.

To put it another way, opting in means that for some consideration (for example, the contest, the white paper, the discount), you allowed the company you are interacting with to send a solicitation that they expect you to take interest in. Rather than just another email address, you've become a potential customer with a real existence.

Opt-in e-marketing has two functions: intelligence and engagement. The first stage, even prior to clicking your mouse on the checkbox, is the forms you fill out with information about yourself. This information is stored along with your website activity, which is monitored as you meander your way through the site. After the form is filled out, at the point that you've clicked or unclicked on the checkboxes, you are engaged. Congratulations!

Opt-in is often contrasted to opt-out email as the more favorable choice. Let's look at a simple example. Which are you likely to be more responsive to, an unsolicited email that says, "If you do not want to receive any more mailings from us, please type remove in the subject line and reply to this email" (opt-out) or a registration form on a site that asks you to accept emails in return for entry into a sweepstakes for $15,000 (opt-in)? The results are a clear mandate for opt-in. Traditional banner ad click-through rates are 0.5 percent, and traditional interruption mail is 1 percent to perhaps 2 percent at most. Click-through rates for opt-in email are 7 to 10 percent as of 2001. For the immediate future, opt-out still constitutes the bulk of email, with opt-in email being only around 38 percent of total email volume as of 2001. The future of opt-in email is very bright, as long as the rules of engagement are clear to the potential recipient of that email. In a study completed by Forrester in October 2001, 41 percent of those who get permission-based email think the email is a great way to learn about a product. A whopping 36 percent actually read all the permission-based email they get and 9 percent actually forward it to friends if it's interesting enough. That is powerful incentive for permission-based email.

Opting In to Web-Integrated E-marketing

Using dramatic carpet-bombing techniques with the hope that survivors will purchase your products is not EMA's métier. That is akin to the idea of creating a commercial so bad that you will be remembered for it. We all know about the 7 grams of fat in Subway sandwiches thanks to Jared.

Using available EMA technologies, opt-in campaigns—or, for that matter, all marketing campaigns—are honed, sharpened, and thrust into a segmented marketplace so that the level of success is potentially much greater. EMA provides the templates and tools for planning, executing, and analyzing these campaigns in real time.

Campaign Planning and Management

E-marketing's great strength is campaign management—the creation of personalized marketing efforts that not only engage the customer or prospect, but also engage the entire enterprise in the effort and provide a single view of the activity to any department or segment of the company. The campaign management features of the technology are end-to-end. They plan and monitor all activity, including:

► Identification of the prospect

► Generation of the lead

► Prospect and customer information capture

► Lead qualification

► Distribution of leads to appropriate segments

► Campaign planning

► Campaign execution (such as promotions, events planning)

► Response management

► Refinement

► Channel management (for example, joint marketing campaigns)

The diagram in Figure 7-1 identifies a typical e-marketing campaign. This is a Web-based offering that gives maximum flexibility to the marketing team.

Superficially, EMA campaign methods don't seem very different from traditional marketing's methods. The difference is the Internet. EMA uses the Internet to capture, extract, and analyze information about each customer and each market segment. It then gives you the design tools to plan, execute, monitor, and refine your marketing campaigns to the level of the individual within the market segment. EMA tools also provide a consistent, continuous representation of a value proposition across multiple channels. The field, the call center, the Web, and internal departments all see a single view of the customer due to the tight integration between the front office—the customer-facing part of the enterprise—and the back office—which controls functions such as human resources and finances. Enterprise marketing automation workflow allows all parties to see exactly what they are permitted to see in all marketing campaigns as they evolve. No one is left out of the loop, and no department is slighted in the process. Thus, mistakes can be minimized—a great advantage in a large corporation. Let's look at a brief example of how it might work.

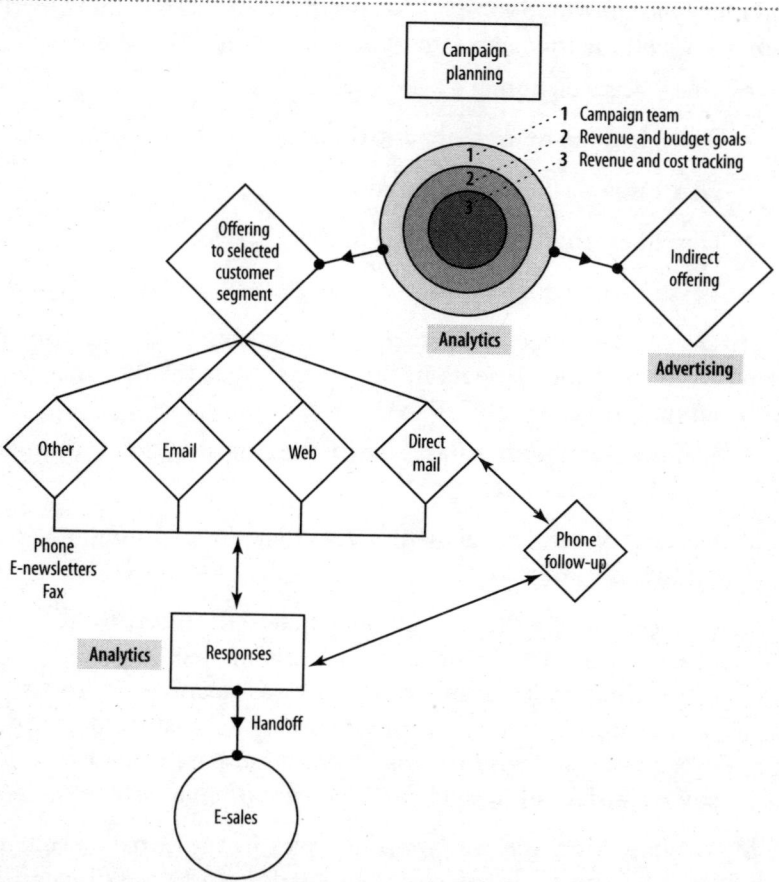

Figure 7-1: A campaign created with enterprise marketing automation tools

Case Study: United Airlines

United Airlines sent me a mailer that began with the following:

Dear Mr. Greenberg,

During the past year, you purchased and flew our expanded United service departing from Dulles airport and we appreciate your business. To thank you, we would like to give you an opportunity to earn free travel and save on United.

Earn double miles and save 15 percent on United.

This seemed short and simple. Not too much information. Not much until you realize that United Airlines has millions of customers and there was information that was specific to me based on my flying habits. To send me this, they had to determine the following:

- That I was a customer

- That I had flown on United Airlines within the last year

- That I was a Mileage Plus member

- That I flew frequently enough to merit the letter

- That I flew frequently from Washington, D.C.'s Dulles airport

This was sorted and extracted from tens of thousands of customers flying from multiple airports in the United States daily. Once that information was determined, they:

1. Identified me with a particular promotion that they thought would appeal to me.

2. Decided on the engagement media that United thought would capture my attention.

3. Using opt-in methods, they then stated "To receive additional offers, join the Mileage Plus email list by going to http://email.mileageplus.com." This was asking my permission in the United Airlines–Paul Greenberg courtship to go from direct mail first base to email list second base in exchange for some consideration, such as 15 percent off and double miles.

My mailing was made even more complex by the disparate systems that United, like most companies, has. In a perfect world, a customer data repository exists, the analytic tools have one place to go to extract the information, and the information has reporting tools that provide clearly readable reports with the thoroughly dissected data. Reality is otherwise. Often there are several systems in place—perhaps an enterprise resource planning (ERP) system, a data warehouse or several data marts, Web-based customer surveys and registration materials, email information, faxes, direct mail responses, and input data from the SFA application. The analytic tools have to capture all this information from sources, deposit it, extract the critical pieces, segment them, analyze them based on templates or customized criteria, and finally, present them in a reportable and useable format. From this, an e-marketing campaign is born.

Business Analytic Tools

EMA tools are distinguished from traditional marketing tools by their ability to capture, extract, and analyze customer information from multiple and often platform-independent sources and realize the results through the Web. This can mean emails, the Web, direct mailing, voice mail, faxes, and a myriad of other sources that may be indirect (such as magazine articles). EMA applications often cost a baseline of $250,000 and up. However, this becomes a reasonable price if you realize that the cost of acquiring a new customer can be 4 to 11 times the cost of maintaining an existing one. Good analytic software can not only reduce the cost of customer acquisition via targeted and segmented results, but can also identify those customers who are potentially going to take their business to your competitors. These tools have to be scalable, since the tools often sift through millions of customer transactions of varying sorts. They have to be rich so they can provide measurements and customization of the metrics to get the measurements. They have to be clear and distinct with reporting tools that provide you with the information you need to utilize the data it creates in a readable, understandable format. They also have to be fast, since they are dealing with millions of transactions from multiple sources in the course of Internet time. The tools interpret in-depth profiles of customers who are accessing websites, responding to emails, answering direct mail campaigns, and accessing what is called "customer touch points" in any way.

Touch points are either active or interactive nodes of customer communication. They are areas of customer interaction that are considered central to the success of any marketing effort. For example, Siebel eMarketing provides extensive prebuilt market, customer, product, and geographical analyses. The EMA analysis provides in-depth profiling information on customer preferences, buying behavior, revenue, profitability, and purchasing frequency. Successful analytical tools give organizations the view of data that lets them interpret, identify, and capitalize on emerging trends in key markets and focus their marketing and sales efforts on the high yielding market segments. The ultimate result of all of this is personalized customer information.

A market leader in EMA analytics, especially with its acquisition of real-time analytics champ RightPoint, is E.piphany. Let's look at what E.piphany's E.6 EMA analytics applications do:

> ▶ Analyze bookings, billings, and backlog information. This means revenue can be segmented by customized sets of criteria, which could be geographical or by industry segment.

- ▶ Leverage data from other CRM and SFA applications to improve sales forecasts, measure sales process metrics, and identify areas of sales focus.

- ▶ Evaluate e-commerce purchasing patterns and website effectiveness. This will allow the user to identify how successful their e-commerce initiative is.

- ▶ Monitor the effectiveness of your customer service agents and systems, such as the average cost and time to service requests and the profitability and effectiveness of individual call center representatives.

- ▶ Analyze your customer base for a clear understanding of customer preferences, buying behavior, loyalty, and profitability.

- ▶ Develop customer segments based on profitability and lifetime customer value, and link these to international, national, and regional marketing programs.

- ▶ Measure the effectiveness of indirect channel partners and programs, including distribution of sales, inventory trends, distributors' profit margins, distributors' sales by product line, and channel backlog trends.

As in any analytic application, this data has to be extracted from somewhere. The development of a data warehouse, such as SAP's Business Information Warehouse (BW), and the creation of data marts as customer repositories are becoming commonplace in the larger CRM implementations. Interestingly, companies like RightPoint, E.piphany's adopted child, developed the technology to extract the data from multiple sources regardless of platform in near real time, allowing for extraordinarily fine-tuned marketing analysis and segmentation.

So far, you've analyzed the data and sliced off your market segment. Using CRM for e-marketing campaign planning and development comes next. Much of this process is like traditional marketing, but the use of new media such as email and the Web makes it interesting. Interactivity, instant gratification (rather than waiting 6 to 12 weeks for a rebate, for example), and little work on the part of the consumer all become part of the equation.

EMA Components

In this section, we'll take a look at the components of the EMA engine and how this transitional mix of traditional marketing processes and contemporary delivery media is composed and how it is leading to new processes.

Promotions

Web or not, opt-in or opt-out, much of what marketing does is the same. Web-integrated marketing provides the same marketing goodies that consumers have always been interested in: promotions, sweepstakes, contests, giveaways, cross-selling of products, up-selling of products, and discount coupons. Loss leaders are still a lure. Buy.com has a model that calls for selling products for 5 percent *under* cost to lure a customer base. Their calculation is that they will gain long-term customer value through repeat customers over time and that the loyal customer base due to *other* things (such as excellent service and constant promotions) will stay loyal despite price increases later on. They are also advocates of permission marketing and marketing e-tools to monitor their sales deals.

Events

Various vendors have developed robust EMA event-management tools for capturing customer information through event registration and online interaction. The Web is the preferred e-marketing delivery mechanism. Registration for seminars, exhibitions, and so on is possible via the Internet. However, even more interesting are "webinars"—seminars that are actually conducted over the Web. I highly recommend one of a series of newsletters called *C.Biz*, by Robert Thompson, the high priest of partner relationship management (more on PRM in Chapter 9). The newsletter is sent in plain text format each week to your email address after you have given permission to do so by signing up on his website, http://www.crmguru.com/. Within the newsletter are embedded URLs for locations on the Web where you can register for a webcast on some future date. A Web-based registration form is filled out, and an email reminder is sent some time before the webcast. Make sure you have the proper tools—either a streaming video plug-in such as Real Player or Windows Media Player or a proprietary player that you download and install at the webcast site—and you're ready to watch either the live or prerecorded webinar. In the meantime, the sponsoring company has captured a qualified prospect—you! The registration page that you filled out on the corporate webcast sponsor's page is part of the e-marketing campaign management toolset, as is the newsletter you received from Mr. Thompson. The site and the newsletter also provide a valuable "opt-in" service by providing consideration for your help in a task. For example, if you give CRMGuru the names and emails of five potential subscribers, you will get an electronic book or a specially derived white paper on CRM or some other form of consideration for your help. This is an important and valuable tool. It is hard to emphasize enough the importance of giving some return consideration when you ask a customer to do something. The phrase "you scratch my back, I'll scratch yours" extends from CRM to contract law. It makes it more legally or psychologically binding if the customer accepts the consideration. It's hard to claim coercion if the customer is getting something they want in return for something the other party wants.

Other registration and lead management features provided by most of the EMA vendors include:

- ▶ Registration page with opt-in

- ▶ Unsubscribe (opt-out) capabilities

- ▶ User-controlled profile management

- ▶ Lead follow-up from tradeshows and similar venues

- ▶ Campaigns on tradeshow floor

- ▶ User group registration and follow-up

It doesn't seem like all that much, but the ability to opt-in and opt-out makes for a far more satisfied and amenable customer and provides the marginal edge a marketing professional needs to both acquire and retain this customer.

Loyalty and Retention Programs

Frederick Newell, in his book *loyalty.com*, states:

> ...we have seen firsthand the confusion that exists between trying to buy customer loyalty with points and discounts versus earning customer loyalty by providing value in ways that are meaningful to the individual customer in her or his terms. We have learned that you can't *buy* customer loyalty.

Very good point. A lot of EMA vendors try.

After all, customer loyalty is much more difficult to retain when all it takes is a different URL and a click or two to switch brands. Customers are constantly bombarded by the next great deal, and access to that deal no longer involves even a phone call or protracted arguments as to the wisdom of staying with the known quantity. Baby boomers and their children are used to easy acquisition of cheap thrills and expensive goods, with sensate gratification easily obtained in a booming economy. The 1980s were the era of free-spending Yuppies, and while they may not spend so freely any more, they have little sense of commitment to anything that's on the market. Even if the product is good, there is going to be a better new generation, something less expensive of the same caliber or simply something cooler very soon. "Here today, gone tomorrow" looks like the business mantra for the 21st century, unfortunately.

EMA applications build in those small, personalized touches that engender loyalty and retain customers (at least until the customer finds the next great deal). For example, Unica's Affinium Campaign Management, has templates for the following:

- ▶ Birthday greetings

- ▶ Holiday and special occasion reminders

- ▶ Delivery of gift ideas

- ▶ Welcome programs

- ▶ Points-based programs

- ▶ Win-back programs for inactive customers

Partner and Channel Management

Partner relationship management (PRM) is covered in detail in Chapter 9. Simplified versions of PRM are embedded into many EMA applications. These include features that incorporate targeted, joint marketing programs to promote both your business and your partner's. Some features are:

- ▶ Cross-sell of a company's complementary products

- ▶ Promotion of new versions or upgrades of a company's products

- ▶ Joint promotions with partners or affiliates

Needless to say, it is important that the partners have the same software.

Response Management

The campaign is in progress. You've had thousands of responses from the targeted markets to different offerings, and many leads have been handed off to sales. Additionally, you've put a series of surveys online so you can truly fine-tune your marketing during the course of this activity. There is a lot of data to look at. How does your e-marketing suite handle response management so you can analyze the data? More complete response management features include banner ads, direct mail, print ads, email, website links, surveys, event registration results, Internet registration, and online survey results.

Traditional response management is tedious, even with the use of computers. The time it takes for response gathering, analysis, and refinement is lengthy and costly, and often unsuccessful. As Figure 7-2 shows, you have to gather the responses from multiple sources manually and enter them into databases. Alternatively, you must store the information somewhere and then do the analysis. After the analysis, you need to work through plans to revamp the next campaign, since the response gathering was often completed after the campaign was completed. This is where EMA shines. Using the Internet as a tool that works in real time, what is now called "closed-loop feedback" has been integrated into the e-marketing toolbox.

Closed-loop feedback is the nucleus of Internet-based response management. At its best, it is response management in real time. It is the use of the Internet and the tools to compile, extract, and analyze information while the campaigns are in progress. It is the augmentation of those campaigns in midstream and the continuous repetition of that development. In other words, information is generating new activity, which is generating new information…*ad infinitum*, as Figure 7-3 illustrates. The time to gather and analyze information and respond to campaigns is notably shorter. The return on investment here is almost painfully obvious:

- Information gathering, extraction, and analysis time is dramatically reduced.

- Refinements to the campaign can be done in midstream, improving the possibility of return within the existing campaign. It is no longer a lesson learned for next time, but instead a chance for success while the original campaign is in progress.

- Automated tasks free up labor time for other marketing tasks that are not tedious or laborious.

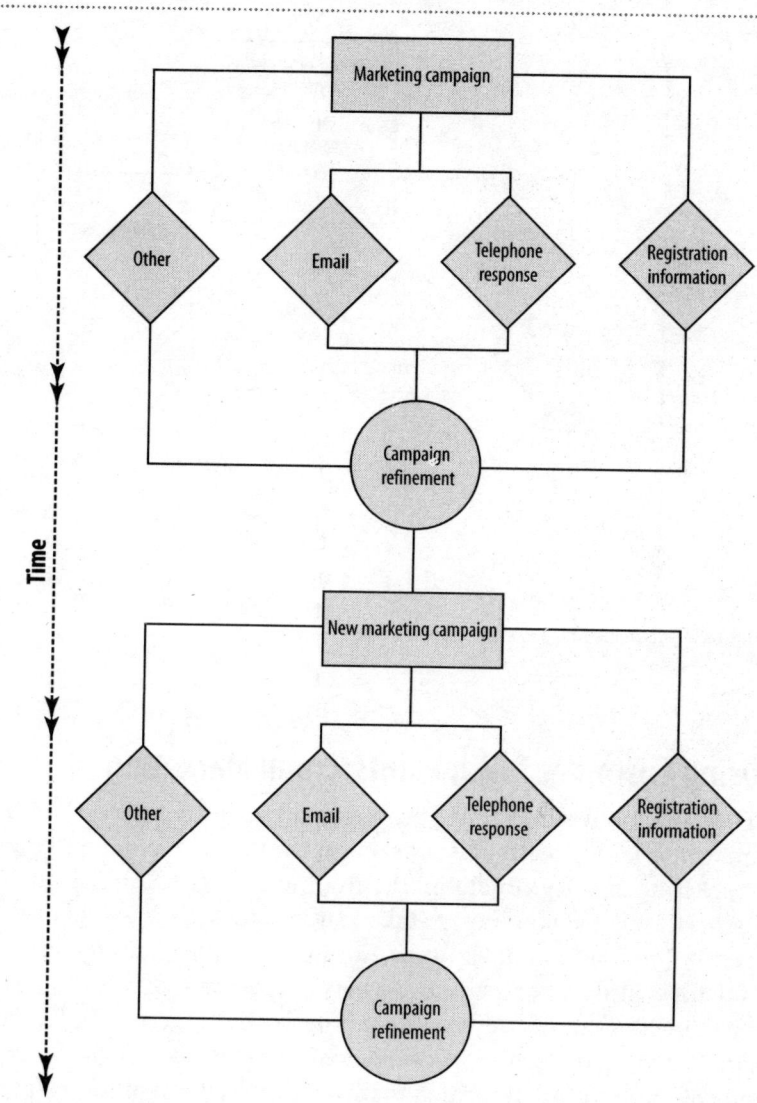

Figure 7-2: Traditional response management

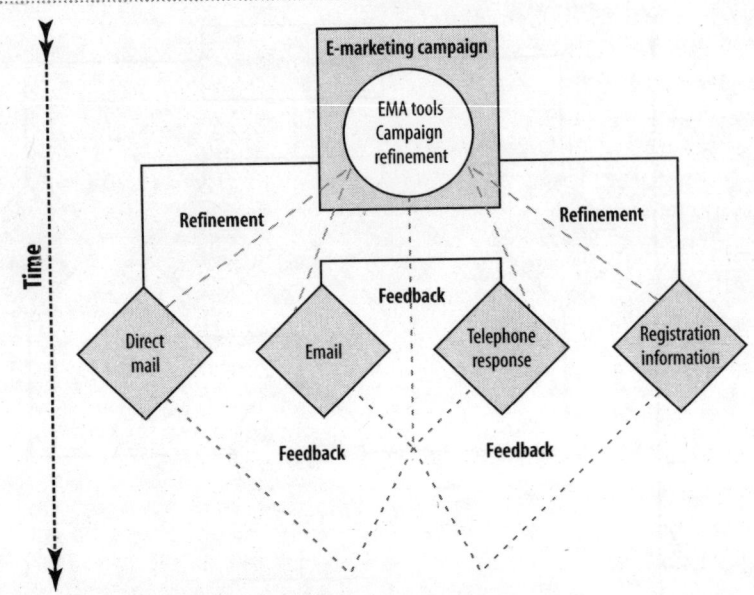

Figure 7-3: E-marketing and closed-loop feedback

Using Customer Touch Points: Email Marketing

This is a touchy subject. The problem with identifying email as a legitimate marketing method is the same as the problem of identifying telemarketing as a legitimate marketing method. It brings up such bad associations that you want to take a swing at whoever would even suggest it. I'm going to duck under the punch and explain it, even if I'm not advocating it here, because whether you use it or not is up to you. First, in 2001, according to a study done by IDC, there were 1.4 trillion emails sent and received in a single year. That is 1.4 *trillion*—every last one of them to you. It seemed that way, didn't it? Email is used grandly and in very high volume—a contention that your email inbox supports every single day. Not only that, but step out of your emotional response for a minute and think about it. How many emails in a given day do you get? How many business-related ones do you get? How many of them do you respond to in some way—maybe click on the URL that it provides for more information or to follow up on an offer? How many of them are interesting enough to read through? On the other hand, how many emails that call you by your first name and come from companies you never heard of who scramble the headers so you can't block them do you trash without reading beyond your first name? "A lot" is the answer to all these questions, isn't it?

Email marketing is valuable when it is targeted. It is intelligent when it is permission-based. It is a cost-effective advertising medium when it is opt-in email and not opt-out pushed email. It works best when it is part of an integrated package that is tied into other communications media. Well, that's a lot of geek speak. What does that really mean? Here's the scoop.

One of the more solid CRM consultants out there, Jay Curry, made a good point in a forum discussing email marketing: "Interesting mail is never junk." He referenced a study done in the Netherlands that involved a questionnaire that PTT and *Reader's Digest* jointly sponsored on customer interests. It was a half hour in length. The consideration returned was simple: We'll send you mail on your stated interests. PTT and *Reader's Digest* then went ahead and rented out the list at $.25 U.S. per name! Yet the response rate was high. In fact, in a study referenced by Siebel as they trumpet their eMail Response Management System, in 2001, there was an increase of 74 percent in customers contacting companies via email. Other notable facts: The response rate in email marketing is roughly 200 percent better than snail mail (the U.S. Postal Service way) and at a cost of 10 to 20 percent of the snail mail campaign (including the stamps). In other words, in a dispassionate sense, there is a great business benefit to using email to market. Yet, on the less dispassionate side, consumer reaction to unsolicited email is swift and brutal: "You're deleted, you filthy piece of spam!" That is the action taken by 77 percent of the spam receptacles (that is about all you can call us humans who get this stuff)—without even reading it. My personal percentage is probably a bit higher than that. If it is permission-based email, only 2 percent delete it without reading it. Those who remain curious enough to read it—permission-based 48 percent, spam-based 4 percent. I could go on, but the point is clear. Emails need to be permission-based, targeted, and well-managed. The results can be smashing. If they are unsolicited, broad, and not well-managed, the results can be smashed.

IMT recommends a very good 12-step process to make email marketing effective. The steps are:

1. Acquire names and email addresses via your normal means—website registration, from existing customer data store, and so on.

2. Analyze and plan an email campaign—this is where you are doing your targeting.

3. Develop creative and interesting (and targeted) email copy. This means not doing something like, "You'll win $50 and a chance at a new Ford Explorer, if you can answer these five football trivia questions, Paul Greenberg." Something tells me that one won't fly.

4. Send the emails out and check on the responses so that the list can be weeded because of changes of address, bounces, and opting-out of the permission-based campaign.

5. Respond to the emails that do get responded to via email or other channels depending on the response.

6. Make sure that there is an integrated campaign across touch points with a consistent message, if not a uniform one.

7. Work with partners and sponsored lists and others to reach prospects.

8. Store all the data gathered, new and updated, in a centralized data repository.

9. Integrate data from multiple customer touch points into this repository.

10. Clean and maintain lists—validate, filter.

11. Set up metrics to track and control the performance of the email campaigns.

12. Finally, make sure there are solid standards for permission and privacy and long-term benchmarks for things like ROI.

These are the basics of the well-planned email campaign, one that can hold the interest of the recipient. Keep in mind, we've been bombarded by emails for a long time and one of the problems that even a well-coordinated and permission-based campaign is going to run into is that there are a lot of poorly coordinated and interruption marketing-based email campaigns sending us emails, too and, honestly, when you are getting from dozens to hundreds a day, they all look alike. In fact by 2006, it is expected that each email user will be getting 1400 spam messages in that year. Nonetheless, it is a time-honored and honorable process. It is also well accepted. Total spending in 2001 on email marketing expenses in the United States stood over $1 billion, and that was expected to skyrocket to $9.4 billion by 2006, according to a study released in December 2001 by Jupiter Media Metrix. That is for list brokers, email networks, software, services, and agencies.

Siebel eMail Response: A Quick Look at a Typical Program

The Siebel eMail Response program is a good example of a sort of "classic" program of this type. It includes a Response Management System, multichannel integration, email voice with CTI integration services, web collaboration and chat-based unique features, integrated customer information, industry-specific functionality, inbound email management, multichannel routing and queuing, a unified knowledge base, email analysis and reporting, enterprise workflow, e-business application integration, and e-marketing integration. It works in a very obvious way. It will route inbound messages according to both provided and customized workflow and business rules. The workflow will allow for automatic escalation if the eMail requires it, down to a specific agent. In fact, it incorporates a self-learning technology by watching the deemed best agents respond to the messages. It will then auto respond to customer inquiries and auto suggest answers to agents. The workflow even provides for multichannel queuing according to customer type. It automates manual processes fairly easily by using a graphical interface that allows non-technical people to establish the means of automation. It has customizable, real-time reporting tools. Siebel eMail Response accepts requests in five different languages. In other words, it does its share and is representative of other similar programs.

Process Flow: EMA Campaign Implementation

You've now seen what the components of this powerful utilization of CRM are. Now we'll run through a sample generic EMA implementation and look at the strengths and some of the potential pitfalls. We'll use a fictional e-marketing campaign implementation, greatly simplified, using the Siebel eMarketing component of their eBusiness 2000 suite and a couple of the best-of-breed software products for particular tasks.

Case Study: AV Electronics

AV Electronics (a fictional company) realized they had to increase their market share, which was rapidly being taken over by Mitsubishi, Toshiba, Pioneer, and other consumer electronics giants. Jobs were at stake. Despite their introduction of an HDTV-ready line of televisions and one of the first progressive scan DVD players, their business had been flagging for months. The one jewel in the AV Electronics marketing crown was their very active business-to-consumer website, which had full-blown retail sales capacity. They had done about 15 percent of their total consumer electronics sales through this state-of-the-art site and managed their opportunities through the use of the Enterprise version of Siebel Sales.

They recently purchased and implemented several new e-marketing tools, including a new Siebel 2000 module, Siebel eMarketing, because it promised them the capacity to do multistep, multifaceted marketing campaigns that could be managed through the Internet and provide a single view of the customer to the entire company so that everyone was on the same (Web) page. All well and good, but they were by no means a sophisticated company when it came to information technology. A consultant who had been involved in several Siebel implementations began to guide them through the steps to successfully use the e-marketing module. AV Electronics had already implemented the sales module of Siebel months before.

Taking the First Steps

AV Electronics' first step was to form an e-marketing campaign team, consisting of the vice-president of marketing, two of his staff, and one person from the sales team. While this didn't constitute all the departments that would have to get involved, it included those who would identify what would best work with existing customers and with new prospects.

The campaign team was given customer data that had been gathered from multiple sources, such as website registration, trade shows, various AV Electronics–sponsored events, and customer purchase information. The information was analyzed by market segment through the use of Veridiem's MPI (Market Performance Indicator) tool so that market segments could be identified by profitability and potential return on investment and through other user-created criteria. This data had been extracted from a data mart that was provided by the core Siebel eMarketing product. After examining their data mart information, the campaign team came up with a proposal to experiment with various types of direct marketing campaigns. For the time being, they decided to scratch any indirect (advertising) offering to the general public. Their campaigns would have a decidedly experimental bent. They weren't sure which of the campaigns would be best for existing customers. They knew they had to get the state-of-the-art techno-junkies, who needed the latest and the greatest as it came out regardless of cost, as well as the customers who needed to improve the equipment they hadn't changed for five years. Additionally, they wanted to bring in the 21- to 27-year-olds who were just becoming moneyed, but were not quite affluent yet. Since the prices of DVD players and multichanger CD players had dropped through the floor in recent years, AV Electronics realized they could now engage this age group, who could now afford AVE's equipment. And Toshiba's. And Sony's. And Yamaha's. And Bose's Life System 3000, which looked really cool and played pretty well, too. Competition was vicious; AVE had to act. Using the eMarketing tools, the campaign team set the criteria for defining the characteristics of these groups. If the group names changed from department to department, the analytic tools would still automatically recognize the criteria, thus preserving the purity of the data and the results.

AVE modeled the campaigns they were going to use and set the models into the applications. There were two campaigns using two separate approaches. First, since the 21 to 27 age group was also pretty Web savvy, it would be easier to get them involved in Web-based promotions and purchases. A major Web giveaway was promoted, with five winners each getting the top-of-the-line AV Electronics complete home theater system. Registration pages were set up through the templates provided by Siebel eMarketing, with a checkbox that asked permission of the registrant to send further information on products. The checkbox had to be checked for this to occur (opting in). AVE had considered having the checkbox already checked so that unchecking would have to occur to *not* receive the information (opting out). The team decided that this was marginally intrusive for 21- to 27-year-olds feeling freedom for the first time.

There were also a number of customized features on the registration pages that were easily created through modifications to the Siebel eMarketing templates, using Microsoft's Web development tool, Front-Page. When the registrant completed the registration pages and clicked the Submit button, the data was parsed and stored by Siebel eMarketing in the data mart. When the data was stored, the registrant was then taken to a separate Web page where there were promotional 20 percent discounted pricing on DVD players and CD multichangers *and* three free DVDs or CDs of your choice from the various Columbia House video and music catalogs.

The second confirmed campaign was a targeted email campaign to existing customers who had purchased equipment in the last three years: 25 percent off on "upgrades" to the A/V equipment the customer owned and a trade-in of $100 or more on the original item, sight unseen. This was to be run through KANA Marketing and iCare Analytics, which could target the audience based on demographic profiles, recency, frequency, monetary value of past purchases, responses to previous campaigns, or any other information of value. KANA Marketing and iCare Analytics would send various targeted trial messages to different audiences. It would monitor the response rates and refine the personalized offers. What the AVE team particularly liked was that KANA Marketing and iCare Analytics could track the level of detail for each recipient down to whether they open messages, click links, make purchases, or use HTML or text as a format. AVE could proactively determine campaign-in-progress refinements. The control samples for these campaigns were randomly chosen by Siebel eMarketing.

The vice-president of marketing, as campaign team chief, then worked with the staff to decide on the revenue goals and budget and enter them into Siebel eMarketing. Once this was done, Siebel eMarketing would allow them to track the cost and revenues derived as the campaigns evolved.

Unfortunately, like every commercial institution, AVE had a chain of command and custody that had to be addressed when money is spent and personnel time is depleted. But, once again, the power of the Web prevailed over bureaucracy (to a point). Siebel eMarketing took the campaign budget and sent it to the finance staff associated with marketing budgets and got their "signature" approval with a date/time stamp. The promotions and contest efforts along with the appropriately attached marketing literature were then sent to the AVE legal department for approval, and within a month, the date/time stamp of approval appeared.

As soon as the legal date/time stamp appeared, the vice-president of marketing checked the Create Activity box in the Siebel eMarketing application. This launched the campaign and triggered a series of enterprise-wide permissions that allow anyone with the campaign-team-determined permissions to see the progress of the campaign (such as the email list and responses to the email via the Web or phone). It also allowed monitoring and tracking of the campaign, including status updates such as active, hold, or closed. It locked in the start and proposed end dates to see the timeliness of the offerings.

AVE didn't want to pass up any possible sales opportunities, so they set triggers at points of handoff to sales through the modularly connected Siebel eSales offering. For example, a former purchaser decides to upgrade his speakers because of the email offering. He goes to the website with the discount offer number and begins the purchase. Another screen pops up and offers him some further bargains. He takes one of them. This is a trigger point that will automatically gather his customer information and send it to a designated salesperson via Siebel eSales.

Getting Something Back for the Investment

But what kind of return on investment (ROI) does EMA give you? After all, these are not cheap implementations, in part or as a whole. A simple, nearly plain vanilla EMA implementation in a large company is likely to cost between $600,000 and $1 million for software and implementation partner services. The costs of e-marketing activities are likely to go up. For example, a study done in late 2000 by Forrester Research estimated that average email spending for companies engaged in email marketing campaigns was $240,000 in 1999 and would be $720,000 in 2004. Roughly 36 percent of those dollars were budgeted for customer acquisition and the rest for customer retention. The click-through rate was roughly averaged to 5.5 percent (with wide variances in the type of email sent), and the average cost per sale ranged from $2 for in-house lists to $465 per sale for sponsored email. This cost is in addition to software costs—product costs often exceed $100,000 and can be as high as seven figures—and ASP costs, which range from a low of $5,000 per month to a high of $40,000 per month. That's just for an email campaign! But the click-through rate, which is more or less equated with a direct mail response rate, is approximately 10 to 50 times the typical response rate for a mailer. Worth it? You have to decide that one.

The difficulty is that there are continuous debates on what constitutes ROI for *any* major information technology investment. One of the reasons for the ERP shakeout was the inability to define the ROI for that large capital expenditure. For example, SAP costs were as high as $100 million, and yet, no one had benchmarks for measuring the return. How would you feel if you were the VP who authorized the $100 million and then couldn't figure out how to measure your benefits?

Similar problems exist with EMA ROI. Marketing has always been a difficult parameter to measure. Its results tend to be measured with market share and mindshare, which are long term and not necessarily attributable to any one functional area. However, there are certain identifiable metrics. While we'll examine general CRM ROI elsewhere in the book, let's look at some of the specific measures of EMA effectiveness.

Customer lifetime value (CLV) CLV is a measurement of the expected cash flow, gross revenue, and margin contribution to revenue over the lifetime of an individual customer. Several available EMA tools build this measurement tool into their suite (for example, KANA iCare). For a detailed look at CLV, see the appendix.

Baseline marketing operations This measures the time and materials cost of customer acquisition. How does EMA reduce this expensive cost? Increase in the efficiencies of the marketing process, reduction in time of the marketing cycle, and reduction in cost per prospect-capture usually determine this.

Implementation costs When does EMA return the cost of an implementation that can be millions of dollars just for the e-marketing modules of more full-blooded CRM applications? This is usually ascertained by looking at the revenue upside—determining a better return per interaction or campaign.

Labor effectiveness Tedious jobs are automated, freeing the staff to do more important work. This means more use value for the dollars spent on salaries/compensation. The trivial work that is often part of the ordinary life of even highly paid employees is automated out of the cost of those dollars.

Unfortunately, EMA is far too new a segment of CRM to be considered an unqualified (or qualified) success. The efficiencies of Internet use are reasonably apparent, but there is no final answer yet.

The Players and the Products

As with all software offerings, particularly those associated with the Internet, there are too many EMA applications. In fact, this CRM subset is so complex that even Gartner Group has two categories for this domain—e-marketing and relationship management. The companies that I'm covering here are more on the "relationship management" side as vendors. But the e-marketing vendors are probably appropriate too. I'm going to briefly outline the two sectors and how they differ so you can wend your way through the complex strands, and I'll list the vendors in each, courtesy of Gartner's thinking. Get used to this. If you're involved in the CRM world, or any part of information technology, for that matter, what the analysts say, right or wrong, makes a huge difference to the companies that are public and that care. Gartner Group and META Group carry particular clout in the world of CRM. This section contains a sampling of the predominant EMA applications so you can get a feel for the marketplace scope and, if you're considering an EMA implementation, which merchant you might look to.

Unica

Two years ago, I didn't even know who these guys were. In fact, they aren't mentioned in the first edition of this book. Now, in 2002, Unica has been named in by *Intelligent Enterprise* magazine's list of "The Dozen," the top 12 IT solution providers that are most influential in the development of intelligent enterprise computing. They have been part of the Deloitte & Touche Fast 500, the *Inc.* Fast 500, the Crossroads 2002 A-List, and several others. They have appeared on the scene like gangbusters and seem to be the up and coming EMA golden crew.

The secret of their success? First, they have an excellent product that does pretty much all that it claims and is not hard on the user. One of the major CRM vendors did a study on all EMA applications and this one was the winner. It is also the first end-to-end product that exists in the ever-evolving world of EMA (or as Unica calls it, Enterprise Marketing Management). Product functionality, usability, integrity, and scope seem to be big reasons for their upsurge in 2001–2002. Second, they have been working on their products since 1992 and have a top flight management team, including their co-founder and CEO, Yuchun Lee, who has either won or been nominated pretty much for every entrepreneurial award out there over the last two or three years. They also have a really good marketing department. While you might ordinarily begrudge that, keep in mind what class of product we're talking about here. Enterprise *marketing* automation. It's a good idea for someone offering that kind of product to have good marketing, don't you think? They even publish white papers that aren't just marketing hype for their products, but have real substance. (Such as their "Maximizing Customer Value," by Jennifer Sullivan. To get it, go to http://www.unicacorp.com. You have to register on the site. Highly recommended.)

Unica has excellent products, substance, sharp management, a good business model, and very smart employees. I'm going to detail their products because they are representative of what a strong EMA product should look like.

Strategy

Unica's strategy begins with a world view that says CRM means many different things to many people. It means call centers to some and EMA to others—or perhaps both, or something entirely different. Each of these CRM markets has a separate collection of buyers that don't necessarily overlap. The Unica target is strictly the EMA market. Within that market, they are focused on a single type of buyer—either the CMO or other head of marketing or the head of the IT support of marketing. This doesn't mean a single type of user, only a single buyer. With the CMO or marketing VP as the buyer, an end-to-end platform is necessary, because that CMO is the strategic figure in the company. As Yuchun Lee said, "This is the pragmatic CRM viewpoint." They admirably achieved their mission with the creation of the Affinium EMA platform. They intend to be end-to-end and best-of-breed in EMA—clear, direct, and pragmatic.

What this has meant is 2000 percent growth over five years and 250 good-sized enterprise customers. In 2001, a year that dramatically hurt many companies, Unica grew their revenues 100 percent and remained cash flow positive.

They have a strong partner-focused strategy. The idea is that they can fill the holes that are there in EMA for larger multifunctional CRM companies. The quid pro quo is that they gain access to markets and customers they would otherwise not be able to reach. For example, they have a partnership with PeopleSoft, integrating their EMA with PeopleSoft's Enterprise Performance Management (EPM) Insight applications.

Culture

Unica's corporate culture is an accurate reflection of their product platform. They have a highly professional staff and management that think that each of the 110 employees is important and professional. While employees are held accountable and need to meet objectives, they are also trusted to meet them and not micromanaged. Unica is a strong advocate of customer service and active customer interaction.

Product

Affinium 4.0 is the current incarnation of the Unica product platform. It is a very user-friendly, intuitive EMA application that has highly integrated campaign management and analytics components. Unica places a very high premium on that user friendliness (provided, of course, the functionality and the engine are there) because you want normal people, not just technophiles, to be able to use the product that makes them do what they do better.

Unica's architecture is a hybrid client/server Web-enabled architecture. They tailor and scale it according to what the customer and they decide are mission-critical elements in the planning stages of the implementation. According to Yuchun Lee, the architecture allows them to deliver the right user interfaces for each role within marketing (such as the right interface for heavy-duty analytics versus the interface needed to create an email campaign). In addition, Web-based interfaces are based on XML style sheets so they can be easily reconfigured (not custom coded) to meet the needs of each individual organization. It also lets them work with the legacy systems of the customer and with the "silos" (an IT term for a narrowly focused application platform or set of applications that does only very specific things) that a customer already has in place. The architecture is even designed to integrate with their competitors. For example, if the customer has the SAS analytics platform already, the various Affinium modules such as Campaign or Interact could be integrated with the SAS offering. To do this, Unica uses a layer called Universal Dynamic Interconnect (UDI) that sits on top of the customer's data sources. So as long as Unica's Affinium modules can read the data, they can hook into it and it will work.

The Affinium platform scales—big-time. It can handle multiple terabytes of data and hundreds of millions of customers. That's a lot of power. Now, let's see how end-to-end it really is.

AFFINIUM PLAN

This is Unica's newest and strategic end-to-end piece—perhaps one of the more impressive EMA modules on the market. This is an actual automated strategic planning application that can handle strategic planning, program management, and project management. If it weren't focused on that single buyer—the CMO—it has such palpable use and features that it could compete and beat any other project management tool. This is a unique and important kind of application to have in an end-to-end EMA suite.

What makes this a powerful application is its ability to develop a plan, design programs that are appropriate to each plan, develop activities and metrics to see that the program is implemented, and create and monitor tasks to see that the activities are carried out. Its strength is due to a powerful embedded workflow. For example, the CMO can see how well or poorly a plan is working and drill down to the activities or tasks level to see why there are problems or what is making it work well. Additionally, using the strength of a flexible roles and permissions engine that characterizes good workflow products (Lotus Notes is a great example of that), simple or complex triggers can be set to notify various individuals automatically, either serially or in parallel, based on any number of conditions. For example, there could be a set of triggers that notifies the VP of marketing that a certain metric has been reached or not reached in a certain time period. He would be notified of either condition and then automatically asked to take certain actions that are based on the results that triggered the notification. The actions that the VP of marketing takes will then set another chain of consequences into action.

The other facet that makes this a unique and powerful offering is the patented analytics embedded in Plan that are focused on optimizing ROI. Plan's optimization identifies which projects, programs, or activities should be prioritized, and allocated resources—such as people, dollars, or even hardware such as computers—are constrained. Optimization allocates resources to deliver the best results (based on the company's priorities). Figure 7-4 should provide you with a good idea of what strategic EMA planning looks like in the world of CRM.

AFFINIUM CAMPAIGN

This is another strong offering with an awesome interface (see Figure 7-5). They have a very customer-friendly drag-and-drop graphical campaign builder—a fantastic feature. Customer segmentation can be done on the fly using this interface. You can not only do the segmentation analysis, but actually plan campaign strategies or define the tactical steps of that campaign by just dragging and dropping. There is a built-in simulation and optimization feature that allows the non-technical to do their testing of the campaigns you created. The techniques are based on statistically valid random samples. This is the kind of feature that can fix the problem before it becomes a problem. They have a patented One-to-One Optimization engine to allow customer behavior analysis at the individual level so that your campaigns can be done effectively and in a well-targeted fashion. You can schedule the rollout of the campaign, execute various campaign "events" using that ever-present workflow trigger, act in real-time response to varying campaign results from purchases (the happy result) to abandoned shopping carts (the sad result). Each promotion planned and executed can be individually tracked with results posted to whatever repository you choose. In other words, you really can plan a marketing campaign with this application—even if you're not a technical guy, but just a marketing professional! Of course, it integrates with other Affinium modules.

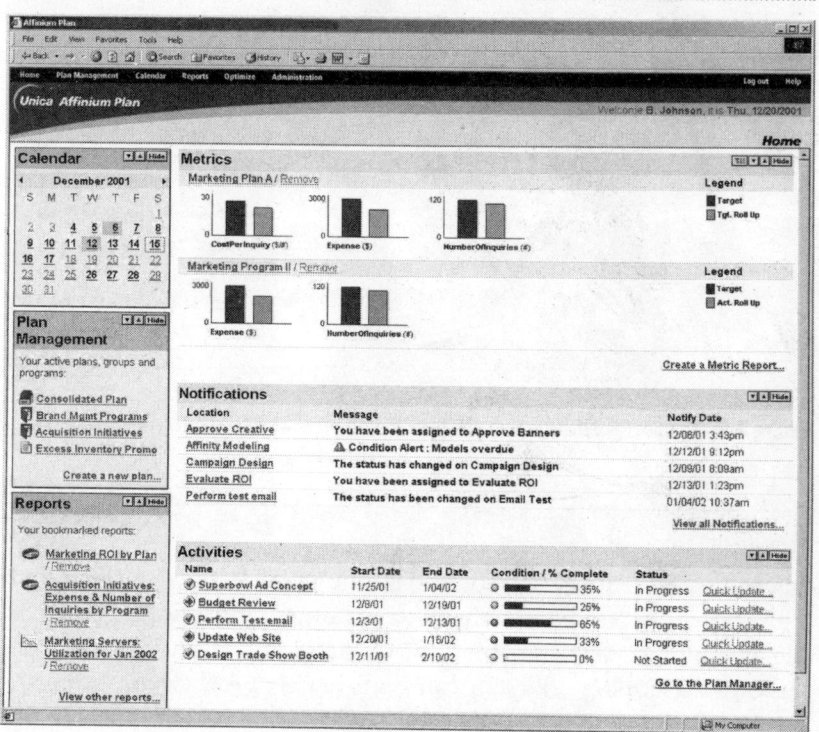

Figure 7-4: The high-level Affinium Plan screen (Copyright 2002, Unica Corp. All rights reserved.)

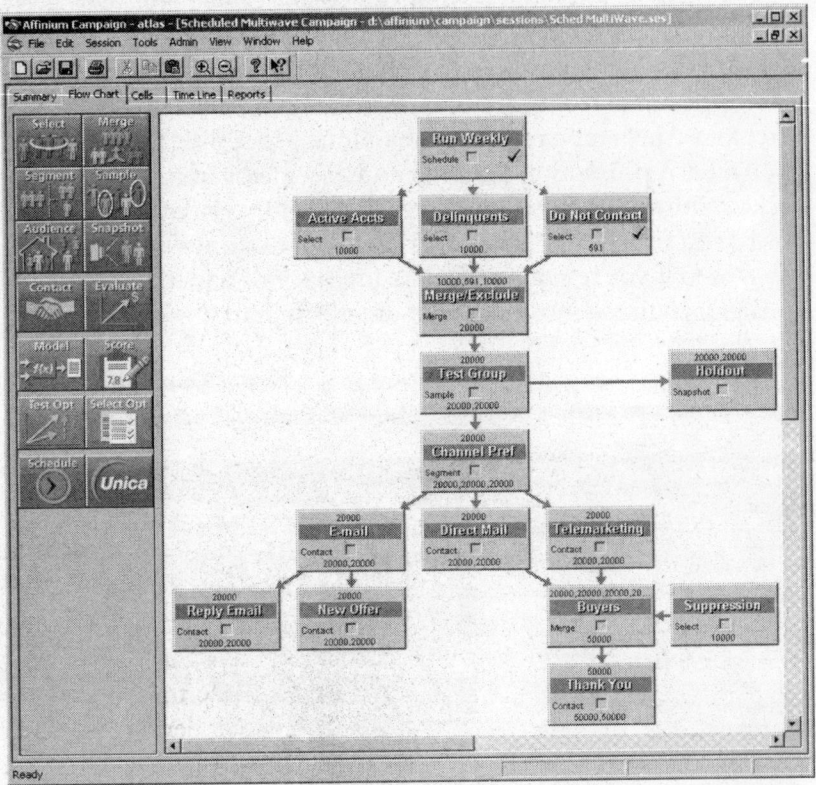

Figure 7-5: Affinium customized campaign page (Copyright 2002, Unica Corp. All rights reserved.)

AFFINIUM INTERACT

Interact is a real-time online personalization tool. It uses data from multiple sources to create individualized customer interactions. For example, it can grab your customer's history and in conjunction with this customer shopping online, it can immediately produce an "opportunity" to cross-sell or up-sell specific products that would appeal to this active customer. It is also gathering data in real-time as the customer is shopping. A good infinite loop. It takes into account such things as RFM variables, customer value, response probability, transaction history, behavior segment, and preferences. It can apply customer-segmented or demographic information to the customer-specific information to produce these opportunities. You can personalize the interaction in as much detail and as individually focused as you want.

The architecture is an open XML architecture that supports all the Internet interfaces you could imagine: HTTP, COM, CORBA, Enterprise Java Beans, Java, and so on. It uses UDI to access data from other sources.

Affinium eMessage

What I call email marketing, Unica calls "personalized one to one marketing." Affinium eMessage is an email marketing package that utilizes personal customer data to set up individualized email campaigns. While you may ask, why not just send an email to the customer, it becomes a bit of a problem when "the customer" is 15 million individuals. An email marketing campaign will generate appropriate automatic emails based on customer demographic, purchase, or similar history. If a customer went to Barnes and Noble in Manassas, Virginia, and bought a CRM book, and then went online and bought ERP books from Barnesandnoble.com, that unique combination of customer data might result in, "Since Paul Greenberg has written on CRM and ERP in the past, this customer would be interested in Paul Greenberg's books. Let's send this customer an email that says, if you buy a Paul Greenberg book title within the next 30 days, you can get 30 percent off the published price." eMessage lets you do that and actually adds real-time response to the feature set. Upon ordering the book online, it is possible to generate the email to the customer immediately, thanking them for their order and providing this great discount for the interesting books.

Another useful and interesting feature of eMessage is the ability to provide content so highly personalized it can include not just cross- and up-selling opportunities, but personalized news and features (links to white papers of interest, for example). It's almost like getting your own emailed mini-portal.

Affinium Model

Unica made its initial splash in the analytics side of marketing, so their offering is very strong here. It has four components that are a good representative breakdown of customer-based analytics:

Customer Valuator This is a predictive model for Customer Lifetime Value (CLV). Working automatically, using rather complex algorithms, it will predict the monetary value and profitability of any single customer or group of customers over a chosen time frame. The benefits of that are obvious, given the 80/20 percent rule of thumb that operates in the business world (20 percent of your customers are responsible for 80 percent of your revenues, or some variant of this).

Market Segmenter/Profiler This determines specific attributes that can be used to segment customers into groups—geography, age, high rollers versus lowballers, and so on. It then uses chosen and identified common characteristics to create what Unica calls "customer clusters." This information will be used to create profiles that can identify common buying characteristics—or "not-buying" characteristics if you prefer.

Response Modeler This drills the customer cluster down to individual levels so that singular customer behavior can be determined. From the models that are developed, what-if scenarios can be run. For example, given that John Smith loves those ERP and CRM books, what if we offered a 15 percent discount, or 15 percent discount on the first Paul Greenberg book and 20 percent on every book thereafter? What would be the likelihood of his purchase of Paul Greenberg titles or the likelihood of his purchase of other titles in that genre? Is he likely to purchase a book on enterprise applications that discusses both front and back office? That is what Response Modeler does. It "what ifs" a probability of result. There's no guarantee of 100 percent accuracy, but it can improve your odds. It works closely with Cross Seller.

Cross Seller This works closely in conjunction with Response Modeler to determine what items that would be the right ones for the individual customer given the customer behavior that the individual has exhibited.

For more on analytics and how the engine works, see Chapter 8.

AFFINIUM REPORT

This product is a strong version of what is typical and necessary in EMA products. Good reporting tools have been discussed generally throughout the book, so I won't repeat that feature information here. Suffice it to say, with good reporting, what you need to know in a form that you can understand is at your fingertips. Flexibility is a big issue in the reporting world—how easy it is to set up a report you want and how much of that is done out-of-the-box.

Affinium Report is a comprehensive Web-based "marketing dashboard" for access to status and results of corporate marketing initiatives, which can be subscription-based. The report tools include a fair number of reports out of the box and a strong, flexible report designer and server using plain vanilla business intelligence technology that is made available to companies that don't use other BI technologies. That is an added plus, not often provided. The BI and the server, in combination with the dashboard, control distribution of these multiple reports, with security and scheduling built in.

Future

Unica's Affinium Suite is as good as EMA gets. Unica's management is smart and competitive, without being vicious in the slightest. They represent the high end of the EMA marketplace and the only complete product that exists in the niche or even among the largest enterprise players. The only glitch in their future is the perceived value of EMA. If the EMA marketplace grows, they can potentially lead that marketplace.

Their website: http://www.unicacorp.com/.

Chordiant

Chordiant is an interesting and successful company. This 430-person (2001 number) company pulled in $75 million in 2001, with $56 million in the bank at the end of the year. According to a 2001 Hewson Group study, they owned a half percent share of the CRM market in 2000 and were projected to double that plus a little by the end of 2001. That's really good for a niche company. They have been a serious, recognized player in the EMA world since their foundation and were successful enough to go public in February 2000. Over the past several years, they have established strong roots in vertical EMA, with positioning in the financial services, telecommunications, and travel industries in particular. Their client list especially supports the financial services vertical market—DeutscheBank, Royal Bank of Scotland, Credit Suisse Group, and 150 other Global 1000 customers.

At the end of 2001, Chordiant added two major players to their management team to try to establish a fully dominant position in vertical EMA and carve out a serious place in the oft-neglected interactive selling space. They hired Jeremy Coote, former president of SAP and general manager of Siebel Systems. They went on to add Paul Burrin, previously the senior vice-president of marketing at Oracle. They also added to their vertical thrust by beginning an insurance initiative.

In March 2001, they bought PrimeResponse, a good move to integrate the Prime@Vantage, though by no means seamless. Realizing that what makes EMA unique is the multichannel approach and the real-time workflow and analysis, in June 2001 they signed a joint development agreement with Hipbone to integrate Hipbone's collaborative browsing software. At the end of 2001, they embedded business rules into their EMA suite. They didn't stop there. On April 1, 2002, they announced the acquisition of Partner Relationship Management OnDemand for cash, adding PRM to their Chordiant 5 application suite. While you may not see them in Chapter 14 as an up-and-coming multi-function leader, that's only because I'm saying it here.

Unlike many companies, their license and services revenues run about 50–50. Normally these days, service revenue outdoes license revenue by up to a two to one ratio. Oracle will even give its licenses away to get the service revenue for a CRM implementation. This makes the Chordiant ratios all the more interesting.

Products

Chordiant's aim at the Global 1000 market hits clients with pretty challenging environments for e-selling and e-servicing, due to the complex procurement processes and sales closings and the higher average monetary value of such transactions. They deliver what their marketing calls the Intelligent Customer Interaction Management (ICIM) platform. This is their enterprise framework. Their architecture announced in mid-2001 for release in the fourth quarter of that year is JX, a Java 2 Enterprise Edition (J2EE), XML-compliant Web architecture that supports Bea Weblogic and IBM WebSphere.

Their product, Marketing Director, is the former Prime Response Prime@Vantage mentioned above. The real-time version is Online Marketing Director and the mobile version is Mobile Marketing Director. If you're looking for the large enterprise EMA application, this one can scale to 100 million records in a single customer database. It can not only store, manage, and use those records to develop campaigns, it can then work through your cellphone with Mobile Marketing Director's support for SMS (Short Messaging Service, those little text messages you see on your phone).

Chordiant is expensive, with average implementations costing between $1.5 million and $3 million. They expect over a three to five year period the customer will spend about $10 million on Chordiant-related products and services. For this high fee, they claim an ROI that turns around in three weeks to a year. This is a strong offering, especially in the vertical space.

Their website: http://www.chordiant.com/.

SAS

This is a great company that produces extremely strong products on the analytic side. They have recently ventured in the EMA space with a good deal of success because of the strength of their analytic offering. This very friendly company, officially SAS Institute, prefers to be called simply SAS because of an (untrue) historic image as a nearly academic institution. In 2000, they purchased campaign management vendor Intrinsic to give them the campaign management functionality basics they needed to develop what has become SAS Marketing Automation. They have a strong analytic focus with their campaign management tools. These tools are heavily aimed at results and analysis, and depend a good deal on predictive modeling to prepare marketing campaigns. They can pull lists, generate customized email and direct mail materials, and track results. Additional tasks include:

- ▶ Selecting, screening, and filtering internal and purchased contact lists to produce clean, nonduplicated target lists, without reliance on the IT group.

- ▶ Coordinating and optimizing outbound and inbound communications, along with external partners such as direct mail houses or agencies, over multiple channels for hundreds of thousands or hundreds of millions of customers.

- ▶ Creating, delivering, and tracking high-volume, opt-in, personalized email messages.

- ▶ Tracking "hard" responses (purchase decisions) and "soft" responses (subtle changes or trends in user behavior) that are captured through conventional channels or varying electronic channels.

- ▶ Providing automatic updates to the central customer data warehouse of customer contact history, response tracking, and analytical processes.

This is an excellent tool for high transaction levels and comprehensive analyses of marketing information. You can plan in detail.

Their website: http://www.sas.com/.

Xchange

Depending on whom you believe, Xchange remains a market leader or is losing its position as a market leader in 2001–2002. In the beginning of 2002, their stock price was at 27 cents a share, but despite that extremely dangerous price, Xchange secured over $20 million in funding in late 2001. That of course doesn't have much to do with the strength of their product, only the strength of their market position. The Hewson Group indicated that Xchange had almost 1 percent of the CRM market in 2000. They retained that percentage hold on the market by year end 2001. Their strategy seems to be to move globally and vertically simultaneously, each of which is a major effort, much less both. One example of the vertical strategy is their alliance with DWL to deliver insurance, consumer products industry, and retail services solutions. But with that has come strong customer relationships, including a major win with Citigroup in November 2001 to use their analytic tools to determine the most profitable customers and to use their e-messaging application to automate responses to customer inquiries.

Products

This is one expensive product. The Xchange 8 product suite starts at $475,000 and goes up from there. However, it is a robust, wide-ranging product suite that has a good history with its customers. The Xchange claim is that a $600,000 investment in their product results in a $12 million average incremental revenue. What does that mean? Not sure, really.

Beyond the typical multichannel campaign management functionality that Xchange 8 provides, its unique offering is their Value in Play analytics. Value in Play pulls data from disparate applications such as sales force automation, call center, ATM, and online customer service apps to determine the value of any customer. The software calculates the cost of interacting with the customer and subtracts that from the amount of money the customer has spent on products. It then can make recommendations on what to do in the immediate time frame with that customer, such as cross-selling a certain product based on past purchasing habits and specific inquiries made to the call center. It even recommends firing a customer! The more polite term is "customer attrition."

Their eMessaging ASP application is also promising. It lets sales staff communicate with customers in both serial and real time. There is enhanced Java 2 Enterprise Edition support and support for IBM's MQSeries and the omniscient, omnipresent IBM WebSphere.

Some analysts say the real-time Value in Play analytics give Xchange an advantage over other EMA players. I'm not sure of that. Even if that is the case, we'll see how the finances of the company fare in 2002.

Their website: http://www.xchange.com/.

The Players and the Products—Part and Parcel

EMA is peculiar. Unlike SFA, it is better known as a niche market that has retained or evolved independent players. But at the same time, like SFA, the enterprise multifunction crowd has its own modules built into its own suites, which in most cases don't have the pure usability or functionality of the independents. In fact, often, when they are wise, the 800- and 600-pound gorillas and orangutans of the CRM world will either ally with the independent or buy the independent. That said, several Sand-box Playmates (the phrase I've coined for the vendors I consider to be the best of the best, which are discussed in Chapter 14) do have their strong EMA modules. Other vendors include NCR (also known as Teradata CRM), MarketFirst, and Protagona. All have first-rate products, and some have really sound corporate vision, particularly Protagona.

KANA Corporation

KANA is a conglomeration of companies rolled into a single entity. It is Silknet, Rubric, ServiceSoft, and, as of June 2001, the most significant is Broadbase. It has had a series of product changes over the last two years that finally seem to have settled on KANA iCare, a product strong in marketing and analytics, especially with the acquisition of Broadbase. KANA has released a J2EE-compliant Web architecture. However, the KANA iCare product in conjunction with KANA's general approach to the world seems to be gaining ground. In November 2001, they came close to a delisting level with a $.92 stock price. I wish I had bought it then because by January 2002, they were at $19 plus. That leap portends 2002 promise, and plenty.

Product

iCare is their product, and in the EMA world, it is a player—a serious powerful product with a high ticket price, as with most of this particular CRM segment. It provides good integration capabilities out of the box with prebuilt interfaces to Web, CRM, and ERP software such as People-Soft. This means data gets into shape quicker and easier. There are more than 100 prepackaged best-practices-based analytics and metrics to help develop targeted programs. It has automated suggestions for promotions, cross-selling, and up-selling based on customer profiles, histories, demographics, and behavior. It has a sophisticated query engine that is SQL-free. It does testing so that the appropriate segments and lists are created and targeted. It creates campaigns for any communications channel and personalizes the campaigns. It handles customer response in real time. It integrates with KANA Response, their inbound email management program (they started in 1996 with just this). The workflow is sound, the update engine works, and triggers are effective. You can measure your results in multiple ways and through multiple channels. In other words, this is the real deal and something that will provide a true option for the more sophisticated EMA customers. More on them in Chapter 14.

E.piphany, Inc.

Of the Sandbox Playmates, this one is the EMA champ. Their EMA product rocks as part of a multifunction suite. In fact, as you will see in Chapter 14, they have consolidated their position as a leader well beyond last year. When they came into the CRM world, it was as a CRM analytics contender. They quickly established themselves as the EMA market leaders, strengthened their offerings in EMA, and began to produce other more diversified modules. In 1999–2000, they went on an acquisition binge, purchasing Octane and RightPoint to address a market that is sometimes called Internet relationship management (IRM). Analysts said that with their acquisitions and their strategic alliances with partners like PricewaterhouseCoopers, E.piphany was poised to become a true market powerhouse. In mid-2000, KPMG committed to 300 consultants trained in E.piphany. In 2001, they strengthened their management team and, despite the global economic angst, still consolidated their position by releasing their E.piphany E.5 suite with Real Time technology and self-learning analytics. That ball keeps rolling through 2002 with the release of E.piphany E.6.

The now superseded E.piphany E.5 system was listed as the only leader among 16 vendors in Gartner's E-Marketing Magic Quadrant study released on October 11, 2001. The company was also positioned in the leadership quadrant in Gartner's Relationship Optimization Quadrant report released on October 8, 2001. Both reports note the critical value of marketing as applied in customer sales and service interactions among, especially, the larger businesses.

According to Gartner, vendors evaluated in the E-Marketing Magic Quadrant can fall into one of four categories: Leaders, Challengers,

Visionaries, and Niche Players. E.piphany was the sole leader in the Leaders quadrant, based on its ability to execute and completeness of vision. The report states, "E-marketing will continue to be a key enabler of an enterprise's overall marketing effort; however, it is becoming part of an overall CRM solution. To optimize the benefits of e-marketing functionality, winning enterprises must address those efforts in the broader context of an overall CRM implementation." (Gartner Research Note: M-14-3136: "Gartner Introduces Its E-Marketing Magic Quadrant," A. Sarner, W. Janowski.) The value of how something stands in the Magic Quadrant is a matter of debate, but what it does do is establish E.piphany's clear market leadership, which I do agree with.

As the market grows and more focus is placed on the value of marketing integrated to the requirements in customer sales and service interactions, E.piphany has a real shot at expanding its market position with its new E.6 product suite. Furthermore, Gartner estimates that through 2002, enterprises leveraging e-marketing data into collective customer repositories will be 40 percent more effective in targeting profitable customers and quality prospects than competitors that do not take advantage of data from their electronic channels. (Gartner Research Note: M-13-3675: "This Is the Best Time for E-Marketing," A. Sarner.) That gives the E.6 EMA products a good leg up on the market, given their success in interaction integration.

Products

I'll cover E.piphany and the differentiators in E.piphany's products in Chapter 14. I'll focus on their two major EMA products here. Their core product is the E.6 suite, released at the end of March 2002.

CAMPAIGN MANAGEMENT

E.6 covers two areas of campaign management: e-commerce and email. They are markedly different in functionality, with e-commerce working with segmentation data such demographics, click-stream, transactional behavior, and scoring time. Needless to say, this data flows to the analytic engine that E.piphany built its reputation on. The current incarnation has strengthened the OLAP and data mining capacity and tightly integrates it to the campaign management application. They use "drill anywhere" reporting and charting to allow marketing pros to find data that they need to design a campaign no matter where on the screen they happen to be at the given moment. The E.6 campaign management module has strong event-triggered, multiwave, and single-shot planning features and functions. What makes it nice is that it uses a graphical tree, arranged logically and easy to read. You can do campaign planning or market segmentation from this tree. You can incorporate business rules and what are called "suppression lists"(filters that eliminate certain messages from certain customers). There is a strong emphasis on permission marketing, with opt-in and opt-out features readily available for campaign creation. For email, the functions are more toward permission-based campaigns that involve capturing information, which can be opt-out rates, click-through rates, and delivery success or failure. E.6 is also able to send personalized email messages through data that is captured and analyzed. Campaigns can be changed on the fly. Results can be analyzed, monitored, tracked, and used to make these changes—all in real time.

There is a separate subproduct called Campaign Management for E-Mail, providing the same services for email marketing campaigns. This is a highly sophisticated product that is excellent for enterprise-level EMA or the upper end of the midmarket. It is also a highly respected product even among its rivals.

REAL-TIME PERSONALIZATION

This is a multichannel capture engine that can make dynamic changes to personal profiles and issue dynamic, flexible responses. It grabs information from click-stream data, customer databases, transaction systems, third-party data, and other sources. The principles that govern this application follow a concept that E.piphany calls Get, Keep, and Grow. It is obvious enough to not need explanation. The idea of the entire application is that there is real-time interaction with an individual customer across multiple customer touch points. What is amazing about this—and something that must always be considered—is the speed at which the engine can deliver a result. We are into the milliseconds range for the results. That has substantial implications. The number of lost opportunities is reduced because there is a proposal to the individual customer on the table almost instantly. The TCO of the campaign and the various materials behind it are reduced because the amount of time producing an individual result that could lead to success is reduced. The wear and tear on a system is reduced. The ultimate result is also a potentially shorter time to a true ROI. In other words, there is a good deal of benefit for a fast engine. Because this happens so quickly, the customer is not waiting for a result, either. His offer is instantaneous, even though a very sophisticated set of processes was executed to identify the best offer for that particular customer. There is a very fast real-time profile being built of the customer. The engine runs a series of "what if" scenarios to see what the likelihood of acceptance of different offers is and then spits out the best offer at the best time. As the customer accepts or declines offers, the system engages in a little self-learning and dynamically adjusts, thus strengthening the likelihood of future offer success.

To do all this takes some serious hardware firepower. There are hundreds of thousands and even millions of decisions in real time occurring every hour. Personalization servers are often symmetrical multiprocessors so there is sufficient speed and scale to handle the incredible volume of transactions being processed in an hour.

If you have a huge customer base, E.piphany might be a heck of a good choice.

Their website: http://www.epiphany.com/.

PeopleSoft

PeopleSoft bought Annuncio in early 2002 to strengthen their EMA offering. That they did. Annuncio has been an EMA market leader since its founding in 1998, though by 2001 they had lost a good deal of their market share to Chordiant and E.piphany and a couple of other EMA vendors, making them a great choice for acquisition. Their products remained very good, regardless of the market setbacks. Annuncio initially gained a significant foothold in the marketing automation world, with a good-sized chunk of EMA mindshare. In mid-2000, they followed what might seem to be a logical step and announced that they had developed a service offering for independent marketing and advertising agencies, marketing consultants, and interactive integrators to provide not only their Web-integrated software, but also marketing strategy services to give these agencies end-to-end coverage. Annuncio's strategy was questionable, but the products aren't at all. In fact, it is likely that PeopleSoft, if it folds the functionality of Annuncio Live and Annuncio Bright into its CRM 8.0 architecture, will have the same success as they did with their purchase of Vantive in 2000.

Products

PeopleSoft bought two products. There is Annuncio Live, its variation Annuncio Live B to B (business to business), and Annuncio Bright. As a whole, they are an e-Marketing Platform. At the end of 2001, they partnered with MicroStrategy to incorporate MicroStrategy's excellent business intelligence platform, MicroStrategy 7, into their Annuncio Bright. This dramatically strengthened their personalization capabilities (see Chapter 8 for more on analytics and personalization), giving Annuncio e-Marketing Platform the ability to discover and analyze customer preferences, response histories, purchase histories, and other CRM-based data from multiple other applications, data marts, data warehouses, and customer touch points. What PeopleSoft will do with this is unknown at the time of publication of this book.

Generally, Annuncio Live and Annuncio Live B to B handle the campaign management for customers. The approach they take is "traditional" (if that's possible in such a young industry), and includes:

▶ Applications that handle customer segmentation so that personalized emails and other media can be sent

▶ Dynamic Web content so that specific offers can be tendered to a customer based on Web surveys and profiles in an interactive environment

▶ Customer profiles and analysis and real-time testing of the campaigns

That, in a nutshell, is Annuncio Live, with the B to B variant focused on companies that do business with other companies.

Annuncio Bright, the result of the purchase of Bright Info Solutions prior to the PeopleSoft acquisition, is a product for the creation of personalized marketing campaigns on the Web, with more than 30 templates for out-of-the-box shopping sites among other things. What makes this an excellent product is that marketing folks can develop the content themselves. The technology is transparent and simple.

With the acquisition of Annuncio, PeopleSoft places itself squarely in the realm of EMA powerhouses and completely fills a hole in their enterprise application suite as they drive toward being the best-of-breed front and back office.

SAP

SAP entered the CRM world significantly in 2001, thanks to about 10,000 possible customers in the SAP installed customer base. They released their MySAP CRM 3.0 product, aimed at their installed base, and by year-end 2001 were projected by the Hewson Group to grab a 6.6 percent market share, making them third to Siebel and PeopleSoft. A major splash. They are now a major CRM leader and will be discussed in detail in Chapter 14.

Products

MySAP CRM Marketing is their EMA flagship. It is tightly integrated with the rest of the MySAP CRM 3.0 offering. What is interesting is that it can draw on the power of the total MySAP enterprise offering to strengthen itself as a specialized part of the offering. It has the standard modular components, campaign management, and e-marketing— their mass email marketing application and marketing analytics. But also included in the offering is telemarketing that uses specialized marketing analytics to qualify leads. It also can manage call lists and monitor campaign progress for the telemarketing person. Within the structure of the EMA offering there is also lead management for sales opportunities that arise through marketing, as well as monitoring the success or failure of the lead generation and distribution, through the "closed loop" structure.

The other very interesting facet of the EMA product is the MySAP Enterprise Portal. The portal is customized and role based, with strong security functions. Thus every view through the portal is individual. These portals are a standard part of the entire MySAP initiative.

What all of this points to is a very strong focus on the sales side of marketing and a product that is profoundly tied to other MySAP components. The benefits of tight integration are obvious. When it works the transparency is fabulous. With SAP aiming initially at its many thousands of installed base customers, this could well be their way to go.

Siebel Systems

Siebel is mentioned in almost every chapter of this book and, in fact, is the giant of the CRM world. Like it or not, they get on the stage in this chapter on EMA, too. With the release of Siebel 7.0 in late 2001, Siebel eMarketing received a makeover—enough to be called a glamour shot. This makeover included adding a whole new module called Siebel eEvents, which can handle the planning, creation, and coordination of multiple seminars, trade shows, and conferences. The module is comprehensive and may even be unique to EMA. Additionally, the analytics have been enhanced to some degree, though Siebel still is weak on the analytics side throughout its applications, compared to its rivals in the marketplace. Their 2001 acquisition of NQuire might be just what's needed to alleviate that, but as of mid-2002, it is still too early to tell. Siebel eMarketing is an internally developed module that is integrated with the marketing encyclopedia of Paragren, a company purchased by Siebel in early 2000, and is well integrated with the other multiple Siebel modules.

Siebel eMarketing software delivers personalized promotions and communications with customers through email and the Web, as well as tools for developing and delivering marketing information and analyzing interaction with customers and marketing campaigns. It is not as sophisticated as many of its competitors, though it certainly is adequate. If you have a Siebel CRM implementation, the integration alone makes it the EMA application of choice for you. Otherwise, there are multiple players that can provide more for either less or the same cost. However, in a couple of years, I might not be able to say that. Let it suffice for now.

Their website: http://www.siebel.com/.

Oracle

Oracle plays hard and is big in the CRM world through its Oracle Applications CRM in 90 Days suite. But their e-marketing applications, done in 90 days or not, don't carry the weight of the other major players. As is puzzling about much of Oracle's strategy, the e-marketing applications seem to be there to sell either other Oracle applications or services. They are strongly connected to the Oracle Sales components of their CRM suite. They sit low in the relationship marketing and e-marketing Gartner quadrants but high in the "aggressive marketing to the potential customer" world. Yet, one can never count out Oracle.

8

Analytics and Personalization

One thing about customers, no matter how you define them: They like being treated like kings and queens. What this means in the age of CRM is personalization—the art and science of creating a unique experience for every individual customer. For example, if I enter a portal for higher education, my class schedule, my financial records, my campus programs, eligibility for awards, access to my particular counselor, and other appropriate information sit on the desktop for me to access. If I were a different student, different options of the same sort might appear. If I were an administrator, entirely different categories relating to appropriate functions would appear, and so on. This is personalization. While this is pretty straightforward, what it takes to create that personal experience is an intricate set of highly complex algorithms. It could take from one to dozens to make the decision on what you should see. These algorithms are slicing and dicing you. You are being segmented, compared, categorized, and qualified. What do you see when you enter your personal student portal? If you're a jock or a groupie who accessorizes, you see that a pair of Nike Air Showcase MAX iDs is available to you. If the algorithms have done the job, it will even suggest a color you might like and tell you the approximate shipping time of these custom-designed and signed (by you) Nikes. All for only $200 of your parents' money. How do they do that? Analytics. These are urbane applications with a high degree of sophistication. There are only a few really good ones out there in CRM-land. This chapter defines personalization, tells you how analytics create it, and who is doing the right things with it.

E-tail, Retail: What's the Difference?

To my knowledge, there are only two ways to buy this book. Either you went the e-tailer route, which meant you went online, did a bit of research, used the search engine, found the book, gave them your credit card in a secure environment, and waited breathlessly for its delivery. Or you took the retail route, which meant you went to a bookstore, searched the shelves, found a copy (of which there were very few left, of course), gave a human cashier your credit card or cash while you chatted with them, went home, and then breathlessly read the book. Or maybe, as part of your personal mission to keep Big Brother on his toes, you researched CRM books online and then purchased this book at your local Barnes & Noble. These are very different buying patterns and different purchase models. Take a look at Table 8-1; it highlights the differences between e-tailers and retailers. The experience is not the same, though that's what the e-tailer is both aiming at and hoping for. The e-tailer wants to provide the same comfort, ease, and personal attention, but also wants to provide the richness and availability of the tools and information on the purchase for you—all at a better price.

Table 8-1: A Brief Comparison of E-tailers and Brick-and-Mortar Stores

Upside/Downside	Amazon.com	BarnesandNoble.com	Brick-and-Mortar
Upside	Cheaper price	Cheaper price (even cheaper than their own stores)	Instant gratification with book purchase
Upside	Convenient ordering (never have to leave home)	Convenient ordering (never have to leave home)	Bookstore ambiance and programs
Upside	Huge virtual inventory (ordinary orders have short delivery time)	National inventory (ordinary orders have short delivery time)	Human attention
Upside	Greater privacy	Greater privacy	Privacy not really an issue
Downside	No personal attention unless problem and then difficult	No personal attention unless problem and then difficult	Higher price
Downside	Subject to blind schemes such as dynamic pricing without knowledge	Subject to blind schemes such as dynamic pricing without knowledge	In-store-only stock means more likely out of stock
Downside	Less privacy	Less privacy	Considerably less variety

What this simple table says is that while there are differences between brick-and-mortar stores and e-tailers, there really are no significant differences between e-tailers selling the same things. So what makes the Amazon.com experience better, in many people's opinion, than the Barnesandnoble.com experience? Looking closely at it, not much. Perception is part of it—how you perceive the value of the site itself. Personalization is a big part of it—how much attention you think you are getting from this cold-hearted Web automaton as compared to Joe who is also surfing the site.

Think about it. As often as you've used Amazon.com, how many human beings have you actually spoken to who are employed by Amazon? How many have you even had a personal email interaction with? The likely answer is none. Yet you've shopped onsite dozens of times and gone back for more and more. Convenience, you say? Good prices, you say? Wide selection, you say? Then why not Barnesandnoble.com or Borders.com or any one of a dozen interchangeable websites that sells books, CDs, DVDs, and such? "Amazon and I, well, we go way back. They know me better." *They* do? Who's "*they*"?

That's the point. *They* know you better because *they* have a data warehouse filled with information about you, based on your personal profile and your past shopping experiences. You are an individual to them as far as the data that is available about you. But so are the other 42.7 million Amazon customers. You are all individuals.

Personalization

In a perfect techno-functional world, personalization identifies the needs and requirements of individual customers *en masse*. It also means that the engagement of named, faced customers has to be ongoing and intimate to the point that the customer hardly realizes that he is not dealing with a person or that he's not actually getting a peer-to-peer response. It must appear to be peer to peer so realistically that the customer wants to stay with you. The benefits are longstanding, happy customers and reduced customer service, marketing, and sales costs.

Wait—engaging individual customers *en masse*? How can that be done? Isn't that a contradiction, both in literal terms and in fact? According to Mark LaRow, vice-president of applications development for software vendor MicroStrategy:

> True personalization of the channel is described as how people want to be communicated to. The idea is to personalize the message or the

offer. Generally, it can be described as, what group of people ought to be presented with what offer? The amount of data that needs to be analyzed to make this accurate and interesting to the customer is complex and high volume. If I were to give it a more formal definition, personalization is the process of customizing any interaction with a customer based on his or her explicit interests and preferences, or interests and preferences that are derived from other data about the customer. The personalization of the interaction can take on any or all of the following forms: personalized offer, personalized message into which the offer is carried, and personalized preference for communication channel.

Mr. LaRow further identified the perfectly personalized techno-functional world, a world in which personalization does not conflict with anyone's concern about his or her personal privacy:

The Holy Grail of personalization would be a world in which all individual customer information is known, but is simultaneously anonymous. While this may sound contradictory, it actually could be done through a personalization service that could guarantee and maintain anonymity between the company and the customer. In other words, every company would see you as user XYZ, but no one could connect XYZ to your true name, email, etc. You still reap all the benefits of a personalized experience, with all the relevant product and service offerings made to user XYZ, without any company knowing who you really are.

Hypothetically, this would mean that all your customer data could be used by L.L. Bean to determine that a cashmere sweater would be the appropriate sale item for you and for people with your data points. An ad for the cashmere sweater in your size and a picture of that exact sweater could be sent to you without L.L. Bean knowing your name until you bought the sweater from their online store. Totally customized, yet anonymous.

Even though, as any Monty Python lover will tell you, the search for the Holy Grail continues, the current personalization technology is sufficiently advanced to get nearly miraculous results—when it works well.

Just How Do Analytics Work, Anyway?

Let's begin by looking under the hood. How do these analytics work to give you that message to buy or to provide you with that information for your eyes only? Weirdly, it's a very impersonal process. We're going to concern ourselves with the layers in Figure 8-1 that are above and below the data warehouse and data marts. Throughout the chapter, the figures will be the SAS Institute version of analytics. SAS is a leading analytics software company from Raleigh, North Carolina. There may be some variances here and there from the way that SAS deals with analytics, but for the most part, their approach and processes are representative of how analytics actually works.

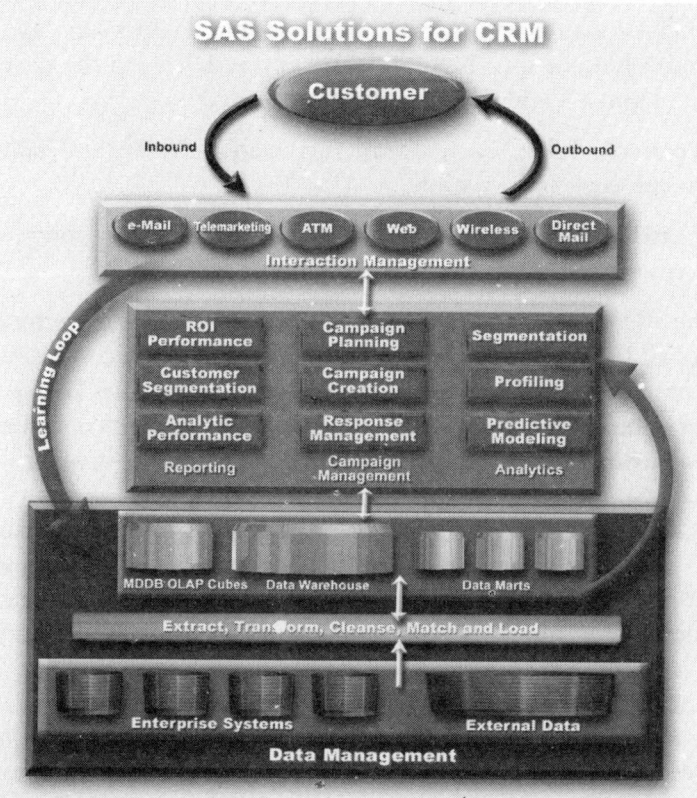

Figure 8-1: SAS CRM analytic workflow process (Copyright 2002, SAS Institute. All rights reserved. Reprinted with the permission of SAS Institute.)

The previous examples are all outputs that come from a marketing automation layer, or "offer engine," that turns the personal information into action. An offer engine is a rules-based series of algorithms, templates, and so on, that takes the data after it is analyzed and applies it to create the offer or message that is appropriate to the individual customer's information. Its components, according to Mark LaRow:

It is goal oriented. "We have to move 200 televisions this week, so find the best bets to buy."

It watches purchase history. "John Smith bought a saw from us two years ago and bought several dozen tools since. The saw should be dull by now, so send this tool-buyer a saw offer."

It is collaborative. "Our analytic algorithms tell us that people who buy documentary DVDs on boxing champions like Muhammad Ali would typically be interested in a 'Fight Club' DVD. Joe Smith bought four boxing documentary DVDs in the past year. Send him a 'Fight Club' notification."

It can schedule. "Each month, run an ad in the *Post* and gather up the response information."

It can handle event offers. "If it is raining, why don't you rent *The Perfect Storm*, since you're stuck indoors anyway?"

The offer engine is (hopefully) the revenue-generating machine that makes all the personalization more than just a gesture of attempted B2C friendship. The key to the offer engine is that rules keep getting added as more and more data is captured and interpreted, so that the actions are increasingly accurate at the customer level—in other words, more personal.

That said, companies need to realize that technology alone can only go so far. I would expect that 10 to 20 percent of these offers would make no sense to the recipient. You can't run the risk of relying on technology too much—exceptions will always occur, and companies that can handle this will succeed handsomely.

One example that shows how results can fall outside the business rules is one of my Amazon.com transactions. I ordered a book on cruises once, when my wife and I were considering a trip. As a result of that single order, though no other book order I ever had is related in any way to travel, the recommended books that keep coming up onscreen for me are always cruise- or travel-related, even though my buying habits (not necessarily the same as my reading habits) are inclined toward technology, business, fiction, and sports. While I understand why the cruise books show up, this falls into that senseless 10 to 20 percent category. However, the other 90 percent of suggestions related to my habits and tastes in music and movies are very accurate, so the pin-pointed personalization is generally working well. Unfortunately, I fall prey to that part of human behavior that tends to remember the mis-cue, rather than the successes. In general, this makes personalization a very tricky road to travel. However, the analytic engines that are used are amazingly good at minding the data store.

What Are Analytics?

In Chapter 1, there is a definition of analytical CRM that I am going to restate a little differently. Analytics are the collection, extraction, modification, measurement, identification, and reporting of informa-tion designed to be useful to the party using the analytics. It includes multidimensional online analytical processing (OLAP) techniques as well as calculations, logic, formulas, and analytic routines/algorithms against data extracted from operational (OLTP) systems (the "T" stands for "Transactional," where the data is too granular to be useful for analysis). This is the slice and dice engine that is used to determine why Mr. Smith or Mrs. Jones should get messages asking them to join a hair dye company's special retirement fund for senior citizens who live in Tampa, Florida, with retirement incomes over $125,000 and who use hair dye to cover the gray.

While this sounds trivial, the reality is that with the appropriate input and data available from some centralized data repository, this could be taken a lot deeper. The analytics capacity out there is that sophisticated. There are hundreds of products that use it and picking one is like walking through a (data) minefield. The wrong one can destroy you. The right one can provide a sharp marketplace edge.

However, before we look at the products, let's begin a drill-down of our own data here. Analytics aren't just analytics. That would make things far too easy.

Descriptive Analytics

This is also known as performance analytics, effectiveness analytics, or, just so CRM definitional confusion can be enhanced, operational analytics. No matter what it is called, these are the analytics of the past and present. These analytics are designed to provide you with a com-plete description of customer history, behavior patterns, and activities up to the present moment. They can track their (and your) perform-ance against the corporate metrics set for monitoring those behavior patterns. If you've seen the movie "Memento," you'll understand the strengths and weaknesses of pure descriptive analytics. They are able to provide a terrific view of what groups of customers (Floridians with incomes greater than $125,000) have done, compared with other groups (New Yorkers with similar incomes). But they don't let you take it beyond the present. They can only show you what led up to the present behavior, or they can work back from the present situation to identify the path it took to get to the present situation. In other words, customer and corporate performance are described, and the success or failure of a marketing campaign can be identified. With purely descriptive analytics, the future *is* hard to see. Yet, descriptive analytics provide the foundation for predictive analytics. (For those who haven't seen "Memento," rent it. I don't want to give away the beginning, but what I'm saying will be even clearer. For those of you who have seen it, you'll note the trick in my previous sentence.)

Predictive Analytics

This is where it gets both interesting and dicey. There are times when jobs depend on the performance successes of predictive analytics. Imagine you are responsible for a million-dollar advertising campaign promoting a new product, and the success of the campaign—acquisition of customers for our new hair dye company's "Wash Out the Gray" product—depends on efficiently spending that million dollars. There are 6.5 million people in Florida. You can't afford to call them all and offer a free sample, but which ones do you call? Descriptive analytics yield a number of valuable insights. In this case, they tell you that 1.6 million of the 6.5 million are Spanish speaking. That's great, but how do you allocate the right number of Spanish-speaking telemarketers? This is the role of predictive analytics, helping you allocate those million dollars to ensure the maximum number of new customers. When they work, predictive analytics save money. When they don't, or when they're not used, they can cost jobs.

The Analytic Process

So how does this work? This, too, is not easy. When the words *profiling*, *modeling*, and *scoring* pop out, what do they actually mean? Are they a strategy for single guys in a bar or do they have some value in the burgeoning world of analytics?

SEGMENTATION

Customer segmentation doesn't mean client body part destruction. It means identifying attributes and behavior patterns that enable a company to group its customers into identifiable and marketable segments. From that point, a company can establish a value and potential return for that segment. These attributes can be demographic, geographic, or pretty much anything thought important. When you have a small number of customers and a limited number of attributes to consider, you may simply rely on your business acumen to determine what's important. When you have thousands of customers with hundreds of attributes, leading predictive modeling products such as SAS Enterprise Miner can automate the "what's important" process for you. For example, Mr. Smith and Mrs. Jones represent a customer segment that has a consistent behavior pattern (beyond retirement to Florida). They regularly dye their gray hair. However, if it were thought important, gender could be separated or the color of hair dye chosen by these customers could be added to the mix. Once the common behavior with these chosen attributes is identified in the group, a value can be placed on how much the company thinks this "analytically optimized" segment is worth, given their behaviors. This is profiling a customer. Keep in mind, the data is not only what is extracted from the customer data repository, but is also potentially purchased from a third party so that generic data on the same customer group can be entered into the mix. For example, if you think that the Mrs. Jones group is really important, you can find out how much of Tampa or all of Florida fits the profile through the purchase of third-party data. This can provide a better view for your target crosshairs. Keep in mind that customer segmented behavior rarely is static, and events can dramatically transform behavior. Think of what everyone went through post–September 11. Segmentation is a dynamic, ongoing process. See Figures 8-2 and 8-3 to get a feel for what segmentation looks like.

There is ongoing discussion in the analytics "community," such as it is, as to when you should do risk analysis. Some say before modeling and scoring, some say after. I'm not taking sides. I'm putting it after modeling and scoring purely as a parallel, not serial, step. Whatever floats your boat is fine with me.

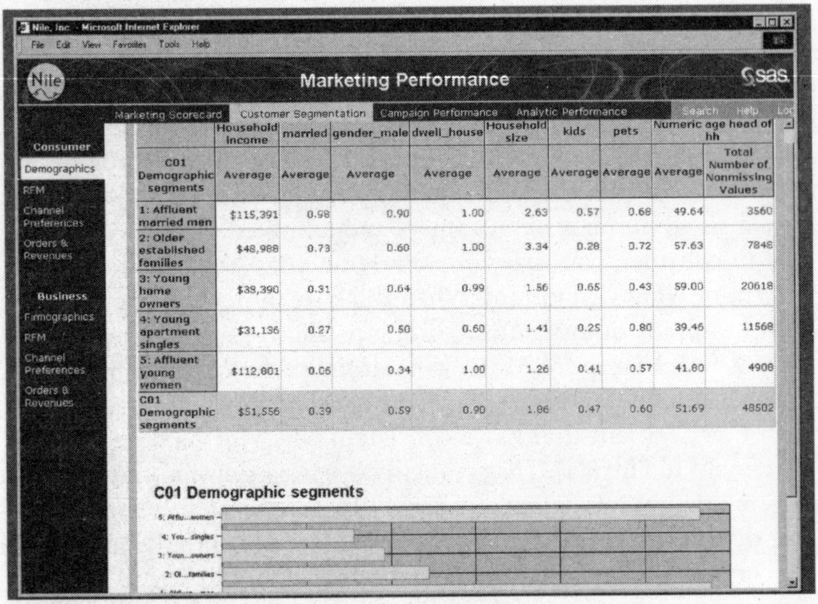

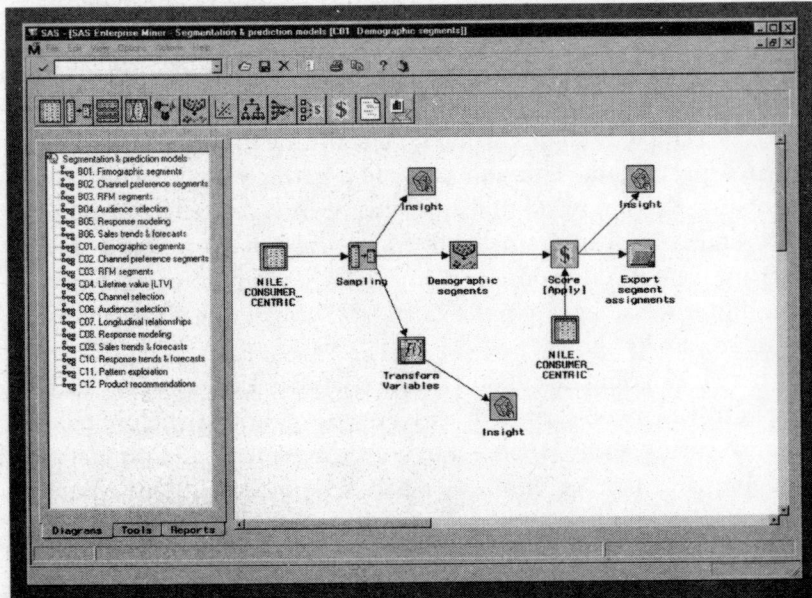

Figure 8-2: SAS customer segmentation demographic data in chart form

Figure 8-3: SAS customer segmentation process flow

MODELING AND SCORING

There are a number of approaches to modeling and scoring, but their definitions are clear. Modeling uses data mining (discussed later) to begin to identify the customers that fit the profile that is best for the planned campaign. Modeling is finding relevant customer segment characteristics that create the best chances for the success of the campaign. The best approaches are those advocated by the serious players. One approach is to use neural networks, which can have good results but may not be intuitive to marketers because it's hard to determine in some neural topologies exactly why some people fit the pattern. A good modeling method can largely mitigate this issue by enabling the analyst to easily compare results from different techniques, such as regression, neural network, or decision trees.

Whatever method is used, the fundamental process involves analytics attached to test campaigns that expose a sampling of the population that has been identified through the initial profiling to the campaign. Valid statistical samplings of specific groups are used and then predictive models are applied to the results. You can see what promotions and channels were successful to which groups, and modify your marketing approach accordingly. You may find, for example, that your million-dollar marketing campaign can reach more people (and generate better results) by using email to some people, instead of the far more expensive telemarketing channel. As a side benefit, you will potentially reduce the number of times you contact specific individuals (down to the customer irritation threshold). Ultimately, no matter what language you speak (sales gobble, market speak, and so on), this is how far you can push a customer before they get mad.

The next phase is scoring. Scoring is a process of applying the model (which is really a complex arithmetic equation) to your target audience and associating a number (score) with each individual. To make things simple, assume you apply your predictive model and it assigns a score between 0 and 10 to every person from Florida in your database. Those most likely to respond to the campaign will have a higher number, thus your target population is effectively weighted and ranked numerically.

Now, if you look at the distribution of scores (and the graph in Figure 8-2 represents such a distribution), you can see that 20 percent of your population has an 8 or higher, and about 30 percent has a score of 5 to 8. How do you apply this new information to your campaign? The high scores aren't just cheered, they are used to qualify customers. Anyone who is 8 or over gets a phone call and an offer for a free four-ounce bottle of the hair dye company's "Wash Out the Gray." Anyone with a score of 5 to 7 gets an email and a coupon for $1.00 off the price of a regular bottle of "Wash out the Gray." Anyone scoring below 5 gets nothing at all. Now you can allocate your million-dollar budget effectively: 20 percent of your population will be telemarketed, and 30 percent will receive an email promotion. The rest probably wouldn't respond anyway (according to your model), and you've saved a lot of money for the company. That, my friends, is scoring.

Validation is used to learn from the results of the modeling and scoring. We don't need to get into the technical details; suffice it to say that you will test the predicted results from your model to ensure that our random sample was not accidentally biased. (Don't take this lightly. Biased samples can have a serious impact; remember, jobs can be at stake here!) This is where descriptive analytics are used to look at the response level of the test sample and actual campaign. Then on the basis of the success of the model, calibration and tuning are done to improve the model for future use. Additionally, by looking at the various response rate changes, recurring and nonrecurring costs, or factors such as new types of previously unidentified customer behavior, this could give rise to new customer segments or brand new models that will work with the existing or new customer segments that are accounted for (see Figure 8-4).

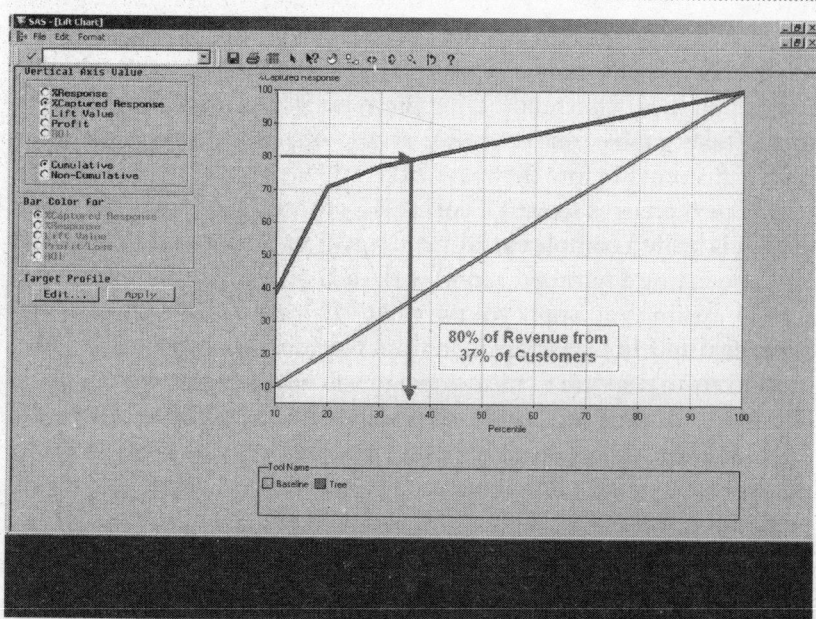

Figure 8-4: SAS lift chart for analytic results

RISK ANALYSIS

Every day we unconsciously or consciously do risk analysis. If I eat this huge pastrami sandwich and an extra large fries and a fudge sundae, I risk gaining three pounds. But if I eliminate the fries, my risk of gaining some weight remains high, but my risk of gaining three pounds is reduced. If I add the after-lunch "run-a-couple-of-miles" factor, my risk of weight gain goes down further still, but remains likely. If I gain the weight and keep doing this over time, my risk of heart problems increases and so on to an omega point of some sort. In other words, human beings are always assessing risk versus reward.

You know those ten offers for the credit cards you're going to need in order to pay off all that pastrami? Each one of those offers has been evaluated for risk—the risk that Capital One or Citibank will eventually loan you money that you may never pay back, whether by intent or happenstance.

Another view of risk that is receiving a lot more attention these days is the risk of losing customers. Customer acquisition occurs. Risk begins. The minute you cheer the entrance of a new customer into your portfolio, the possibility of losing that customer begins. For any customer to become dissatisfied is a process that takes place over time and with certain factors more likely than others to cause that dissatisfaction. For example if Mrs. Jones uses this hair dye company's product and her hair falls out, odds are good she is going to be dissatisfied. On the other hand, it could be less dramatic. She could buy a bottle of hair dye that is old and dried up and not get good customer service around that. It could be the failure of the hair dye company to answer an inquiry. Anything can get anyone angry and make them more and more likely to bolt. So risk analysis factors in things such as perceived quality of service, not just actual quality of service against expected quality of service. For example, a rebate offer may say it takes four to six weeks for the rebate to be delivered. If it takes seven weeks, dissatisfaction in the quality of delivery increases. If it takes five weeks, there is no discomfort, because the perceived quality of service falls within the expected range.

Other risk factors taken into account by this process include loyalty, competitive offering, payment, credit and fraud risk, and changing economic conditions.

Risk analysis in the analytics world is a lot less fluid than the human mind, but it can do great things—if you construct the appropriate questions and use the right methods to figure out possibility. Know this, though:Risk analysis is risky. You are using analytics to identify what consequences a potential result or action might have for you. The methodology you are using has been created and tested with the awareness that the methodology itself has the risk of failure built into its fiber. If Citibank had a perfect risk model, they would have zero net credit loss on their portfolio of credit card customers. Citibank wrote off (acknowledged as unlikely to receive) millions of dollars in net credit loss in 2001. Kind of an Alice in Wonderland endless loop in the reasoning behind it, isn't there? However, there is enough proven success to create, as they say in the legal profession, foundation. Use it at your own risk.

MEASUREMENT AND TRACKING

This is the analytics "scorecard." To put it in non-analytic terms, imagine that George Steinbrenner, owner of the New York Yankees, pays Jason Giambi of the Oakland A's $120 million for seven years during his free agency. This is based on the strength of his performance (descriptive analytics) over the past two years, which was roughly a .342 batting average, 40 home runs, and 130 runs batted in. You have certain expectations, given those numbers, as well as other information: the short right field porch at Yankee Stadium of 314 feet; the way he hits to right field a lot; his leadership in the Oakland clubhouse; his love of the Yankees through his life as a fan; his father's love of the Yankees; his willingness to bend to Yankee clubhouse decorum and professionalism; his age; and so on (predictive analytics). You're willing to spend $120 million because of the seven-year rate of return and return on investment your club will get in endorsements, attendance, and TV contracts. Plus the World Series victory, which means more merchandise, brand recognition, franchise ticket sales, and TV and radio contracts. This simple model has worked as well as other models you tried.

It is the 2002 baseball season. Giambi is mired in a slump and is batting .242 with 5 homers and 31 RBIs. Gack! The model seems to be wrong. Attendance is down. The analytics seem off. You change Giambi or you change the model so that they are in conformity with one another. The metrics aren't working.

I wouldn't change the model; I'd let the coaches change Giambi, because your data has been good. The descriptive analytics are good. The predictive modeling might need some tweaking, but what it really indicates is that there is some kind of flaw. That means the campaign has to be tweaked, which means get the coaches to change his stance, already!

Actually, human decision making mirrors these analytic behaviors and modeling. We look at the history of something, we decide what is the best possible course of action under the circumstances, and then we see if the course of action works. If not, we fix the mistake wherever it seems to show. Analytics are the automated form of a limited type of cognition. It is not creativity, and it is not human. It is a linear or non-linear automated form of decision planning. Simple in comparison to the human mind, so it is used as a tool, not a substitute. We measure success and failure by the performance to a preconceived measurement of some kind. If they don't match, fix it. If they do, congratulations.

DATA MANAGEMENT

This is the underlying transactional substructure of analytics. Data management is what is done to make sure that the data is usable and available for the analytics work to come.

Procedures occur that keep the data "pure." In this case, the data is gathered from multiple sources (customer databases, prospect lists, call center records, sales notations, customer activity histories, and so on) and is "cleansed," which means CASS certified name and address standardization is applied. SAS suggests that the newly refreshed data is stored in analytical data marts, which contain the statistically useful samples. It is easier to prepare data for use when the time comes because the data is prepared in advance and available. Then scoring and model tuning can be done routinely on these analytical data marts, contact histories created, and so on. Makes for a well-organized system, doesn't it?

Data Mining: Better than Gold

Data mining is the automatic or partially automated analysis of large quantities of stored data to uncover significant rules or patterns. The analytic algorithms that are applied to the data provide information that can get as complex as the most valuable customers, using dozens of criteria, or as simple as the customers in Virginia over 50 years old who buy Jell-O. This is automation of the traditional functions often carried out by marketing research and advertising firms, which is why these same agencies are acquiring companies that do data mining. The data mining tools are dependent on development of predictive models. These models are evolved from the core business questions of individual companies: What kind of customers do we have? What kind do we want? How are we going to keep them? What can we do to capture new markets?

The results of data mining demand more than just simple automatic responses, however. Human intelligence and campaign design are vital to making something of the results of the data mining activity. Ultimately, it follows the time-honored principle that says the more useful information you have, the more successful you can be in meeting your objectives.

However, there are a number of regular procedures that are carried out in data mining. There are multiple models for data mining, but for the purposes of this edition, we're going to very briefly look at SAS's SEMMA process. It is a good example of how data mining works. SEMMA stands for:

Sampling This is the process of picking a statistically valid representative data set to model. There are multiple sampling methods that can be used.

Exploration This is actually what we ordinary people call "taking a look." It is a visual way of looking at the data to find out what the landscape actually seems to look like. Imagine using binoculars on terrain to find terrain patterns.

Modification These are changes to the data due to newly discovered information from the exploration stage. This is also the stage of manual cleanup, when data that would obstruct an accurate conclusion is removed or changed to be more appropriate to the sample.

Modeling This is the same as the modeling above, so I won't repeat it.

Assessment Analysts use different techniques to develop models, such as regression, neural nets, and so on. Assessment involves comparing results to determine which technique works best.

Analytics and Personalization

When you surf to Amazon.com or some other personalized site and see, "Welcome back, Paul Greenberg, here are some book, DVD, VHS, and CD recommendations for you," you may either get annoyed or marvel at the accuracy of the choices they are suggesting. When done optimally, the choices are going to be uniformly meaningful and you are going to buy something.

Logins to portal sites have unique user names and unique passwords that are attached to a profile of the portal user. Each time users log in, they find a specific view with specific information that is related to them on that site. For example, if I log in to Oraclesalesonline.com, it provides me with information that I need, such as the meetings I have scheduled, the plane flights I have to catch, the database of my customers and the recent interactions with those customers, and customized news and services designed to make my Oraclesalesonline.com experience useful and personal.

The technology that sits behind the personalization of the information is extraordinary. The amount of data analyzed and the number of ways that it is analyzed is extensive, often in multiple terabytes. In the optimal system, a customer data warehouse will gather information on individuals from all customer touch points. These touch points could include:

- Website information gathered through forms

- Point of sale (POS) information

- Information from ERP data warehouses such as SAP's Business Intelligence Warehouse Call Center data

- Sales force automation customer information

- Information gathered in varying marketing venues:

  - Data from marketing automation applications

  - Attitudinal data collected from surveys

  - Responses to direct mail campaigns

  - Email marketing feedback

  - Demographic data feeds from departments such as marketing and sales that might be directly inputted

- Any other customer data source

For the dissected and configured data to be useful, there has to be some action taken to give it some value. That action could be campaign management, email, direct mail management, further information capture, message creation, or a myriad of other actions. However, to get to the point of action, there has to be some transactions going on under the hood that provide appropriate and meaningful information to a chosen audience, such as marketers or strategic planners.

As Cold as Analytics Are, They Get Personal

How does all this left-brain stuff create a right-brain warm and fuzzy experience? On the surface, it seems almost sacrilegious to think that what you feel with Amazon.com is nothing more than a machine-created experience. But think about it this way. In the last quarter of 2001, Amazon turned a (gasp!) profit for the first time in its history. There are all kinds of reasons for that, some of which are pretty cold—such as laying off 1,300 employees to reduce costs and various accounting tricks—but one of the reasons stated was that a much better CRM system "squeezed" a fair number of extra sales out of the last holiday season. This was due to a continuously improving individualized experience. That was done without ever really meeting you, wasn't it?

What models are used for personalization? There are two or three that float the industry pretty regularly. The most frequently seen one is an offer-based personalization model. That is the one that is also most familiar. Mrs. Jones and Mr. Smith, based on the scores we mentioned earlier, get a free sample of hair dye. They are part of a target group that has a high purchase probability and a low irritation factor. They are measured and tracked for response, and the model and processes are refined to improve the chances of success and lower the risk of failure in round two. Do it again for round three. *Ad infinitum.*

More recently, though, newer systems that offer real-time interactive personalization products are beginning to appear with the accession of the Internet as a mission-critical addition to communications channels. In this context, interactive means they can be used for proactive, outbound communications such as a direct marketing campaign, as well as reactive, inbound communications, such as when a customer initiates a session with your e-commerce website. SAS's version is called Interaction Manager. Interaction Manager ensures that your customer is treated consistently across every communication channel, or touch point, regardless of who initiated the dialogue. Real time is a challenging area in the context of analytics. Remember the scoring process we discussed? How long do you think it takes Amazon.com to score 42.7 million customers on their likelihood to buy Product X? Since Amazon doesn't really respond in real time, how does it react more quickly to your purchase activity, and prompt you with new and accurate recommendations? That is the essence of interaction management, the ability to make qualified decisions right now, when the customer is searching for a good book to read this weekend. The data gathered provides the data for mapping offers to the activity, so there is context-specific interaction being identified along with the customer activity. Then an offer is made. Ideally, there are multiple touch points involved in this. If you know the same customer's activity via phone, fax, email, and the Web, you can then send that customer an appropriate message or offer via the communications channel most favorable to your company. In other words, if I call in to take an offer that I received in direct mail and pay over the phone via credit card, but refuse a similar offer that I received in email and could have paid over the Web, guess which communications channel I am more likely to use to purchase something?

One of the newer (and very challenging) approaches is interaction management. Many companies would love to use interaction management to coordinate the analytic work. When a trigger goes off and identifies a point that needs a decision based on customer behavior, information could be sent to an interaction manager who receives the customer ID, the touch point information, and the activities that triggered the decision-making need. Based on business rules, predictive model scores for that customer, customer history, and so on, an interaction manager might be able to make a decision that is then delivered through the appropriate communications channel. This is more real-time and personal than the older offer-based model. It is also founded on that dream objective: the 360-degree view of the customer, available across departments, across customer communication channels, and to those who need to see it. It has weaknesses, of course. For example, it would be quite easy to extrapolate a one-time bonanza result from a customer as a behavior and make wrong future decisions. You need to carefully include the descriptive analytics and customer histories so that one-time events occurring in real-time get a proper response.

SAS Institute

SAS is quite the company. It's one of those companies that I knew had an excellent reputation. But when I saw the actual workings of the place, spoke with customers and partners, saw the products, read the buzz, and met the people, I realized I had severely underestimated this enterprise. It is a terrific company with terrific people and terrific products. My enthusiasm comes after a long, hard look at it. There are so many companies with analytics and so few who can do a good job. Trust me, SAS may be the place to go for your CRM analytic and business intelligence needs. I'm going to take a look at SAS's CRM-related analytics products because of their reputation. Long-time CRM veteran Prasanna Dhore, senior vice-president of The Dreyfus

Corporation, and leader of one of the more successful CRM projects ever undertaken, said it well: "There is no one else that is flexible enough. No one can compete with SAS. SAS is the one package that provides us with real value." This seems to be an industry customer mantra, so before I examine the analytics process, I'd like to give you a brief glimpse of this fascinating company.

Company Specifics

The SAS Institute is headquartered in Cary, North Carolina, which is a suburb of Raleigh, North Carolina. SAS is one of the largest privately held companies in the world, with revenues of more than a billion dollars and nearly 9,000 employees in 190 offices in 53 countries. It has also been around since 1976—a long time in the IT scheme of things. They have more than 90 products, many related to the analytics and marketing side of CRM, but they encompass far more than even that. They even have their own hosted ASP products called Intelivisor. SAS has more than 37,000 business, government, and university sites using their product globally. Customers include 98 of the Fortune 100 and 90 percent of Fortune 500 overall. They are a well-capitalized company with annuity streams for 35,000 instances of those products. They are a world-class leader in business intelligence and more recently are becoming a serious player in the CRM universe.

All that said, what I find most remarkable is this statistic: Their personnel turnover rate in 2001 was 3.9 percent. They are consistently voted one of the 20, 30, or 100 best places in the United States to work, and they buck an industry that has a 20 percent or higher staff turnover and is known for its lack of loyalty. In fact, *Fortune* magazine, for the entire five years of its "100 Best Places to Work in America" list named SAS as one of only two companies who have made it every single year. For the 2002 list, they are number three! This is quite an achievement, especially given my emphasis on the importance of corporate culture in determining customer relationship to vendors. SAS has a 1,000-acre campus in Cary that has its own onsite healthcare, with two doctors and several nurses. They have two onsite daycare facilities and three gyms. They even have a privately funded Cary Academy (funded by founders James Goodnight and John Sall) that has 650 children enrolled. They have a natatorium with ten lanes for swimming, five miles of paved running trails, subsidized cafeterias, and two soccer fields. They pay astounding attention to their employees.

Because they are an analytics company down to the fibrous levels of being, they have statistical justification for that. By having onsite health-care, they've saved $4 million in medical costs, thanks to early treatment. Because of their low turnover, they save $75 million a year in headhunters, training costs, and so on that they would spend on getting new employees up to speed. They are a left-brained company with a right-brained sense of thought and a big-hearted culture.

SAS Case Study in Brief: The Dreyfus Corporation

This is perhaps one of the most successful stories in CRM. A benchmark of success in the financial services universe is asset retention. For reasons of retirement, customer dissatisfaction, or reinvestment in instruments not offered by the financial services company (among others), people will pull out their assets and go elsewhere. The industry average has historically been about 22 percent. When Prasanna Dhore began his CRM project at Dreyfus in 1997–1998, the company was at the industry average. This attrition rate was affecting a company that manages more than $130 billion in more than 180 mutual fund portfolios nationwide. His objectives? Reduce asset attrition (increase retention) and increase sales. He developed a road map that was premised on several things:

- ▶ Align the corporate culture to the changes that were going to inevitably happen

- ▶ Hit singles every three to six months, rather than a grand slam homer

- ▶ Use the SAS products to handle modeling, forecasting data mining, recording, and overall analytics

It worked. The Dreyfus Corporation's asset attrition rate is 7 percent, what Mr. Dhore calls "a natural attrition rate." Their sales went up considerably in 2001, a year that showed almost a complete downward trend for all other financial services institutions. Success indeed.

Key CRM Analytic Products

I'm not detailing SAS products here the same way I detail the products for the highlighted companies in other chapters. The reason for this different look at the product line is that their approach to product building is 180 degrees away from most other companies. Their out-of-the-box, plain vanilla functionality in products—like marketing automation—is custom built. What? Let me explain.

Most vendors build their products from the top down. There is a certain amount of out-of-the-box functionality with the capability to customize using a set of tools that is added in. This approach works just fine. For example, PeopleSoft provides PeopleTools with its applications, Siebel has a toolset, SAP has a toolset and highly specific APIs to make the customization and integration easier, and so on. SAS takes a very different look at it and builds their products from the ground up. Their engines are flexible and customizable out of the box. You can make them do what you want as long as you put together the appropriate applications out of the many they offer. For example, they have a data mining product seen as one of the best, perhaps the best, on the market, called Enterprise Miner. It selects, explores, and models data and provides patterns for interpretation based on criteria set. It is pretty vertically and horizontally neutral. But applied to CRM or, in particular, EMA, it can be an invaluable tool in plumbing the depth and breadth of knowledge that sits quietly in a customer data repository. It can be customized for use with the SAS Institute Marketing Automation suite, a set of applications that were SAS-native and acquired with the purchase of the United Kingdom–based Intrinsic in November 2001. As a good example of their approach, Intrinsic provided the campaign management components of the suite, while SAS itself provided Enterprise Miner 4.2 (as of 2002); Warehouse Administrator 2.2, which does data extraction, transformation, and loading, and then manages the use of the data; and AppDev Studio 2.0 to build Web-based reporting applications. There are also several optional components.

This is a typical SAS approach. They have highly customizable CRM products that allow for creating vertical applications, such as Churn Management for Telecommunications. Forrester Research considers their flagship CRM product, Marketing Automation, to be wonderful when complex data analysis is needed. The Forrester comment: "It excels at managing complex customer segmentations."

Their website: http://www.sasinstitute.com/.

PeopleSoft Enterprise Performance Management (EPM) and the Customer Scorecard

PeopleSoft's analytics are something to behold because they are the strongest of the enterprise application vendors (see Chapter 12 for more on enterprise applications). They are one of two vendors that build the Balanced Scorecard into their analytics offerings (the other is SAP) through the use of their EPM applications, and they offer embedded reporting of those analytics in real time. If you want to see the results of some of the modeling that is being done, it will show up directly on the page that you enter through the use of a portal customized to you. For example, if you are a vice-president of marketing, the results of the customer satisfaction modeling will appear on the page in the format that you chose for it.

PeopleSoft's approach is to embed key performance indicators (KPIs) into a Customer Scorecard that is measured against. There are analytic templates for Profitability, Sales Activity, Marketing, and Support. At the end of 2001, they released customer behavior modeling (CBM) software—their take on predictive analytics. In an article from SearchCRM.com, Robb Eklund, vice-president of CRM product marketing for PeopleSoft, used a hockey analogy: "The idea is to skate where the puck is going to be, not where it just was."

The repository for all their data is the PeopleSoft Enterprise Warehouse (EW). Their analytic applications have earned the Balanced Scorecard Collaborative certification. They are also deemed architecturally compliant with the Customer Information Factory standard (CIF). These are sophisticated products and a true differentiator for PeopleSoft.

Personalization and Privacy

With all the individual data captured and stored, privacy remains an issue. Privacy is an ongoing battle being fought on the Internet as a whole. How much information captured and what information stored constitute a violation of privacy? Cookies—those little files that are generated by the website that feed data back to the site when you return—are the subject of the general battle. So much so that Internet Explorer and Netscape Communicator have cookie managers as standard parts of their browsers.

Personalization is a much more comprehensive data-gathering process, and far more information about you, the individual, is ensnared over a long time from many sources. Do you want the info-kidnapping site to know that you download shareware constantly that is related to wills and estates? Do you want all your credit cards on file after you have used them? Do you want www.dot.com to know that you are an elder in your church—information gathered from your downloading a white paper on the nature of the Trinity? Even more, do you want to be besieged with offers for estate-related legal services or religious articles? How much information about your family do you want stored in someone else's database?

Net Perceptions, a real-time personalization specialist, has developed an exceptional privacy standard for customers. Two excerpts will highlight the privacy issue:

Net Perceptions supports the individual's right to protect their online privacy, thus we collect minimal information. As part of Net Perceptions' commitment to privacy, we actively support or are founding members of several privacy standards. These include:

- ▶ Active membership in the Online Privacy Alliance

- ▶ Licensee in good standing of TRUSTe program

- ▶ Authoring membership of the ICE (Information Content Exchange) standard

- ▶ Full compliance with OPS (Open Profiling Standard)

- ▶ DMA member compliance with the DMA Privacy Promise

Net Perceptions, like others in the business of personalization, takes privacy seriously. Each of the organizations and standards mentioned is a medium for the protection of the right to privacy of all citizens. By no means should this be treated lightly.

The Online Privacy Alliance (OPA) is an organization that crisscrosses the entire private sector, not just the information technology world. It not only includes companies like 3M and Bank of America, but major associations as diverse as the Information Technology Association of America, the Motion Picture Association of America, and the American Institute of Certified Public Accounts.

As an institution, OPA is creating a privacy standard for its hundred-plus global corporate members to adhere to, which provides powerful protections for privacy. OPA distinguishes the singular components that should be part of any security or privacy package the corporate executive is considering purchasing or using, as well as personalization tools to be aware of. There are five rules for an organization:

- ▶ Publicly adopt and implement a privacy policy.

- ▶ Give notice and disclosure of the privacy policy (such as Net Perceptions' easy-to-find disclosure).

- ▶ Give individuals the choice on how their personal information is going to be used online, especially if the use is unrelated to the purpose for which it was collected (opt-in). Minimally, allow the individuals the ability to have it not used (opt-out). Consent to use by third parties should also be an opt-in or opt-out choice.

▶ Secure data that is gathered and develop standards to guarantee the reliability and accuracy of the data. If the information is to be transferred to third parties, it should be in adherence to this data security standard or procedure. The third party should protect the integrity of the data transfer.

▶ Take steps to ensure the data is accurate, complete, and timely. Mechanisms for correction of problems and for protection against unauthorized alterations should be established.

The TRUSTe program is a highly visible, trusted source in which many e-commerce Web publishers are enrolled. It is directed solely at the online community. Commonly identified by websites that carry its privacy seal, the "trustmark," TRUSTe has developed stringent standards that not only define protections for consumers, but also provide strong proof of regulatory compliance to government officers. This is a profit-making, nonpartisan venture that has been generally accepted in the online community. Members of the TRUSTe program are actually subject to oversight procedures. Reviews are conducted initially and periodically to see that adherence to TRUSTe compliance is occurring. Seeding, the process of creating a dummy consumer with traceable personal information (sometimes called a "red dye test"), is part of the oversight, so that TRUSTe can see firsthand that the site is complying. Finally, they depend on online users to report violations, and they've created a watchdog form to make that process easier.

To further ensure customer privacy as more and more personal information is publicly harvested, there are standards groups, such as Information Content Exchange (ICE) and the Open Profiling Standard (OPS). ICE, run by the same folks who are heading up the CPExchange CRM standard, is a standard for management and delivery of data and content between networked partners and the "syndicator" (creator of the information) and "subscriber" (receiver of the information). The OPS is a model championed by Netscape that provides a foundation for the creation of "personal profiles" on the Web and at the same time protects customers from egregious use of those profiles, through permissions and opt-in/opt-out behaviors.

Now the second excerpt:

Privacy Standards for Net Perceptions Customers:

Net Perceptions develops and sells a variety of tools designed to help companies offer personalized suggestions of products or content to individuals. Net Perceptions' products do not require the collection of profiling information, such as name or contact information, to serve personalized recommendations. Net Perceptions encourages all of its customers to adopt privacy standards of their own and make those standards freely accessible.

(Both excerpts are reprinted from the Net Perceptions website, http://www. netperceptions.com/.)

What makes this second quote comforting is that Net Perceptions has, to some extent, found a piece of the Holy Grail: anonymous data collection for accurate personalization. Looking at it from the perspective of privacy commitment, they are creating the paradigm.

Wireless Personalization

The epitome of personalization in the early part of the 21st century is doing it on the small screen. The small screen is no longer the television, but rather the PDA or cellphone. The mobile salesperson is already being attended to by SalesLogix or Siebel or other such companies through wireless versions of their sales force automation applications, but what about the mobile customer? What if I realized I had forgotten my anniversary and had to order flowers, but I was in the car out of town? What if I logged on to my Palm M505 or Compaq IPAQ 3870 (after I'd pulled the car over and parked) and saw a message that said there was a special on roses for customers who had used the flower site before? Click. Click. Click. Roses are ordered and sent instantly. The stored personal information pushed the appropriate offer to me on my PDA, and the stored personal information was used to reply to the offer with an order. This is a likely scenario for the very near future and is being enacted in a small way now.

Web shopping is growing into a major segment of the retail industry. The projected size of the B2C ecommerce transactions revenue is expected to grow from $88 billion in 2002 to $361 billion in 2007 according to a study done in 2002 by Ovum, an international research and consulting firm. Additionally, the handheld market is still a faster-growing hardware market, despite both the economic downturn and the fall-off in Palm sales. International Data Corporation expected the market for PDAs to grow by 55.9 percent in 2000 (up from 26.6 percent growth in 1999) with an expected annual growth rate of 27.8 percent for 2000 to 2004. While that hasn't happened so far, there has been significant market growth at about half that rate. The combination of increased Web shopping with the growth of handheld sales is deadly for the purse strings of American consumers and has lip-smacking potential for merchants. No longer is stationary or enclosed the prerequisite for shopping. Now purchasing can happen on the go, anytime, anywhere. All the prominent PDAs—the Palm, Visor, Pocket PC, and Blackberry—have wireless capabilities, either native to the device or attachable through snap-on modems from companies such as Go America (Pocket PC) or Omnisky (Palm or Pocket PC). Personalization is ideally a wireless application, able to communicate with any wireless device, from your PDA to your cellphone to your pager.

As it stands, even in 2002 this remains a long way off. Many of the companies that formed to deliver some sort of personalized news content—sports, technology news, business, world events—to your wireless device have failed with the dot.com bomb and the recession of 2001–2002. Some of the online major presences like ESPN and others have raw forms of this kind of personalized content for delivery to wireless devices or at least for viewing over wireless devices. While better than the 12-character news bites that appeared two years ago, they still leave a lot to be desired for the viewing. There is no real killer application for this yet. There are some significant portals opened that have this potential, nonetheless. For example, Oracle has Oracle Mobile, a wireless portal that delivers content to your PDA. More germane, though, is that most of the major CRM vendors now have these portals and have integrated wireless modes into their latest applications as of 2002.

What makes the wireless world exciting for personalization is that there is nothing more personal than the cellphone you carry or the PDA that sits in your pocket or in your purse. Unlike a desktop computer, which is a fixed, immobile instrument unless you throw it out a window, the cellphone is ubiquitous and the PDA is yours and rests on your person somewhere. Both travel with the user constantly. Same with pagers. By creating the small footprint software to broadcast information to you, the service you are getting seems so, well, personal. It's on your cellphone that rings on your belt or sings out that Beethoven tune when the personal information is delivered. That is not only useful, it's cool. Don't think that the personalization companies of the world don't know that. Useful and cool both sell.

Wireless personalization is the ultimate sexy personalization venue. Each individual has a device that is customized to provide information and actions for that person alone. Makes you feel wanted, doesn't it?

How Personal Is Business?

"Well," you say, "how does this benefit my business? I know how it benefits Amazon.com." In this configuration, you're forgetting one thing. Amazon.com is a business, too, whether its appeal is to consumers or to other businesses. It is a needs-to-be continuously profit-making entity, pure and simple. Keeping customers (you) is central to their business model, and I assume, yours. Personalization and analytics provide you with a marketing tool to give you an extra sword in the battle for customer market share.

There are millions of people who shop online and in stores who will soon be shopping via cellphones and PDAs. Personalization tools make it cool, make it easy, and make it an individual experience. They work well when they are seen as an aid to creative thought, not as a substitute. But they do really work.

9

Partner Relationship Management: The Other Significant Other

As the "Neoclassic" economy begins to evolve to greater complexity, and as it increasingly penetrates the so-called Old Economy, the need for managing partnerships becomes increasingly important. There are several reasons being used with legitimate justification. They run something in this vein:

▶ The economy is tight. We have to focus on core business functions. We can outsource much of the rest.

▶ The economy is tight. We can't invest in new areas of expertise. We need to find partners who can enhance our overall offering.

▶ The economy is tight. We can't hire a sales force much bigger than the one we already have. We have to look at alternatives to direct selling.

These are compelling reasons for partnerships and channels as the economy emerges from the recession of 2001 and early 2002. These kinds of indirect channels account for between 30 and 70 percent of sales revenue worldwide and cost an estimated 40 percent less than selling directly. This is enough reason to develop what can be a tricky set of partner relationships. The ROI is right there. In fact, Bob Thompson, the founder and president of Front Line Solutions, Inc., a consulting and research firm specializing in PRM, sees that good partner relationship management systems can return something on the investment potentially in as little as three months. (Yes, CFOs, as *little* as three months, not as long as three months.)

IDC, a leading analyst group, estimated that 85 percent of the Fortune 500 companies sell through channels and that over 60 percent of all IT business in 1999 was done through indirect channels. That's $120 *billion* of a total of $200 billion. And that's just information technology. That's a bit of a trick statement since IT is most likely to be involved in partnerships and channels because of the complexity of the solutions and the inability for all but the largest companies to be all things to all people. For example, SAP is nearly all things to all people in the enterprise applications world, and it has one of the largest partner programs of all companies of its type. It depends on partners in different niches and vertical markets for leads and sales and other collaborative ventures.

SalesLogix, now a subsidiary of The Sage Group PLC, a leading mid-market sales force automation company, built a 4,000 plus–customer list, with the channel responsible for almost 80 percent of all their sales. They had, as of mid 2002, more than 300 partners who operated as resellers of their software, Web offerings, and services.

Beyond the software world, insurance and auto companies depend on the networks of dealers who are their partners to drive their revenues. McDonald's depends on a combination of company-owned stores and independent franchises to drive their bottom line. In other words, we have a partner-based world. Imagine a Big Mac without Mack to run the store.

With the growth of a ubiquitous Internet, the channel also becomes part of the corporate ecosystem, an independent segment integral to and dependent on the overall ecosystem built around a company. The channel helps a company broaden its penetration in new geographic and vertical markets more efficiently, strengthen customer relationships, scale to meet customer demand, maintain competitive advantage, and increase market share and brand loyalty. The channel needs your products/service offerings to sell to the customers; you need the channel to sell your products/service offerings to their customers, who indirectly become your customers. Symbiotic? Yes. Very hard to manage? Yes.

Aye, there's the rub. They are very hard to manage. In fact, though most businesses see the value of partnerships, more often than not, the purpose of the partnership is not met. Optimism abounds regardless of results, oddly.

B to B magazine (http://www.btobonline.com/) did a survey with PepperCorn, Inc., released in January 2002. This survey addressed the issue of partnerships. Their findings were telling, but not terribly surprising.

Of the several hundred respondents, 77.6 percent thought that partnerships and alliances were helpful in the current economy (recessionary at the time). The types of partnerships most popular were Web-based content and links (27 percent) and geographically distributed partnerships (16.1 percent). The goals that were most important were increasing sales and revenue (66.1 percent) and, a distant second, expanding visibility and sales (43.9 percent). Other goals were building brand, enhancing credibility, and a few that barely appeared on the radar screens. What is fascinating is how unsuccessful the partnerships were. More than 72.1 percent of those who wanted to increase sales and revenues failed. More than 64 percent of those who wanted to expand visibility and sales failed. Beyond that, an average of about 75 percent of all other objectives failed. Not exactly a good track record, is it?

So why be involved in partnerships at all? Because you can. That might sound glib, but the reality is that partnerships, when successful, provide a natural value to the company that even affects corporate valuations positively. But, like everything else in the business world, they have to be managed properly.

The Path to PRM

There are fairly simple precepts to success in the partnership game. Some are pretty typical and some aren't, but they all are necessary. Stick to the path and the partnerships will work.

Evaluate Your Potential Partnership

Evaluate how effective the partnership is likely to be before you enter it. That might sound commonsensical, but the reality is pure. It's not hard to find partners. There is always a company, small or large, that has some reason to want to partner with another company. The issue is how appropriate the alignment really is. For example, Live Wire, the company I am employed by, has partnerships with a small number of systems integrators, both extremely large and modestly sized. Each one of those integrators has an "offering" that complements the strengths of Live Wire. Live Wire's strengths complement each of them in a different way. Most of these partnerships are successful so far. The objectives are well aligned. Another company I worked at wanted to partner with every IT vendor under the sun at varying times, and most of them failed because they were spread far too thin. Align with those that make sense.

Compare Company Cultures

Make sure the cultures of the partners are complementary. This is a simple but absolutely critical rule. Don't get into the waters with a shark if you're not a shark. If you are, shame on you, but that's your partner. You have to have a common outlook, and even more simply, you have to like your partner. Any partnership where the principal stakeholders and those who will intermingle don't like each other is doomed.

Identify the Key Personnel

Make sure there are stakeholders on top of the relationship. These are not the stakeholders I describe in Chapter 4 on strategy. These are specific to partner management: a key point person, perhaps an alliance manager or vice-president. Make sure the sales forces of both companies are fully aware of the offerings of the other company if increasing sales revenue is the objective.

Establish Procedures

Make sure there is a clear cut set of rules of engagement and a procedure to fix broken parts. There are going to be glitches along the way, especially if you are managing a channel that has several partners who do the same thing. Who gets the leads and why? Someone at some point might feel slighted. Have a structure to deal with that and a procedure to correct wrongs. Anticipate those wrongs beforehand and build corrections into the system. Make sure that each partner understands what it is getting and not getting out of the relationship to minimize the misunderstandings.

Collaborate

Collaborate, collaborate, and, oh yeah, collaborate. Remember you're actually partnering with people at times who are your competition in other areas and who partner with your competition. Take a look at the Siebel partners list and the PeopleSoft partners list. Note the significant number of the same names. However, who the partners partner with is not your concern unless it really can create a conflict. Decide how much the partnership is going to mean to your company and then work collaboratively with the partner. Don't begrudge them their other partnerships. You have more than one, too.

Partner Program Confusion

The preceding suggestions are some of the correctives and "regulations" of partnerships that enhance the possibility for success. But partnerships still break. Managing complex relationships takes more than the rules above and goodwill. Take a quick look at Siebel's partnership program and levels to see an example of complex:

- ▶ Siebel Consulting Partners
- ▶ Siebel Platform Partners
- ▶ Siebel Technical Partners
- ▶ Siebel Content Partners
- ▶ Siebel Software Partners

Within each of those are three categories of programs:

- ▶ Technical
- ▶ Marketing
- ▶ Sales

Within each of the five categories there are also varying levels:

- ▶ Strategic
- ▶ Premier
- ▶ Base

Each of these has individual rules and regulations. Within each category, there is a commitment—financial, manpower, or other—required to keep the partnership. In other words, if not managed properly, a mess ensues. Siebel has a lot to manage. No wonder applications to make partnerships manageable and successful have been growing dramatically for the past two years. The term for this is partner relationship management (PRM).

PRM was not unlike CRM in its conception. Bob Thompson says:

PRM is a business strategy to select and manage partners to optimize their long-term value to an enterprise. In effect, it means picking the right partners, working with them to help them be successful in dealing with your mutual customers, and ensuring that partners and the ultimate end customers are satisfied and successful. But PRM is where CRM was two years ago. Nobody's got the whole thing yet.

Bob Thompson is also the creator of the superb CRMGuru website (http://www.crmguru.com/), devoted to PRM and CRM.

Sometimes you will see the term "e-partnering" used interchangeably with or alongside PRM. PRM and e-partnering are not identical.

E-partnering represents the all-encompassing system—the combination of strategy, processes, e-tools, and methodology. PRM is the strategy and tools in the equation.

PRM is one of those smaller, but fast-growing segments of the CRM world that has just begun to realize its superb potential. In the year 2000, it was about a $500 million business, which was to double to $1 billion by 2003 according to Gartner. IDC said it will be over $2 billion by 2003. In fact, in 2001, it was nearly a billion in licenses and services. Gartner recently gave the genre its highest honor by recognizing PRM as a distinct software category with its own famed "Magic Quadrant." And Robertson Stephens Technology Research noted in its April 2001 report, "Channel Commerce Software," "The channel represented thousands of fragmented, independent entities that were difficult to manage. This perception is changing, however, as manufacturers increasingly recognize the value of optimizing channel relationships— pointing to what could become a $3–$5 billion software market over the next five years." In other words, PRM is hot!

It's not just hot, though, it's also mission-critical. Look at this forecast released by Gartner in early 2002: "By 2005, Gartner believes that 90 percent of failed CRM projects will have focused solely on internal organizational collaboration, rather than extending the process to partners and to creating an improved customer experience." In other words, using the (Greenberg) definition of customer, if you don't realize that CRM involves your partner as well as your internal organization and clients, then failure is very possible.

Businesses are now integrating their supply chain with their demand chain out of sheer necessity. As I mentioned in Chapter 1, the definition of customer includes suppliers, vendors, partners, and employees and is now encompassed by the corporate ecosystem. Some like to call it a value chain.

There are some major benefits to partnering, some apparent and some not. The META Group research firm identified the following advantages in a series of 2001 reports on PRM:

- Creating a single selling experience across multiple organizational boundaries

- Increasing market share and overall brand loyalty

- Synchronizing, optimizing, and understanding sales and demand impacts across channels

IDC identified three benefits in a report on PRM sponsored by Allegis Corporation, a leading PRM vendor. They cite the following:

- Expanding market coverage
- Offerings of specialized products and services
- Broadened range of offerings and a more complete solution

I would add to that:

- Your possible competitors become your allies.
- Your company can concentrate on its core capabilities and still have full service coverage.
- The "my staff is your staff" principle governs your relationships, so you can call upon your partners to work with you to cover your gaps with your customers.

This actually can enable businesses that use PRM solutions to tighten their communication and collaboration with selling partners, improve lead distribution and follow-up, sharpen revenue forecasts, decrease channel conflict, and reduce channel management costs.

Take a leading telecommunications company like Qwest Communications International. Qwest was driving a significant and growing share of sales through the channel and decided to build a branded, collaborative marketplace to improve their partners' sales performance. This meant helping its partners to deliver an end-to-end communications solution, which clearly was to Qwest's benefit. Using PRM software from ChannelWave Software, Inc., Qwest built the Q.Marketplace, an online lead sharing and collaboration tool for the Qwest Business Partner Program (QBPP) members. One strong advantage to Q.Marketplace is collaboration between partners so that the appropriate (Qwest-driven) communications solutions can be provided to customers. According to Qwest's website, members can:

- Receive prequalified leads from Qwest
- Find and share business opportunities
- Collaborate with other members to augment existing capabilities and create complete solution offerings
- Gain valuable exposure with other QBPP members and end-user customers, creating stronger channel opportunities for individual solutions

▶ Access new solutions and increase sales opportunities

▶ Share best practices

Qwest told Forrester Research its PRM investment has paid off in less than one year, and Q.Marketplace has been recognized as one of the most comprehensive partner programs within high-tech and telecommunications. "It's a solid investment on our part," Craig Schlagbaum, senior director of the Qwest Business Partner Program told *Interactive Week* magazine. "We've already put in close to 3,000 leads, and 70 percent have been followed up. That's the kind of interactivity you can get on this. Before, we'd send out a lead and hope it would be followed up. We'd never know the result." Results like this within a year of rollout are awfully impressive. Is that norm with PRM ROI? Not necessarily, but the fact that there is more than one example of this kind of return tells you why PRM is a constantly growing sector within CRM: results.

Managing Your Partners

The problems in managing partners are far different and far more complex than those of sales management. Each partner has a business interest of its own, a set of business processes that are endemic to their company, a group of their own partners and paying customers that may or may not overlap with yours, a business model that is most likely not identical to yours, and a group of personalities that vary as widely as the different corporate cultures. Thus, the way they allocate their time and the intensity of their partnering effort will vary from partner to partner. The contractual obligation of each partner will vary to some degree. However, each partner is essential to the infrastructure of your ecosystem and vital to the offerings to your customers.

An additional degree of complexity is added when you have to figure which partners are appropriate to which customers. The number of partner programs will vary depending on the category. Is your partner a value-added reseller (VAR) selling your product and adding services? Is your partner an independent software vendor (ISV), developing a software solution that is founded on your product? Is the partner a training partner? Is the partner a joint business partner who is providing a software solution that you don't have from a third-party vendor? These are functional and cultural concerns. What about technical issues? Is the IT architecture that your partner uses able to integrate with your architecture? With you at the hub, this becomes a mission-critical question for each partner, usually each using a different configuration due to their corporate needs and each trying to juggle architectures with their partners from their hub.

Look at a company like IBM. They have thousands of partners with multiple roles and programs and purposes. For example, IBM Global Services has so many subcontracting partners that they have established a program outsourced to 22 subcontractors to subcontract other subcontractors to either do or administer all of IBM Global Services subcontracting assignments—unless there is a niche need such as ERP so that an "other than the 22" subcontractor can work with IBM Global Services directly. Even those arrangements are impacted by the nature of the alliances IBM has with companies such as Siebel, which has its own service organization, which doesn't stop IBM from working with SalesLogix, and on and on.

Complicated? Yes, it is, and that is precisely the purpose of Internet-integrated PRM applications: to manage what can be a plethora of complex partner relations that are often conflicting. Mr. Thompson again:

> A channel strategy is a prerequisite to effective PRM. Internet-based technology is often (but not always) a part of PRM because it's the only practical way to manage hundreds to tens of thousands of partners in large complex channels.

Effective PRM requires a channel strategy and a portal that gives each partner a customized view of their partner programs, leads, opportunities, forecasts, objectives, news, and so on. Take a look at Figures 9-1 and 9-2.

PRM Is Not Just PRM

As the market for PRM grows, the complexity of what PRM is and what it isn't increases. While Cro-Magnon PRM evolves to contemporary man, its Neanderthal brother, Enterprise Channel Management (ECM), with its somewhat stricter channel management programs, automated tools, and strategy, begins its trek toward civilization. While ECM branches, the corporate ecosystem begins to expand and envelop PRM strategy by creating collaborative commerce through the use of what the Forrester Group calls Partner Hubs. These Partner Hubs consist of:

- ▶ A PRM strategy with PRM tools

- ▶ The addition of partner scorecards for measuring the success or failure of partners

- ▶ Contract negotiation tools

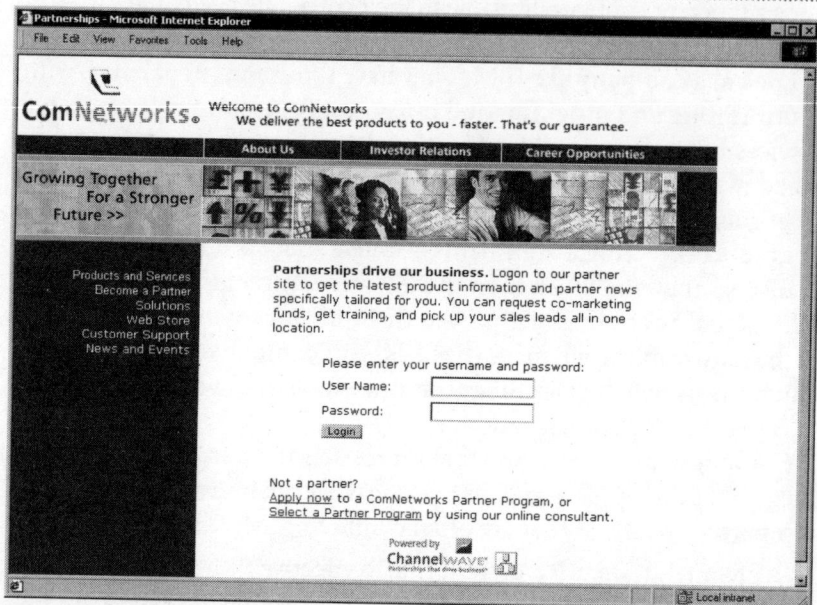

Figure 9-1: The entrance to the Magic Partner Kingdom: a look at the ChannelWave portal gateway (Copyright 2002, ChannelWave, Inc. All rights reserved.)

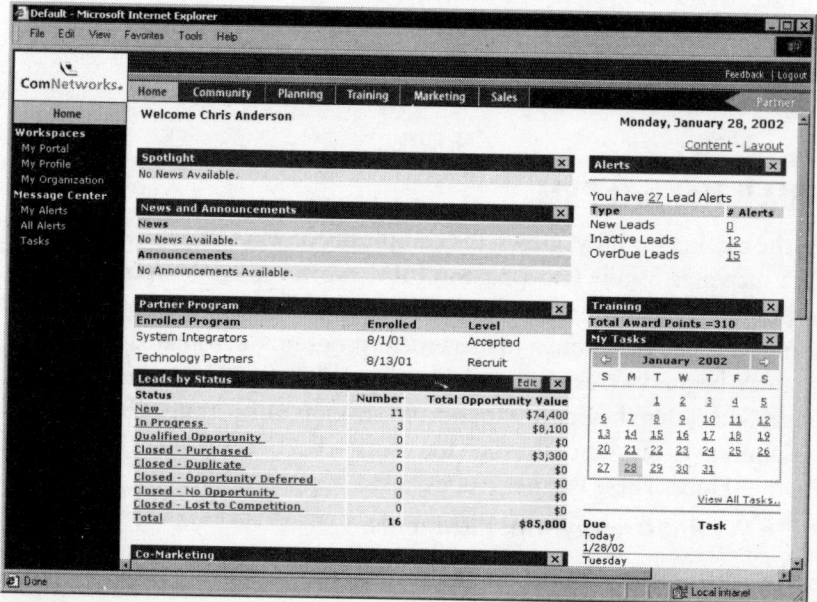

Figure 9-2: What you see when you get inside the ChannelWave portal. (Copyright 2002, ChannelWave, Inc. All rights reserved.)

Additionally, the verticalization of PRM is a natural part of PRM since channels and partners (and their metrics) vary widely from industry to industry. That means strategy and programs also vary widely from industry to industry. How you deal with independent insurance agents as part of the Century 21 network is fundamentally different from how you deal with your services partners when you are a software vendor. Yet the PRM or ECM software has to be flexible enough to handle any kind of strategy. The market complexity has grown greatly in the last two years. But the fundamental composition of what makes this PRM or ECM hasn't changed.

PRM Is Also Not Just Sales Force Automation and a Partner

PRM has some similarities with sales force automation applications, but not enough to delete the subfolder. In order to understand the differences between SFA and PRM, let's begin with another comment from Mr. Thompson on the necessity of integrating SFA with PRM to develop a more complete PRM:

> Not unless there is true team selling when direct and indirect reps are collaborating on deals and need to communicate what's going on with a specific opportunity. Then it makes sense to connect SFA with PRM applications, or find one application that will serve both parties well. Another example is distributing leads that may come out of a CRM/SFA application and need to be forwarded to a PRM application. So, yes, there can be connection points, but not in every case.

> In a nutshell, SFA with partners is not PRM.

PRM Means Partner Network

PRM applications handle considerably more than simple channel management. Channel management ordinarily covers the simple partner relations that characterize the days gone by. Robert Thompson calls the channel a "st..tic, linear distribution process." In fact, the channel has been most closely identified with value-added resellers, more than any other type of partners. *Smart Reseller* magazine, recognizing that the tides of indirect channels were shifting, renamed themselves *Smart Partner*. The magazine projected a strong future for PRM. "Virtually every company that sells indirectly is a candidate to use PRM software, which enables you to manage ties and work with partners, share leads, and make collaborative sales forecasts," it noted. (Sadly, as of 2002, they are no longer *Smart anything*, having gone out of business due to the economic downturn.)

The new definition of the channel is probably characterized by the Yiddish term *shadchen*, which, in English, roughly translates to "matchmaker." The demands of the corporate ecosystem call for a network of partners spawned or redefined by the Internet, chosen by the corporate network members, that can deliver a true solution sale or end-to-end service offering for the customers of any one member of the network. However, with the advent of the Internet version of PRM, the role of the indirect partner increases even more. Mr. Thompson says:

> One thing that I do feel is often overlooked is the role of "influencer" channel partners—those who don't purchase products for resale, and may not earn an agent fee, but nevertheless are an important channel for companies to support. Integrators, consultants, and industry analysts are good examples. Customers buy based on recommendations of these influencers, but since the purchase is made directly, the role of the influencer is hidden.

What is the authority of these influencers? As the economy becomes more customer-intimate, the authority of the indirect partner—the influencer—becomes increasingly important. Industry analysts such as the Gartner Group, IDC, and Aberdeen do reports on who the players are, and the new mindshare champion is crowned in that market. For example, Allegis paid for the PRM report I quoted earlier from IDC, and there is a significant segment on the now superseded Allegis Sales Partner as a market frontrunner for PRM. The "Paid for by Allegis" stamp tends to dilute IDC's conclusion a bit, but there are unmistakable PRM truths being stated by IDC and they carry credibility. A consultant who has established himself in the IT world in a particular discipline carries a lot of weight in the recommendations he proposes. And just as much as an additional category—friends. How frequently do you as an IT manager seek the counsel of knowledgeable friends and pay close attention to their recommendations? This is the value of the *shadchen*.

Assessing PRM

PRM functionality is multifarious. Because of its intricacy, there are a significant number of different attributes that any company assessing a PRM system must consider. What are the processes that should be embedded in the application? Let's look at the partnership cycle.

Partner Program Development

Siebel's aforementioned partner program deserves a more intense scrutiny to grasp the level of partner management that these kinds of programs involve. The basic requirements for a typical Siebel partnership type, Consulting Partner, illustrate these issues.

Services provided include business process redesign (using Siebel, of course), end-user training, project management, systems integration, systems administration, and training. Other characteristics are geographical focus and vertical market expertise to fill Siebel gaps. Dedicated Siebel-certified resources ranging from 1 (Base Partner) to 50 (Premier Partner) to 300 (Strategic Partner) are also required. The fees are significant—from $7,500 to $50,000 annually—and there is a marketing development fund commitment ranging from nothing for the Base Partner to $1 million per year for the Strategic Partner. The benefits are logo usage, varying levels of training appropriate to partnership level, partner posting, getting on the inside with Siebel, joint success stories, partner area access, marketing, demonstration, development licenses (though for the Base Partner there is a fee for this), technical support, attendance at the Siebel annual user conference, and of course, plenty of advertising, especially for the upper levels (they *are* paying for it!).

In the other categories, such as Software Partner, while the requirements and benefits vary from type to type and level to level, there are even more layers of interwoven intricacy—such as the Siebel Validation program that will certify your software product, which is different from the Siebel Certification program that certifies the successful training and completion of the testing of Siebel consultants, which is different from the certification accorded varying partners after customer audits are conducted annually, which is different from the certification accorded partners for… you get the picture. This is not an easy process to manage.

Partner Recruitment and Profiling

Partner recruitment has undergone a dramatic shift since 2000. If you look at major vendor partner recruitment or global services company partner recruitment, there have been drastic changes in time and method for all but a handful of companies. In the pre-2000 era, partnerships were "granted" by the vendor to an elite group of VARS, ISVs, or consulting services companies who gave the vendor something of significance—a place in a vertical market, a significant presence—and who brought business to the vendor as an offering. Typical ERP partnerships took eight months to build unless you were Accenture or IBM, and getting into them was harder than admission to Harvard. But now that the corporate ecosystem is relying increasingly on partners providing those goods and services they lack, those eight months have become one to three months, and though most companies are still selective about who their partners are, they are far more forgiving on the criteria for entry. Now, time to partnership is shortened in many cases and the "rules" of partnership are being eased. These, in combination with a shortage of qualified manpower and a very crowded domain-expert vendor field have led to hundreds, even thousands, of companies trying to become partners or create partner programs to fill the gaping holes. For example, dozens of EMA vendors on the market vie for your company's attention since they don't have the staff to implement their own software nor do they have the sales force to approach the markets you are attacking. You are now a valuable commodity to a vendor, rather than a potentially blackballed member of an elite society. But keep in mind one thing; the rules of partnership that remain are opportunity- and revenue-driven. Most other partnership criteria are more ephemeral. But in this case, revenue is the master.

Companies are using PRM solutions to streamline the recruitment process and manage contracts and other partnership functions such as registration, qualification, and program enrollment. What follows is how it does that.

Partnership Goal Management

Of course, the problem with making the entrance requirements easier is that regardless of the program in place, the partner performance quality may be considerably lower than planned for. Remember that famous Groucho Marx line, "I'd never join a club that would have me as a member." One good example is Siebel. For all the complexity and cost of their program, they have a tremendously high rate of partner "firings" because of non-performance. For example, in 2001, they fired an incredibly large number of their mid-market partners due to what Siebel saw as a less-than-impressive performance level. While I can't speak to the fact that some of the blame could have been other than the partners', what it does point out is that regardless of how comprehensive a program can be, if a strong part of this PRM strategy is not goal management, then failure is likely, if not inevitable.

Once you have a partner, expectations must be established. What are the objectives for the partner? Do they have sales requirements to maintain the partnership? What kind of marketing development funds (MDF) do they have to commit? How does the application assign goals, manage tasks, and set metrics for determining success? How does the application flag under-performance or trigger responses to over-quota performance? Joint planning of the mutual goals is necessary. For example, in order for a company to become a PeopleSoft partner, a mutually agreed-upon set of specific metrics is identified prior to the partnership so that when (and if) the partnership is done, the objectives are already clearly defined. Then the partner needs to define a plan to execute toward the objectives. Take a look at Figure 9-3.

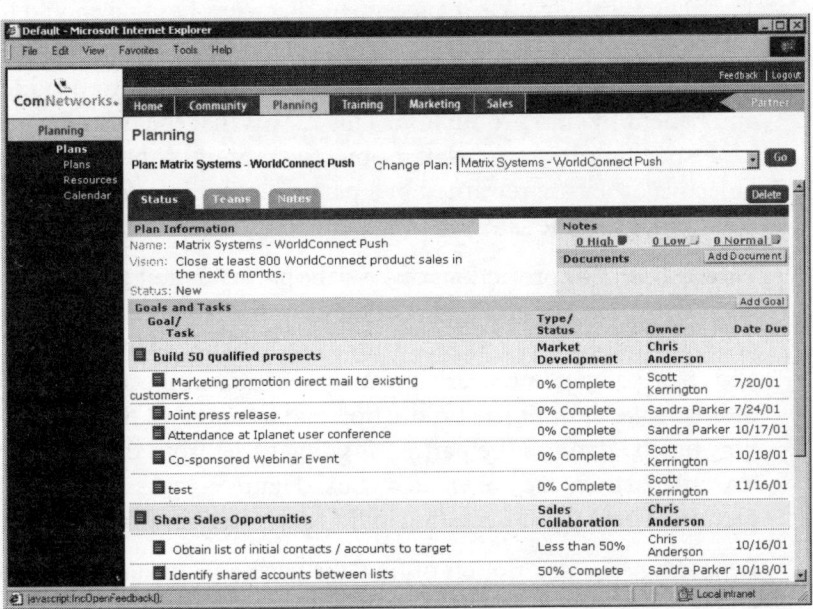

Figure 9-3: Partner planning toward objectives (Copyright 2002, ChannelWave. All rights reserved.)

Sales/Marketing: Lead Generation and Distribution

Let's face it—a lot of partners are in it for the business leads the partnership generates. There's nothing wrong with this as long as they are prepared to bring in business as well as take it. However, it's a fairly dicey proposition for the hub partner to distribute appropriate leads to the appropriate partners, since others may feel they are being left out or being burned in the process. Criteria for distribution and management of lead distribution are part of the package as it is presented.

Partner Life Cycle Management

Partner life cycle management is PRM's core functionality. This is where the partner is proven to be a partner, not a leech or a trophy-spouse.

Life cycle management is a buzzword in the IT world now for customers, partners, employees, and any other social or economic category of people that you care to think of. Simply stated, it is the entirety of the engagement with that group or individual, long and deep—long in the sense that it extends the entire lifespan of the relationship, deep in that it covers all areas of the partnership, including the risks and rewards for that particular arrangement. PRM life cycle management characteristics that should be part of the application include:

Productivity and rewards How the partner is going to produce and benefit by that production. This means that the partners will have specific program-related objectives. Should they hit those objectives, they are rewarded in a particular fashion, for example, a percentage of the sale or a premium partnership status.

Forecasting The projections on how the partner is going to produce and benefit. An important part of life cycle management is what the company thinks it can expect from its individual partner. Vendors and their partners need to accurately monitor and predict future indirect sales to optimize production and inventory. This addresses how much attention the partner is going to get from the company since all partners are not created equal. Figure 9-4 gives you a good picture of how that forecasting looks to the anxious brand owner.

Reporting The description of how the partner is going to produce and benefit, using reporting tools endemic to the functionality of the application (Seagate's Crystal Reports is often integrated with the application). Organizations are seeking real-time visibility into the entire life cycle of channel presales, sales, and postsales activities in order to make better-informed business decisions. Life cycle management reporting is critical because how you formulate the report is key to the understanding of the report results by the reader of that report. Corporate decisions are made correctly or incorrectly, often based on how well-structured the report is. Figure 9-5 shows you how a brand owner can look at performance reports via the PRM application.

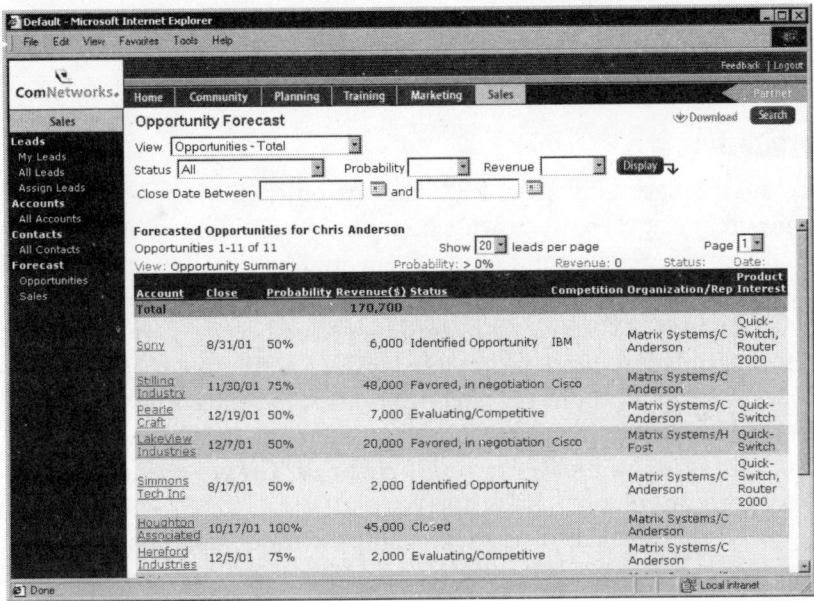

Figure 9-4: Brand owner view of an opportunity forecast (Copyright 2002, ChannelWave, Inc. All rights reserved.)

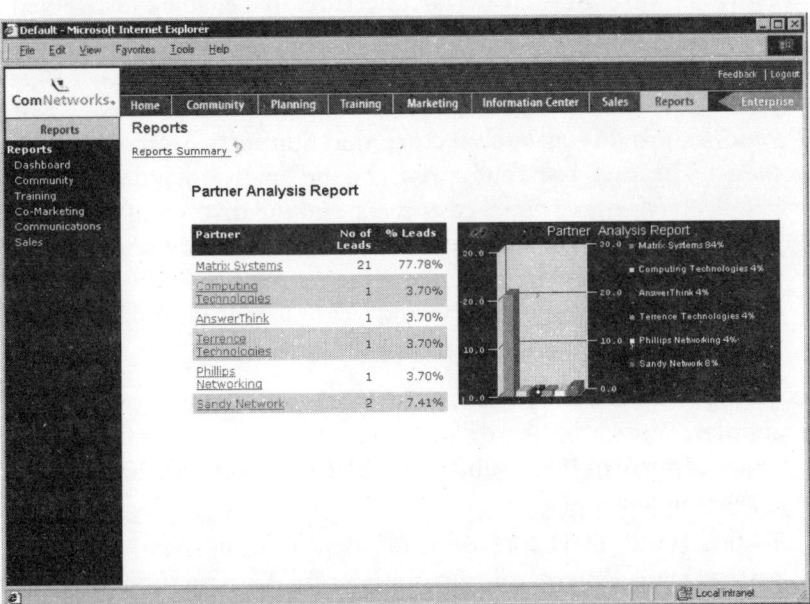

Figure 9-5: Partner analysis report for the brand owner (Copyright 2002, ChannelWave, Inc. All rights reserved.)

Contract management How the partner is legally obligated to produce and benefit by the partnership. This is a tracking function to make sure that contractual obligations are met.

Architecture

Perhaps the biggest difference PRM has with other CRM applications lies in the architectural requirements necessary to gain full visibility across an enterprise's demand and supply chains and support dynamic collaboration across a complex network of vendors, partners, and customers. SFA and other CRM applications are designed with a one-to-many architecture facilitating direct selling relationships within the organization. When these applications are extended outside the enterprise, they cannot readily adapt to managing the selling and servicing of products and solutions across multiple distribution channels. The next generations of PRM applications, such as ChannelWave 5.0, are designed with a many-to-many architecture to manage complex multi-tier relationships throughout the entire value chain and define multi-tiered, ad hoc, or permanent communities consisting of multiple vendors, distributors, partners, influencers, and customers.

Gartner noted in a 2001 report, "PRM vs. CRM":

> PRM vendors...have created architectures that enable a distributed network of business partners to create and maintain value-added services for their customers and complementary partners (i.e., support for a many-to-many business model).... In contrast, CRM vendors provide an architecture that supports a one-to-many model. The "one" is the enterprise, and the "many" include the salespeople, call centers, direct customers, and the first tier of a partner channel. Without the support for a many-to-many relationship model, enterprises will experience higher total cost of ownership due to extensive customization and technology that inhibits, rather than enables, partner relationships.

According to Gartner, 90 percent of CRM vendors do not provide these capabilities.

The research firm IDC found a similar distinction. In a 2001 report on PRM, it noted:

> To date, traditional CRM software has typically been limited in the partner management functionality because it is optimized for a different sort of relationship. CRM treats the partner as a customer

rather than as an active sales party, thus requiring extensive customization to meet partner requirements.

The Internet's open standards are pretty much the only way for an "e-hyphenated" package to go. That means able to handle HTTPS (secure HTTP), XML, and various Java encodings, plus perhaps Active Server Pages (ASP), and Java server pages (JSP). This plus good old HTML should do the Web-trick.

Integration

Integration, which is covered in Chapter 12, is of paramount importance unless you have never done anything with information systems at your company. Since that is highly unlikely for anyone reading this book, what is more likely is that your company has invested between tens of thousands to tens of millions in information systems. Dennis Ryan, president of Allegis, noted in an interview that most Allegis customers had some CRM or simply an SFA application in place prior to their purchase of Allegis Sales Partner. Additionally, most companies may have ERP up and running, legacy client server best-of-breed applications, mainframe applications, if they lean toward the Pleistocene era, and who knows how many other Web applications their sales and marketing forces already employ.

Ease of Deployment, Change, and Use

How important is this one on a scale of one to ten? Ten. Getting the application up and running, customizing it without the consulting firm that implemented it, and then using it without teeth-gnashing is vital to successful implementation of what can be a costly piece of software.

Chris Heidelberger, president and CEO of ChannelWave, noted in an interview that PRM applications are defining a new software business model. He equates its importance with the paradigm shifts from mainframe to client/server and client/server to Internet/browser-based platforms. With the move to Internet architectures, PRM solutions that are built on the open, flexible J2EE platform, using XML technology, are designed to deliver faster deployment, easier integration with existing enterprise applications, and a lower cost of ownership. "Companies are not going to spend the kind of money that they spent on the last generation of enterprise software. Under the new model, we can put up meaningful applications in 45 days that start immediately delivering millions of dollars in ROI for our customers and their partners." That is a heady claim with some basis, as problems in PRM applications are being worked out as the sector matures and the need for channel and partner management skyrockets.

For example, Partnerware's extended Enterprise 2000 (XE) automates many of the PRM processes through eXtensible Module Designer templates and design tools, which eliminate most of the coding. You don't have to pay for custom coding every time you change your partner programs or business processes. This is important for the return on investment expected. Being able to implement and deploy the application and then simply go to the Web and go to work is essential with the need for speed that governs the world of business-to-business. PRM isn't quite there, but is approaching "the Heidelberger Paradigm."

Security, Performance, and Reliability

When the system is up and running, it has to stay up and run.

Return on Investment

There are differences of opinion on both the metrics for ROI and the validity of the ROI at this stage of the PRM game. But the growing consensus in this field is that unlike a couple of years ago, PRM now provides among the best ROI of any CRM sector. Gartner's "PRM Business Benefits Model" found that enterprises can justify the benefits of PRM deployments on cost savings alone—particularly from reductions in customer service costs—but that the revenue-enhancement potential of PRM was six to eight times greater than these cost savings. The strongest revenue benefits include:

- ▶ Increased conversion of prospects into active sales opportunities by partners through a PRM system's closed-loop lead management capability

- ▶ Increases in sales wins attributable to improved online partner training and certification

- ▶ Larger order sizes through sales content management capabilities that improve the distribution of sales and marketing information for partners

IDC published a case study on the experience of Internet infrastructure software vendor Tarantella with PRM. Tarantella used ChannelWave to manage its partner program and has improved partner follow-through on leads from 10 percent to 69 percent, resulting in more effective forecasting and opportunities. IDC reported:

> Tarantella is able to justify the implementation from a return-on-investment perspective…. The Tarantella implementation is exactly the kind of success story PRM vendors…will need if this market is going to fly. PRM vendors need to create return-on-investment stories, and the return won't always be as clear as it has been in Tarantella's case.

Those analysts and pundits who have made prognostications about the PRM field have all agreed that PRM has or will have a tangible benefit, but *when* seems to be in question. IDC cheerleads for a rapid ROI that they think is not only possible but absolutely necessary in making the determination to purchase PRM. They make statements like these:

> Companies need to be able to see results and recoup their investments. The days of lengthy implementations without accountability are over. They also need to project future investments accurately.

And:

> PRM also allows companies to better measure and improve their return on investment (ROI) in channel programs and activities. (Source: International Data Corp., "Partner Relationship Management: Enabling eBusiness for the Channel.")

Robert Thompson, on the other hand, took a more cautious approach in our interview:

> There is a tangible ROI for PRM, sometimes in as little as three months, but while there are a growing number of case studies, the results aren't fully established yet. However, some companies like Cisco Systems are well known for employing PRM systems in dealing with partners. Although their technology was homegrown, the results have been impressive in terms of sales productivity and reduced support costs. More important, however, is that Cisco has created loyalty relationships. Many of the companies I've interviewed are chasing similar goals, but haven't achieved Cisco's level of results.

Research shows that Mr. Thompson is perhaps closer to the tempered mark.

The Technology: Who's Who and What's What in PRM

Despite PRM's relative newness, there are a few established names in the field that have fully functional, well-developed, often expensive applications. While there are several other players mentioned at the end of this chapter, ChannelWave 5.0 is, by my estimation, the best of breed in the PRM market with a nearly complete package and a very clean, usable interface for the channel managers among you who don't care what is under the hood. The breakdown of their product provides a very useful look at the components of what actually constitutes a PRM system. Think about these features and the interaction between them and you'll begin to get a sense of how complicated task partner management actually can be. Ease of use is a real and important focus in PRM's domain.

Interestingly, there is no particular pressure to use a single PRM solution. Take a look at this quote from an article on ZDNet:

> [Hewlett-Packard] already uses PRM solutions from Allegis Corp. [for managing dealer registration and rebate programs] and ChannelWave Software Inc. [for partner training and certification programs]...Hill said HP could find the technology in [OnDemand's] Demand Center useful.

Three of the four major players in a single company. Where are you, Partnerware?

ChannelWave

This is a really good company. They have put some serious time into thinking about the partner and one of the more old-fashioned virtues of partnership: loyalty. Their platform is built on the idea that loyalty matters a great deal and the relationship of the partner to partner, whether a brandholder or member, is of the essence.

ChannelWave 5.0 is the current incarnation of ChannelWave Software, Inc.'s PRM suite. ChannelWave 5.0 is one of the first with an open Java-based platform and a suite of Web-based applications that spans the life cycle of indirect presales, sales, and postsales activities. ChannelWave's customers including AT&T, BEA, Cable & Wireless, Hewlett-Packard, Motorola, and Qwest.

ChannelWave 5.0 includes four broad applications—Partner, Market, Sell, and Service—and, within each, specific solutions that can streamline the multiple collaborative and complex business processes of partner and channel management.

Partner

ChannelWave's Partner solution is designed specifically to improve the performance of partners by providing the business planning, collaboration, and support resources required to achieve indirect sales goals. The ChannelWave Partner solution maintains critical information about every business partnership, including details on partner organizations, solution offerings, and individuals involved. It handles those highly fragmented, multi-tiered partner programs that we all know and love. Its components are as follows:

Planning Manager Features include:

> **Business Planning** Allows businesses and partners to set mutual goals, define objectives, assign and manage tasks, and set metrics for determining success.

> **Demand Planning** Monitors and predicts future indirect sales to enable production and inventory optimization, if that's what is needed.

Relationship Manager This is perhaps the core piece of Partner. It includes:

> **Recruitment and Renewal Manager** Streamlines the recruitment process and reduces recruitment time.

> **Recruitment Advisor** Intelligent, interactive recruitment tools that automate partner application registration, qualification, and program enrollment.

> **Program Manager** Assists lower performing partners and provides continuous incentives for top performing partners to stay productive, loyal, and motivated.

> **Agreements Manager** Manages and tracks partnership contracts and other commitments such as service level agreements online. This is a particularly important piece and is often missing in PRM applications.

> **Certification Manager** Defines and tracks partner certification requirements and status. Updates certification status manually or automatically.

Partner Reports Reports can provide real-time visibility into the recruitment, planning, agreement, and forecasting activities of partners.

Partner Metrics Produces analytics-based reporting by drawing from a data warehouse containing information from ChannelWave applications, as well as back- and front-office enterprise applications.

Market

ChannelWave's Market solution enables businesses and their partners to collaborate and coordinate joint marketing activities on a local, regional, or worldwide scale. Partners gain access to a variety of marketing resources at one centralized location. Enterprises can track and monitor the effectiveness of demand creation programs through a closed-loop lead distribution system and provide partners with automated one-to-one communications. The components of Market include:

Communications Manager Features include:

Collateral Distribution Manager Manages distribution lists, marketing messages, and collateral distribution. Announces events through personalized communication broadcasts via the Web or email.

Survey Manager Builds and administers online questionnaires to collect feedback on any topic and generate professional reports.

Content Manager Provides partners with access to a library of personalized content, including presentations, product and pricing information, special offers, and promotions.

Events Manager Views and registers events online and creates personalized event calendars and reminders.

Campaigns Manager Creates, manages, and organizes marketing campaigns that support specific marketing goals or objectives. This is a very versatile module.

Solution Advisor Gives customers access to an online, virtual equivalent of a company's best salesperson, and, in turn, gives partners highly qualified leads. This is a very good module for new partners because it is essentially a way of knowing best practices and has embedded corporate culture to the extent it can be embedded.

Literature Fulfillment A straightforward feature. It fulfills and tracks distribution of marketing literature to partners.

Incentives Manager One of the valuable partner program creation features, it creates and manages incentive programs to increase system usage among partners.

Marketing Funds Manager Handling marketing funds is a sensitive and difficult task, because in the world of partnerships, these are *co*-marketing funds. Marketing Funds Manager creates, tracks, and manages funds and views partner activity for marketing initiatives. Partners can track approval requests, claims, accruals, and adjustments.

Market Reports Produces real-time information on marketing campaign and promotions performance, including cost analysis and return on marketing investment.

Sell

ChannelWave's Sell solution automates and streamlines the indirect sales process. Businesses can automatically distribute and track leads and access real-time information on channel sales activity, opportunity forecasts, and sales transactions. Its components include:

Opportunity Management Features include:

Lead Management Captures and manages leads automatically or manually from a variety of sources and distributes them to the most appropriate partners based on defined rules.

Opportunity Forecasting Tracks lead opportunities by close date and measures them against projected sales goals.

RFP Manager Allows partners to establish subcontractor relationships with other partners. This feature is particularly thoughtful and is one of the few available in any PRM software that actually benefits staff augmentation, professional services, and government contractor businesses.

Team Selling Allows partner teams to collaborate on sales opportunities with a direct sales force. Assigns opportunities to multiple partners and enables them to share resources and expertise to close deals. Again, another feature that can encourage partner collaboration.

Order Management Enables partners to view product catalogs and price lists, and enter, configure, and process orders through direct integration with ERP systems. This is important because one of the weaknesses of the immature PRM market was its lack of ability to integrate with back-office systems.

Partner Locator Manager Provides partners with access to other partners with complementary sales and service capabilities.

Sales Report Tracks status and partner activity on distributed leads. Runs opportunity and order summary reports based on partner organization, territory, product, and other attributes.

Service

This is a hardcore customer service application. It would be easy to separate this from PRM and view it as online help, but this particular feature set is aimed straight at partners. They get access to online customer service information and resources. Its stated purpose is to alleviate reliance on call centers, but that is always a questionable result. Most of the benefit of this type of partner application is to enhance the customer service offerings, and in that it succeeds. Call centers may become more effective and efficient, but that is where I would leave it. Its components include:

Training and Education Partners gain online access to downloadable self-study materials, course schedules, and registration.

Self Service Features include:

Problem Diagnosis Advisor Provides instant 24/7 access to online support expertise.

Service Bulletin Distribution Provides online updates about key information to your customers and partners. The updates can be newsletters, bulletins, or targeted emails.

FAQ Manager Consolidates and posts common questions that are, of course, frequently asked.

Content Manager Provides partners with access to a library of personalized content including presentations, pricing and product information, special offers, and promotions.

Channel Support Manager Features include:

Support Request Manager Enables customer service representatives to process and escalate service requests from partners and customers.

Peer Support Provides support tools for partners or customers without making requests directly to the vendor organization.

Post-Sales Support Manager Features include:

RMA Manager RMA requests can be automatically logged and checked prior to issuing return authorization. Support staff can issue RMA numbers, approve appropriate repairs, and provide refunds to accounts or initiate shipment of replacement products and parts. This is more of a back-office function and actually is often a component of enterprise channel management (ECM) systems.

Warranty Manager Real-time online registration and tracking of warranty information. Again, an excellent back-office function and ECM system component.

Survey Manager Builds and administers online questionnaires to collect feedback and generate professional reports.

Service Reports Each major set in ChannelWave 5.0 has reporting capabilities. This one will provide reports on productivity gains as a result of call center offload through the addition of self-service capabilities. It reports usage analysis of FAQs, document library downloads, guided problem resolution, and support requests.

This is about as end-to-end as you are going to see in the PRM world. It handles indirect sales, co-marketing, partner service, and the hardcore partner relationships. It hasn't missed much and has a clean interface, too—an alliance manager can actually use it. Partners can get what they want. Makes collaboration a bit more frictionless, doesn't it?

Their website: http://www.channelwave.com/.

Allegis E-Business Suite

Allegis Corporation is among the leading PRM players in the marketplace, providing a fully Web-integrated e-channel management solution. In the last couple of years, they have lost some ground to companies like Partnerware and ChannelWave, but they still provide a more than substantial product. Their most recent product suite, E-Business Suite, is a PRM version of multifunction CRM. The product is complete and has a strong bent toward channel management. It is broken down into Partners, Marketing, Sales, Services, Network, and Intelligence subsegments. Each of these subsegments has multiple modules and features to cover pretty much any of the possible day-to-day activities. It is well organized. For example, in a single subsegment, Allegis Partners handles:

Registration This feature qualifies new partners by enabling online registration. It defines approval processes and even handles self-registration.

Ramp-up This feature standardizes ramp-up processes and activities, and has a strong workflow. Roles and permissions are assigned through this feature.

Corporate profiles This identifies who your partners are, what they sell, where they sell, what industries they focus on, and what certifications they have.

People profiles This is the same as corporate profiles except it is profiles of your partner or your individual organization members. This determines what functions they can perform in the system, what content and tools they receive, and how sales opportunities and marketing programs are targeted to them.

Business planning This feature is for the assignment of objectives, targets, metrics, and the timeframes to reach these goals and to compare actual results against the objectives.

Territory management This is always a dangerous minefield because territory to a partner sales team is, well, territorial. The care that has to be built into how it is handled with multiple partners makes for one of the more vexing PRM problems to be solved. When done well, the application will build and manage territory plans by mapping your partners to your channel territory structure. There are analytic tools in the Allegis version to slice and dice your partner coverage and your channel sales results across geographies.

Call planner Also as part of Partner, the call planner tracks communications and interactions with the partners and provides a built-in methodology for tracking communications objectives, expected outcomes, and key issues.

This should give you an idea of how rich their functionality actually is. Here is a quick summary of the rest so that you can see the depth they now have.

Marketing This is the suite piece that handles the channel programs themselves including allocation of co-marketing funds and joint campaigns, and provides collateral material to the partners.

These modules are Communications, Funds, Promotions, Campaigns, Sales, and Marketing Library.

Sales This modular offering is all you ever need for lead assignment, joint opportunity management, products, and pricing, including special deals and partner-specific lead assignment. The modules are comprehensive: Oppportunities, Account Management, Special Pricing, Team Selling, Post Sales Management, Product Catalog, Needs Analysis, Partner Locator, and Pipeline Forecasting.

Services This is exactly what it sounds like. They are the modules that provide the services that can make the partner a more effective participant in the partner programs—from making sure there are online services to partner-initiated request fulfillment. It also offers the various means for improving partner skills from training to libraries of best practices. The modules here are Training and Certification, Partner Requests, e-Services, and Best Practices.

Network In a way, this is the slickest of all the applications that Allegis offers. This is the partner-to-partner set. It allows partners to team on proposals, to list their complementary services and solutions, to work with each other directly on opportunities via this network, to advertise to each other, and to just do what partner programs should—provide increased opportunities for business among the members. This is the Allegis Club as far as I can see. The modules: Partner Network, Multi-Vendor Catalog, Solutions Stacks, Request for Proposal, Network Request, Partner Team Opportunities, and Network Communications.

Intelligence This is the Allegis partner engine that could. This is where the success and failure of the metrics and benchmarks set for each partner are looked at. How is the program as a whole doing? How is partner A or B doing? What can we look at as the revenue stream from the partners? In addition, there are sales data capture and surveys. The modules are Channel Analysis, Custom Analysis, Channel Forecasting, Point of Sale, Surveys, and Feedback.

Their website: http://www.allegis.com/.

Partnerware's Total Channel Experience (TCX)

In February 2002, Partnerware officially shed its skin and entirely rebuilt its company. They dropped their ASP business model and the "one software fits all" approach they had that meant out-of-the-box functionality with tools for customization and a hosted solution. They got new management and a new product line called TCX. They phased out their 20 ASP customers and are attempting to convert them to TCX. Their enterprise business model is built around providing a solution (not hosted) that could be fully customized to the business processes of the application purchasing company from the beginning. They built this offering around an Enterprise Java Beans XML-compliant architecture for easy communication and transactions via the Web. In other words, Partnerware is now Partnerware: The Sequel.

They have two offerings—TCX Foresight and TCX Insight:

TCX Foresight TCX Foresight is a service and a set of configuration tools that involve a workflow engine and a rules processor. Partnerware partners work with the clients to identify the business processes that make the client company work. During the consulting stages, they actually benchmark the client company's existing systems and processes against business objectives. If they find a broken set, they help reconfigure those processes so they become functional. An implementation would be consulting in combination with the identification of the workflow and the configuration of the business rules to the processes via the rules processor. Depending on how dysfunctional this environment is, the configuration could take between 90 and 120 days, and has been known to be as short as 60 days in a few cases.

TCX Insight These are the actual applications that are implemented following the planning through the Foresight services.

Configurable Workflow Definition This is the tool for creating the workflow that is mapped to the various modules.

Partner Profiling This module links the brandholder's corporate objectives to the actual performance of individual partners.

Partner Acquisition This creates the criteria for the partner programs. Then as potential partners apply, see how well they score against those criteria. If they score well, they are partners. If not, not.

Lead/Opportunity Management This is one of the golden modules for partners. It is a closed-loop lead management system that covers everything from lead generation and distribution through opportunity management and follow-up to closing.

Funds Management Another golden module, the funds management module handles the administration of marketing funds. It takes multiple factors into account in the allocation process including program types, partner types, and revenue targets by expertise, budgets, discounting structures, and disbursement rules.

Knowledge Management This one is the same as many other programs, but a vital one. It is the tool for reporting and analysis.

Customizable Queries and Reports This is exactly what it sounds like. It can produce customized reports and answer specific queries in real time.

How well this new application and new business model will perform is clearly up in the air. While it seems to be pretty darned full featured, it has no real track record yet. Good luck, Partnerware.

XE can be hosted via application service providers and thus keep the costs to a minimum.

Their website: http://www.partnerware.com/.

OnDemand

PRM star analyst Bob Thompson mentioned OnDemand's Partner Accelerator as one of the PRM top ten vendors (others included ChannelWave, Allegis, and Partnerware). There are five parts to Partner Accelerator: Partner Center, Opportunity Center, Demand Center, Campaign Center, and Acceleration Services. What is amazing about OnDemand is that it is providing a sophisticated product that starts at $12,000 in cost (other related costs *may* total an additional $30,000 for startup), when most other PRM applications are in the hundreds of thousands or at least the many tens of thousands, even at the low end.

There are two functions that are unique to OnDemand. The first is Acceleration Services. These consist of a series of software, consulting, and managed services that are designed to provide complete integration and real-time response with an existing e-business system. The other function is the Demand Center. This provides the brand owner and the partner with a real-time look at each other's inventories. It also provides a partner entitlement system that rewards the partners for accurate forecasting with incentives such as rebates, discounts, or even marketing development funds and price protection.

OnDemand is a bargain. Apparently, not only to the customer. On April 1, 2002, Chordiant purchased OnDemand for what looks to be $12 million. Of course, now comes the dance of cultural and product integration between Chordiant and OnDemand through the rest of 2002. Let's see how much of a bargain this remains.

Their website: http://www.ondemandinc.com/ (at the time this was written) and http://www.chordiant.com/ (in the near future).

Enterprise Channel Management (ECM)

Enterprise Channel Management (ECM) is actually non-linear management of a product distribution channel. It is a hub that normally is used for Internet distribution of a product or other brands that work through distributors, vendors, or value-added resellers (VARs). ECM manages the marketing, sales, and services of a brand. It is different from PRM because it concerns itself less with indirect sales and more with product supply and demand through integrated marketing channels. It's sort of a sophisticated inventory delivery and control system for product distribution through channels. It is entirely applicable for the manufacturing or automobile sectors, for example, and can control vast networks of distributors or resellers or whatever. Catalogs, warranties, and orders are part of the ECM lexicon, where they are less likely (but not entirely unlikely, as you saw) to be involved in PRM. It reaches its most sophisticated form through companies like Comergent, which provides a customizable marketplace for multiple distributors of a single product or multiple products. ECM is probably the place where CRM overlaps most closely with e-procurement. ECM order and fulfillment management functions are generally very strong, and there are strong product configuration, proposal management, and quote generation capabilities in the ECM domain.

To give you the visual here, imagine manufacturing a product that someone wants to buy. He goes to a website and fills out a form—as brief as a zip code or as sophisticated as a buyer preference survey. He clicks on a Buy Product button, which either gives him a list of appropriate partners or transparently takes him to a site with the buying information, which is the single partner that fits the criteria chosen. Easy and transparent to the potential buyer, with integrated manufacturer/reseller activity. Voilà! The partner is now the manufacturer's strategic asset, not just a reseller. Imagine what it takes for Ingram Micro or Merisel to maintain 2,000 or so products from hundreds of manufacturers. They have to distribute those products to between 150,000 to 200,000 resellers of different sizes. Each of those 150,000 to 200,000 has a different value to Merisel and each is also valued separately by Ingram Micro. What is important to Merisel may not be to Ingram Micro. For further illustration on the scope of what resellers, distributors, and manufacturers are dealing with daily, imagine the following: The food and beverage industry had 31,293 manufacturers and 741,304 partners as of 2001. ECM can handle that.

Comergent

Comergent calls its Distributed E-Business System a sell-side channel commerce system. It is a very sophisticated series of customizable private and public marketplaces that are coordinated by the workflow engine of Comergent's applications. Its footprint spans the customer segment of customers/suppliers/partners. In fact, there are elements of both CRM and supply chain management embedded in this product. The Comergent engine will handle traffic in the marketplaces. It handles a customer to the manufacturer site for a single product, the customer to a private marketplace to buy multiple products, or the customer to a public marketplace to buy multiple products from multiple sources. They were smart to also have strong integration capacity, especially with SAP, the ERP leader for the manufacturing industry. Elements of the Distributed E-Business System include needs assessment, product recommendations, product comparisons, configuration management, proposal management, and complex quote generation. Its SCM side is provided by a very strong order and fulfillment engine.

Customers include Cisco, Maytag, Black & Decker, Dupont, Ingram Micro, and Tech Data, among many others. They have a strong presence in the High Tech industry and its distribution channels.

Their website: http://www.comergent.com/.

ClickCommerce

ClickCommerce is one of the growing Microsoft .NET stables. They have placed their sell-sell ECM solution squarely in the Microsoft initiative's camp. Their solution, Click Commerce 4.3 (as of early 2002), is especially good for Microsoft-compliant companies that have extensive customer data investment already and need strong integration to existing corporate and industry portals, ERP, product data management, production planning, CRM, or logistics back ends. They have an open XML-compliant architecture that has made them one of the ECM leaders. Their features are designed for the nontechnical. One of the best assets of Click Commerce 4.3 is the ability to make changes in business rules through a graphical interface so that developers don't have to make those changes for the user. There is even wireless access through extensions and Web services. Good stuff.

Their customers include such giants as Black & Decker, Peterbilt, Mitsubishi, Hyundai, Emerson, and Motorola. Clearly a strong presence in the manufacturing world.

Their website: http://www.clickcommerce.com/.

Other ECM Vendors

Check out InfoNow for now. While not covered here, they are worth a look. Their website: http://www.infonow.com/.

CRM with PRM Functionality

CRM companies are all realizing the benefits of partner management. As a result, several of the CRM leaders are incorporating some PRM features into their applications. A few examples follow.

Pivotal PartnerHub

Pivotal products will be discussed in Chapter 14. However, one part of their offering deserves to be heard in this chapter. Pivotal's PartnerHub component focuses on the channel. While it's not nearly as robust as the applications from the pure PRM vendors, some of the fundamentals are covered. PartnerHub is comprised of four modules that are reached and regulated through either of the two major browsers. Their focus is more collaborative and cooperative, which, while certainly adequate, is more a function of direct marketing and sales than indirect channels. One of PartnerHub's values is its use of the Pivotal Lifecycle Engine, a three-tiered, XML-compliant, transaction-processing beauty that is eminently scalable. Of course, it is fully integrated into other Pivotal eRelationship products.

PartnerHub creates a virtual sales team that combines the online capabilities of each of the partners. Collaborative information-sharing on competitors, placement of orders for collateral or products from any given partner, co-marketing collaboration, and monitoring of the joint customer orders are done seamlessly, regardless of the partner's physical location. PartnerHub provides reporting tools and a robust customization and development tool. The platform it uses is the Pivotal LifeCycle Engine, a three-tier XML-based platform that makes communications between partners and brandholders rather easy and flexible. This is not a true PRM application, but more a collaborative set of applications for partners.

Their website: http://www.pivotal.com/.

Siebel eChannel

eChannel is one of Siebel's most popular modules, growing revenue at the rate of 80 percent per year since its inception. It covers all the basic needs of partner-oriented institutions, such as lead management, MDF management, service requests, and order/quote online. Prior to the release of Siebel 7.0, Siebel recognized the shortcomings of the Siebel 6.2 version of PRM, so they partnered with PRM industry heavyweight OnDemand, working out the integration with OnDemand's Partner Accelerator 8.0. What will become of that premier alliance is up in the air, with the release of Siebel eChannel 7.0 in late 2001 and the acquisition of OnDemand by Chordiant. Its core components:

Partner Manager Used by managers to address issues related to managing and enabling partner relationships and operations.

Partner Portal Gives partners individualized access to programs, news, and other transactions via the Web.

Partner Analytics Provides brand owners with algorithms to measure partner performance. There are more than 200 prebuilt reports and extensive customization tools.

Partner Planning and Motivation Tools Allows both the partner and the brand owner to jointly plan strategies, develop objectives, align programs, and agree on metrics.

Partner Performance, Forecasting, and Reports Not only allows the tracking of partner performance, but gives the brand owner visibility into the appropriate partner sales pipeline. The report engine is Actuate.

Access to Product Information and Sales Tools The equivalent of the marketing encyclopedia. Partners get the brand holder's prebuilt proposals templates, existing presentations for their use, and current brandholder product catalog information, including product availability, pricing, etc. This provides easy access to much of the same information that the brand holders' internal sales teams have.

Of course, for a partner program as complicated and difficult as theirs, Siebel would be better off using someone else's PRM application. For a multifunction CRM company, they have a good product with total integration into their own suite, of course.

Their website: http://www.siebel.com/.

Onyx Partner Portal

Onyx's Partner Portal takes an intriguing approach, but certainly falls short of a full-blown PRM application. Actually, it is a full-time self-service product that uses the Web to deliver partner services. The application focuses on sales, with lead generation, joint sales capacity, and sales pipeline management. There is a library feature that allows the partner to download appropriate partner marketing collateral and send it to their clients. However, like the other CRM companies that had a start in sales force automation, it is highly concentrated on the selling aspects of the PRM application world.

Their website: http://www.onyx.com/.

10

C(RM)SPAN: There Is More to Life than Just Plain CRM

There is no doubt that the definition of CRM is broad. The only thing the analysts and pundits can agree on is that CRM means customer facing. Otherwise, there is no entirely consistent, satisfactory definition, except, I hope, those mentioned in Chapter 1 of this book. However, the CRM market is maturing and individual corporate needs are becoming increasingly unambiguous. That clarity is making one thing pretty obvious. CRM needs not just customization, but specialization—whether that means out-of-the-box solutions, tools that are focused on vertical markets, or add-ons that bolster the specialized piece of the application.

The type of customers that an oil company deals with, for example, are oil distribution companies, trucking companies, refineries, and the like. Those are quite different from the customers that an insurance company deals with, which can be underwriters, buyers of the insurance, and independent insurance agents. What each of them needs from CRM is quite different. With the Dreyfus example in the analytics chapter (Chapter 8), the objective was reduction of asset attrition. The aim of the insurance company could be to increase the up-selling or cross-selling potential of their insurance holders. The aims of the oil company could be to increase the numbers of distributors.

But vertical CRM systems aren't the only things that are specialized in the CRM world. There are add-ons that enhance specific aspects of CRM. These are frequently, but not solely, standalone applications that make CRM a better place to be. They might be a time and expenses program, a proposal development and management program, or an application that has a CRM-related strategic planning focus.

Then there are the "CRM-like" applications such as mail management applications that are specific to a horizontal aspect of CRM, but don't really qualify as subsets of the genre. Be careful here, though, because many vendors will characterize themselves as CRM vendors because it's the "in" thing to do. They may not be. The helpdesk is the helpdesk, not CRM.

There are an awful lot of verticals, horizontals, and add-ons that claim to be CRM-related. Rather than a comprehensive look at all of them, we'll look at a few that show promise, reveal a unique fresh perspective, or are at the cusp of explosion and are qualified to call themselves CRM.

Verticalization: Business to Business

Verticalization is a concept gaining increasing credence as niches that need to be filled define how the Internet is increasingly used. That "vertical market as a niche" is seen everywhere, with portals for chemical, auto, trucking, and other traditional manufacturing industries springing up. CRM is a flexible system that allows for vertical customization fairly easily, since its foundation is customers and customized definitions of customers that can be easily programmed. This is leading to a proliferation of verticals that are founded on the CRM platform, such as Live Wire's student relationship management (SRM) solution for campuses. This expansion also includes the extensive number of vertical industries that SAP, Siebel, and SalesLogix have in their customer base because of either easy customization (SalesLogix) or vast knowledge and history (SAP).

One Size Does Not Fit All

"One size fits all" could not be further from the truth in the CRM space. Every company has its own needs based on the unique characteristics of their customers and markets where they compete. Ask any ten experts in the CRM space to describe in detail what features and functions an ideal CRM system should have and you are likely to get ten significantly different answers. At first glance, these systems seem to follow the same basic principles and patterns, but an investigation at any finer resolution will show that one ideal system may be dramatically different from the next. So which one is correct? They all are.

When a company implements a vertical version of CRM, it must be tuned to account for the unique blend of characteristics found in their customers and the industry in which they compete. These characteristics must be identified at an early stage in the implementation cycle and factored into the solution to avoid project failure and ensure the maximum ROI.

To illustrate, a semiconductor equipment company should have high per-transaction value, low-volume, business-to-business transactions with its customers. It would be relevant to track information such as the type of facility the customer operates and its hours of operation. If the company were running a 24/7 300mm facility, it would be important not to attempt to sell them 200mm equipment and to ensure tech support was available during off hours. It would also be important to have a formalized problem escalation process integrated into the CRM, as customers who make multimillion-dollar purchases typically require this.

In contrast, a company that sells books and CDs would have low per-transaction value, high-volume, individual consumer customers. It might be important to track the birthday of the individual so a "birthday special" promotion could be sent to him once a year, or perhaps to provide a Web-based or automated email-based response system that allows the customer to request shipping status on his last order, thus reducing a potentially overwhelming volume of phone calls.

It can quickly be seen that the requirements of CRM differ substantially from industry to industry. However, while most of today's solutions do not target any vertical industry niches primarily, there is an increasing understanding that vertical CRM solutions out of the box are essential pieces leading to future revenue.

A Case for Verticalization

In the 1800s, if you had chest pains you would likely visit the same town doctor who pulled your aching tooth last week and delivered your wife's baby last spring. He would probably be the same person to prescribe remedies for any other ailments you may have, from blurry vision to back injuries. Today, you use a general practitioner for a preliminary diagnosis, but any one of a dozen specialists such as cardiologists, dentists, or obstetricians may be engaged to address specific medical issues.

The specialization of medicine is analogous to the verticalization occurring in the CRM market. The rapid adoption of CRM technology has sparked an evolution in the sophistication of this space and is now serving a very broad range of business models. While every vendor understands and must deliver the basic components of CRM and, to some extent, CRM, similar to a general practitioner, there is a growing need for specialization. For CRM products, this specialization is the creation of vertical solutions along the lines of industry segmentation such as healthcare, technology, transportation, finance, or communications.

The main advantages to purchasing a verticalized solution are the reduction in tailoring to make it fit your business and the comfort of having a software vendor who truly understands your business. After all, if you were operating a semiconductor business, how comfortable would you feel about a product that was recently installed for an online toy store or an insurance company? The way customer relationships are managed is one of the most critical competencies in your company—could your operations be so generic that this same product will meet your needs? Of course not. That is why you will pay thousands, or even millions, for integration consultants to configure the system until it does meet your needs.

Who Is Going Vertical?

CRM vendors who understand the value of industry specialization are already capitalizing on the vertical approach. Thus, SAS has Churn Management for Telecommunications, SAP has multiple vertical solutions, Siebel has Automotive and Pharma for the automobile and pharmaceuticals industries, PeopleSoft has CRM for Local Government, and so on.

This has led some analysts to speculate that the underlying software of CRM will soon become a secondary consideration to the industry expertise of the vendor. This could put the current market gorillas at a significant disadvantage against smaller, highly focused companies. For instance, in a target market of semiconductor companies, how well could Clarify's generic High Technology vertical offering compete with a hypothetical brand like Semiconductor CRM Inc., a company run by recognized semiconductor industry experts who focus exclusively on solutions tailored for that industry? Semiconductor CRM Inc., in addition to their highly specialized product, might differentiate further by providing value-added, industry-focused services such as content aggregation, competitive equipment databases, a preloaded semiconductor FAB database complete with contacts, reports that adhere to Semitech consortium specifications, a prewired semiconductor-focused trading hub, and a turnkey EDI network with all major vendors in the semiconductor industry—just as a start. It is not inconceivable that this type of laser-focused vendor could chip away at the CRM market-share pie one small niche at a time.

However, the most important vendors (or the Sandbox Playmates, as I refer to them in Chapter 14) are aware of this and spent part of 2001 planning and executing vertical strategies and developing vertical products. The justification for this is easy. Between 25 and 30 percent of the functionality of the general CRM suites is customized for the clients who buy them. Vertically specific CRM applications are only customized to the tune of 10 to 15 percent—a big time and cost savings on customization right there. It doesn't need much more justification than this.

Vertical CRM solutions are certainly a special tool for a special job. Only the industry itself will determine the level of specialization that it needs. Companies that play in these small niches will have a much narrower customer base, so it is likely they will have to find other value-added services to augment their revenue lines. But these same value-added services are exactly what will help them differentiate. The value proposition for this type of product remains extremely compelling. However, remember, that very compelling case means that CRM charlatans will be entering the marketplace. Additionally, shortsighted vertically challenged companies that cannot keep up with the specialization will begin to tout their "highly configurable" nature and "powerful API" to the specific industry—translated, this means lots of expensive custom consulting work.

Quick Peek at Industries

Before we launch into a major discussion on the CRM vertical that has the most global impact—the public sector—let's take a fast look at a few of the industries that are using CRM today.

Financial Services

Financial services is such a diverse category that it almost isn't a category. Retail banking is a financial service. Insurance is a financial service. Securities trading is a financial service. Financial services to consumers differ from financial services to other financial services.

CRM vendors are faced with a conundrum. What should they emphasize when they are building specific applications for this particular vertical? This is critical because financial services is one of the most CRM-hungry industries in the United States. According to a joint study done by Peppers and Rogers Group and *Financial Services Marketing* magazine in 2001, nearly 47 percent of all financial services institutions have a CRM initiative in place, and 56 percent of the remaining institutions are planning one now. The range runs from

51 percent of retail banks with initiatives to about 33 percent of insurance companies at the low end. The maturity of this particular vertical market is evident when you see that major players such as Thomson Financials, American Skandia, Charles Schwab, and H&R Block have implemented CRM solutions from various vendors already. In fact, Thomson Financials began its implementation of CRM in 1993. The TowerGroup's Retail Banking services division projected in 2001 that retail financial institutions would spend about $4.3 billion on CRM through 2005, with exactly half that coming from the North American side of this industry. It is seen to be growing at a compounded annual rate of 6 percent, particularly in the campaign management and personalization domains.

So the stakes are high on how you approach the financial services market because the market covers such a wide range of retail financial institutions. For instance, take retail banking, securities, and insurance. What they commonly have is customers. How they service them is what makes them very different. Each company has a different approach to a different segment. For example, Pivotal and PeopleSoft are looking at traditional banking/credit unions as a functional partner for their financial services vertical application (among other segments). This is an industry that cries for CRM and is very aware of it, providing low-hanging fruit. However, it is a complex industry that demands serious knowledge of its workings from the CRM vendors. Some of the companies handle multiple financial products such as Prudential, which has annuities, 401(K)s, health insurance, and life insurance among its dozens of offerings. Some of the companies build their own applications. Besides PeopleSoft and Pivotal, Siebel and SAP provide specific vertical CRM applications for this industry. Companies such as Chordiant are building life insurance–specific CRM applications with specialized data models for the particular financial service.

Hospitality

The hospitality industry is not exactly one of the early CRM adopters. Traditionally, the hotel markets were focused (pre–September 11) on group business and just assumed that transient business (individual or family customers) would be returning or that there would be sufficient volume of transients to cover bases. However, forward-thinking hotel chains like Hilton and Marriott began to work on doing such things as identifying individual customer likes and dislikes or developing programs for the best customers, using different criteria to determine what is "best." CRM for hospitality is just beginning to come into vogue. This has been a product/services-oriented market forever and is very slow to become customer-focused, but changes are in the works as 2002 rocks on.

CRM products for this industry that do exist are few and far between.

Automotive

The auto industry is one that has been CRM-savvy for a while, primarily due to the competition being so extreme. In fact, there are companies out there who do nothing more than automotive CRM. One prominent player (working in conjunction with EDS) is DIVA, which provides a product called Auto-Vision. Its claimed automotive CRM-specific functions are:

- ► Salesperson and manager desktop that organizes day-to-day activities

- ► Electronic Showroom, which includes log books for each customer type

- ► Logbook, which also includes appointment and sold logs

- ► Web-enabled, including email merge functionality

- ► Letter processor

- ► Export to Excel spreadsheet for print capability

- ► Auto Scheduler, which enables you to fully customize your letters, prospect, and owner followup

- ► Daily Planner, which has all daily scheduled followup for each salesperson

- ► Report generator, which enables reporting for salespeople and managers

- ► Auto Scheduler reporting, which allows printing or email preset reports to the dealer or management company

You'll note that a lot of this functionality is strongly geared toward contact management–types of solutions—calendaring, scheduling, reporting, contact organization, and so on—though it does exceed that in a few places.

The CRM automotive vertical is advanced enough to develop its own board game, called "ReTension," developed by Cap Gemini Ernst & Young Consulting for CRM training.

The multifunction vendor with the most visible CRM automotive application is Siebel. The package they use is a number of their more generic applications such as Siebel Call Center or Siebel Sales, but they add Siebel eDealer, which provides fairly robust opportunity management, marketing materials management, joint marketing management (assigning dealers to campaigns), and very strong service management.

Other verticals that are impacted by CRM include telecommunications, healthcare, retail sales, professional services (entirely new category of business applications called PSA are emerging now—guess what it stands for?), consumer packaged goods, manufacturing, energy, life sciences, and a myriad of others too numerous to mention.

CRM and the Public Sector

The single most undeniable vertical with a need for CRM is the public sector. This includes federal, state, and local government agencies, quasi-public institutions like Fannie Mae, and citizens. Because of the current war against terrorism, there is more support for government than ever, and at the same time, there is a greater need for CRM in the public sector. Studies done in March 2001 by the Center for Digital Government indicate that over 80 percent of state and local executives surveyed say there is increasing pressure to use technology to manage their constituents' interactions with government. Those are *very* significant numbers. These days, public sector entities are trying to do more with less. They would like to drive costs out of transactions, or at least reduce them, and they are aimed at generally improving the quality of their customer service and interactions. Especially now, citizens won't stand for chronically poor service from the government, so the government has to respond. As our expectations continually rise, government is actually working hard to ensure higher quality customer service. Government agencies are trying to make sure the right information is available to support each customer transaction and that each transaction builds on previous transactions for a particular customer. The government is also increasingly recognizing that it is in the customer service business. Says Scott McIntyre, managing director of Public Services CRM for KPMG Consulting in McLean, Virginia:

> Most government agencies are committed to dramatically improving customer service. They are making great progress in achieving this by first identifying who their customers are, then placing them at the center of their businesses, and finally adopting solutions that address customers' needs.

Despite its monopoly on the market for delivering government services, the public sector is committed to improving customer service. Government agencies at all levels are concerned with identifying their customers, accurately recognizing and addressing their needs, and improving the quality of customer transactions. While commercial entities have aggressively pursued CRM excellence in the name of enhanced customer loyalty and the attendant increases in both revenue and profit that can come from a loyal customer base, the public sector is not sitting still. Government is taking the lessons learned from the commercial world and applying them to their unique environments. They are working to ensure high quality customer transactions by embedding business intelligence, workflow, knowledge management, and enterprise data access into the customer support function.

Examples of the public sector's aggressive move to improve customer service during 2001–2002 include a wave of contact center overhauls, the increased use of case management and campaign management solutions, a flurry of self-service customer service portals, and a general strategic and operational focus on the customer. The size and magnitude of these public sector investments can be tremendous. In mid-2001, the IRS went so far as to award a $15 million contract to PeopleSoft for a PeopleSoft 8.0 CRM implementation, one of the first federal agencies to make such a move. This is the tip of the iceberg as government agencies continue to see the value in adopting CRM solutions to solve their customer service challenges and the solutions continue to mature for this developing market.

Public Sector CRM

Studies being done in 2002 indicate that federal government CRM spending could reach as much as half a billion dollars by 2006 (source: Input, Chantilly, VA, 2002) and will markedly increase from the 2001 spending of $233 million with a compound annual growth rate of an estimated 17.5 percent. Keep in mind this is just federal spending. This doesn't include state or local governments or agencies, which are potentially a much larger market. When all is said and done, this is a very big potential market. Very, very big, easily stretching into the billions.

No wonder the big systems integrators like KPMG and other Big 5—which are already serving the public sector with everything from strategic planning to ERP implementations—are focusing their efforts on developing strong CRM practices. Additionally, those integrators that have not traditionally excelled on the government market are now creating public sector practices to go after these opportunities. The software vendors are fully geared to build public sector–specific applications or to integrate their other public sector products (such as back office) to the CRM products. But while this is a potentially lucrative market, it is also a navigator's nightmare. Not only do you have to deal with the vagaries of each public sector segment, agency by agency, you have to contend with interagency rivalries and politics, different bureaucracies, major entanglements with multiple laws, regulations, and compliance issues, and vastly different operational methods and practices.

One brief example. Many years ago, I landed a contract to exclusively do Lotus Notes work for a federal contractor laboratory with a large contract at NASA. This was NASA-related technology. When I received this lab's contract, it was seven pages long. Not bad. But government passthrough regulations—those regulations that are required to be part of a vendor contract or subcontract—were an additional 94 pages! This was after the Reduction in Paperwork federal mandate! Sadly, occurrences like this are not unusual.

This all gets complicated by the CRM vendors or integrators who glibly miscast what public sector CRM is all about. If you are a public sector official looking into public sector CRM, beware of vendors and integrators who cutely call CRM either Citizen Relationship Management or Constituent Relationship Management. This is painfully wrong. KPMG Consulting's McIntyre says:

> In the commercial sector, a primary objective of CRM is to provide seamless multi-channel customer service by ensuring that regardless of the channel selected by a customer, all previous transaction information is always available and each transaction builds a comprehensive customer profile. In the public sector this is still a laudable goal, but government agencies must also seamlessly share information with numerous other agencies at the state, local, and federal levels. This contributes to the enormous complexity and also the tremendous opportunities presented in the public sector.

These relationships within and between governments are obviously complex and very different from the relationships in the commercial or consumer marketplace. When it comes to understanding public sector CRM, equally as important—perhaps far more important than the relationship between the government and its individual citizens—is the relationship between agencies of the government or intergovernmental relationships between state, local, and federal government units.

I was returning on a shuttle from Baltimore/Washington International airport about a year ago and sat next to a treaty negotiator for the Department of Agriculture, who negotiated international export treaties, among others. As a senior level negotiator, he had liaisons with the departments of State (general international issues), Defense (agricultural issues in warfare), and Commerce (obviously, trade issues), as well as several agencies within Agriculture. He also consulted with the CIA regarding the status of the nation he was negotiating with, state officials concerning the food that was being exported, and shipping entities who were involved in cargo movement. In addition, there were various bodies involved with the nation or nations he was engaged with and a few commissions of the United Nations. This is typical of what our very large government has to deal with every day. It is also a prime example of how CRM would be beneficial by simply coordinating the agencies through this effort. By calling it Citizen or Constituent Relationship Management, CRM's real value in the public sector is viciously undercut. Being able to renew my driver's license online at the state DMV, while valuable and useful, just doesn't have the value that working with that Department of Agriculture matrix does.

Another example. In the wake of September 11, immigrant tracking became a much bigger and more volatile issue. CRM vendors all began brainstorming how their software could engage in such tracking, primarily through the field service components of CRM. Agents of the INS in the field could get valuable "customer" information on immigrants and the whereabouts of those particular immigrants. One of the biggest issues in these discussions was how to handle interagency cooperation at the federal, state, and local levels, given the frequent jurisdictional battles. This is the minefield you walk through in this very lucrative market.

CRM Public Sector Needs and Solutions

Enough with the negatives. What should be the ten goals for CRM public sector success? I identified some of them in a section that I wrote in the book *Public Official's Guide to E-Government* (Thompson Publishing Group, Inc., 2001). With some modifications since, here they are:

- ► More effective government services.

- ► Single point of entry for problem solution or citizen/agency interactions.

- ► Consistent look and feel to provide consistent user experience.

▶ Easy full-time availability—24 hours a day, 7 days a week, 365 days a year.

▶ Consistent dialogue for the citizen or other agency, which means information is centrally accessible to any government agency needing it, including interactions with other government agencies.

▶ Communication reciprocity.

▶ More citizen channel availability and, thus, selection.

▶ Creation of necessary vehicles to ease the process of compliance for the citizenry.

▶ More effective interagency cooperation and efficiency at the state, local, and federal level.

▶ Better monitoring and tracking; better reporting.

These goals are premised on a very telling statistic: Over 50 percent of government interaction is with other government agencies. That's a very significant number.

To address the items above and effectively adopt CRM, the public sector must keep a few key things in mind. First, government entities need to develop CRM strategies that cut across the entire agency. Second, they should recognize that in order to get the maximum value from CRM, certain elements of the bureaucracy may need to give up the power associated with information hoarding. And third, they need to realize that public sector privacy requirements can restrict the information an agency can gather regarding customer transactions.

SAP, MySAP, and Your CRM

SAP made its reputation in the ERP world as the 800-pound gorilla. It was the giant 17,500-customer, multibillion-dollar enterprise with powerful centers in Germany and the United States. It was the fourth largest software company in the world, after Microsoft, Oracle, and Computer Associates. Most germane to this chapter, SAP had a vast presence in the vertical world. In fact, it had dozens of industry solution maps that had industry-specific applications, fields, templates, methodology, and embedded process knowledge for the B2B vertical world. When the MySAP initiative, a strong Web-client/server hybrid, portal-focused revamp of SAP basic applications, began more than three years ago, SAP began to also aggressively develop a CRM product. It got it right in 2001 with MySAP CRM 3.0. The combination of their extraordinary installed customer base and a solid product led SAP to capture about 6.6 percent of the CRM market by the end of 2001. That places them squarely at number three in market share, behind PeopleSoft and Siebel. This is remarkable for the short time that they've been involved. SAP's CRM product is designed to utilize its back-office strengths in the verticals. The Gartner Group reports that SAP says the CRM features are strong for B2B manufacturers in such sectors as automotive, oil and gas, consumer packaged goods, and chemical/pharmaceuticals. Tight back-office integration is critical in these industries, and SAP is the leading back-office vendor for those sectors. For example, SAP has incorporated an incentives and commissions module for their CRM sales components. All of the customers they have for it are in the insurance or financial services markets. Every last one of them. That is not surprising. SAP vertical strengths are paramount to their success in the CRM world.

SAP's industry solutions maps aren't just regurgitated, industry-specific demographics and statistics. They use highly evolved, fine-tuned methods to create these maps. First, they develop a Customer Interaction Cycle. This is the identification of the specific customer groups that a particular industry might interact with. For example, the pharmaceuticals industry has multiple customer groups: the end-user (directly purchases the medication), doctors, healthcare organizations, wholesalers, and retailers. There are separate processes for dealing with each. The way the end-user ordinarily interacts is through direct marketing such as television ads. For the doctors, the interaction is with sales representatives, who not only show up at the doctor's door with free samples, but go the extra mile (tough life!) to play golf with them as well, making the relationships personal, not just salesy.

Once this set of processes is identified, the next set is the C-Business (collaborative business) map. This shows how the pharmaceutical companies might work with multiple customer groups to affect other customer groups. Interaction points are identified between these groups and then a case is developed for an ROI at these points. For example, Dell Computers works directly with original equipment manufacturers (OEMs) to provide software and an operating system that is built into their computers, which are then sold to the public.

When these processes are identified and mapped, SAP creates the industry solution map, which deeply embeds the processes rather than simply changing the names of fields. So the CRM processes are embedded with the historic data and content accumulated by SAP in its investigation of the particular vertical and its business processes and methodologies.

Stay tuned. There will be more on SAP CRM in Chapters 12 and 14.

CRM as a Platform: xRM

Relationship management is perhaps the most important factor in building any successful business. This factor has been driving the proliferation of xRM solutions, where x is a variable that represents the role of a target audience, such as a customer or supplier. The more specifically x is defined, the more vertical the solution. For example, where x equals customer, you find traditional CRM products that are marketed to a very broad audience. Where x equals student, you find a student relationship management vertical solution with a niche market of academic institutions. When x equals tenant, you find a vertical solution targeting real estate organizations, and so on.

Essentially, CRM is evolving into more of a platform for developing focused applications rather than being an end solution itself. Once the basic relationship management components have been developed, it is not difficult to program specific business rules that define the x in xRM. Some basic components of the xRM platform include:

Account management Track and manage people

Case management Capture, trace, and route issues

Knowledge management Mine knowledge from previously closed cases

Interaction management Manage communications with the audience x either via email, Web extranet, or other communications channel

There are hundreds of possible flavors of xRM. In the first edition of this book I said "It is quite possible that by the time this book has gone to press there may even be a software vendor that provides a framework for new ISVs to build their vertical xRMs." There still isn't any specifically that I've found, but the advent of Internet architecture makes the vertical solutions more accessible than they were.

Mail Management Solutions

In addition to the traditional CRM solutions, there are a number of mail management products on the market that are also well equipped for managing customer interactions. These products primarily focus on email management by providing programmable rules that allow you to define how inbound emails that target corporate addresses—

such as support@mycompany.com—should be dealt with. Vendors in this space include Brightware, eGain, and Quintus.

In addition to routing messages to the appropriate individual in your organization, this type of product can potentially reduce the support burden on your staff by filtering and automatically answering certain questions. The target customer for vendors in this space typically includes companies who deal with a high volume of customer email traffic. While most products in this space are typically implemented as a traditional enterprise deployment, vendors like eGain provide their solutions as a hosted service, reducing implementation costs and headaches.

Add-ons: More than the Sum of Their Parts

CRM is a complicated system because it is a combination of highly personal human interactions and the extremely impersonal use of technology designed to enhance those personalized interactions. If that isn't enough, CRM technology is loaded with an incredible amount of functionality. To make it even worse, much of that functionality is never used by a company that bought it. There is a new 20-80 law in CRM (I'm inventing it purely as a metaphor here) that says that you will use 20 percent of the functionality that you buy and 80 percent will sit on the shelf. There is no science behind this statement.

That makes an add-on market kind of peculiar. Why increase functionality when you have more than you can use? For the most part, you shouldn't. But there are a handful of add-ons that provide features that increase the value of CRM measurably. They are *not* Swiss knives with zillions of different functions in a single package. They usually have a single purpose and add a certain kind of value. Those are the add-ons I want to bring to your attention—a Henkel knife, not a Swiss pocket knife.

For example, one major strength of a good sales force is its ability to get out a well-written, to-the-point proposal. Proposal development and management are not normally part of sales force automation and has to be included as an add-on. However, imagine the importance of getting out a potent proposal in half the time that it would normally take. The odds of winning that proposal are increased by the timeliness of the effort. To do that effectively often takes both best practices and a knowledge base of useful proposal information that has evolved over a considerable amount of time doing those kinds of proposals.

A good add-on could automate parts of the proposal development process and, if sophisticated enough, could even automate some of the process involved in responding to requests for proposals (RFPs). RFPs are highly detailed documents, with an operating set of rules that have to be followed and requirements that have to be met to be considered responsive to the proposal. In larger government contracts, the response to an RFP is often done by teams of anywhere from 2 to 20. For example, I was on an IBM team in the early 1990s that had 140 people who worked in three shifts of eight hours so that all 24 hours would be covered for more than six months. The RFP we were responding to had to be in compliance with MilSpec (military specification) 2120, a formatting template. If the proposal wasn't in compliance it would be summarily thrown out. So not only was responsiveness to content important, but consistent and very specific formatting rules were in evidence as well. The proposal response effort cost IBM $10 million. This was an exceptionally large effort, but it reflects the difficulties of managing an overall RFP response or developing a proposal quickly. Two and a half years after submittal, IBM won the deal—worth $1 billion a year for 11 years. I suspect that if *any* of the processes could have been automated beyond the MilSpec 2120 template, we could have cut down the proposal response time and size and thus the proposal cost.

Imagine the value of something like a proposal automation add-on for sales force automation or enterprise marketing automation applications. Invaluable. But how does that work? Is there enough of a market for it in the CRM world? In a word, "no," but let's look at a specific useful example of why there is still a need for the add-ons.

Pragmatech

New Hampshire–based Pragmatech Software has been in business since 1993 and has built up a blue chip clientele for its *standalone* proposal management applications. They are a highly successful company and one of the few companies that can claim a serious revenue increase last year (more than 10 percent) despite 2001's disastrous consequences for most businesses. They were named on the 2001 Inc. 500 list of the fastest growing companies over a five-year period in the United States, showing revenue growth of 2127 percent during that time. Their 1,500-plus clients include stalwarts throughout any number of given industries. For example, in the high-tech world, PeopleSoft is a client. In the financial services/retail banking world, ABN Amro is a client. Any company that writes proposals is a prospective client. They are not cheap, but they provide a very valuable tool, with a short and easily measurable ROI. For example, in 1999, DST Innovis, a provider of customer management solutions to quasi-public institutions (utilities, telephony-based companies, and so on), responded to 73 RFPs. By the end of 2000, after installing Pragmatech's suite of proposal automation products, they had nearly doubled their response rate, with fewer personnel.

Numbers indicate that sales teams spend 30 percent of their time pulling together information for proposals in one way or another. That is a very significant amount of time that could be spent selling or doing things that lead to more immediate revenue generation. The Pragmatech suite not only automates the creation of proposals, but actually creates a library of reusable content that can be imported into any proposal and professionally produced within seconds. Slick querying capabilities and a repository/library handle large amounts of information in various formats. All of this is done in the familiar and omnipresent Microsoft Word so that sales folks or marketing folks or whoever is using the product can be comfortable with it.

But keep in mind this is an add-on, not an add-in. It is a set of products that stand alone. They are by no means plug-ins, integrated APIs, or anything of the sort. They are independent products that can be conjoined to the products they are working with. This particular product suite is one of the most useful products in the add-on marketplace: well thought out, rapid investment return, and a great company with excellent people running the show.

The Products

Pragmatech has several excellent products that I will very briefly outline:

The RFP Machine This is both the engine and the car's interior. It is a centralized repository for common responses to questions. It has a highly evolved expert systems language processor that answers questions asked appropriately, drawing from this database and dropping that answer into the proposal. It is easy to integrate into SFA or EMA applications.

The RFP Express This is the Web interface for the RFP Machine (in effect) so that distributed sales forces and the like can access the features of the RFP Machine.

The Proposal Assembler This is the core of the core. It is a document assembly system that automatically generates on-demand proposals. It handles the elements and the design of the proposal, has a sophisticated query engine, and puts together appropriate language for the document.

Proposal Express This uses SmartDocs technology. I've used it before and it is an excellent technology that uses a document format containing the form, blueprint, and any associated logic. It is almost like having an embedded intelligence with your document. Proposal Express uses this technology to publish a self-contained proposal that can be distributed to sales and marketing. They can use it to automate some of the routines they would ordinarily have to use the Proposal Assembler for.

The RFP Tracking System This is a management tool for all the proposal activity within an organization. It can allocate resources, schedule activities, provide comprehensive reports, and generally track and improve the effectiveness and efficiency of the proposal creation process.

Web Publisher This is a way of accessing the knowledge base via the Web by turning the knowledge base *into* the Web or, at least, a website.

e-Proposals These are development tools that provide for the design of Web-based forms that make it easy to pick and choose content for proposal creation and delivery via the Web.

All in all, this is an excellent add-on for sales and marketing professionals and anyone who has ever had to develop proposals. CRM benefits from precisely these types of add-ons—add-ons that enhance and automate fundamental pieces of a CRM system.

Summary

So what does all this vertical and add-on material mean to CRM? CRM is a sophisticated and maturing realm in the world of business and information technology systems. As CRM matures, the companies that are considering it need more specialized ways of using it so that there is both cost savings (less customization, more focused out of the box) and more value available (proposal automation as an add-on). There's no debate there. This is one of those situations where the customer says, "Jump," and the CRM vendors, integrators, and specialists say, "What do you specifically mean by 'jump?'" Then they build the diving board.

11

Call Centers and Field Service: Nearly Head-to-Head

@#$*(@#*#. Isn't this the first thing that usually occurs to you when you think of customer service? Who hasn't cursed someone at a customer service center or on a service phone call? You who are without this sin may cast the first phone. The cost of this @#$*(@#*# is not cheap. Studies have estimated that the cost per PC of an internal helpdesk operation that is dysfunctional is between $6,000 and $15,000 per year. The other tangible costs are customers lost due to poor service and deals not closed by telesales reps. However, with the technological evolution of the customer service sector, @#*(@#*# may be a thing of the past.

First, there was the customer service counter—the place where you would (and often still do) return to live human representatives. Then came the helpdesk, which you would call to get help on Word because it crashed when you typed the word *lotus*. Then there was the call center, which used the voice technologies of the 1990s to provide your service representative with enough information so he'd hear you out on why your computer wasn't working again. Now as we move through the Internet Age, we have the customer interaction center (CIC), also known as the customer contact center or multimedia call center. CIC sophistication lets you call in on your phone (and soon with wireless transmissions, courtesy of your PDA) and walk through a website that will handle the most common problems easily, with online information at the ready. The functionality is deep, the technology is complex, and the results are strong.

Keep in mind that a customer interaction center or a customer contact center doesn't necessarily mean a customer service center. It could apply equally as well to a telesales center or a field service operation.

Many of the really big players started out in the customer service market. Vantive (since purchased by PeopleSoft) and what was then the independent company Clarify (since purchased by Nortel Networks and then Amdocs), in particular, were known for their call center strengths and incorporated other functions later as they grew to prominence. Nortel Networks, given its telecommunications history, seemed to be an obvious partner for Clarify's call center qualifications. It has been speculated that CRM started with call centers, though as I mentioned in Chapter 6, sales force automation is likely the real grandfather of CRM. Customer service is either the great-uncle or the step-grandfather.

Calling this facet of CRM a customer interaction center or a customer contact center is not something to treat as a marketing pitch. There is a lot implied in the statement. It is recognized that, in the twenty-first century, it is no longer valid for the customer just to be a transmitter or receiver of information. Collaborative activity is one aspect of what makes this a CRM application. The customer directly interacts with the company through a customer service representative and a variety of communications channels, and both use tools that make the interactions valuable. The customer could be interacting with the website through self-service applications. If a human being isn't involved directly as a customer service representative, there are virtual service representatives. Now that all but the most difficult and complex problems can be automated, customer satisfaction has been improving dramatically.

One of the problems in this world of rapidly changing customer expectations is that the evolution of the call center to the CIC or contact center is slow, though its rate of change is accelerating. The Gartner Group expects that only 20 percent of the existing call centers will have integrated live Web contact points or some form of automated email response by the end of 2002. It is expected that by 2005, it will be at 70 percent—a monstrous leap. However, we have to get to 2005 through 2002, meaning that for the most part, call centers, regardless of what they call themselves, will still be call centers with human operators for awhile yet. This is not to say that the changes aren't already underway.

What does this segment look like? What can it actually do? How is it intertwined with the other parts of CRM and when is that not a good thing? Let's take the plunge.

The Functionality

Think about a typical call you might make to a computer company technical service representative.

1. You dial the computer company's number.

2. You press several buttons on the telephone that gets you through menu options, ordinarily guided by a human voice.

3. You wait for a customer service rep while music plays.

4. If you haven't punched in an ID of some sort prior to this on your phone, you are asked for an ID.

5. The representative, reading off a screen that outlines your entire history with the company, including the recent calls or email inquiries you made, the level of difficulty of your problem, and the success or failure of the results, queries you on the nature of the problem, request, or concern.

6. Once you have spoken with the rep, the rep enters the information, checks several possible results that show up on a screen, and if one of them resolves the problem, marks it off. If none of them resolve the problem, you are sent to a new level to undergo a higher level of customer service (a manager if it is not technical, and a level 2 support technician if it is), with all the new information on what didn't work or what problem wasn't resolved.

Whew. That's a lot of potentially frustrating activity. But think about all the functionality involved in this call. There is call routing, assignment management, queue management, call tracking, entitlement processing, workflow, problem resolution, performance measurement, and service management, among other things. There are activities that are going on without the knowledge of the customer, such as logging and monitoring. There is also an audit trail that is keeping track of all the information through a log. For example, if a call is opened, it is tracked and a record is kept of its disposition.

The Technology

The technology for CIC and customer contact centers is complex and involves a mix of telecommunications and other communications channels, such as email, the Internet, faxes, or CRM software. By adding advanced telecommunications and Web-enabled CIC technology, the ante is upped heavily. How can media traffic flow be handled so that there are dynamic interactions with what could often be an emergency or at least an urgent situation? The bottom line for *any* CIC technology, classic phone center only or Internet-enabled, is its effectiveness in helping to resolve a customer interaction successfully. This means that the technologies are designed to create a collaborative environment for the customer and the customer contact representative (CCR). It also means self-service.

What are some of the technologies that are involved? On the classic telecommunications side, we are looking at the acronyms ACD, IVR, and CTI traditionally, and now, with the ascendance of the Internet, VOIP—all voice related. But what do these acronyms mean?

ACD (automatic call distribution) This is phone call workflow, which is how a call gets routed based on the defining characteristics of the call.

IVR (interactive voice response) You're entirely familiar with this one. This is the one that drives you nuts with the menu-driven voices that specify which choices you can make by hitting numbers on your telephone pad. Its actual benefit is that it can handle routine transactions without the benefit of a live agent—for example, when you call in to a credit card company and get your balance automatically.

CTI (computer telephony integration) These are the technology applications and interfaces that allow data integration with telephones. For example, CTI-enabled functionality allows both Internet-based information and phone-based information to be gathered and sent to a particular agent or routed to a particular desktop.

Using inbound and outbound call-routing software has been the traditional means of handling call loads effectively. However, the Internet has changed all that. Now, because of the ubiquitous role of the Internet, Web-enablement of the call center is of paramount importance.

Call center Web-enablement is a substantial investment. The first thing you are dealing with is the overall social change in the perception of acceptability of the customer. What was an acceptable level of frustration on the telephone (x minutes before ballistic missiles went off in the customer's head) is no longer acceptable because of the multiple channels available to the customer. That adds huge complexity to the issue of how agents handle phone calls. There has been a substantial amount of effort put into customer response time. There is actually an algorithm, developed early in the 1900s and refined in recent years, called the Erlang-C equation. This equation finds the optimal number of agents required to handle call loads. Its recent incarnations not only take into account historic call reception and agent skill sets, but also busy signals and call abandonment. That might not sound like much, but think about it. If you have 100 agents and only receive enough calls for 50 agents for six months and receive calls for 75 agents for four months and for 25 agents for the other two months, you are spending a lot of money on agents who aren't needed. Now, what if you receive 50 calls in the hours from 10:00 to 1:00, 150 calls from 1:00 to 6:00, and 85 calls from 6:00 to 8:00? What's the right number of agents, since you can't shuffle the agents' numbers very easily? Also, if you underestimate the number of agents, including during the call spikes that are expected as part of a given time period, how are you going to handle the overload? You'll have lots of unhappy customers—again, a cost you can't afford.

With the Web now ubiquitous, the complexity increases by manifolds. You have new communications channels that have to be dealt with, such as the Web, email, fax, chats, instant messenger, automated voice, voice over the Internet (à la Net2Phone), and others. Web-enablement is a priority.

Web-Enabling the Call Center

Keep in mind a cardinal principle: CIC means customer *interaction* center. Web-enabling the call center is in agreement with the New Economic principle that customers want control over their decision making. They don't want to be forced into their vendor's rules, nor do they want to be railroaded into a decision. Self-service becomes a critical psychological component as well as an effective one.

Self-service has existed for awhile with IVR. The problem with IVR is that it involves time for a virtual human voice to provide you with information that could be visually understood in a millisecond, so it becomes frustrating. Nested menus on the phone are very irritating, and IVR has created as many problems as it solves. Normally, when someone is on the telephone, unless she is calling in for something absolutely routine and attainable (like the aforementioned credit card balance), she is calling because *she needs to talk to someone real*. She isn't looking for self-service. She is looking for service.

The Internet is another matter. It is a place for solitary interactivity. You don't ordinarily need a voice on the Web—though that is now an option, albeit a very primitive early-stage one. The Web's greatest strength is comfortable self-activity that provides a true measure of control. For service centers, this is vital. Frankly, too, it is easier to sell on the Web (to someone who shops on it) because a cross-sale or up-sale is impersonal. If I'm on the Web and trying to solve a problem by going to a FAQ (frequently asked questions) list on my problem and I see an ad for something I am interested in that is related to it, I might buy it. But if I'm talking to a human being about my problem and the CCR tries to sell me this same object, I would be mad. One is my choice without pressure. The other is an attempt to railroad me, at least according to my perception. With self-service, I'm solving my own problem and am happy with the company that posted the ad to save me the trouble of dealing with customer service. A buy is more of a possibility. I'm more satisfied. If I am talking to the CCR, I just want the problem (and the beleaguered CCR) to go away.

Okay. So how do you Web-enable the call center? Start by planning around certain concepts:

- ▶ Though it is a technology being implemented, the customer is the focus. The customer is calling the center to get answers to issues and questions—in other words, resolution is the central focus of the entire process. Even while problem resolution is the purpose, the experience has to be pleasant for the customer, which means that the customer needs as much interactive control over the multichanneled process as possible.

- ▶ The technology chosen to "e-ize" the call center is the one that is most appropriate to the business rules of the company.

- ▶ Web-enablement is time consuming, not just for functional and technical implementation, but in the retraining of support personnel, the increased intricacy of the job, and the change in the mindset of the personnel necessary for success. This means learning email management, how to understand multiple channel information and use it, and what appropriate response times are, not just based on "traditional" New Economic criteria (service level, customer value), but also based on knowledge of New Media response times. Documentation skills become hyper-important because of the email responses.

- ▶ Use the existing tools, if possible. Don't build from the ground up. Integrate the existing tools with your legacy system. For example, why not use PeopleSoft since they have years of experience in how customer contact centers work and have the best practices often built into the software? Better that than building your own. There are packages like PeopleSoft and Siebel Call Center for the enterprise and there are packages that handle pieces of the puzzle. For example, a package was released in 2000 called Virtual Hold, by—what else—Virtual Hold Technologies. It works like this:

1. Customer listens to recorded message while waiting for an agent.

2. If he doesn't want to wait, he chooses a phone option that tells the system to make a call as soon as an agent is available or allows the customer, via the phone number pad, to schedule a date and time up to seven days ahead.

3. The phone number is captured and holds a place in the ACD queue for the customer.

4. The Unified Queue Module does the same thing for the Web. If your agents are busy when the customer clicks on the website, a similar choice is available: telling the system to have an agent call back as soon as one is available or a calendar pops up to allow the customer to schedule a time and date up to seven days ahead. The two formats (phone and Web) converge in the Universal Queue so there are no conflicts. It takes care of ACD and inbound routing issues and provides the Web-based customer with the maximum experience, even to the point of letting the customer know when the next agent will be available (updated every 15 seconds). Niche covered. Would you want to build that from the ground up?

▶ Plan to give higher-priority treatment or some other reward to the self-service Web users. Encouraging that behavior is important because two things have occurred with the use of the Web. First, the user normally isn't interacting with a live agent. Second, the information captured is a lot more effective and there is simply more of it, providing a quicker ability to put the publicly available problem resolutions back up on the Web so that more and more people can be solved by self-service.

▶ Don't assume it will take the place of the human being. It won't. It is an alternative that is valuable and useful, but can't be forced. Not everyone uses the Web. Contrary to popular belief, not all Web users want to use it for something like this. Sometimes a human voice is better than a mouse click.

▶ Try to implement software that will capture information well enough to constantly improve your knowledge base. (See Siebel Call Center example on the next page.)

▶ Keep the interface simple. It is important that the customer sees the same interfaces that the CCR sees. That way, customer interaction with the CCR is consistent, either on the Web or on both the Web and the phone. Explanations of what one is seeing are useless.

Assume you've Web-enabled your call center and have a full-featured CIC now. Let's look at the technology behind a phone call that is made by a customer to the CIC (this is Siebel's take on it, so it may be a bit different for other software, but generally it's about the same).

The customer phones into the service center for the first time. He gives the corporate configuration ID, which is matched against a table that shows the customer's company is a Gold Service holder, thus providing the customer with the highest level of service offered by the company running the CIC. Then the individual gives name information and is assigned a unique configuration ID (called a config ID for short) that is attached to the config ID of the company. Once that occurs, it will be used for recording the call, as well as logging and monitoring future calls through what is called the Siebel Audit Trail. The customer service representative (CSR), who for the sake of the "Neoclassic" Economy and Greenberg's Political Correctness, I'm going to continue to call the customer contact representative (CCR) for the rest of the chapter, then asks the customer what level of urgency the problem has. The categories are Low, High, and Urgent, which are available to the CCR through a pick list. Each category has business rules and workflow attached to it accordingly. When the choice is made, the workflow and rules automatically kick into gear. For example, if the call is categorized as Urgent, there are three people, including the CCR who answered the call, who are responsible for getting the question resolved within two hours. If it is marked High, there might be six people who get serial routings, depending on where the call has to go, and who have 24 hours to resolve the question. The status field is automatically flagged as open when the call and config ID are logged. It remains open until it is marked as resolved, and the information is then logged and stored in a table that is attached to the customer's corporate and individual config IDs.

The workflow is a very important part of the Siebel, PeopleSoft, or Clarify call center operation because it handles the automatic routing that is critical for timely resolution of problems. In the previous example, if the first assigned engineer fails, the problem is escalated automatically to a specific person called the "backline"—really the level 2 support—and this goes up the predesignated chain until the problem is resolved or there is final failure to resolve the problem. If the issue is closed successfully, screens pop up for the ultimate CCR who solved it that ask him questions to be answered, such as what the problem was, how it was resolved, and who resolved it. The name of the person answering these questions auto-populates the Assignee field, under the assumption that the final resolution lay with that person. There is a date and timestamp field that is auto-populated once the "resolved" flag is checked.

Should the same person from the same company call in with the appropriate config IDs later, several things occur. The information that was entered into the system at resolution (and along the way) will pop up for the use of the CCR now dealing with the newer call. Additionally, there is the capability for a query to find like defects that may have occurred either within the customer's company or from other companies that are being serviced by the same service provider. The fields with this information are attached to a business object, which is attached to a table with the information that answers the query.

Automated Intelligent Call Routing

What is the importance of call routing? It seems simple enough. You call in, you wait a few seconds or minutes, and you may or may not speak to someone or carry out something with a touch pad. You are then directed to a particular person. It sounds pretty easy, but it is one of the functions most prone to failure in the world of volume transactions. Intelligent inbound and outbound traffic direction is a central condition of an effective CIC. Call routing gets difficult when email, chat, VOIP, and Web routing get involved. High volumes make it scarier yet.

Managing this means using call-routing software that can handle increasing volume, geographical dispersion of the CCRs, multiple channels, and workflow. Typically it would identify who is calling and why they are calling (see the Siebel example), use the customer database to identify the history, and then find the appropriate party who is available at the time the caller calls. The software should have integrated IVR so that some of the processes can be routed to automatic responses. It should have CTI to capture information and use the databases effectively. Its distribution should be multichannel, which means an open architecture. It should be easily scalable, since call volumes will vary widely between companies, times of day, year, and month. It should be able to capture real-time data and use it in conjunction with the historical data on the customer that exists in the customer data repository (or customer case repository, as the "case" may be). It should be Web-enabled so that Web-based routing to the appropriate menus can occur and so that the information given is easily captured and centrally stored. It should allow live collaboration on the Web. It should provide remote agent support so that branch offices and small office/home office (SOHO) agents can be utilized in the problem resolution. That means that the home agent and the branch offices can access most of the functionality that is provided to the HQ agent. This eases the weight of the high-volume days without tying up valuable HQ real estate.

The software should have strong scripting capabilities and an open interface. This means the interface can control IVR scripting that is governed by applied business rules.

Finally, it should integrate workforce management tools with its call-routing capacity so that the CIC's agent capacity and scheduling forecasts can be integrated into the use of the call-routing functionality in micro specific ways.

The larger companies outlined build much of this functionality into their CIC software. However, there are other vendors who do nothing but this. One award-winning example in an uncrowded field is Telephony@work's CallCenter@nywhere intelligent routing applications. This is unique, cutting-edge software that is recognized for its advanced nature by the industry that spawned it. It won multiple awards in 1999, with the most significant being Product of the Year from both *Computer Telephony* magazine and *CallCenter Solutions* magazine.

What makes it at least a significant step in evolution for the CIC is that it is easy to install. It offers literally all the pieces of the call center puzzle in one preintegrated suite of applications. The platform gets its name from the fact that it can queue and route interactions from anywhere (phone, fax, and Web), it can be installed anywhere (through support for T-1, E-1, ISDN, and analog lines), and it enables call centers to deploy and seamlessly blend agents and supervisors from anywhere (local, branch office, and remote locations). Not bad for a start. But take a look at their "Programmers Not Required" technology. The users can install CallCenter@nywhere's complex routing system! Not just the "you get the call from Joe because Joe is a Gold Level service customer" functions, but also IVR scripts, multimedia queuing, and skills-based call routing. Think about it. You can install it and you aren't even technical.

Workforce Management Software

In a manner of speaking, workforce management (WFM) software is what lies on top of the call-routing software. The two features that are most important are call volume forecasts and agent scheduling. Remember the Erlang-C equations that I mentioned a few pages ago? They are built into the good workforce management software programs. Equally as important is sophisticated pattern recognition. The foundation for pattern recognition is not recognition of patterns, oddly enough. It is recognition of the pattern anomalies. For example, if, over a year, there are exactly 250 calls per day every Monday but three, it recognizes the anomaly in the three days and tries to figure out how those anomalies come to pass. If those anomalies are explainable, the basis for a different number of agents assigned to those three days is there and thus, the money is saved or the customer is satisfied. Logging and monitoring are also part of workforce management. By capturing and collecting the data day to day, the ability to manage performance and schedule appropriately is increased by multiples. The more depth defined, the better the system.

Genesys, of whom you will learn more later, has a great take on this domain. They are pushing for what they call "Multimedia Workforce Management," which means that in a CIC, there are multiple media channels through which interactions take place. For example, an email from a customer might initiate either a return email or a phone call that leads to a Web collaboration. One example I've been asked to review is a new CRM software package. The first notification came in an email. The second set of interactions was a series of phone calls. The third was two emails with attachments. The fourth is a Webex interactive presentation of the software.

The channels of communication are vastly expanded since the 1990s and the factors that morphed the call center into a customer interaction center are at play in workforce management, too. The functionality beyond the forecasting and agent scheduling mentioned above also includes reporting, what-if scenario planning, and compliance with rules and regulations. Other features can include comparison between the forecasts and the results, and most importantly, multisite support. The most important part of this is that it is done via multiple communications media.

Keep one rule in mind: Workforce management applications are only as good as the data gathered to use them. For example, if you are planning for customer contacts via various media, you have to collect at least a month or two of contact data. You could collect data from your automatic call distribution (ACD) system, which will show you the peaks and valleys of call volume over time, call duration, abandon rates, and other important facets of contact. Wherever you get your data, know that WFM is still software, and if the data is bad, so will be the management.

LOGGING AND MONITORING

Logging and monitoring software provides the granularity needed to do precision scheduling and improve performance management. Besides such obvious things as collecting information that is based on caller IDs of some sort, there are several other features that good logging and monitoring software has:

- ▶ The means to develop criteria to capture appropriate samples across the entire CIC network
- ▶ Extensive and very flexible reporting tools
- ▶ Universal connectivity to ACD systems
- ▶ Strong interfacing with the WFM applications
- ▶ Analytic tools that can score data so that weight can be assigned to captured information
- ▶ Easy export to other systems

One company that specializes in the performance management domain is e-talk Corporation (http://www.e-talkcorp.com/). They provide some of the most comprehensive logging and monitoring tools in the business and have four applications. The two that are apt for this usage are:

Recorder Enables customer contact centers to record and evaluate customer interactions simultaneously through telephone, email, and Web interaction. It even allows for live monitoring and recording sessions. What makes this particularly powerful is a deep search engine that can provide call selections based on any number of criteria. Recorder can be accessed from a touchtone phone.

Advisor A tool that measures agent or agent group performance. It imports productivity data from your ACD and other business systems and combines it with your quality criteria to give you a complete picture of your agents' performance. This is a Web-based evaluation tool.

The Measurements

At the time Robert Kaplan's *The Balanced Scorecard* was published in 1996, the metrics that defined success or failure in business tended to be quantitative. *The Balanced Scorecard* was one of the reasons for the move from purely quantitative analysis for success to combinations of both the tangible quantities and the less tangible quality measurements.

This, a bit more slowly, has affected the CIC world as well. Traditionally, the measurements of success were quantitative:

- How long is the average handling time?

- From the time the customer dials in to the end of the call, how much of the time spent is idle time?

- How many of the calls hang up before the call is completed (abandonment rate)?

- How much time is the customer in the queue before a representative speaks with him/her?

- How quickly is an agent available from call to call?

- Once the caller is engaged, how much time until the call is completed, either successfully or unsuccessfully?

Grab a waiting call that was on hold a short time and complete the call successfully in under a minute and you did really well. The problem with these measurements, particularly in the customer service world or even the telesales world, is that no metric really defined whether the problem was solved. The measurements were strictly on volume. The assumption was that some percentage of the calls were successful.

These days, the Web, email, and fax play a role in this, so the quantitative measurements have to change. The other part of the equation comes into play too: How do you manage the inquiries regardless of the channel?

What is often proposed is a ratio of customer profitability to number of calls. One step further for measuring the ROI here is to differentiate service levels in conjunction with the number of calls or visits, or the involvement of CIC-employed labor with that customer in relation to the customer's profitability. Perhaps the best example of a successful program in that realm is the frequent flier premier programs that all the major airlines have. Fly with us for 25,000 miles or 30 segments and we will recognize you as someone we want to spend more time with and give more value to because you are sustaining our airline substantially.

The Internet makes these measurements a bit more difficult because the Web pages a customer surfs on the company site and how email responsiveness is handled play an important role in the measurement of the metrics. Logging and monitoring software can handle the quantifiable side of these measurements.

The Cost

ContactBabel did a study in 2001 that identified the cost per transaction for each communications channel in a CIC transaction and, by comparison, for an in-person salesperson. This resulted in some interesting numbers. The mean average for each category:

Automated email	$0.25
IVR	$1.10
Web self-service	$0.50
Text chat	$5.00
Assisted email	$2.50
Telephone	$9.50
Unassisted email	$9.00
Web collaboration	$15.00
In-person sales call	$700.00

The numbers are actually astounding, at least by comparison to the mean average cost of an in-person sales call. What is noticeable is the difference in cost between the transactions that involve humans and those that don't. Those that do: $5.00, $2.50, $9.50, $15.00, $700.00. Those that don't: $0.25, $1.10, $0.50, $9.00. You people are expensive! It looks like we're going to have to do without you. To keep down costs, of course.

Actually, this clearly points out the value of automating what you can in the CRM CIC space. But what is the ROI time for CIC CRM?

The ROI

Okay, we have some measurements and benchmarks. We have some actual costs. The question is how real is the ROI for the kind of bucks that you're putting out for significant feature upgrades to make your call center a CIC? Let's take a look at a study that was done by *Call*

Center magazine in November 2001 on ROI for different telephony and CRM features and the projected time to get a positive ROI.

Automatic call distribution	18 to 48 months
Interactive voice response	3 to 18 months
Outbound dialer	12 to 36 months
Computer telephony integration	6 to 36 months
Intelligent call routing	3 to 9 months
Customer service and support call tracking	24 to 60 months
Campaign management system	3 to 18 months
Analytics	9 to 24 months
Knowledge management	10 to 60 months
Remote agent	Not yet determined
Wireless	Not yet determined

So what can we conclude from looking at these numbers? For the most part, not much except that it takes a *long* time to get a return on any investment in CIC technology. Anyone implementing it has to be prepared for a long cycle. However, judging from the ultimate cost per transaction, it is well worth it. The savings potential is huge.

Who Handles the Calls?

There are a number of established and newly minted companies that form the bulk of the CIC market. Most of the CRM multifunctional solutions companies—those that offer end-to-end services—offer a CIC or customer contact center. However, there are some that either have long roots on the software side (such as PeopleSoft or Clarify) or come from the telecommunications end, like the new Lucent spin-off, Avaya Communications. When it comes to the enterprise-level multimedia call centers that these represent, certain technological standards and metrics prevail:

- ▶ Response time to each transaction has to be subsecond.
- ▶ High transaction volume has to be handled easily.
- ▶ Scalability is critical.

▶ There needs to be a common architecture across all interrelated applications, preferably a single framework.

▶ A common data model should prevail—one dominant model that allows a single view of the customer to all agents. This data model should be concurrent across call centers, not just a sole call center.

The marketing approach that all of the companies seem to be taking is interesting. It is something akin to, "Your customer interaction center can become a profit center if you do it our way." How that's the case is pretty uniform, with direct links to sales and marketing and giving the customer service representative the ability to cross-sell and up-sell. From a technological standpoint, this is doable. From a human standpoint, customer service representatives aren't necessarily going to be good salespeople. There is a reason that some people go into sales and others to customer service. But I guess pure, good customer service is no longer enough.

PeopleSoft

PeopleSoft's heritage comes from the Vantive call center. While they have come a long way with PeopleSoft CRM 8.0 Support applications, they owe Vantive's success in the CIC marketplace a great deal. With the rewrite of all the code for PeopleSoft CRM 8.0, their CIC applications that are part of their Support and Field Service modules got a good makeover architecturally and, to some extent, functionally. PeopleSoft's offering includes:

Support PeopleSoft CRM Support is a pretty complete contact center solution. It automates call tracking, entitlement processing, workflow, problem resolution, revenue generation, credit card authorization, customer self-service, performance measurement, and service management, which covers the gamut of basic CIC activities. They differ from Amdocs Clarify in both philosophy and focus, though the ultimate result is much the same. While Amdocs has a strongly mercenary bent, PeopleSoft CRM Support's philosophy is aimed at increasing the quality of interaction with their customers. They are directed at identifying a customer's lifetime value and then steering the effort toward maintaining lifelong, profitable relationships with those customers.

FieldService This is one of the better field service applications on the market, because of the PeopleSoft CRM 8.0 architecture. Internet access provides a normally mobile workforce with customer information from just about anywhere and any time. It is coupled with their Mobile FieldService applications so that allocation, scheduling, and dispatching are under control of both the individual field representative and the dispatcher at the headquarters. Some of the more useful features include:

- ▶ Tracking and logging service requests, including required skills, activities, return material authorizations (RMAs) inventory requirements, and configuration updates.

- ▶ Assigning, scheduling, and dispatching both internal and third-party service providers with automatic notifications.

- ▶ Accessing customer records and case histories from a single location.

- ▶ Managing service agreements and warranty coverage.

- ▶ Relating predefined task actions with actual service orders; tracking and logging actual time, materials, and expenses of service technicians.

- ▶ Managing spare parts inventory and requisitioning functions.

- ▶ Integrating with back-office information management systems such as manufacturing, distribution, inventory, and accounting.

- ▶ Of course, integrating with other PeopleSoft modules. No big surprise there.

HelpDesk This particular module delivers problem, change, and asset management and, best of all, has a Web-based self-service helpdesk for the employees. Features include:

- ▶ Initiating, tracking, and resolving internal customer requests for support.

- ▶ Automating workflow, escalation, and notification processes.

- ▶ Tracking and supporting company assets, including hardware and software.

▸ Performing root-cause analysis to quickly diagnose problems and provide resolutions.

▸ Aligning helpdesks and business models with change management capabilities.

▸ Measuring key performance metrics with excellent enterprise-level reporting tools.

This is a very solid CIC Support set of applications; they do good work.

Amdocs Clarify

There is a reason that Nortel Networks bought Clarify for $1.2 billion. There is also a reason that Nortel sold Clarify to Amdocs in 2001 for $200 million. Most of those reasons have to do with Nortel, not the Clarify product package. I won't comment on that, other than to say that a market leader was dropped to the bottom of a deep well due to a horrible fit, though it seemed good at the time. It tells you something when it is sold for a roughly 83 percent discount.

That is not to say that they don't have an excellent product. It is just unclear what and how well Amdocs is going to do with them, though Amdocs itself is a sound, smart company. They see the March 2002 renamed ClarifyCRM as a package they can sell to the communications industry. Call centers, which are the spinal column of ClarifyCRM, fit well with a telecommunications backbone. They seem to be maintaining the Nortel vision that their call center applications are the centerpiece of all their solutions. That means, as Nortel did, they are bundling ClarifyCRM Call Center with their sales and marketing solution, which is a bit of a stretch, but doable. However, conceptually, what they are attempting to say is that a call center, if properly administered, technologically sharp, and customer-focused, can become a profit center rather than just a cost center. This is a good thing. There seem to be some deals that indicate an aggressive CRM posture in the telecommunications market. In February 2002, Amdocs announced a five-year CRM outsourcing deal with Verizon and a deal with Dominion Telecom, a regional carrier that provides broadband products to wholesale customers throughout the eastern United States, for the full Amdocs ClarifyCRM product—SFA (sales force automation), marketing and campaign management, and call center management. So things seem to be picking up.

In March 2002, Amdocs also announced a new architecture for their ClarifyCRM product—an "Internet-enabled" version, written in Java and XML that is also J2EE compliant. It can support both thin and "thick" clients, applications, and browsers. They have positioned this architecture as an easy migration path for individual "as-needed" migrations to a Web-based environment. This way the entire infrastructure won't have to be overhauled. At least that is what they are saying at release time.

So what are the CIC-related applications that Amdocs is presenting in Clarify, their ISM 2002 award-winning suite?

ClearCallCenter Straight from the website: "ClearCallCenter is a turn-key business solution for creating and managing sales and marketing processes that increase call center profitability." The Amdocs vision for Clarify is the same as Nortel's, which is to turn the CIC or the call center into a profit center. That seems to be a blatant part of their direction. They don't hide it. ClearCallCenter is designed for sales, marketing, and call center and universal agents to manage customer relationships by identifying, qualifying, and closing sales opportunities. Customer service is a part of it, but, at least according to what I've seen, is viewed as something you provide to increase profitability. I suppose that this is pretty much what all customer service is. Providing the service for the sake of good service is not really part of the equation. Amdocs is not cynical; they're just being "realists" in a world defined by profitability. This product has workflow organized around order entry and quote generation. It even tracks inventory. Why it's called "CallCenter" is a bit beyond me, actually.

ClearSupport This application has strong customer service features. ClearSupport service representatives can log cases, set priorities, route cases, verify contracts, review case histories, manage configurations, and track case-related costs. It has very good feedback capabilities so that customers can interact with the representatives.

ClearContracts ClearContracts provides a powerful set of features that can both create and identify service level agreements (SLAs). It overlays the individual customer records and automates the levels of service available to each customer when a problem or request arises. Once again, it is blatantly aimed at cross-selling and up-selling: "It enables sales representatives to quickly quote and sell complex services through the automation of key contract information and processes, including complex quoting, renewals, financial management, and entitlement tracking."

ClearHelpDesk ClearHelpDesk functionality includes call tracking, diagnostics, service level agreements, change management, integration with network management systems, integration with off-the-shelf knowledge bases, and reporting. What makes this interesting is that it is designed for internal use, primarily.

ClearQuality This is an integration-dependent features application. While it can stand alone, it is much more powerful when integrated with other modules such as ClearContracts and ClearSupport. On its own, it creates change requests to handle bugs and service enhancements. When integrated with ClearContracts, it ensures adherence to SLAs that might say something like, "Bug fixes must be turned around in 10 business days," assigning priority and urgency to the requests. It automatically notifies customers of the status of bug fixes or enhancements called for by contract or in general.

Task Manager Task Manager seamlessly integrates with ClearHelpDesk and ClearSupport to automatically schedule and track moves, additions, and changes to configurations. This application manages commonly occurring requests, tracks the status of individual and group approvals, and maintains a complete audit trail of changes.

Script Manager This module is a matter of taste. Personally, I'm not a big fan of scripts since I believe that they restrict human thinking and put human personality on automatic. Script Manager uses drop-down menus and natural language to craft personalized scripts that are tailored to individual customer profiles, including demographic information and purchase histories. Once again, on the mercenary side: "Script Manager improves the quality of customer service interactions and provides agents with a more professional, personalized, and flexible scripting to promote up-selling/ cross-selling."

Account Manager Account Manager provides a comprehensive, enterprise-wide view of all activity, inquiries, service requests, and problem reports using all media. The strong workflow features of this module allow account activity to be turned into proactive actions.

CRM Navigator This application is the front end, fully integrated to the entire suite or whatever modules are implemented. It has a strong workflow, and it moves inbound and outbound customer interactions to the appropriate places. For example, if a customer requests x, it can route the request to y, and then (of course) bill that customer for the service, depending on the SLA.

e-care Ah, the perfect world. The customers can pay bills online, replenish prepaid accounts, view bills, update accounts in real time, and watch the progress of their own requests through the system. Using the analytics that Clarify provides, it can also give personalized messages and screens to the individual customer.

This is a comprehensive former market leader in a tenuous situation with a solid company. The CRM suite is perhaps the most openly mercenary of all the suites, but then if business isn't to make money, what is it for?

Genesys

Genesys is vendor-agnostic. It has no fervent belief in any particular vendor, creating products that can be used regardless of vendor. An apt analogy would be a high-end pair of speakers that do nothing more than pass the pure sound out to the listener almost entirely distortion free. They pass the sound through regardless of how it is recorded— CD, LP, DVD. None of that matters. The sound is as pure as the medium allows it to be. There is an enormous amount of technology that is behind this transparency. This is Genesys. They provide CRM-enabling technology that handles the routing of interactions between customers and the CCRs of any company. They build an agnostic business logic into their hardware and software that handles the routing and queuing of incredibly large amounts of calls, regardless of which CRM technology is being used. Their products can handle such huge call volume that it has a customer that measured at 209 calls per second in a live environment. They don't even know their theoretical limit.

They have the Gplus Line of products that provide both hooks to existing CRM applications—currently Siebel and PeopleSoft—and a toolbox that provides both customization tools and already created APIs to integrate their products. They also have prepackaged certain business processes used by CRM vendors such as SAP and Broadvision. They integrate voice portal software and technology from companies such as Siebel-favorite Tell Me and Telera. Genesys handles the routing hub for these voice portals. They have strong vertical integration with telecom and financial services.

One unique facet of Genesys products is an engine that incorporates natural language analysis. In other words, it learns from the activities of the CCRs and other service agents—their problem solving and their answers—and builds a knowledge base that provides the most likely answers. This is an automated process to build a standard library that is based on the real-time and real-life agent responses. That is the cool part of techno-agnosticism. It might not bow to any CRM icon, but it responds to the real humans who do the work by automatically building something that makes their work easier—a secular version of heaven.

At the higher level, Genesys products provide tools to build routing strategies. They have the Interaction Router Designer for developing the workflow and the strategies. Once created, these are loaded into the router being used and compiled and integrated. Thus, a call flow is born.

Genesys Products

Genesys has a *huge* product set with multiple industry plaudits. I'm going to concentrate on two, Genesys Suite 6 and the Gplus Adapters.

Genesys Suite 6 Version 6.5

This version was released in early 2002 and was a significant upgrade. It focused on making sure that down time from service interruptions was considerably reduced. Internationalization was increased with GUIs for multiple European and Asian languages. In addition, there was increased support for both VOIP products and Web servers of multiple stripes and hues.

Network Routing Customized routing strategies are developed that allow customers to call from toll-free numbers and be delivered to the appropriate agent.

Enterprise Routing This is a vendor-neutral feature that uses real-time stats, customer data, or customer-defined business rules to develop a routing strategy that is executed by the engine. A new universal routing engine actually allows the creation of a universal routing strategy that can apply to both network and enterprise routing when the two are being used.

Internet Contact This takes advantage of the multichannel or, as Genesys calls it, multimedia features of Genesys applications. Email management and Web-based interaction are integrated into the call center which is, thus, magically transformed to become a CIC, because of the manifold channels.

Outbound Contact This is fairly obvious. It handles outbound contact management with a strategy.

Workforce Management This is the Genesys version of WFM, described earlier in this chapter.

Universal Workflow This engages the front and back offices with the customer interactions over a wide variety of channels, and handles transactions through the CIC operations, regardless of channels.

Campaign Sequencing This simply is the coordination of several outbound campaigns, saving the normal time it takes to manually intervene.

Additional notable features of version 6.5 are Internet Contact (automated email content analysis) and Advanced Schedule Modeling within Genesys Workforce Manager (what-if scenarios for testing staffing configurations).

GENESYS GPLUS ADAPTERS

These are the bridges beyond vendor neutrality. The Gplus Adapters are integration hooks to various CRM applications that link them to the Genesys framework and its Universal Queue[2]. Currently they have adapters for Siebel, BroadVision, SAP, and PeopleSoft that are unique application codes so that integration between Genesys products and the four vendors' applications goes a bit more quickly.

Gplus Adapter for Siebel This product connects the Genesys Suite with Siebel 7.0.

Gplus Adapter for SAP As of the publication of this book, Genesys had the T-Gate, which is the adapter for the ERP side of SAP. They plan on developing functionality similar to the PeopleSoft adapter in the near future (see immediately below).

Gplus Adapter for BroadVision This connects the Genesys Suite with BroadVision's One-To-One Enterprise.

Gplus Adapter for PeopleSoft This is the most feature rich of the adapters, connecting the Genesys Suite with PeopleSoft CRM 8.0 applications. It offers intelligent queuing and routing of customer interactions across all media channels, multiple sites, and switching platforms to a unified agent desktop with customized business rules and customer profiles.

Normally, a company mentioned in this book is a clearcut CRM company offering vendor-specific solutions. This isn't Genesys. Their vendor neutrality (or for those of a religious bent, vendor agnosticism) is very different from a "typical" CRM vendor. Regardless, they are an important company in the world of CRM customer interaction centers and customer service. They have even written a small book called *20:20 CRM, A Visionary Insight into Unique Customer Contact*" (by Steve Morrell and Laurent Philonenko) that is an excellent exposition on CIC-based CRM. It is not a general discussion of CRM, but you can't beat it for the basics of the call center or CIC. It is surprisingly free of marketing material. Its viewpoint is the one that Genesys espouses (obviously), but they have the experience and the savvy to espouse this view, so it is a plus not a minus. If you'd like a copy, contact me at either pgreenberg@live-wire.net or paul-greenberg3@comcast.net and I'll get you one.

Siebel

Siebel is playing the field, with both enterprise and midmarket editions of their Call Center software. Siebel is following the strategic path of the other enterprise-level players, which is to turn the service center into a profit center, be it enterprise or midmarket. In fact, with the applications—Siebel Call Center and Siebel Service (plus, of course, their "e" variants)—one of the most obvious facets of the applications' screens is that they have views that include all the sales opportunities in the entire enterprise (viewed with proper roles and authorizations), all the marketing campaigns, and all the service tickets outstanding, all from within Siebel Call Center. It even shows some of the SFA attributes such as contact and account management—a bit unusual for a call center application.

Siebel also has push broadcasting to the desktop so that the CCR's manager can send messages that will pop up to the desktop for one reason or another. The interface can narrowcast details specific to a single CCR, if so desired.

Siebel Service and Siebel Call Center have powerful response templates that are customized. Let's say an email comes in from me, and I have a history in the database, a config ID, and a particular identified problem. A simple click on Reply preloads my email address, gives the option of greetings, and offers an extensive pull-down list to pick out the answer to the problem identified and a choice of closings. Three clicks and a "Dear Mr. Greenberg, if your problem is xyz, you need to…" and I'm done. The problem resolution list is dynamically added to as more new problems are solved. If the CCR wants a more dynamic proactive process, he can use SmartScript, another slick feature that compiles all the information on Paul Greenberg and his problem, verifies his entitlement to service, identifies the problem, and puts together a suggested list of steps to settle the problem. It also identifies such information as how much time there is to solve this particular issue and how far along in time the issue is. SmartScript also will then check on the current promotions associated with the asset or customer that would be appropriate and even sends the notifications of those up-selling and cross-selling opportunities to the customer. Again, I'm no big fan of this, but it is a sales opportunity. SmartScript can even prepare the quote and tell Paul Greenberg to go ahead and hit Auto-Order—voilá, a sale.

Siebel Call Center can also conduct customer satisfaction surveys and compile the results, charting peaks and valleys in call center activity. It has strong telesales and telemarketing functions that I won't cover in this section.

Avaya

These guys are the year 2000 spin-off formed from Lucent's Enterprise Networks Group. They are not exactly a startup, with thousands of customers and $7.4 billion in revenues from the get-go. Their original CRM product, CRM Central 2000, came with them from Lucent but has evolved into much more over the past two years. They have serious alliances with companies like Siebel in the CRM world and have become an important force in CRM. They are in the CIC market from the telecommunications and networking side.

Avaya Product Offerings

In the year 2000, this was CRM Central, a powerful framework for CRM applications. It has evolved considerably in the last year and a half and now has multiple products, rather than a centralized framework. I'll group these loosely into management products, solutions, and business intelligence:

Management Products Management products are Avaya Interaction Management, which both integrates and captures inbound and outbound customer "experiences," and Commitment Management, which basically keeps track of your promises. With these products, you'll be able to handle distribution, tracking, and measurement of the promises that you make to your customers and so will your boss, so be careful what you tell those customers. With this product, you're going to have to keep those commitments.

Solutions   They have two that are appropriate for this section, though a bit odd in their separation into two products. They are MultiVantage Call Center Solutions and Multimedia Contact Center Solutions. The MultiVantage Call Center Solution is straightforward classic call processing software. Beyond the marketing hype, it processes calls and routes them appropriately. The Multimedia Contact Center Solution is linked directly to Avaya's Interaction Engine so that multichannel transactions can be processed and routed through a single control point. That means universal routing strategies can be applied to this system at the control point and do its deed. It is fine-tuned enough to handle personalized marketing campaigns and is optimized to this end, making it a great companion to some of the EMA suites out there. This is the "cost center to profit center" bulls-eye for Avaya.

Business Intelligence   This is what it always is when you hear these words, whether the words are from Avaya, or Cognos, or SAS, or whoever markets business intelligence applications. It captures and analyzes customer data and then uses it to optimize a customer experience. That may sound like jargon, but, in a simple form, that's what it does.

KANA

CSC Consulting chose KANA as their call center partner. That means that KANA is probably doing something good because CSC is an important player in CRM. While the logic of this statement isn't necessarily impeccable, it does indicate a prominence in the customer service CRM subset for KANA, one of my chosen best—the Sandbox Playmates. I want you to know they play big in this domain, but I'll cover them in Chapter 14 in more depth.

12

CRM + ERP = Enterprise Applications and Then Some

As we move through 2002, the prevailing winds of implementation philosophy have gotten downright gusty, blowing in the opposite direction from 2000–2001. Business is taking a "pain cure" approach toward CRM. In other words, buy the CRM pieces that will solve immediate problems and worry about the larger enterprise rollouts later. With the development of Internet architectures and other open frameworks such as SAP's Unification Framework, released in 2002, the larger vendors have less of a problem with this approach than you might imagine, enterprise-level solutions or not. The larger enterprise rollouts are the plums but no one is complaining about the small berries either. Analyst after analyst is reporting that the mood has shifted to solving the "pain domains," and there is some variance on exactly how that is playing out. For example, unlike many of the other analyst organizations, Gartner is saying, "Yes, it is 'cure the pain' now, but it will still shift back toward enterprise rollouts as the economy improves." I agree with this.

What does this have to do with what are called enterprise applications, also known as the collaborative enterprise? They are the multifunction CRM vendors of the future. Why? Let's go to a time long, long ago and a land far, far away....

Enterprise Resource Planning: A Brief History

Enterprise resource planning is a highly integrated (and highly expensive) system of back-office functions, particularly human resources and financial applications that are integrally customized and linked to all existing office business processes. In the late 1980s, SAP AG, a German software company, now the fourth largest software company in the world, came out with SAP

R/2, a huge piece of software focused on manufacturing companies that were using mainframe applications. What made this a revolutionary breakthrough was the integration of best business processes directly into the guts of applications and the whole office integration of business functionality. For example, with SAP R/3, the client/server version of R/2, sales and distribution were interlocked with financials, which were intertwined with production planning, which was intermeshed with materials management. SAP had very successful sales despite an extremely high software and services implementation price (sometimes as high as $100,000,000!) and implementation times that could take up to three years. By 1998, they had more than 4,700 customers in Germany and 1,800 customers in the United States and generated $5.5 billion in revenue.

This SAP success led to dozens of real and pretend ERP companies, the most notable real companies being PeopleSoft, Oracle (with its ERP Application suite), J.D. Edwards, and Lawson Software, each aimed at different markets and each simultaneously competitive. Hundreds of other companies such as Great Plains and Macola, formerly known for their accounting packages, revamped themselves and began styling themselves as ERP mavens. Cottage industries that linked ERP packages to almost any other form of application grew up as tens of billions were being spent on implementing ERP by most Fortune 1000 companies. The middleware market, which had been modestly successful with products like IBM's MQSeries, Casahl's Technology's Repli-caction, and so on, was transformed when companies who had implemented these vast ERP systems realized they had a lot of data they needed to link to and use that they couldn't spend the time "translating." The enterprise application integration (EAI) market was born, with major players like Mercator and NEON entering the fray and doing very well as the EAI market expanded rapidly to many other areas.

After a banner year in 1998, which was reflected by PeopleSoft growing from a small company with $227 million in revenues in 1995 to $1.4 billion in revenues in 1999, ERP troubles began to show on the horizon. All of a sudden, corporate vice-presidents who had authorized millions of dollars for an ERP implementation that was supposed to take a year to 18 months were clutching their throats when the implementation just didn't seem to be able to get finished—18 months were turning into 24 or even 36 months—and the process was well over budget. The benefits of the ERP return on investment weren't all that apparent, either. Unfortunately, as with all quasi-revolutionary applications and changes, ROI has no metrics. So how was the senior vice-president for information technology going to explain to a CFO who was concerned with both costs and return that it was very costly and the return couldn't be measured?

The climate was changing at this time, too—ironically, partially due to ERP, but primarily due to the Internet. Globalization and the dramatic escalation of transaction speed irrevocably changed the way the customer looked at the supplier. Customer demand for immediate response to inquiries and rapid shipment of orders, increasing competitive fervor, and the "need for speed" to market, created a new form of customer demand. Personalized goods and services should be deliverable almost instantly upon request nearly anywhere in the world.

ERP wasn't suited for this. While there is a lot of value in the back-office functionality it provides, it is not designed for rapid, nimble action; it is made for integrated functionality. SAP R/3 is a good example of that. Throughout the late 1990s, there were complaints that SAP R/3 versions from 1.0 to 3.0 were inflexible and forced you to adapt to their business rules, rather than provide you with applications that could be customized to those business rules you used as your best practices. SAP retooled and by 1997 came out with SAP R/3 4.0, an object-oriented version of the product that allowed the flexibility, but the mindset took a while to change.

Despite being seriously affected by the ERP market decline in 1999, PeopleSoft recognized the change that was occurring in the marketplace. In 1996, they acquired Red Pepper, a company that specialized in supply-chain software. With that acquisition, they began to push ERO (enterprise resource optimization), a philosophy and method they claimed was necessitated by the increasing real-time customer-driven economy. Perhaps the best example of this is the current "build-to-order" model used by most of the major computer system manufacturers (Dell, Micron, Gateway, and so on).

The ERP Market Declines Suddenly

ERP entered a dramatic market decline in early 1999. What was expected to be a banner year for the major enterprises became an unmitigated disaster. Dramatic stock price loss, with flat revenue growth after nearly 40 percent annual growth, major corporate upheavals and key management changes, thousands of top employees jumping to the dot-com world where flexibility, nimble footwork, and IPOs were the order of the day, all led to major soul-searching and reorganization. Stock prices plunged. For example, within a year, PeopleSoft's stock price, which had been as high as 53 in 1998, dropped to a low of around 14. However as of early 2002, due to very strong sales and several strong profitable quarters, it had climbed back and held at around 35. In ERP, only Oracle weathered the stock price storm on the strength of its database sales and its foresight into the need to retool the database and all products to the Internet, not just on its adaptation of them. As 2000 approached, the ERP companies blamed Y2K concerns and the near panic to complete Y2K projects as one of the major reasons for the decline of their revenues.

ERP companies began noticing the fast-track growth of Siebel Systems, a company that had been around since 1993, promoting CRM. While ERP enterprise-wide software went into a steep market dive, Siebel Systems began to promote, not the back office, but the front office (customer-facing) applications necessary to meet the globalized and personalized real-time demands of customers. Siebel, founded and still run by ex-Oracle executive Tom Siebel, climbed as spectacularly as SAP and other ERP vendors fell. Table 12-1 shows revenues for 1997 to 1999 for ERP and CRM vendors and the striking changes in the applications landscape that occurred virtually overnight. Keep in mind that the fiscal year ends vary in this chart.

Table 12-1: Revenue Comparison for Major ERP and CRM Vendors from 1997 to 1999

Company	Revenue 1997*	Revenue 1998*	Revenue 1999*	Growth Rate 1997–1998	Growth Rate 1998–1999
SAP	3,345.5	5,073.3	5,146.0	51.6%	1.4%
PeopleSoft	815.0	1,313.7	1,429.1	61.1%	8.7%
J.D. Edwards	647.8	934.0	944.2	44.1%	1.1%
Oracle	7,143.9	8,827.3	10,130.1	23.6%	14.8%
Siebel Systems	118.8	391.5	790.9	229.5%	102.0%
Clarify	88.2	130.5	230.7	47.9%	76.8%

* In millions of dollars

The differences are startling. The winds had shifted and the market was fully aware of the impact. While the ERP market leaders still gained a bit over the long run in a very uneven roller coaster ride, other ERP companies plunged to the bottom, and only in late 2000 were beginning to return. The pure CRM market leaders had spectacular growth. PeopleSoft made a fairly spectacular recovery in late 2000 due to PeopleSoft CRM sales' dramatic growth. SAP gained all told, but that is deceptive since part of the increase in the stock price was their opening on the New York Stock Exchange in 1998. From that opening through 1999, their actual percentage increase was zero. Oracle, who had an industry-leading database to fall back on, showed major growth. All stock prices are rounded to the nearest whole and reflect a month of activity in December of the year in question. They all show what CRM was becoming and ERP wasn't.

ERP was inextricably (and inexplicably) linked to CRM by industry press and pundits as CRM rose spectacularly. After all, Y2K-tainted data rested in the back office of financials and human resources, not the front office of sales and marketing, so the connection was peculiar. Witness the headline and first paragraph of an article in *Information Week* on July 21, 1999:

> **Earnings Reports: ERP Down, CRM Up**
>
> Quarterly results from SAP, PeopleSoft, and Siebel Systems confirm the obvious: The market for enterprise resource planning software is continuing its free fall, while the customer relationship management software market continues to climb.

This was typical for the time.

ERP Tries to Catch CRM

Beginning in 1999, ERP companies decided that perhaps CRM was the way to go. However, there were considerations. How were these behemoths going to compete with the head start that Siebel had? How could they retool to beat the young pups that were entering the CRM space Internet-ready? Not an easy task.

They also had to look at their historic investment in their own ERP software and thousands of clients. They had an attractive base, but many of the clients hadn't yet seen any real return on ERP implementations, so they were reluctant to trust their implementation partner. ERP implementation cancellation and failure stories were rampant. However, if they moved quickly, they could reap huge benefits as they reinvented themselves for the twenty-first century. Their installed base with the fully integrated back office could also have a fully connected integrated front office. Liz Shahnam, vice-president of Infusion: CRM for the META Group, said in an article in *CRM* magazine:

> Not only do [customers] value these pre-integrated solutions, but they're willing to pay a premium for them, because this integration is really hard.

CRM-ERP Integration

What does integration between ERP and CRM mean? Back during the ERP troubles of '99, another buzz acronym enjoyed a short reign of popularity: XRP. This stood for extended ERP, which was another way of looking at what the Yankee Group calls the "Extended Enterprise." While the acronym was short lived, it reflected the ERP vendors' tentative foot out the door to CRM and integration with the front office when they realized that what they had been building for the last several years was in jeopardy.

There are two distinct chains in the corporate ecosystem: the supply chain, which covers the back office to external suppliers and distributors, and the demand chain, which extends the front office to the customers and the channel. The back office includes departments and processes associated with finance, human resources, and, often, manufacturing. It includes multiple functions ranging from inventory management to accounts receivable to shipping and logistics. The front office includes sales, marketing, and channel management and all customer service functions. Its reach is out to the customer or partner, not through to the supplier or vendor.

However, there is a lot going on between the back office and the front office. For example, a closed product sale to a customer generates a bill or invoice and creates an account receivable that has to be taken into the ERP or financial package being used by your company. This product has to be physically created and moved from inventory to shipping and distribution. All this is accounted for in the back office, though the transaction originated in the front office. If the front and back offices are integrated, this works well. Easier said than done. How do you integrate this well enough so there is no duplicated data or repetitive data that has to be entered into the system?

The natures of ERP and CRM are not at all similar. As modular and flexible as it has tried to become, ERP's foundation evolved from earlier manufacturing-based manufacturing resource planning (MRP) applications and its later incarnation, MRPII applications. This foundation is based on creating *internally* stable business functions and predictable process control. The concept of ERP was the integration of all back-office functions so that the bottlenecks responsible for interruptions and breaks in the processes were smoothed and the incompatibilities of the best-of-breed applications (homegrown or commercial off-the-shelf software) were eliminated or reduced. This doesn't work with CRM, which is *external*. How can you be in command of the processes when they are based on your customers' behavior? Conceptually, one important reason for CRM is real-time (or near real-time) response to the constantly liquid shifting of customer demand, which is not controlled internally at all. It also means the psychology of the front office is quite different from the psychology of the back office. Despite all your efforts to create a uniform, employee-friendly corporate culture, you have two functionally different subcultures within. It would be like mixing yogurt and cheese. Both are dairy products, both have bacterial cultures, but together—ugh!

Integration presents a real challenge to the enterprise. Micron and Dell, with "build to buy," are the proof that integration, daunting as it may be, can work. While ERP predecessors, MRP and MRPII, functioned in the "build to forecast" world, that model is now dead. The challenge of CRM-ERP integration is, in one regard, to keep it dead. This has progressed very well over the last year, but still has important issues and questions.

ERP, CRM, and the Web

There were two other major problems with ERP vendors' incursion into CRM. Before they could enter this agile market, they had to reinvent themselves as business-to-business enablers. To get e-business panache and to actually become e-commerce-focused enterprises, they had to revamp their entire applications because none of them had Web-integrated applications of any note. For example, in order for Oracle to deliver Oracle CRM effectively, they had to convert their Oracle 8.0 database so it would work with the Web and then convert a series of other products to make them Internet-ready. Since mid-1999, all of them have serious Web initiatives. The most prominent three are:

SAP With the release of SAP version 3.0 of their CRM product, they have integrated the product with their MySAP platform. This is still hybrid architecture, but adds a unified Web portal with an open architecture (the Unification Framework) to the mix.

Oracle They have fully rebuilt their world-class database, Oracle 8i, Web-integrated their applications suite, Oracle 11i, and revamped their CRM package to be what they claim is 100 percent Web integrated. However, there are some vestiges of non-Internet architecture such as Oracle Forms, keeping the back- and front-office integration from being entirely seamless.

PeopleSoft With the release of PeopleSoft 8.0, they have a seamless back- and front-office capability. This is probably the single most advanced, fully integrated ERP-CRM collaboration.

With the development of Internet architectures and Web-integration, the ideal of seamless integration between back and front offices became that much closer to a reality. Some of it remains a dream yet, but the PeopleSofts of this world are getting there.

Options for ERP-CRM Integration

The simplest option is to hire a systems integrator to come in and integrate the systems. However, the obvious pitfall here is that they are not only dealing with ERP and CRM applications they may not know much about, they are also dealing with your legacy systems, which they know nothing about. But integrating all of that is what they are paid the big bucks for. And the bucks will be big.

You could hire the ERP vendor and implement the ERP vendor's CRM solution. This is increasingly becoming an option for CRM implementations. If the framework for the back office and the front office are built on the same architecture, integrated back- and front-office functionality is a lot simpler and more seamless. The caveat here is that these enterprise-wide applications are expensive, and the need for integration with legacy and third-party solutions can be daunting. However, companies like SAP and PeopleSoft do have open frameworks, allowing for an easier road than otherwise would be there. So the future bodes very well for integrated enterprises.

The third solution is what many companies are using already: enterprise application integration (EAI), which remains particularly valuable in client/server environments, but less so in a pure Internet milieu.

Middleware: Enterprise Application Integration

EAI applications, previously known as middleware, is the most cost-effective way of integrating the back and front offices in a client/server surrounding. EAI ranges from full-blown applications, like IBM's MQSeries or Mercator's Mercator, to adapters that are application specific such as the highly touted SalesLogix-to-SAP adapter from Scribe Software. Scribe is a particularly good company to be dealing with on integration between the front and back office, having come into the world as a company devoted to just that. In addition to the above-mentioned adapter, they have adapters for Siebel, SalesLogix, Onyx,

Great Plains, SAP, Solomon, J.D. Edwards, Invensys (Baan), Pivotal, Oracle, and Epicor. They are used with Scribe Integrate, the all-purpose framework they provide for these adapters. They have an XML adapter for integration with external applications. They cover all four bases. The limitation is that they are adapters for what they are adapters for, where Mercator can pretty well handle anything that can be mapped from one data source to another.

EAI's purpose is razor thin: to integrate data between disparate applications that don't natively speak with each other. That can mean off-the-shelf applications, legacy systems, ERP, and CRM. It means virtually any data. The adapters, which carry a lot less load, are even more specific. They move information from one specific application to another specific application. For example, SeeBeyond's Intelligent Bridge can handle up to 80 percent of the functional integration between Siebel and SAP R/3. Data synchronization works with everything from front-office sales functions to the back-office inventory and pricing. To hand-carve that level of integration could be a multimillion-dollar project over months. The price for Intelligent Bridge is six figures. For basic efforts, SeeBeyond offers eWay Adapters, priced considerably cheaper, for Oracle, SAP, Siebel, and such.

XML

XML is perhaps the most important emerging standard in Internet "languages." With universal applicability, it makes internal and external integration possible. Even though the standard is never complete and there are currently competing standards bodies, the promise of XML in integrating suppliers, customers, and back and front offices is monumental and could actually solve integration problems. Some capable XML applications leaders include WebMethods and Vitria, though XML integration is becoming increasingly a standard part of any application at the front- or back-office level. Take a look back at Chapter 2 for the companies that are using Internet architectures. They are pretty much all XML-compliant.

ERP Vendors Deal with CRM

So how did the ERP vendors deal with the onrush of CRM? See Table 12-2 for some of the strategies. Initially, most of them just made their pacts with the CRM devils. Now, after testing the winds of change, through internal development (SAP), acquisition (J.D. Edwards), or simple partnership (Lawson), they all have CRM suites. In fact, the case can be made that they are no longer ERP vendors with CRM suites, but to differing degrees they are enterprise application vendors—the leaders of the collaborative enterprise.

Table 12-2: ERP Vendor Strategies for CRM

Company	Approach	Actions
SAP	Internal development	Development team building SAP CRM with initial release planned in 2000. Integrated with mySAP.com. Announced alliance with the then Nortel-owned Clarify in early 2000 so they could integrate call center software into the mySAP.com offerings. Ended the alliance by the middle of 2001. Released their own MySAP CRM 3.0 in late 2001.
PeopleSoft	Acquisition	Partnered with Vantive, and then bought them in 1999.
Oracle	Acquisition, internal development	Purchased Versatility and Concentra in 1999. Still struggling with CRM product (most recent version 11.5.7 in early 2002) to get it right.
Baan	Acquisition, internal development	First to see CRM as important with purchase of Aurum in 1997. Created Baan Front Office. In 2002, as part of Invensys, announced iBaan, an integrated back- and front-office product with much stronger CRM features than previous attempts.
J.D. Edwards	Partnership, acquisition	Siebel strategic partnership in 1999 and announced integration of ActiveERA software with Siebel eBusiness suite in 2000. In 2001 bought YOUcentric to provide an enterprise application aimed at AS400 market. Ended Siebel partnership, though maintains reseller status.
Lawson	Partnership	1999 partnership with Siebel and use of Siebel Sales, Call Center, and Field Service as part of enterprise relationship management.

The ERP Players Take Center Stage

Who are the ERP vendors in the running for possible success? In the first edition of this book, I said Oracle, SAP, PeopleSoft, and Baan. Now J.D. Edwards is welcomed, with caveats, to this rather small group of potentially dominant players. That means Lawson is out of the race for the gold because this small and medium business (SMB)–focused ERP vendor is providing Siebel as its CRM applications. In fact, their CRM suite is downright funny when you look at it on their website. Lawson's "CRM suite" is Siebel *everything* and an adapter to integrate Siebel with Lawson's very good back-office software. But they don't rate for this group of enterprise applications. Sorry, Lawson.

Also, note the absence of Siebel in this group. Yes, they are CRM industry giants, but they have absolutely no back-office functionality at all and do not belong anywhere near this category. They have tried to disguise this by calling themselves an "e-business" suite, but the reality is they are a CRM *only* front-office product company. Not even e-business as they claim.

PeopleSoft

PeopleSoft did it the "easy" way. They acquired Vantive and its products, now called PeopleSoft CRM 8.0. Vantive was one of the top CRM applications on the market (third after Siebel and Clarify) when PeopleSoft took the plunge and purchased the company in late 1999. They saw an immediate increase (68 percent) in Vantive revenues from the third to the fourth quarter of 1999, while PeopleSoft sales rose 37 percent during that same time period. While there was an issue of whether the cultures could commingle, that buzz became minimized with the release of PeopleSoft 8.0 and Vantive eArchitecture 8.5 in July 2000 and a complete non-issue by the June 2001 release of PeopleSoft 8.0 CRM. The Vantive name and culture disappeared into the ether, though Vantive talent remained as many PeopleSoft employees. These are both Web-based architectures, rebuilt from the ground up, for back- and front-office functions that could fully integrate the offerings. There is more on PeopleSoft architecture in Chapter 2.

What this relatively seamless integration does is to allow the back-office products such as Human Resources or Financials to be fully and transparently integrated with the front-office products. Is it easy, given that they are both governed by the same architectural framework? No, but it works very well together when it is successful. For example, you not only can see the pipeline status of your corporate customers and their up-selling and cross-selling potential, you also can easily check on their invoices and payments and the commissions that the customer is generating. The best part? It can be done without you really having to care how it's done—or being reminded how it's done by glitches.

SAP

With the release of MySAP and the CRM 3.0 product, SAP has accomplished what they ambitiously set out to do. They have been able to integrate their CRM product with their back-office product. It can work extremely well with other SAP modules, such as manufacturing modules. Thus, it provides a very coherent, full enterprise solution. It is not yet to the level where it can seamlessly integrate with non-SAP products out of the box, but they have developed what they are calling the Unification Framework, which will allow easier integration and customization for both SAP and non-SAP products. Additionally, to deal with the external products, SAP has always had their Business APIs, connectors, hooks, and other small pieces of code that are designed to integrate with other applications, be they front office, back office, or in between. These are a long-standing part of SAP. It is a company that knows the enterprise applications market.

In June 2000, SAP announced an alliance with then Nortel-owned Clarify, a leading CRM call-center vendor. That alliance ended in 2001 with SAP releasing its own CRM suite and Clarify going down the tubes temporarily (I hope), sold by Nortel for $200 million to Amdocs. (See Chapter 11 for more on Amdocs Clarify.) Sadly, when Nortel acquired Clarify it cost them $2.1 billion. Because Nortel handled the Clarify product line so poorly, despite Clarify's history as a market leader, Amdocs got it at a bargain basement price. SAP did the right thing by building their own and leaving that temporary, expedient, and very limited relationship. The benefit shows (see Chapter 14 for more on SAP as a market leader).

Oracle

Oracle has always known how to be a player. Oracle Customer Management integrates e-commerce with more typical CRM functionality. It is Web-enabled, though not a pure Internet architecture. It is generally well integrated with other Oracle offerings. For example, not only is there an Oracle Sales module, but there is also Oracle *i*Payment, a module traditionally lumped with e-procurement solutions such as those presented by Commerce One, Metiom, and Ariba. This allows the procurement back-office functionality to work effortlessly with the sales force automation functionality that Oracle provides. That means not only do you close the deal, but the Accounts Receivable office (Oracle Financials) can track customer payment, which then can be integrated with Oracle's strong commission management functions (Oracle Sales Compensation).

Each of the Oracle Customer Management modules has a series of subsets within it. For example, Oracle *i*Sales contains the following:

- ▶ Oracle Sales Online

- ▶ Oracle Telesales

- ▶ Oracle Field Sales for Mobile Devices

- ▶ Oracle *i*Store

- ▶ Oracle Sales Compensation

- ▶ Oracle Order Capture

- ▶ Oracle Sales Intelligence

- ▶ Oracle Configurator

Big Five systems integrators and consulting firms are working closely with Oracle on their CRM solutions. For example, KPMG successfully implemented Oracle CRM at the Public Broadcasting System (PBS) in 2000. The Oracle 8*i* client base is a terrific foundation for Oracle to play significantly in the world of enterprise applications.

The Others

There are market leaders and there are pretenders to the throne. Occasionally, one of the pretenders reaches the throne. Here are some of the current pretenders who are heading in the right direction.

INVENSYS BAAN AND AURUM

Oddly enough, troubled ERP vendor Baan was also perhaps the most CRM foresighted when it purchased Aurum Software in 1997, far ahead of any other ERP company in the CRM game. Baan's CRM has been totally acquired, with the CRM suite from Aurum Software, product-configuration software from Beologix of Denmark, and sales-force support software from Matrix in Holland. Unfortunately, "Baanvision" had been blind to market reality for more than two years until its acquisition by Invensys in 2000. In April 2000, Baan announced that, contrary to all other ERP companies, it was spinning off its CRM applications. As with everything Baan, analysts questioned the whole idea. By comparison, SAP, Oracle, and PeopleSoft were integrating their CRM applications into their overall offerings. Baan's approach flew in the face of conventional wisdom—another odd move from what was a seriously shaken company.

However, after its acquisition by Invensys, there were a number of promising signs that brought sighs of relief to Baan-lovers around the world. The U.K.-based Invensys was a well-capitalized firm that had a wide reach and a wider vision for the Baan product lines. The results?

The announcement of the iBaan line of products and solutions and, most germane to this chapter, enterprise strategies. The iBaan product announcement in January 2001 was also an announcement that Baan was back. They announced multiple product lines (such as iBaan e-Procurement 2.1), frameworks (including iBaan OpenWorld, an XML-based integration framework), and enterprise solutions such as CRM. They announced an iBaan CRM strategy for the enterprise in January 2002 that is based on the collaborative use of the Web. The idea is to aim at the CRM verticals that Baan has among its installed base of 15,000 customers. That would be aerospace and defense, automotive, electronics, and industrial machinery. They even have established a marquee client base for their collaborative applications such as Hitachi Data Systems, Flowserve, Barco, and A-Dec. In other words, they are driving hard and back with a vengeance. They have a capable strategy, a stronger product line, and a powerful installed base. The only real remaining question is their ability to overcome the taint of the troubles of the last few years. If they can do that, with their enterprise applications, they can be a player with their version 4.2. We'll see. Good luck, Baan.

J.D. EDWARDS AND YOUCENTRIC

When J.D. Edwards established a partnership with Siebel in 1999, it was a bit of a surprise. J.D. Edwards as an ERP vendor owned the AS400 market. If you had an AS400 system and needed ERP, you went to J.D. Edwards. The Siebel partnership seemed forced because Siebel was never very good in the midmarket, which is where the AS400 is used primarily. So the purchase of YOUcentric by J.D. Edwards was no real surprise when the completion of the acquisition was announced in November 2001. This seemed to be a valuable and smart purchase because the architecture of YOUcentric was Java-based. Denis Pombriant, research director at Aberdeen Group, commented in a Line56.com article in January 2002:

> They're going to bring CRM to their small and medium-sized business (SMB) customer base. I think it's a good idea, because that area seems to be underserved. Traditional CRM vendors haven't been successful with SMBs.

This is one to watch, but it doesn't yet compete in the league with PeopleSoft, SAP, or Oracle. Someday, in the upper regions of the SMB market that have historically been the AS400 user base, it very well could. (See Chapter 13 for much more on the SMB market for CRM.)

LAWSON

This is a repeat of the earlier mistake of J.D. Edwards. Their entire CRM offering is Siebel. Siebel doesn't understand the midmarket, regardless of their claims and their so-called midmarket product. Lawson is one of the best ERP solutions for the small and medium-sized businesses in the United States. Go figure. I can't.

Summary

Enterprise applications vendors are the future for large enterprises in particular. They have a complete suite of all applications, minus the esoteric, quirky, or downright bizarre, that major corporations (the companies that are over a billion dollars and even those between half a billion and a billion dollars) will ever need. Companies like Siebel who play at this level don't carry the same overall functionality. They have no back-office applications. If you need the back-office functionality and you're a big guy, don't let marketing fool you. Talk to the enterprise applications big guys—PeopleSoft, SAP, and Oracle. They can most likely be of service.

13

SMB CRM: When Small and Medium Is Better than Big

There is a line written by Shakespeare that goes "Ay, there's the rub." This means, "That's the problem." While it is easy to say General Motors is not the midmarket, defining the midmarket is the rub. As we will see later, larger vendors don't understand what midmarket is despite their general tendencies in that direction. As a result, they define the midmarket in terms of the revenue size of a company that they feel they can sell their products to and still look like they are dealing with the "little people" out there. The reason they are anxious to do this is that they are aware that the midmarket as it really is (small and medium businesses) is probably the best place for CRM sales for the next few years. After all, the Global 1000 is only one thousand businesses, while the midmarket and small businesses number in the millions. But the extreme caveat here is that this is a unique market with its own set of problems and a much different general set of business practices, processes, and principles. For the purposes of this chapter (and future reference and universal acceptance), we are going to call the midmarket by its rightful moniker: the small and medium business (SMB) market.

The MidMarket Is Hot...Very Hot

The SMB market potential has CRM vendors and integrators of all sizes and shapes drooling. There are millions of businesses that fall into this category—the number I've seen is 13 million. While certainly hundreds of thousands of them may be too small to be that interesting to most CRM purveyors, it still leaves hundreds of thousands of others to get into. According to IBM, this mushrooms at the rate of 13 percent per year, considerably faster than large enterprise growth. The Gartner Group and Arthur Andersen claim that only 15 percent of SMBs have deployed even simple e-commerce functionality and only 5 percent have deployed complex e-commerce solutions. Plus they barely use (10 percent) email marketing. This fruit could be easy pickings.

What SMB Isn't

SMB isn't big, mature, consistent, similar to others in it, of one mind, easy to deal with, capital comfortable, resource rich, or all that knowledgeable about what CRM system it wants. It isn't a market that is easy to define or understand. It isn't a place that you want to be unless you truly do get it. It isn't a $1 billion entity or even a $500 million entity, which are the revenue values that the larger CRM companies use to give us their wisdom on what this market is.

Imagine the Los Angeles Dodgers saying that the Pittsburgh Pirates or the Cleveland Indians are the minor leagues. Or that the San Francisco Giants are a Triple A Pacific Coast League team. That is pretty much what Siebel-sized CRM players call midmarket when it suits them. The vendors identify the midmarket range from the low end of $300 million (at the time of this writing) to the high end of $1 billion. Wouldn't you, small business owner, like to grow up to be like the midmarket? The reason I say "at the time of this writing" is that many of the larger vendors frequently change the definitions to suit their current sales need. I've seen it go from $250 million to $500 million and back down to $300 million within the past 18 months, and in between $750 million and $1 billion, depending on which vendor you choose to believe. Let's take a brief look at who fits this version of the definition, given the revenue size. Consider the following: In 2000, Amica Mutual Insurance had revenue of $1.2 billion. What makes this significant is that they are number 1000 on the Fortune 1000 and they fall barely outside CRM vendors' standard for the midmarket! Or this little nugget: One of the largest companies on *Industry Week*'s Growing Companies 25 list is the $195 million ONI Systems Corporation. That is the biggest revenue number for the midmarket according to *Industry Week*, which is decidedly not a CRM company.

What SMB Is

Let's take a look then at what SMB is. We've already done away with the term "midmarket" and substituted small and medium business market, because the differences in the characteristics of the small business and the medium business are matters of degree. But small and medium businesses, similar in their natures, both differ very much from the large enterprise world—so much that they are a separate entity in more than just size.

As you can see in Table 13-1, SMB is a vastly different creature from the Global 1000 or larger enterprise. They are barely post-pubescent, if that, in terms of their business practices. Here are some of their characteristics in detail.

Table 13-1: Differences Between the SMB and the Global Enterprise

SMB: Small and Medium Business	Fortune 1000+: The Large Enterprise
Under 200 million dollars	Often a billion dollars or more
Fewer than 1,000 employees	Several thousand, up to hundreds of thousands of employees.
Multiple roles for individual employees	Highly defined responsibilities by title
Underdeveloped business processes; best practices often nonexistent in any organized way	Often inflexible business processes, well-established best practices
Sometimes publicly traded, sometimes privately held	Rarely privately held (Cargill and SAS Institute are privately held exceptions in this enterprise category); almost always publicly traded
Nimble, but not big	Powerful, not nimble
Modular CRM strategy	Enterprise-wide CRM strategy
Implementation strategy: accelerated, fixed price	Implementation strategy: Long term, either cost plus or time and materials
Likely to implement and manage CRM applications in-house for cost savings	Likely to outsource the implementation and, on occasion, the management of the CRM solution

SMBs Are Small or Medium-Sized, Not Large

While that sounds self-evident, remember what I said about the self-serving definitions above. For the purposes of human thought processes, we can define the SMB as a company with less than $200 million in revenues, or fewer than 1,000 employees, or both. While $200 million is a revenue number devoutly to be wished for for most SMBs, the common characteristics of the smaller enterprises tend to hold with some stretching to this level. Even the $200 million range seems high, but it is an appropriate compromise for now.

There is a level that is between $200 million and $500 million that is "young adult" in nature, with best practices newly established, incrementally increased differentiation of job descriptions, and so on. The largest vendors address this space more effectively than they do the SMB space, but they still don't have a clear understanding of the difference between these corporations and the large enterprises. These vendors tend to create programs and applications that are smaller versions of the large enterprise, rather than demonstrating a clear understanding of the significant differences in culture and business processes that exist between the SMB category and the global corporation.

SMBs Are Responsible Only to Themselves

The SMB is relatively rarely traded publicly—that is, a much smaller percentage of them are publicly traded than the Global 3500. That means they don't answer to Wall Street. For example, if they have a rough year, they lay off people, implement pay cuts, do nothing, or choose another path as dictated by their conscience, not their stock price and shareholders. This statement must be modified a bit when private investors are involved, especially venture capitalists who invest in the smaller firms and often have quite a bit of say in what goes on. So individual cases vary, but overall, SMBs work according to their business plan and conscience.

Job Descriptions Are Not as Clear

I'm the executive vice-president of an SMB. My job description tends to be somewhat operational, but I don't do operations. That is the function of the president of the company. I do business development and marketing with one hat on. I do CRM strategic consulting with another hat on. I do handholding if and when necessary with a third hat on. Our national sales director will help out when necessary with human resources and assist with collections for finance because she has a good background and history in that. This is typical of a small established company.

If you work in a small company that is large enough to provide you with a formal job description, but small enough to ignore it or to have a clause in it that says "and other responsibilities from time to time," when was the last time you adhered strictly to the job description? If some executive of your company came to you and said, "Hey, can you fill in and do this?" do you say, "Sorry, it's not in my job description"?

Or do you routinely do that "out of job description" task? If you still have the job, I know the answer to that rhetorical question.

The processes embedded in good SMB CRM software applications have to be flexible enough to recognize these constantly shifting roles and responsibilities. Permissions and roles cannot be tied to job titles without the ability to override the default versions of those assigned roles and permissions. Flexibility has to be built into the larger enterprise versions too, but it is life and death to the success of the CRM system for the SMB.

Best Practices Could Change Overnight

The SMBs are often a *meschugas* (crazy mess) of business practices. There is often no well-established knowledge base of best practices because most of the companies haven't been in business long enough to establish them or have had an informal culture or underdeveloped content management forever. In other words, a new salesperson coming to the company for the first time is on his own as far as how to sell. The business methods are not in place, nor are all the formal processes yet cleared. For example, if an SMB decides to upgrade sales functionality from, say, the limited Salesforce.com functionality to the more complete and complex SalesLogix, they normally have to shift how they do business to do that. Forecasting becomes a much more important part of how the pipeline is utilized. The TCO probably increases even though the ROI increases, and that redefines the cost structure and refines the way the company does its accounting. It means the salespersons are taught something they didn't know before. SalesLogix has a product catalog that is essential to understand in order to create pricing and determine the cost of deals and so on. Creating that catalog is something that makes the SMB personnel think along new lines. The practices embedded in SalesLogix become the practices of the company.

That seems good, and it is. However, let's look at it a little differently. Suppose the company grows from $10 million to $75 million in a year. That will dramatically transform the way the company does business. Inventory management with 35 salespeople is dramatically different with 6 salespeople. The back office and the supply chain become more critical to operations and sales. The level of competition changes, and marketing becomes a different thing. Now it takes $100 million to have a good year rather than $15 million, and the pressures are that much greater. Providing incentives for sales and other personnel has to change to make them reach these much greater numbers than before. The corporate culture has to be transformed to a much more collaborative one (or shark-like one, depending on the inclinations of senior management) to make the numbers work. The pressure to perform is accelerated and the stress levels increased. Then an IPO is being considered because of the great success of the company and the need for capital. To get to the next level, self-funding is no longer the way to go. Maybe investment capital. Maybe "The Street" (heaven forbid!). Then all of a sudden, cost savings and total cost of ownership and employee efficiency become a matter of IPO, rather than business...ad infinitum.

I could have spun this scenario a million other ways—and that's the point. Because of its more dramatic rises and dips, and its considerably more immature nature, the SMB market doesn't have established processes and practices. It is subject to equally dramatic changes in corporate culture in shorter time periods than the enterprise behemoths who are happy with profitability, 5 percent overall growth, and accounting procedures that let them drive up their stock prices.

SMB-focused CRM applications have to understand these mercurial and volatile shifts and must be built to both withstand and absorb them as they occur. The very large enterprise is dealing with long-established ways of doing business and best practices that are generally similar and easily customized. SMBs are not.

SMB Customers Buy Smaller

Simply put, the reason SMBs are SMBs is they have smaller companies than the big ones. That's fairly straightforward. Their customers tend to purchase their goods or services or both at smaller levels. They have simpler systems and are less compulsive in what they track. EBIDTA (earnings before interest, depreciation, taxes, and amortization) is a foreign concept to many small companies, until it is time to acquire them. Their need to integrate the back office and the front office, while as great as anyone's, is also a less difficult task since they are ordinarily tracking less complex transactions. Good to know when you think about SMBs.

SMB Partner Relationships Are Not Typically Served by PRM Solutions

This is interesting. Usually, the SMB is the partner and not the brand holder. It doesn't run the partner program, but it does have partnerships with the brand holder. For example, one small company I know is partners with Unique, Microlog, Oracle, Sun, Microsoft, IBM, Intelisys, Corio, Siebel, FileNet, and Vignette. They have no channel programs, but they have multiple partnerships with software vendors and with integrators not named here. They have a sort of "inverse partner relationship management."

In the non-IT world, the SMB is often the distributor of someone else's product, or the owner of several franchises of McDonald's, or the insurance agency that handles multiple insurance providers' products. If they are brand holders, that create widgets, they are handled by a small number of distributors, if not just one. SMBs in the services world are often subcontractors to multiple partners or other companies like them. What the SMB doesn't have (or really need) is a channel program.

This is by no means unusual in the SMB market, yet, to my knowledge, it's not really addressed by CRM vendors. How do you manage the multiple partnerships SMBs have with the companies that have partnership programs? The functionality of PRM or channel management applications really doesn't fulfill the need here. They have the wrong (or far too much) functionality for partnership juggling. Rather than partner relationship management, most SMBs need partner*ship* relationship management. Hopefully, someone with SMB expertise will come along and build this into their CRM applications.

SMBs Are Nimble

In the late 1990s, there was a significant push by the larger denizens of the commercial world to "get with" the Internet craze. The reason? It seemed to be the future and the way that everyone was going to make oodles of money. One byproduct was the attempted restructuring by many of the gargantuans to become lilliputian in their practices. They figured "nimble = Internet." They figured wrong as we later found out, but I heard the following comment from my senior management buddies at the major corporations more than once: "We want to partner with (or be like) the smaller companies, because they are nimble."

The following became clear:

▶ The Internet was nothing more than a mission-critical communications channel and not the road to wealth and fame.

▶ Big companies really didn't have to imitate small companies and be "nimble" unless they truly wanted to jump over a candlestick. Big-company departments were often larger than the entirety of the SMB.

It became even clearer that small companies were flexible and could move more quickly because their organizational hierarchies were flatter, less complex, and not so benchmarked or bureaucratic at each step. Approvals moved faster through the chain of command simply because the chain of command had fewer links. The president was that multi-functional guy who could approve things easily since there was one office, no administrative assistant, and maybe a vice-president or two who could easily be circumvented because they were out on a client site delivering a project.

This flexibility is important to understand in terms of the corporate culture of the small firm. Vendors selling to larger firms are used to long sales cycles and multiple levels of approvals. (In the wake of caution since September 11, 2001, the sales cycle for enterprise CRM packages can be as much as 18 months.) Their applications have a very complex workflow built in when simplicity needs to be the rule of the day.

What the SMB Needs in CRM

Vendors use a sales model for small businesses that is based on the assumption that the primary concern of the SMB is price and fast ROI. That is, of course, the primary concern of large and small companies in the economic environment of 2002. The strategy employed for the sale by the more savvy vendors is the "cure the pain domain" strategy (my terminology). In other words, don't try to sell them everything, just solve a particular problem for the potential SMB customer. Ironically, in the latest craze to imitate the little guy, the problem-solving modular approach to CRM sales is also the means that vendors are using to sell to the big enterprise.

Because the smaller enterprises don't have very much money, the quickest return on investment that they can show is an expenditure that solves some CRM-related specific problem. With this small victory, the CFO of the small company can justify the cost. Some examples of areas of pain are:

- ▶ The sales pipeline is haphazardly available to managers and is in an Excel spreadsheet that is updated when the salespeople get around to it.

- ▶ Opportunities for up-selling and cross-selling are routinely found by call center representatives, but they aren't followed up because there is no incentive, nor is there any method of getting the leads to the appropriate parties.

▶ Partner relationships are dysfunctional, and no one seems to be taking that too seriously.

▶ Customers are leaving the company and going to competitors, and no one seems to know why.

▶ Finally, no one has any idea which customers are more valuable than any other.

All of these can be solved by a module or two of CRM without implementing a full multifunctional package. All of them are problems that any company can have to one degree or another.

If the SMB Needs the Vendor...

SMBs are pretty much dependent on the vendor. They don't usually have the bandwidth to buy the services of neutral strategists or package selection specialists to help them determine what packages to buy. They normally use their own internal staff. Even if they have no experience with CRM in their work histories, the staff may have been reading *CRM at the Speed of Light* in depth or finding out how CRM works from other sources, but haven't had the benefit of experts coming in to assess their business processes. This is dangerous. While the desire is often there, the experience often isn't.

For example, in 2001, after *CRM at the Speed of Light's* first edition came out, I got an email from a fairly large (upper edge of SMB) company in an Asian nation. The managing director of IT had read my book and wanted to implement CRM using the book. While flattered, I asked him to please stop immediately since I hadn't written the book for their company particularly and thus the book was a bad substitute for onsite CRM expertise. The approach of using a generalist book on CRM is not wise. Nor is the idea of doing it 100 percent internally unless you are absolutely positive you have the internal expertise to pull it off. There are successful implementations in the SMB market and even beyond, but they are the exception by a long shot. The rule is, find the expertise somewhere else.

...Then the Vendor Should Make the SMB This Offer

If the SMB, after all the work is done, is still reliant on choosing a vendor internally, then the SMB needs to look at what the vendor actually offers to a company of their size and in their industry as they are choosing the package. I am going to outline some of the basics here. Please remember that the fundamentals will differ somewhat from company to company.

Fixed Price and Customization (or the Lack Thereof)

Licensing fees and service costs for implementation for normal bigger-market CRM don't work here at all. The cost is prohibitive and the functionality that is provided for the cost is just simply too much. In an article in *Line56.com* magazine, January 10, 2002, Dennis Pombriant of the analyst firm Aberdeen Group said it well: "As far as implementation, there's so much there they don't need or won't use. Their first choice is what to turn off."

Consequently, many vendors have a package for the SMB that offers a fixed price and accelerated methodology. The caveat to the deal is that, if it is effectively done, there is a clear statement of work or of what the SMB customer gets for that fixed price. Substantially, the fixed price covers plain vanilla, out-of-the-box functionality geared toward midmarket needs. Anything else costs and is subject to other pricing schemes such as time and materials. Customization allowed for this fixed price is minimal.

ACCELERATED METHODOLOGIES

Accelerated methodologies are just what they sound like. They are implementations in shorter time periods using a templated system to complete the methodology.

The advantage is that you're up and running in time periods as short as 12 weeks, as with PeopleSoft's Accelerated CRM. Salesnet had 650 salespeople in multiple nations up and running, trained in their online SFA, in only six weeks.

One of the most well-established, accelerated methodologies is ASAP—the SAP accelerated methodology that has been around for years from the ERP side and is now being applied to the CRM marketplace. It is a good example of how an accelerated methodology works. It provides CDs that have built-in process maps, evaluation tools, instructions for preparing an ASAP implementation, best practices, and blueprints so that the implementation can be done in an almost "wizard-like" fashion, following onscreen steps.

Sounds good? It can be, but keep in mind that "accelerated" also can easily mean "shortchanged." What you get is what you get. There is no more and no less than the templates provided. Customization is done with some of the methodologies, but only in a minimal fashion.

"You get what you pay for" tends to be the standard in all this. Sadly, what an SMB will often find in an accelerated implementation is that they have needs, too. Needs that are very much like the larger enterprise they aren't. This means loads of customization. Just because they're small doesn't mean they don't have character and culture. CRM is a customer-facing system, so the character and culture need to be obvious to the customers. It is precisely that, which can be the differentiator for the SMB.

SMBs need to beware of the pitfalls of the accelerated CRM methodology. If you can live with them, go for it, but be absolutely sure you can live with those pitfalls. It hurts if you fall to the bottom of the pit.

Architecture

The Internet tends to be a mission-critical channel for SMBs. While there is a high development cost associated with creating a good e-business site, it is the most convenient channel because the costs associated with maintenance are lower and automation is at a much higher level. The value of a good website is incomparable. For example, how do you first find out about a company these days? Do you write away for their marketing literature? Do you call and question a friendly customer service representative? Do you wait until they advertise in an industry magazine or on TV, or just read the industry magazine? No. You go to their website.

Optimally, for the SMBs, a Web-based architecture works best for CRM, since an integral part of their CRM facilitates their e-business strategy. Is that the only possible architecture? No, of course not. But it is the most effective. Architectures that encourage self-service tend to be good things for SMBs. The SMBs are less burdened with massive legacy systems than the large enterprises, though they often have some form of legacy and third-party investment to deal with. However, they are not nearly the issue that they are with the large enterprises.

In Chapter 2, I made mention that there aren't that many CRM vendors that have true multifunctional CRM Internet architectures. Pivotal and Onyx do, as far as the companies with the best understanding of the midmarket go. SalesLogix does when it comes to sales. Companies like Applix do for call center Web-integrated applications. But there are a few emerging vendors that provide modest functionality (in the SMB world, this is a good thing) and are built as either in-house or ASP solutions. Let's look at the ones that seem to understand this marketplace.

Vendors That Understand the SMB Market

There are companies that do actually understand how the SMB market works. I can't possibly list all of them (TriVium, I'm sorry), but I will identify those that have a clue. These are the ones that know that shopping for petite sizes is not the same as shopping for a small in a regular clothing store. The whole structure is different.

Established SMB Vendors

This is the vendor segment that is comfortable with their knowledge in the SMB market and has architected solutions for it. However, that doesn't mean they are comfortable with their place in that market. Some have pretensions—often real, sometimes imagined—to bigger things.

SalesLogix

After some flirtation with a larger enterprise strategy, SalesLogix, one of my Sandbox Playmates (see Chapter 14 for details), settled comfortably in the place where they are easily one of the strongest vendors—the SMB house. The vast majority of their clients are small and medium businesses for this hybrid, architected, function rich, and technically tight sales-focused multifunctional solution. Whew. That's a handful of phraseology.

SalesLogix has always been one of the best buys for the money if you're looking for a strong sales application for your company. Live Wire, the company that employs me, has implemented it internally. Chapter 4 details the decision-making process for this choice. A friend of mine who is the chief sales person at a Midwestern wholesale furniture company has overseen a successful internal implementation using only employees to do so.

J.D. Edwards

This is an interesting new entry to the SMB CRM market. J.D. Edwards's purchase of Youcentric is positioning them to be a true player in this market. Their pedigree is AS/400-dominance in the ERP world in the 1990s. They have 6,300 customers and a substantial presence in the manufacturing midmarket/SMB space. In fact, they are nearly as dominant on the back-office side of that market as SAP is in the large enterprise domain. J.D. Edwards understands the AS/400 market like no one else. The one stipulation to keep in mind is that AS/400 users are the larger side of the SMB market—more of the "M" than the "S."

As of early 2002, only 6 percent of J.D. Edwards's installed base had a CRM solution in place. J.D. Edwards is in a position to lick its lips as 2002 progresses. The question will be the functionality of Youcentric being appropriate to its client base and the usual issues of cultural integration. We'll see, but I'm betting on these guys to make a splash as big as they made in the ERP world.

Onyx

I am not going to say much about Onyx here. They will be covered in Chapter 14 on the key vendors, "The Sandbox Playmates." Suffice it to say, they have a second-generation Internet architecture that makes them ideal for the SMB market.

Pivotal

Onyx ditto. Except that they have third-generation Internet architecture and are Microsoft .NET-invested up to Mt. Everest's peak. More in Chapter 14.

E.piphany

Again, more in Chapter 14. I want them on your SMB radar screen for multifunctional CRM, heavy in the analytics and marketing space. They are exceptionally strong products.

The Established New Breed

These are the *dramatis personae* that have begun to make a splash on the SMB stage because they are built for the small community theater, not Broadway's glamorous productions.

FirstWave

Oddly enough, this "new breed" company is an 18-year-old. Starting its life as Brock Control Systems in 1984, it has been a stalwart of the CRM industry since then. It recently has re-emerged, never quite capturing the imagination as some of the other companies have. But even though it hasn't gained the traction of the current crop of major players, it has mature n-tier Internet architecture, going through its seventh version. It is an XML-compliant, COM+ compatible architecture.

There are some concerns about its Microsoft-centric approach. To add a bit of fuel to that fire, it only supports Internet Explorer, and the two databases it integrates with are Microsoft SQL Server and Oracle, leaving out the big and fast-growing DB2 marketplace. However, to its credit, its eFramework architecture can work with adapters to other systems and databases. This is fortunate, as studies show that many SMBs are looking toward the possibility of implementing Linux and most companies are creating Linux versions of their applications. Microsoft-centrism isn't bad at this juncture, but the future holds all kinds of possibilities to go beyond it.

Recognizing the financial constraints of the SMB marketplace, First-Wave offers an innovative leasing program for its software and services in addition to the more standard hosted and purchase options.

Talisma

Talisma has a strong channel for its sales with more than 50 VARs (value added resellers) by the end of 2001. They are even more Microsoft-centric than FirstWave, with a Microsoft look and feel, and a resemblance to Outlook that is more than coincidental. Of course, this look and feel is actually a good thing, given the wide exposure to and comfort level with Outlook for most computer users in the business world.

The architecture is written in HTML and JavaScript, with the client side in Microsoft Visual C++ and Microsoft Foundation Classes. It supports native Talisma databases and Microsoft SQL Server 7.0 and higher. Seeing a pattern here?

In the SMB market, being Microsoft-centric is not a big problem at this time because the vast majority of those millions of companies use Microsoft products and operating systems. It's why Talisma was one of the first CRM vendors that announced support for Office XP when it came out (along with Microsoft .NET-heavy Pivotal). Concern for this is in the future, not the present.

Up and Coming: The Gen-Z of CRM

There is a small and upcoming group of vendors who are taking advantage of the maturity of the CRM market and the increasingly knowledgeable stance of the potential and current customer base. There aren't a lot of contenders for the major leagues yet, but there are a few that show promise. I'm going to highlight one of them so you can see how the newer generation of CRM applications for the SMB market is evolving.

J-Curve

This is an intriguing company. Founded with a solid management team in 2001 by E. Patrick LaVoie, the former National CRM Practice Leader for Deloitte & Touche and former CSO for Interact Commerce Corporation (aka SalesLogix), J-Curve has a really good take on CRM and the SMBs. They recognize that they can't be all strategic things to all CRM people, so they take a reasonable (read: warm and fuzzy to SMBs) approach. What J-Curve provides is Cogent—a multifunctional CRM package that is aimed squarely at the SMBs and only the SMBs. J-Curve puts it this way: "CRM holds tremendous value as a strategic program and CRM software can be an integral tactical facet of this strategy... Cogent realizes CRM software's place as a critical tactical system that supports facets of a strategic CRM initiative."

This sound insight is coupled with SMB experience. Mr. LaVoie, as CSO of Interact Commerce Corporation, was immersed daily in the SMB marketplace through the products of Interact/SalesLogix (see Chapter 6) and the ever popular ACT. The rest of the CxOs were also veterans of Interact Commerce Corporation.

COGENT

What distinguishes Cogent from the pack? Rather than a dumbed-down enterprise edition of a larger package, it provides functionality in SFA, EMA, and customer service and support that is built for the SMB market only. Their architecture is open hybrid architecture with an application layer that generates XML-based forms. They are entirely PDA friendly with an application that supports SMS text messaging, wireless browser access, SmartPhone integration, and wireless synchronization. Cogent is completely compliant with both the Palm and Pocket PC operating systems.

The product has four flavors. Personal Edition is free. Professional Edition provides increased functionality, the above-mentioned PDA application, and access to multiple templates for customization. It then steps up to a higher level with Cogent Small Business Edition, which provides even more functionality for all CRM segments, full bidirectional synchronization with Outlook, and a SQL-based Sync Server. Cogent Enterprise Edition is for those of you with geographically dispersed offices and larger enterprise-level databases such as Oracle and DB2, thus reducing the reliance on Microsoft applications, but with the full awareness that most SMBs use Microsoft applications.

So what do you get out of Cogent that is very SMB-ish?

- ▶ A concept that reflects the thinking of the SMB market—the software is tactical and needs to be usable, not just have functionality.

- ▶ A system that is easily internally customized through templates and easy to use toolsets, allowing for the possibility that the cost of customization is normally very high and if there is an internal IT staff that can do it, well, then, by all means do it.

- ▶ A system that allows for internal growth. It goes beyond the use of the Microsoft applications (Outlook, Word, and such) and allows use of the Oracles, DB2s, and Lotus Notes. It claims to be very scalable, too.

- ▶ A system that allows external SMB growth—a version that is aimed at companies with remote locations.

- ▶ A small footprint system. It can use as little as 10 megabytes of storage—a refreshing change from the multi-gigabyte midmarket versions of other vendors. Even the multiple remote office versions use no more than 100 megabytes for the applications.

- ▶ Open source code customizes it any way you want. Build all the hooks you want.

- ▶ Self-configuration. Users can do what is almost a self-needs assessment. The product varies according to the needs of users and organizations, reducing the need for complex customization.

- ▶ Self-healing capabilities that improve reliability and reduce the need for IT support. Cogent dedicates over 50 percent of the code base to error detection and trapping.

- ▶ A system that encourages end-user adoption through metrics that line employees find useful daily, instead of just metrics that place a data-entry burden on end-users so managers can play Big Brother. This plays on the fears of end-users in the SMB segment that they are participating in CRM only for management's benefit.

I could go on, but this gives you an idea of what the newest generations of CRM for this market will look like. A responsive CRM application, beyond the normal self-interests of business, is not self-serving. It is focused on what the SMB market is, not what they want it to be. Good things are coming for the SMBs.

Up and Coming: Microsoft Looms Large

At the end of February 2002, Microsoft came out with a long-expected announcement, nonetheless surprising in its timing. It will be entering the CRM fray with a product called MSCRM, which will focus on the 100 to 1,000–employee market. What is scary about this is that once again, Microsoft got the thing, at least conceptually, right. A corporate giant that understands the SMB market. This initial positive thinking, like all things Microsoft, is clouded by the fact that their Great Plains partners, the ones who were handling the SMB market for Microsoft, weren't told of MS's entry to the CRM marketplace and thus were caught unawares.

The initial application is, of course, Microsoft-centric and is focused on the SFA marketplace with the functionality we all know and love. However, Microsoft EMA and Customer Service are the next to be released (though not as of this writing). In fact, their EMA module, which will have campaign management, telesales, campaign planning, and an analytic engine, won't be on the horizon until 2003.

Summary

The SMB market is huge. Addressing the specific needs of this market is crucial to the future of CRM in general, because of the crying need of SMBs for CRM and the sheer size of the market. This is contrasted with the simple fact that the Global 1000 is 1000 companies—delimited by definition.

The largest vendors have no real grasp of how SMB companies work, though they could (and do) sell successfully into those markets. There are several companies well suited to acting in this drama because of how they are built, but even they have to look to the future of this play, not the present.

Anyone even interested in CRM for any reason needs to understand this market, whether they work for a large enterprise or an SMB.

14

Top CRM Vendors: The Sandbox Playmates

The CRM landscape changes almost daily. The ebb and flow of the economy, the rhythm of decision making, the timing of budgets, the power and buzz over this or that company vary almost by the nanosecond. Vendors show up on the horizon and keep going until they fall off the end of the earth. There are keepers—the real vendors—and bandwagon types—the pretender vendors. Keeper or short-lived, vendors are often quirky. You are lucky if you get a vendor salesperson who is not just selling to you, but who is genuinely trying to establish a relationship. Even then, you have to be careful that the promises of the vendor are tempered with a realistic offer as opposed to what they would love to claim.

There isn't anything wrong with good marketing. No one should really have a problem with it. It's a fact of business. Don't people and companies want to be seen in the best light possible? It matters to me whether I'm a credible honest force in my world. It matters to a CRM vendor salesperson whether he is selling product or services that he can believe in. Human beings are incredibly interested in how they rank or what their rating is. Who doesn't give credence to a company in the 91st percentile or to a company that can say they achieved a 4.2 of 5, which placed them second in the overall rankings? What advertisers don't pay attention to the Nielsen overnights and longer-term ratings of TV shows? Yet the reality is that these numbers are based on a small sampling of representative TV watchers who are watching something in particular at a particular time on a particular night. Someone at Nielsen decided what the criteria were going to be for determining what type of audience member was representative. So a very subjective set of attributes became a representative viewer so that a quantified sampling could be done. Hopefully, they used analytics!

When humans look at standings or rankings, they see quantified comparisons of what seems to be how good some group is at the thing that is being ranked. CRM vendors routinely issue press releases when they win awards or are ranked in the upper-right box in Gartner's Magic Quadrant for their category. This is considered a sign of excellence, leadership, and depth based on the criteria that Gartner used to rank them. But Gartner had to earn respect in CRM for the ranking to mean something. If you look at Forrester Research, ISM's ISMGuide, the *Fortune* magazine 100 best places to work in America, or *Working Mother*'s best places to work for working mothers, they all have different criteria for their choices. If the award giver's criteria are acceptable to those who are paying attention to it, their award choices carry authority. Validation is absolutely essential for the awarder, so that the award is important to the recipient and to the community at large, even if it is a segmented community. If I gave out an award for the 100 best places for working mothers to work, I don't think I would be taken too seriously.

User-Focused Criteria: A New Approach to Validation

As you've seen throughout this book, I'm user-focused when it comes to CRM. I'm of the mind that CRM is the most personal—not just the most personalized—of systems enhanced by technology because it is based on *human* customer interactions. I believe there isn't a CRM system out there that will work without dramatic changes (in the vast majority of cases) in the corporate culture of the implementing company. I also believe there isn't a CRM vendor out there with the perfect solution, and in fact, their lackings are pretty severe in some instances. So my criteria aren't based on the depth of functionality or the purity of the architecture. I'm looking at the products and their differentiators, the culture, the market position, the strategy and the management of that strategy, and lots of stories on satisfaction or the lack thereof. Other criteria include how much the company is liked or disliked in the sales cycle and during the implementations; successful implementations; perceived ROI by the customer; and how well the company meets its promises. What kind of corporate culture the vendor has is vital because my mantra is "when you buy the application, you buy the vendor." The nine vendors presented in this chapter were chosen because of predominance in these various criteria.

With the products, rather than list all the different features of every product for these companies, I'm going to examine the key differentiators, good and bad. Most of them have all the functionality that has been outlined throughout this entire book in the separate sections. Enterprise-level CRM has the SFA, EMA, PRM, analytics, call center applications, field service, and so on built into the suite, in varying strengths. I'll spend some time pointing out those strengths and holes, and what the companies might be doing to fix the holes.

The other criteria for these choices involve financial stability and survivability. Will they be survivors or go the way of the more than 80 CRM companies that folded in 2001?

Who Isn't Included

There are two companies that were in this list in the first edition that are no longer here, and I'm going to say why. It is not because they have become bad companies in either case.

MicroStrategy is the first of the companies dropped from my list. While they have a wonderful product, this list is really for the multifunction CRM players who can make a case for enterprise-level implementations. MicroStrategy is first and foremost a business intelligence company and, despite the fact they have a CRM product, they are not a primary CRM vendor, though I would unhesitatingly recommend their product for business intelligence and personalization.

Second, Amdocs Clarify is on hold from the list. Clarify is also a robust, rich, and deep product that is of huge benefit to the telecommunication companies and others who need major call center, CICs, or customer service. However, while Nortel had Clarify, they became damaged goods. Amdocs may well be a good home for them and seems to be doing well (see Chapter 11 for details), but as of mid-2002, it is too soon to make that determination. However, this is no reflection on the quality of their products. I'm merely waiting to see how Amdocs handles them.

Now for the happier side of this chapter.

Simply the Best

There are nine companies in this section. These nine represent the crème de la crème of the multifunction vendors. They are the ones you can look to for full-blown enterprise-level implementations, and, in most cases, a willingness to uncouple modules from the enterprise suite to allow your company to solve a particular problem. This is, in a way, the best of both worlds, since it gives the potential customer budgetary control and a quicker ROI for confidence building and, at the same time, retains the integrity of the applications with the seamless integration that is theoretically the case with the enterprise suite. I say "theoretically" because integration is never seamless, with factors like legacy systems, mobile users, and remote offices all playing a part in the differences between theory and practice. This doesn't mean there is equal strength in each segment. Some are stronger in the analytics side than the sales side; some are better with EMA than PRM. It depends.

There are a few interesting trends that have emerged in the 2002 versions of the applications. One is that selling methodologies are being embedded in the different applications. The method may vary from vendor to vendor. "Solutions selling" is the most commonly incorporated methodology with the Sandbox Playmates, but there are others like Miller-Heiman and even a homegrown one for Siebel. (See Chapter 6 on SFA for more details on these selling solutions.)

Additionally, there is a significant increase in products for customer self-service, which is how the Web customer touch point is being used these days. This stems from a smart growing awareness that the customer needs to participate in the customer experience and see the same view that the customer service representative sees. The desire for consistency across communications channels means self-service on the Web.

Even though the basic functionality is the same, there are also differentiators. Some of them are just marketing fluff—calling CRM something with a different acronym doesn't make it a new evolutionary stage in the development of CRM. On the other hand, the release of a Quality Management module for Service with PeopleSoft 8.4 or the significantly increased use of the Real Time engine and Active Pass navigational guides for E.piphany 6.0 are true differentiators that are worth the difference.

The CRM Superpowers

There are four companies that I've chosen for this segment. Each of them has market position and is a corporate giant themselves. They all have massive CRM enterprise suites that can scale to tens of thousands of users or, in an Internet mode, beyond that. They are functional superpowers and are each "nationalists" in their own right. Competition in their market space is fierce and aimed at Fortune 3500.

Over the long run, three of the four—PeopleSoft, SAP, and Oracle—have a market edge here, despite the significant market share of Siebel. Their potential customers are very large corporate entities with thousands and tens of thousands of employees, potential terabytes of customer information, and sophisticated back-office processes. To be able to provide usable front- and back-office functionality that is integrated is a distinct advantage over the need to link with someone else's back-office products.

PeopleSoft

"PeopleSoft was conceived on a beach in Maui." This quote was in the foreword of one of my earlier books on PeopleSoft and is from David Duffield, who "conceived" PeopleSoft in 1987. It is a comic quote, but true to the initial spirit that founded this company as one with high-quality products and an incredible family-like culture. Talk to a PeopleSoft veteran, whether at the company now or somewhere else, and the commitment to the David Duffield–led family culture of the 1990s is still amazing. Customers and partners have that same commitment. It is truly remarkable to see a corporate giant that people adore working for and with. Even with the early relaxed "PeopleSoft casual" business environment, their products were of the highest caliber and pioneering. As the 1990s came and went, this unique company expanded to other back-office products covering such areas as financials, student administration, and manufacturing, and continuously improved their n-tiered architecture and their PeopleTools customization kit.

With its purchase in March 2000 of Vantive Corporation, the number 2 or 3 player in the CRM market, PeopleSoft started to focus on the total enterprise experience, what they called "collaborative computing." They were one of the few companies that could offer end-to-end solutions, both customer-facing and cubicle-facing (back office). There were some concerns at the time about the integration of the cultures of Vantive and PeopleSoft. The sale was difficult. Vantive key personnel didn't really want it to happen, but they understood that they were in a difficult financial situation so it was important to accept the acquisition. The industry watched this one closely and a bit cynically. Could it work?

On the PeopleSoft side, its culture was becoming considerably more corporate—a necessity in a competitive environment. To its credit, it artfully retained some of the patina of the "PeopleSoft casual" culture. But Vantive was a different bird altogether, though also relaxed. While it was a tough road, the cultural integration between the two companies worked better than expected because of diligent work, a little bit of assertion, and the common interest that now existed in creating successful CRM products. With the release of the PeopleSoft CRM 8.0 product under the Internet architecture that had been released in 2001 for the back-office products, the merger was officially complete. Highly talented Vantive employees finally became highly talented PeopleSoft employees, and the Vantive functionality plus added functionality became PeopleSoft's CRM hallmark.

The overall success of PeopleSoft comes with the success of the CRM product, but probably more importantly the acceptance of their PeopleSoft 8.0 Internet architecture. While I doubt the users really cared about the zero code on the client message that PeopleSoft was pushing for so hard last year, those in charge of total cost of ownership did care. The users cared about the comfort of using the familiar browser as the interface and the rich functionality that the products offered. As a result, PeopleSoft increased its revenue from $1.74 billion in 2000 to a remarkable (given the year) $2.07 billion in 2001. In the fourth quarter of 2001, they logged 41 major (over $1 million) deals, up from 27 in the third quarter. They tapped well into their customer base, with 58 percent of their license revenue that quarter coming from existing customers, thus adhering to the most functional strategy of 2001, customer retention and account expansion. They had 147 new customers in the quarter, nonetheless. These are all signs of a healthy and very smart company. Let's just see how smart they are.

Strategy

PeopleSoft has been under different management since 2000. The current president and CEO is Craig Conway, an Oracle veteran, who brought a considerably more button-down—though still personable—style to PeopleSoft. He did it with the blessing of David Duffield, one of the more remarkable CEOs in the late twentieth century. Mr. Duffield is living proof of what I earlier called the *shadchen* principle, which says that you can be successful and also an outstanding human being. You don't have to be a shark. Mr. Duffield is not only a kind man who made PeopleSoft a billion-dollar company—a major achievement—he is also a huge philanthropist on both the human and animal front. He spent

$200 million of his own money to establish Maddie's Fund, (http://www.maddiesfund.org) an animal foundation that advocates kill-free zones for cats and dogs. In addition to his philanthropy, he is one who recognized that the tanking of the ERP market in 1999, the subsequent crash of PeopleSoft's stock price, and the size of PeopleSoft meant time for new leadership, and he didn't have too much ego to step aside. Craig Conway assumed the mantle and has done well, though with quite a different management style. It seems to work. During the downturn in 2001, PeopleSoft not only consistently beat expectations but achieved record revenues throughout, directly against the rest of the market. By comparison, Siebel revenues dropped in the fourth quarter from $496.5 million in 2000 to $428.5 million in 2001, with a commensurate drop in net income. The year-end numbers for PeopleSoft in 2001 were the above-mentioned $2.073 billion in revenue. Mr. Conway won multiple awards for excellent performance under the economic circumstances. David Duffield, who remains the chairman of the company, has always stood by his choice, and PeopleSoft has the revenue to prove how wise Mr. Duffield's choice was.

With this success, PeopleSoft has established itself as the likely number two player behind Siebel. They have an estimated 6.8 percent of the CRM market under their banner and have an aggressive, big vision. Their only real competitor here will be SAP. But PeopleSoft thinks it has the strategy to grab the slot and hold it. Until they become number one, of course.

"We are aimed at Enterprise CRM," said Stan Swete, long-time PeopleSoft veteran and CRM Global General Manager, "that is, we want to take CRM from a siloed set of solutions into an enterprise strategy that ties these solutions across the enterprise."

What makes their strategy potentially successful in this time of caution and small budgets is that it is based on a realistic view of the enterprise, not just a "wouldn't it be wonderful if" scenario. PeopleSoft knows that, for now, the budgetary restraints make it difficult to sell a "buy it all now" approach. Consequently, as Stan Swete so poetically put it, "We have to at least complete the thought across the enterprise." Gartner calls it "the enterprise experience end-to-end."

There is a lot of industrial-strength underpinning to this comment. The strategic implications include:

▸ Flexible ties to legacy products and third-party products. Integration is essential.

- ▶ Merger of customer-facing activities and supply chain transactions.

- ▶ Stronger use of analytics in determining a strategy. The use of what PeopleSoft calls "insight" into what is going on at a company.

- ▶ Establishing a clear and particular ROI within the enterprise strategy.

- ▶ Focus on customer profitability rather than efficiencies, though efficiencies will result naturally.

This is just a brief look at the complex undercurrent to the "thought across the enterprise."

PeopleSoft uses a product strategy of buy or build. While planning roughly four acquisitions in the year 2002, they recognize that acquisitions don't do everything. On the one hand, they acquired Annuncio to fill a substantial EMA hole in their product offering and will spend the next few months integrating and enriching the formerly-known as-Annuncio-Live product into their suite. On the other hand, Stan Swete recognizes that this isn't always the right way to do things. PeopleSoft has a PRM suite gap (take solace, PeopleSoft, you're not alone here). Because channel programs and partner relationships permeate all aspects of the CRM business processes, Mr. Swete thinks it is probably smarter to build here, rather than buy. This is a smart man. Just think about co-marketing funds and campaigns built around that, and partner opportunity and lead management and partner MBOs and data access. This alone should give pause to the person thinking of buying the functionality and integrating it. It might be doable, but it's more expensive than simply building the right stuff yourself.

Product

PeopleSoft is not resting with its recent successes in the marketplace. In March 2002, they released the newest version of the PeopleSoft CRM 8.0 applications, PeopleSoft 8.4. They are planning a rollout of PeopleSoft CRM 8.8 by year end. Their strategy is frequent substantial upgrades to both fill holes and kick up the competition with Siebel, Oracle, and SAP. Like it as a strategy or not, it is ambitious and puts PeopleSoft head on into the race.

The PeopleSoft CRM 8.4 upgrade recognizes a few market realities. First, the nature of the workforce, especially since September 11, is increasingly mobile and remote. In recognition of this reality, PeopleSoft released CRM Mobile Sales and Mobile Field Service. The idea is disconnected access to customer info on any wireless device. The key is that this is a very thin technology so that the data synchronization is very fast and the footprint is miniscule. The way they deal with that is to focus the synchronized data around the transactions chosen for synchronization. While mobile solutions have clearly been around for a while, the speed that PeopleSoft's solutions works at is truly fast. For example, they are claiming that users can synchronize a year of updates in six minutes. That, according to analysts such as Wedbush Morgan Securities, is "impressive performance relative to Siebel System's solution."

Aside from the standard Sales, Marketing, and Services modules offered, PeopleSoft is offering new applications. The first, Quality Management, is unique to PeopleSoft and is focused on product manufacturers or vendors. It tracks product defects or requests for product enhancements online.

Going with the flow, they have joined the growing crowd that is producing CRM applications that involve what most vendors are calling "interactive selling." PeopleSoft follows its naming convention here, calling the application Collaborative Selling. All told, it integrates needs analysis, recommendation, configuration, pricing, quoting, and order capture, and makes scalable product and services configurations a lot easier. What makes this interesting is that it handles fulfillment, moving over into the back end. This reflects the true strength of PeopleSoft as an enterprise application, not just pure CRM. The other component of Collaborative Selling is self-service, so the customer can do his or her own thing here. This is also recognition of a growing trend in CRM toward Web-based CRM interactivity, which tends to translate to personalized self-service.

PeopleSoft is also realizing, a little behind the curve, that industry-specific applications are an essential short-term focus. According to an article on the CRMdaily website, Robb Eklund, vice-president of CRM Product Marketing for PeopleSoft, says, "Industry solutions are a huge focus for PeopleSoft in 2002. We will be looking to release one or two industry verticals every quarter." To that end, with the release of PeopleSoft CRM 8.4, they released PeopleSoft CRM 8.0 for Communications.

Additionally, PeopleSoft released a message broker as part of PeopleTools 8.4 that can translate messages between disparate applications and guarantee delivery better than FedEx or UPS. It supports Simple Object Access Protocol (SOAP) and Universal Description, Discovery, and Integration (UDDI), which are the universal structures for the messages, and it incorporates XML coding. That means no coding is necessary for translation and delivery of those technically testy messages.

Culture

This is the most recognized and perhaps the most copied culture in the software industry. Long known for its benevolence and family-like environment while under the ownership of David Duffield, the PeopleSoft culture engendered fanatic loyalty from its employees and its customers. With a beautiful campus in Pleasanton, California, and amenities such as bus service to the door, pick-up service at Bay Area Rapid Transit (BART), and daycare, PeopleSoft seemed more like something from the 1960s than a hard-driving corporation of the 1990s—which it was. It was a remarkable place to even visit and the stuff that legends were made of, as I know from my many visits to the campus and meetings with PeopleSoft staff who had nothing but peace and love and software to dispense. I'm not knocking this. It genuinely glowed.

Alas, times change, loyalties change, and corporate cultures change. With the switch in management at PeopleSoft—and the need to compete when you are a billion dollars rather than a couple of hundred million dollars—there was a sadly necessary and absolutely essential change in the culture. It became more typically corporate. At the same time, with Duffield-era veterans like David Thompson as CIO, Stan Swete as the senior vice-president and CRM general manager, and Robb Eklund and Laura King as the VPs of marketing for CRM, it remains a very friendly and highly customer-focused place—still a good place to work.

Future

With a strategy of "the thought across the enterprise," which is a realistic recognition of the market conditions in 2002 without a loss in vision, and the frequent releases (two a year so far), PeopleSoft is making a bid to not only catch up to the curve in some instances (such as vertical markets and mobile technology), but to get ahead of the curve and become *the* industry leader. They are out to capture the hearts and minds of the people now, something they have the admirable possibility of doing because of an interesting corporate culture that retains some humanity, while recognizing the realities of corporate life. The step after this heart share is the market share, which can be a tough road up against Siebel. But PeopleSoft has two things going for it: front-office and back-office products that are integrated very tightly—a claim that Siebel can't make.

Siebel

Like them or not, there is no denying Siebel. They have the market share; they are aggressive and smart about the way they sell. Where other CRM vendors often will give canned demonstrations of their general functionality to a potential customer, Siebel is quick enough to know that customers need demonstrations of products that are personalized to the company that is viewing that demonstration. They win deals because they do things like that. They also have the product strength to pull the deal off. There is little functionality that they don't have for general CRM applications. For example, of the CRM superpowers, they have the strongest partner relationship management (PRM) module. But they have a problem. They are so dominated by the personality of Tom Siebel that he is the only executive listed on their website's list of company executives! This doesn't exactly lead to a comfort zone, when the other management is not even recognized. A true enigma of a company.

Strategy

Siebel is the dominant player in the CRM universe, with over 26 percent of the market share. They've gotten there by being a step ahead of the competitors more often than not, both in product release and in salesmanship. They have a strategy defined by none other than Tom Siebel that says if the conditions are right to get a jump on your competitors, then jump. Those conditions were defined in November 2001 in an article in *Forbes* magazine as:

> The market is mature, full of tired competitors, ready for technological revolution.

> The potential for the market, post-revolution, is big enough to grow the company.

> Siebel can sweep in first and capture a defensible 50 percent of market share before competition arises.

This is why Siebel is the most functionally rich application suite on the market, because they have quite often been first to market with their features.

In healthy economies, this works well. For example, Siebel was the first serious player in the sales force automation market, though certainly not the first player. Siebel has been developing its mobile capabilities for five years, far ahead of the rest of the industry, and has even been able to patent several technologies in the Siebel 7.0 mobile solution that also remain in front of the industry, even if not revolutionary.

Their current strategy is to "get verticalized" (my term for it). They are moving quickly to establish themselves as the "siloed industry" player in the field, though they have some intense competition with SAP and will probably be second to SAP in the long run. Siebel already has Siebel 7 industry-specific products in the software bazaar and in the queue. They cover industries such as healthcare, retail, energy and utilities, apparel and footwear, communications, financial services, insurance, media and publishing, automotive, pharmaceuticals, transportation, public sector, high tech, travel, and clinical medicine. Their only competition in sheer vertical scope is SAP.

Product

The breadth of their product offering is staggering, probably the greatest of any vendor. They excel in providing mobile solutions and partner relationship management in a suite. Their Siebel 7.0 Web architecture is not the leader of the pack by a long shot and is known to take some performance hits, but it is fairly strong Web architecture with the advantages of such. They have a most comprehensive approach to employee relationship management (ERM)—one of the newest CRM facets defined by the contemporary definition of the customer. This is a potential multibillion dollar play for Siebel. They claim a possible $26–$30 billion waits for the plucking in this slice. To that end, they have defined an ERM product with a very rich feature set that is expensive, as all their products are. At the same time, it is a strong differentiator in a crowded CRM fair. The product covers five areas:

Planning Performance management, incentive compensation

Training eTraining, training administration, including transcript management, curriculum planning, curriculum management, reports and tracking, enrollment, skills testing, certification management, distance learning

Inform Customer content, distributed content management, company and department news, InfoCenter, eContent services, page creation and layout, advanced search

Collaborate Teams (shared workspace), calendar, sync, including problem resolution tools and automated assignment and escalation

Self-Service Travel and expense reporting, time management and reporting, quality management

This is a broad list that isn't even complete. For those of you who would like to know what each of these features does in detail, please email me for more information, though a lot is self-evident. This should give you some idea of how full Siebel applications really are. A complete description of the functionality of all their Siebel 7 products, not including the verticals, can run about 500 pages.

This doesn't mean they've got no weaknesses. Even with the purchase of nQuire, their analytics are nowhere near the best on the market and still a major area of concern. However, their biggest competitive lack is that the other members of the CRM superpowers have the back office and they don't. No financials, no human resources, no other back-office functions. This could mean trouble for their future.

Siebel is on a relentless drive to incorporate substantial Web services into the Siebel 7.5 release, expected in the summer of 2002. If they complete their product development, they will have incorporated Simple Object Access Protocol (SOAP), Web Services Description Language (WSDL), and support for Java Connectivity Architecture (JCA). Support for other protocols, languages, and standards like UDDI is expected later on.

Culture

This is a unique culture, and not a particularly good one. While perhaps not quite as heartless as it is made out to be because of the Siebel public face, it is a button-down, shark-like culture that says that what drives the human being is economics. Revenue is the key and nothing but revenue matters. They have a set of core values that read very well, but they don't always seem to be the way they live. However, to their defense, they actually do tie compensation to customer satisfaction. There also are some exceptionally bright and very decent people who work for Siebel, though it's been said that it's mostly for the options, given the way that internal pressures are put on to produce. They also have a strong support engine and technical account managers who are both technical and customer service trained.

In mid-2001, Siebel formed an e-government political action committee (PAC) and raised some $2 million to seed it from its employees.

They have been actively engaged in a drive to lobby governments around the world with their agenda. This is an unusual move, but again, knowing the aggressiveness of Siebel and its culture, not a surprising one.

On the other hand, this is an arrogant culture. A small blurb in *BtoB* magazine last year mentioned that Siebel had a policy of not allowing any executives but Tom Siebel to speak to the press. Sadly, the incident with *BtoB* is not only commonplace, but indicative of the level of arrogance and the commensurate dislike with which they are viewed by the world outside their management's boardroom. Ordinarily, these kinds of incidents are not mentioned in the press, because they are just that—incidents. But with Siebel they are mentioned, because they're just asking for it.

Future

I didn't choose Siebel for any reason but breadth of offering and market position. They have functionally rich products and substantial market position. They didn't make it on my most important criterion, the corporate culture and its relationship to customer satisfaction. Despite Siebel's claims, there are too many people in the CRM universe who are not happy with them, in all walks of customer, vendor, employee, analyst, and consultant life.

Siebel is the dominant player in the CRM market. They will remain so for quite a while yet, but eventually the shark will begin to eat its own tail. SAP, PeopleSoft, and Oracle have made inroads into Siebel's prospective base with their enterprise offerings, and will continue because Siebel simply can't offer the back office. However, Siebel's obsessive drive to be number one will keep them there for now.

Where they might get damaged is their attitude. Companies are made up of human beings and they emotionally interact, regardless of product quality. Arrogance hurts in the long run, even if it can dominate in the short term. While Siebel's applications and market position deserve respect, their behavior doesn't.

SAP

This is the fourth largest software company in the world (after Microsoft, Computer Associates, and Oracle) and there are good reasons for it. They have an installed base of 17,000 customers globally. They are easily the most sophisticated when it comes to understanding the specific industry markets that buy software. They dominate several of them nearly completely, such as oil and gas, chemicals, and much of manufacturing. No one even comes close. They made their dollars in the ERP world with the release in 1992 of SAP R/2 for the mainframe and the more seminal ERP breakthrough release of SAP R/3 for the client/server several years later.

Strategy

SAP's CRM strategy is SAP's supply chain management strategy, is SAP's ERP strategy, is SAP's global strategy. CRM is on an on-ramp to an ambitious ten-year vision that looks at what they call pre-integrated capabilities out of the box. This means that CRM is fully integrated with SCM and ERP and is also cross-functional. They are building their CRM products with an increasingly open architecture. Their strategy is the "open end-to-end enterprise" unlike the proprietary end-to-end enterprise of Oracle.

They are committed to this fully integrated open set of applications as applicable to the industries they have already serviced and new ones on the map as they progress. The IT architecture that their products use simply maps to the business processes, whether general or industry specific, so that their product strategy has remarkable flexibility.

SAP's CRM team is run by Michael Park, a Siebel veteran with an excellent personality and a strong strategic mind. He is building up his CRM team with veterans from around the industry. The overall success of SAP's CRM on-ramp strategy meant $220 million in CRM license sales the first year. They are currently chasing their installed base, and have ambitious plans to meet the market head on.

SAP is taking an interesting route to the midmarket. They bought the Israeli company Top Manage, who produces a CRM application that is aimed at SMB. This will be their line of approach into that midmarket and small business environment. This is a bit unusual for them, since ordinarily, SAP produces its own products, but this is a better way to go. In other words, if you don't get it, buy it.

Product

SAP CRM 3.0 is SAP's first real CRM product suite and it is why they are now a Sandbox Playmate. What makes this set interesting is that the architecture is open and is meant to integrate with any SAP application or any third-party application. Imagine, if you will, three layers. The first layer is the portal. These portals are user-based, have an open architecture, and have role-based definitions. From inside the portal, views of multi-enterprise and unstructured data can be viewed according to roles and permissions granted.

The second layer is the Web applications layer. "Think of cubes," says Michael Park, vice-president of SAP's CRM. "These cubes are labeled CRM, SCM, PLM (product lifecycle management), and ERP." There are also what Park calls "black boxes," which are the third-party applications. All of them sit beneath the portal, ready for use, tied seamlessly through the user roles built into the portal structure.

With these two layers in place, you can do what SAP calls "drag and relate," a very useful proof of the value of integration. Imagine this: You have three applications open in your portal view. The first is a PeopleSoft customer record with a payment history. The second is an SAP application showing you the invoice status of current outstanding balances for this individual. The third application is some Web-based thing showing that this customer is on a website paying a bill and buying new items. You can drag the invoices from the SAP application right to the PeopleSoft view and drag this customer's new purchases to the SAP invoicing screens. They will all update automatically to show that the old bill is paid and the new purchases are in the queue to be invoiced. All the data systems that hold this information at whatever level are automatically updated.

The third layer is the Markets technology. This is where the corporate ecosystem is integrated, not just the applications. Divisions of an enterprise can communicate with other divisions through an exchange layer so that data, views, and activity can be shared according to roles and permissions established in the workflow. This ability holds well beyond the division level. It can be intra-enterprise, inter-enterprise, or extra-enterprise. Your suppliers can talk to you, you can talk to your partners, your partners can talk to your customers. This is truly the glue of a corporate ecosystem. There is an IT infrastructure across any business process at any company involved in your value chain. The architecture of the SAP system in its own grand way can handle pretty much any scale here. That is quite an achievement. CRM to SAP is just the on-ramp to this convergence that is critical to the enterprises of the next few years. I'll cover more on this in Chapter 18.

SAP CRM products are multiple and widespread. They are fully featured and cross-functional and built with the practical vision laid out above. They are 800 pounds and counting.

Culture

There have been dramatic changes in the culture of SAP over the past few years. Eight-hundred-pound gorillas can be ponderous and even non-responsive if they control the (ERP) market. Their weight made them less than nimble. But to their credit, they were a research-oriented culture, publicly stating that they spent over $1 billion per year (nearly 25 percent of their revenue) on research, which was more than many companies they competed with made in that year. They turned out excellent products. Even though they were hard to understand sometimes, one thing was certain. While they were building their own products, they understood that to market those products, they needed partners.

SAP has always treated their partners with respect. Once you made it past the difficult partner application and acceptance process, you were given the SAP "world as your oyster" industry road map. To highlight this point, one of the partner programs they built was called Certified Business Partners (CBS). This was a national network of partners who were handed all of the opportunities that SAP got with companies below the $200 million revenue range. This is not exactly chump-change business, but SAP gave it away. Needless to say, the CBS partners are thrilled to be in this position. SAP got licenses; the partners made money—sometimes lots of it.

In recent years, SAP has become more accessible, more friendly, and an easier company to work with. They continue to treat their partners with respect. The CBS program still exists. In fact, partners are so important to SAP that in their public sector practice alone, in 2001, the SAP partners drove over $20 million of revenue to SAP with public sector institutions. Respect does get you business.

Future

SAP is definitely a player and a dominating and dominant one. They are well situated with a massive installed base, a worthy enterprise application, an incredible grasp of and application to the verticals, and a lot of money to go after it. Their only weakness has been a historically slow gear-up and response time, which makes them come from behind more often than they should like. However, they are in a situation where the 800-pound ERP gorilla is gaining CRM muscle mass pretty fast and is seen as a key force in the CRM market. I'd say that's pretty amazing for a company that didn't even have a CRM product worth the name a year ago. Their CRM 3.0 product now is worth the SAP name and a fore-runner to the realization of a ten-year plan and vision.

Oracle

Tough situation for this database champ in 2002 and beyond. They are the producers of the world's greatest database, Oracle 9*i*, where their only real scalable competition is IBM's DB2. They have a large enterprise application suite that has been around for a long time; the current incarnation is Oracle Applications 11*i*. They are super marketers, aggressively putting their products out there as well as—and often more powerfully than—anyone else. Yet, as of mid-March 2002, they are positioned by analysts at financial services firm Hambrecht and Company with a projection on the order of a 29 percent decline in license revenues between 2001 and 2002. According to Hambrecht, this "is toward the conservative end of management's guidance of a 25 to 35 percent decline in license sales." Oracle is concerned with losing market share in the database market. Their Oracle 11*i* applications have more than 6,000 patches, with Oracle CRM being responsible for more than 1,000 of them, which indicates they are going to have technical troubles in the enterprise applications market, too. They are currently at version 11.5.6 in CRM and still counting.

Strategy

Oracle's CRM strategy seems to be pretty rigid in a way that could work with the size of its installed base: Integrate the CRM applications as part of the overall enterprise suite and try to push the concept of the end-to-end enterprise. They are maintaining it as Oracle database-centric and not particularly open, but they have enough muscle in the database world and a decent enough product to make that a go for them, though it might hurt in the longer term. There are many deals that Oracle wins because the database is already theirs.

They are also making a very visible bid for the SMBs and the price- and time-conscious enterprises with their "CRM in 90 days" initiative. This has been a powerful thrust and far more publicized than their competitors' versions of accelerated CRM implementations. These 90-day, fixed-price, fixed-time implementations are tied into the Oracle strategy of "War on Complexity," which has four bullets attached to it:

- Single database instance
- Suite of integrated applications
- Software configuration, not customization (such as an out-of-the-box solution)
- Software as a hosted service

Using these, a 90-day CRM implementation in marketing and/or sales is certainly possible if you buy into the "all Oracle, all the time, big or small" approach. That means using Oracle's out-of-the-box business processes, too. This has value because it saves money and time. It is tricky because it is completely Oracle-driven CRM with no open standard, and that creates difficulty.

The other part of this strategy is the use of forward flows. These are nine out-of-the-box business processes such as Call to Resolution, Contract to Renewal, or Plan to Campaign—fixed processes that identify a workflow that has best practices built in. This works if you accept the premise that these are the processes you want in your business.

Product

Oracle's products are classic CRM applications. Here they are grouped typically for an enterprise-level implementation:

TeleSales

Sales Online

Incentive Compensation

Sales Intelligence

Teleservice

Service Online

Field Service

Service Intelligence

Marketing Online

Marketing Intelligence

CRM Foundation

Customer Support

This is by no means the complete set of applications. Oracle is also market-savvy enough to provide some unique CRM features that their competitors haven't even thought of. The two that come to mind are classics if you understand the revenue-driven culture of Oracle itself. They are Oracle Contracts, a contract management module, and, most interestingly, Oracle Collections, one of the first CRM applications to use the back office as well as the front. This is a true enterprise hybrid and a forerunner of things to come with customer-centric convergence (see Chapter 18). This is a Cro-Magnon application that expresses the trend toward back- and front-office integration in its DNA.

Culture

Driven by revenue objectives, suspicious of their own partners, and suffering substantially bad press and buzz, Oracle's reputation as an unfriendly place to work and work with dramatically escalated in the mid- and late 1990s. Oracle's culture was not the domicile you wanted to occupy. Better to work from home. However, they still built up a substantial partner network because of the success and value of the products, which were outstanding. My own experiences with them sadly reflected the problems with the culture at that time.

However, in the last few years, their culture, while still not ideal, is better, and Oracle is doing some good with some of the cash they accumulate. For example, in 2001, they donated $10 million to the United Negro College Fund (UNCF)—a small but important gesture as Oracle attempts to do some outreach into the community.

Future

There is no question that Oracle plays among the biggest in the sandbox. Their database is top notch, though even there they are losing some market share. Their CRM applications are not as top notch and while functionally robust, are not of the technical quality of the other three playmates here. Their strategy depends on their Oracle-only success more than the strategies of their competitors. The Oracle strategy won't be as successful if the customer wants to use both Oracle CRM and other vendors' products. I'm leaving the jury out to deliberate for a while. The instructions to the jury couldn't be any clearer: "All Oracle, all the time." But the verdict is uncertain.

The Champ in the Middle

This category is E.piphany's and E.piphany's alone. They are the CRM fence-straddlers, working their product magic on the upper end of the SMB market and the lower to middle of the large enterprise market. Odd place to be, but advantageous to them.

E.piphany

E.piphany closed 2001 with $125.7 million in revenue, maintaining their position in a revenue-starved climate. They got 47 percent of their revenue from their existing customers. More interestingly, they continued to grab significant large enterprise clients such as Caterpillar, Nestle, and Cigna. This retention and acquisition split reflects something good about this excellent company. They are able to get both something new and keep what they get. They are among the most innovative and creative of CRM vendors—and among the nicest, in a business sort of way, and there's nothing wrong with that. Some of my best friends are nice in a business sort of way.

Joking aside, E.piphany is a solidly led, powerfully cast company that has leadership shaped by CEO Roger Siboni (see Chapter 1 for a piece by him), a former deputy chairman and COO of KPMG Consulting, and Jeff Pulver, executive vice-president of marketing, and a former PeopleSoft senior management guy, who carried the David Duffield family culture with him. They have veteran senior management from Oracle and Lotus, the latter very much a friendly culture in its heyday. This is the right blend of skills and experience to propel E.piphany to great heights, at least from a management standpoint. They are newer to the multifunction CRM market than some of the others, coming from the world of slice and dice. But they do really well on the multichannel, multifunction planet.

Their products originally were analytic products that were considered contenders from the beginning. In 1997, they became, if not the absolute first, one of the first CRM companies to go to Web architecture. It was coupled with campaign management and other EMA-related offerings, strong enough for Gartner to catapult E.piphany into the upper-right leaders' box of their Magic Quadrant for 2001. With the release of E.piphany 5.0 in May 2001, they added an SFA component by updating Moss Software's ActiveSales SFA. Moss had been acquired in February 2001 to plug the SFA hole in the E.piphany suite. With the release of its E.5 suite in 2001 and then E.6 in March 2002, E.piphany took further steps forward. Its focus became more concentrated on its enormously innovative Real Time personalization, self-learning, real-time data mining engine that provided super-powered personalization capabilities. More on that later.

Strategy

E.piphany doesn't have a traditional strategy that says we are going to go after this market to get that result and that market to get this result. It is defined heavily around the customer experience and how to maximize its effectiveness and thus, prove profitable to its CRM customers.

The size of the potential customer is not a concern, though as Jeff Pulver says, "The more complex, the better we do." In fact, the reason they have their own Sandbox Playmate category is that they actually straddle both the SMB and the large enterprise markets. It also means that while they prefer to sell the E.piphany EMA and SFA offerings or the entire E.6 suite, for example, they have created an architecture for what they call their Real Time products, which is open, so that Real Time can be embedded into any CRM application. "The key here is to make people more effective," says Mr. Pulver, "The architecture allows for the application of Real Time with any CRM product."

Rather than just streamlining and efficiency, effectiveness is the core of E.piphany's strategy. It is characterized by the corporate vision, "providing insight and action across every customer touch point in real time." The SmartCRM Real Time components of their products are at the heart of the strategy.

Product

The release of E.piphany E.6 in March 2002 was a watershed in the company's product history. This was the first suite that allowed them to fully concentrate on the Real Time components of the product offering. The use of an engine that pushed a self-learning and real-time personalization is branded as SmartCRM and it truly is. The product that delivered this capability with E.6 was E.piphany Dialogs. The Dialogs product is a combination of guided navigation, real-time analytics, and multichannel integration. What makes this a cutting edge product that still remains practical is that it builds on the heritage of E.piphany's analytic strength, but takes intelligence to a whole new paradigm. It learns from both customer history and real-time customer behavior as the customer interacts at any touch point, and comes up with sophisticated suggestions or guides for the customer in real time. It is long past the extract, transform, and load approach to data. It is more like ready, aim, fire.

Guided navigation is a process that runs through many of E.piphany's products. In their campaign management applications, it directly helps the marketing professional set up campaigns that provide real-time feedback and real-time tweaking on the basis of these results. In the call center, it can give the agent or the customer the tools to help the customer purchase or upgrade products or solve problems through intelligent wizards that essentially understand you as you move through them. They are using their built-in intelligence to analyze your customer history and your current interactions to define how they think you will behave and what would be of value to you that you would respond to. If you think about how complex this is, you can appreciate the level of intelligence that is built into the products. For example, your behavior and history indicate that you know that spinach is good for you but you don't like the taste, and that you love the taste of ice cream but know it isn't particularly good for you. What passes for intelligence in many current CRM products is that you will get an offer for spinach ice cream. The difference with E.piphany ActivePath guided navigation and the intelligence that underlies E.piphany products is that it will come up with the up-sell to better nutrition with a good taste that might not include either spinach or ice cream.

Their product suite is multichannel, multiplatform with support for many flavors of Windows and Unix and databases such as SQLServer, Oracle, and DB2, which pretty well covers the standards. There is no reliance on a single platform. They offer marketing, sales, and service that are integrated through their Web-based open architecture and XML-compliant services with back-office applications regardless of the software producer.

Their analytics products, E.piphany Insight, have complete access to all data stores, regardless of where the data comes from. The highly evolved algorithms are directly connected to well-known CRM processes. They are:

- ▶ E.piphany Insight for B2B Marketplaces

- ▶ E.piphany Insight for Contact Centers

- ▶ E.piphany Insight for E-Commerce

- ▶ E.piphany Insight for Indirect Sales

- ▶ E.piphany Insight for Real-Time Marketing

- ▶ E.piphany Insight for Direct Sales

These are coupled with both the Dialog product, mentioned previously, and the Real Time product.

The Real Time product uses information from multiple data sources—real-time behavior, customer demographics, transaction data, customer clickstream data, and any place that you can get your hands on data in your data "ecosystem." It then builds a real-time profile for each customer. To do this, the system calculates acceptance probabilities and selects the best offer using up-to-the-second information. As customers accept and decline offers, the self-learning engine continuously adjusts its real-time predictive model.

Their product weakness? Like most everyone else on this list (Siebel being an exception), it is PRM. They take the "neither build nor buy/acquire" approach. They partner with ChannelWave and Comergent to get their PRM fix. Hey, it's a partnering world. For example, Pivotal licenses the E.piphany engine for their analytics. They have few competitors anywhere near their quality in what they do produce. They even pick really good partners.

Their future is in deeper integration via the Web services they already support such as SOAP and XML. More SOAP interfaces, deeper intertwining with ERP, supply chain management, and other Web services-compliant websites are what we can expect from E.piphany.

Culture

Bill Walsh was COO of E.piphany. Jeff Pulver is the EVP of marketing. Both were veterans of PeopleSoft during the era of David Duffield. Roger Siboni spent 23 years in the white shirt cultures of the Big 5–type of consulting firms. The combination makes for a company that drives revenue and likes its employees and customers. Not a bad combination. They spend time with their employees, doing things like renting a Greyhound bus and taking an entire department on a ski trip. A great time was had by all.

Even more so, though, they have excellent relationships with their customers, and that is worth its weight in gold. One customer told E.piphany that the reason they beat their competition in the deal was that they loved the people and felt that they could partner with them. In 2001, AOL/Time Warner named E.piphany Vendor of the Year because of their responsiveness to the client. This goes along with a host of 2001–2002 product awards such as *Customer Inter@ction Solutions* magazine's 2001 Product of the Year award. It was awarded the "Best of Show" award in the category of "Best CRM Product" at Advanstar's Call Center & CRM Solutions trade show in Las Vegas. In 2002, E.piphany was named one of the top CRM software packages by ISM, Inc., a leading CRM consulting firm at the DCI's CRM Conference and Expo in Chicago. This is quite a list of achievements.

Future

E.piphany's strategy has been successful because of its unusual thrust. They realize that, even with the release of the E.6 Suite on March 19, 2002, they still have something to prove. "We know that we have to continue what we are doing," says Mr. Pulver. "We have to continue to deliver financially and to execute. We need to be profitable and to generate cash."

By providing architecture in E.6 that has reusable business logic and open APIs that can easily be registered in a Web framework, they are enormously flexible and able to pick up incrementally large pieces of non-E.piphany CRM business. They are also are well positioned to take advantage of the increasing interest in Web-based CRM self-service.

E.piphany has managed to straddle the two worlds of SMB and large enterprises and remain innovative, despite the internal differences in those worlds. Their strategy—that is, their increased focus on the Real Time personalization engine, in combination with the strength of the E.6 suite—means they can play in any world they choose. Couple this intelligent product offering with their strong management, their classy demeanor, and their honest self-assessments and add a warm corporate culture and customers who are simply happy to work with an outfit that can partner with them, rather than just sell them. If they can execute on their vision, they will win big time.

The Midmarket Champions

These companies are the midmarket leaders. There is no issue here. For the most part, they actually understand the nature of the differences between the large enterprises and their smaller brethren.

SalesLogix

In 2001, SalesLogix was acquired by Sage. At the time, I worried how the acquisition by Sage would affect this excellent CRM company. It did affect them. There was some management fallout, as is expected. But there was something else put in place: huge access to the European markets, a vast VAR network for the Sage products, and very deep financial pockets. SalesLogix now has serious bucks to do what they have to do and a vastly expanded scope. Pat Sullivan, voted one of the 20 most important men in CRM history, remains at the SalesLogix helm, and they are poised to go toe to toe in the SMB market over the next several years. (By the way, in the United States, Sage is known as Best Software.)

Strategy

For a while, SalesLogix flirted with the thought that they could scale to the largest enterprises and maybe compete with the CRM super-powers. They changed their minds before they went too far to market with this idea. They are firmly ensconced as an important presence in the mid- and larger-sized SMB companies and can service the lower end with either SalesLogix or ACT! Gartner, in one of its sessions at its 2002 CRM Excellence Awards conference, said that they thought SalesLogix was one of the few, if not the only, CRM vendor that was "comfortable in its own jeans." That, of course, is the SMB market.

Their focus in 2002 is on the integration of the front office and the back office in this market space. With the rather large back-office prod-uct line of Sage, this is less of a problem than it has been in the past. The long-term strategy is to tightly integrate the architectures of Sage products and SalesLogix. In the interim, creating the integration points via hooks developed by SalesLogix and its partners will be the way for them to go.

The other major parts of the SalesLogix strategy are familiar if you've been reading this chapter so far. These include a set of highly flexible mobile components and real-time interactions. They have developed a Pocket PC product you can see at http://www.saleslogix.com/pocketpc/. It is a very good-looking, richly functional version of their desktop product that works with any mobile PDA-like component, including the tablet PC or smart phones, besides the most obvious PDAs.

SalesLogix has competitors: Pivotal, Onyx, and their newcomer on the block, the well-funded Salesforce.com. In 2002, Microsoft entered the fray. However, "Apathy is our number one competitor," says Joe Greenspan, marketing director for SalesLogix.

They are not aimed at the vertical markets particularly. Because they have such a highly partner-focused strategy, where the partners repre-sent a very significant part of the SalesLogix stream, they are leaving it to the partners to penetrate the verticals. What looks to be the future in 2003 or 2004 is a partner-based "vertical marketplace" where the part-ners can peddle their industrial SalesLogix wares online. This doesn't rule out SalesLogix entering the vertical markets, it just diminishes the possibility. This is a marked departure from the strategy of most of the vendors. SalesLogix has the strength in their partner community to carry this off. Most other CRM vendors don't.

They are also focused on a 2002 strategic initiative they think will give them a strong play deeper into their markets. That would be the Quickstart initiative, which is their version of accelerated implementation. For the SalesLogix variety, it means:

- ▶ Fixed price

- ▶ 30 days implementation time

- ▶ Software

- ▶ Training

- ▶ Project guarantee and risk sharing

- ▶ Pre-implementation signoff

The interesting part of this is the project guarantee and the risk sharing. It is not something you usually see in this sort of deal. That distinguishes it and makes it worthy of a look. Ordinarily, I'm not a big fan of these accelerated implementation plans, but if there are guarantees from the vendor, that vaults it to a different realm.

Product

The new SalesLogix product lines for 2002 are characterized by flexibility and speed. The hardcore functionality of their Sales and Support applications has been embedded in their suite for years and is solid and geared to their SMB sphere, so I won't reiterate it here (see Chapter 6 for more discussion on this). I've mentioned the wireless technologies previously, so I won't repeat myself. There is so much more to their new product releases. They have added solutions selling methodology to the application suite, due to an apparent customer demand that doesn't particularly surprise me, but always perplexes me. I'm not a strong believer in selling methodologies, embedded in applications or in human habit, but apparently this is a feature devoutly to be wished for since several of the vendors are doing this. At least the feature is available to the SMB with the SalesLogix offer so I commend them for that.

Far more interesting to me, and useful, are the new functions built around alert services. These services are built around the new SalesLogix KnowledgeSync, an add-on that actually monitors system activity and customer transactions to identify and respond to conditions that are user-identified in user-specified ways. The alert system sits on top of the CRM applications and is based on what they are calling "extended workflow." SalesLogix has two unique types of alerts:

Integrated Service Alerts   This is a slick add-on for support teams. It can do things like analyze email and create automatic open tickets and then route them to the appropriate persons to take care of. It uses a powerful workflow to then notify chosen personnel when a ticket hasn't been closed in time or needs to be escalated or whatever knotty service problems crop up. It can also alert salespersons that a services contract is about to expire.

Business Alerts   This is a variation on a KnowledgeSync theme. It is the same as the Integrated Service Alerts but aimed at the sales and marketing teams. The notifications here could include new leads entered into the system, opportunities that are growing stale, up-selling or cross-selling opportunities, or pretty much anything that you want to permit and direct.

SalesLogix does have a couple of major holes, such as analytics, which they are moving to overcome in the future. They are actually currently developing an analytics tool that is aimed at developing algorithms that are useful to the SMBs and don't require a Ph.D. to comprehend. SalesLogix's analytics tools in development are designed to be used by non-academics. They will have a very easy-to-use feel about them, but will still extract and interpret the most essential data for the SMB market when completed.

What SalesLogix has in SFA functionality is unsurpassed in the SMB market. There is no one better and no one smarter on that. For example, with version 5.2, they added Advanced Outlook Integration. Anyone who lives in the SMB market doesn't need to hear another word.

Culture

SalesLogix has been making major adjustments to their culture since their acquisition by Sage. Once they realized that they were going to remain focused on the SMBs, they also realized the kind of cultural alignment that this implied. They had been organized to be big with a very large org chart with lots of management titles, regardless of management activity. They have leveled that org chart considerably. They also realized that this meant encouraging innovation and creativity inside a nimble and flexible environment, so they brought in Tim Fargo as their new general manager, a man greatly respected as someone who listens to his employees and inspires them.

To show they were serious about changing what had been a stale culture for the better, as 2002 progresses they have launched both a customer and an internal initiative that are tied to each other, called Customer First and Who's Your Customer, respectively. Ultimately the purpose of both is to provide better interaction with the individual customers and to get to know them as well as you know your fellow employee. Part of the plan will be to align individual objectives and compensation at every level with long-term customer satisfaction. The second part is to realign business units around the customers that the unit should serve.

SalesLogix was always a pretty happy place to work, with less than 10 percent employee turnover, even when the culture got a little stale. Their management has always been accessible and continues to be even more so.

Future

SalesLogix has an exciting new product suite. They have deep pockets and long-term stability due to their acquisition. They have a newly revamped culture that is more customer-centric. They are highly partner-focused and have that extended Sage reach to Europe as well as North America. They are comfortable in their jeans, which is more than I can say for me. All told, if the product holes don't bug the customers, their future is looking bright.

Onyx

Onyx is focused solely on CRM. Their entire revenues and staff support CRM. All CRM, all the time. This is their message and it is a good one. As of December 31, 2001, Onyx employed slightly more than 450 people. Total 2001 revenues were approximately $19.23 million.

Strategy

For a while, I was concerned with Onyx and their seeming absolute focus on the Microsoft. NET platform and SQL Server as their back end. To me, that was a possible death warrant, because any company dependent on a single platform lives and dies with that platform. Then I was concerned that, with their acquisition of Revenue Labs, they were so over-focused on their "business value proposition" that they would forget they were a CRM company and not a management consulting firm. Then I was concerned that they were setting their market sites too high in the headier days of CRM in early 2001 and were going to try to compete with Siebel, PeopleSoft, and the like. That would have been ludicrous.

I am happy to say with the pending release of Onyx 4.0 in early summer 2002, their strategy seems to have become intelligent: "We are a CRM company that is strong in the upper end of the midmarket and can function on multiple platforms." Tight revenues slapped them to their senses and I'm glad for that.

While they may have gone strategically awry for a while, the quality of their products never did. They were and are excellent portal-based products with highly robust offerings based on the appropriate definition of the customer—customer, employee, and supplier.

They have made significant gains in Europe. In fact, in 2001, they announced an alliance with Deloitte Consulting in the U.K. to work on what they are calling citizen relationship management, which will be powered by Onyx. They will focus on local government and financial services and healthcare overall in the U.K., allying with vertical specialists in each domain, beyond Deloitte. This is an important forward movement by Onyx.

Product

Onyx 4.0 is their new product release in 2002. The Onyx product line has always been a Web-services-based, portal-driven CRM suite. In fact, it takes a different tack when it comes to how it views a suite. It is a set of portals that have specific strong functionality built into the offering. As I detailed in Chapter 2, there is an employee portal, a customer portal, and a partner portal, all based on the Onyx e-business engine. The functionality for sales, channel management, services, helpdesk, marketing, and so on that characterizes the "traditional" multifunction suite is under the portal hood rather than the guiding interface.

The release of Onyx 4.0 will be aimed at diversifying the support of the applications to Oracle's 8i database and the Sun Solaris operating system. It will also provide a user interface toolkit that will allow a no-coding integration with third-party applications, following the trend of almost all the multifunction playmates to leave the proprietary and go to the open architectures and common standards. To bolster this, Onyx 4.0 will be XML-compliant.

Don't get me wrong. This doesn't mean that they are moving away from the Microsoft-centric characteristics of product line. In fact, they are strengthening it so that third-party Web services can be leveraged through the Microsoft Hailstorm platform, a platform that uses the now well-known Microsoft Passport, Instant Messenger, and other normally consumer-focused Web services.

They are not leaving the realm of the proprietary, either. Included in the Onyx 4.0 Employee Portal is a proprietary selling model called Opportunity Manager, which for some reason is not available in the Windows client. This is coherent with the current trend within the multifunction CRM players to incorporate various selling methodologies into their application. Siebel, PeopleSoft, SalesLogix, and now Onyx 4.0 have all done this with their 2002 releases.

Analytics is not their strong suit. With companies that have high caliber analytics (such as SAS and SPSS) offering OEM deals to CRM firms, it might be wise for Onyx to see what it can do here.

Culture

This is a tough one. Onyx has a somewhat schizophrenic culture. On the one hand, kindnesses to employees are not infrequent. Brent Frei, the founder and CEO, is a very fine human being who has successfully built an important company in the CRM industry. On the other hand, for a company in the $100 million revenue range, the politics are pretty intense. This makes me scratch my head. Companies this size shouldn't have the level of internal political activity they do.

Future

Onyx is a leader in Web services. They have settled down their strategy. Their message has been refocused. This is all very promising provided they continue on the newly paved road they seem to be on. Gartner thinks they are a long-term acquisition target and that may well be true. But for now, if the release of Onyx 4.0 lives up to its promise, Onyx will likely do the same. But when it comes to staying the strategic course and settling their culture, two areas that are important criteria to these Sandbox choices, the "if" remains.

KANA

KANA began its CRM career as an email management company in 1996 with a nice chunk—$27 million in venture money. It was smart, sophisticated email management, with one of the first uses of artificial intelligence in that genre, but email management is all it did at that time.

But founder Mark Gainey had other plans, and that meant acquisitions. Starting in 1999, within 15 months or so, they had acquired three more companies—triple the rate that they had done since 1997. The acquisition of Silknet in 2000 was the turning point for KANA, bringing them into the world of XML-compliant, n-tiered architecture with open standards and open protocols. The Silknet product, in combination with KANA's other products, gave KANA its CRM heritage. Silknet's product managed all aspects of customer interaction. For example, the customer representative can see an entire history of customer preferences and support requests, sales order status, and other customer history while speaking to the customer. This customer information was gathered through multiple customer channels. As if this wasn't enough, KANA then went out and merged with Broadbase (or acquired Broadbase, depending on who you read or hear). That created KANA Software, which has gone on to become a very important CRM company with 425 employees and a sound revenue stream.

Strategy

The KANA strategy is one that differs from the run-of-the-mill CRM strategists. "Our belief set is that the Internet changes the game," says Bud Michael, executive vice-president of marketing at KANA. "It has changed customer expectations. It can be used to educate large populations of systems users. There had been a wall between customers and service providers and vendors. The customer has been a victim to the vendor." Ultimately, KANA sees the consumer as the end customer and the Web as a low cost means of shifting information around. Think about this. Age is not a discriminator when it comes to the interest in using the Internet for something, even if it's just email. "The accelerating adoption rate of the Web works by the half generation now," says Mr. Michael, "and the information is expected to be free."

This interesting perspective actually shapes the KANA strategy. They deliberately are building a suite of applications that not only takes advantage of the Internet with its architecture, but that will "commoditize" point solutions as suite features. That allows KANA to build a cost-effective suite whose very functions and modules are process-focused point solutions and yet still can be built out to the enterprise.

What that means is that the enterprise can be automated. However, the basic underlying principle to an automated enterprise in CRM is to work with continuous customer interactions. The business paradigm that Mr. Michael uses "allows your customer to be their own agent— i.e., I did the Web, now I want to talk to a real person." The KANA iCARE suite is built around self-service through CRM Web services.

Product

KANA's iCARE stands for Intelligent Customer Acquisition and Retention for the Enterprise. Obviously, there was a very smart marketing team on top of this one because not only does it give a message on its CRM purpose, but it also says, "You do matter," which fits their smart "customer in charge" approach to the suite and its heavy Internet focus. It smacks of the idea that the way to retention or acquisition is to make the customer feel good. The product is broken down into two major components that I'll briefly mention: the services applications and the marketing applications.

Customer Service This is both self-service and assisted services.

Contact Center Request management, workflow, personal views, solution publishing.

IQ The foundation for customer self-service or assisted knowledge-base access.

Response High volume email management. This is their heritage application.

ResponseIQ Email management enhanced with a knowledge base.

Connect Proactive event-triggered notifications; important workflow product.

CTI Conduits Focuses on integration of CTI into the CIC.

Service Analytics Analytics geared toward multichannel CICs.

Marketing Hardcore and basic EMA applications.

Marketing Automation Campaign planning application.

Marketing Analytics Campaign analysis module.

Commerce Analytics Application that analyzes individual website activity.

For now, that will be enough to give you a flavor of their strength in the contact center. They don't have a PRM or SFA module. However, their customer service applications are just knockouts.

Culture

KANA's culture is extremely interesting. It starts from recognizing that the values of the company are the values that are done in partnership. That means at every level. For example, the driven, results-oriented executive style of one portion of senior management is coupled with the more "great place to work in partnership and harmony" side of another portion of senior management. This combination drives corporate initiatives to the employees who are valued for their input to that combination of management. To make this even more fascinating and consistent, KANA has embarked on an initiative they call the "Drink Our Own Champagne" project. This project highlights partner cooperation in a most unusual way.

KANA's partner strategy is to use their strategic partners for implementations, rather than their own professional services. What that means is that they have a chosen few strategic partners: KPMG Consulting, IBM, Accenture, and CSC. In Chapter 16, you'll note that three of the four are among my five major choices for service providers, so this bodes well. KANA deviates widely from the normal approach to strategic partners, which I call the "blah, blah, blah" approach, because the initiatives are so blah. What KANA does is to use the partners to get KANA up and running on KANA products. KPMG Consulting, Accenture, and IBM all are working in house, with offices on the premises to implement KANA. The partners have onsite senior managers to handle the implementation. They are trained on KANA products. They have on-the-spot problem solving. It is an interesting and unique approach.

Their culture is consistent, valuable, and entirely focused on delivering success through partnership and teamwork. That is an outstanding way to go. Balance, harmony, and KPMG Consulting and Accenture working together.

Future

KANA's culture is on the whole aligned with the meaning of CRM. While each member of management may have a very different management style, they still figured out that it takes a team to make things work in conjunction. Even with the enormous churn of merging two companies, KANA and Broadbase, that had already done six and five acquisitions respectively, KANA has emerged streamlined, strong, and profitable. The upward thrust of this company will continue in spades.

Pivotal

I'm going to treat Pivotal a little differently, but not because I think differently about it. It is a member of the Sandbox Playmates and a prominent one. In fact, in the first quarter of 2002, they were given the upper-right section on the Gartner Magic Quadrant as mid-enterprise CRM leader. I am turning the Pivotal section over to a guest speaker:

Paul Steep of Toronto-based Yorkton Securities, one of the leading technology investment banks in North America. Mr. Steep is an excellent CRM analyst who understands Pivotal thoroughly. Yorkton Securities is a financial agent for Pivotal. In fact, I have agreed to include the following waiver at their request and in the interests of disclosure: "Yorkton Securities has acted as agent for financing of or financial advisor to Pivotal Corporation within the past three years." I find what they say about Pivotal to be informative and will defer to them so you can see what analysts do when they look at a company. They are more right-brained than I am, and very capably so. Getting an analyst's view is instructive because the perspective is different from what this book is ordinarily focused on. Here is Paul Steep until the end of the section on Pivotal:

Pivotal Corporation started to focus on CRM in 1994 and has been active in selling to midmarket enterprises for the past six years. The company has managed to accumulate a suite of CRM applications through internal development and several acquisitions. Pivotal established itself as one of the leading CRM choices for midmarket enterprises based on its Microsoft architecture and flexible agent-based software.

Strategy

Pivotal, like many CRM vendors, is currently in transition as it attempts to stabilize its operations following a severe downturn in the CRM market. The company, like other fast-growing enterprise software vendors, was caught up in the market downturn of 2001. Pivotal had been pursuing an aggressive expansion strategy as it attempted to (1) expand into new markets with the opening of new offices and establishing a local sales presence in new countries (for example, Europe and Asia) and (2) focusing its sales and marketing efforts on larger organizations with hopes of starting to sell into the Global 2000. On August 28, 2001, Pivotal announced a series of management changes with the appointment of Bo Manning as CEO, Divesh Sisodraker as CFO, and Rob Douglas as vice-president of sales. The new management team has spent the past six months [through first quarter 2002] restructuring the firm's operations with a series of staff reductions, office closures, and new management hires. Pivotal is now targeting "entrepreneurial enterprises" and is no longer targeting Global 2000 firms, which remain the domain of Siebel Systems and other ERP companies. Pivotal has launched a new marketing campaign, "Pivotal versus the humongous," in an effort to introduce customers to its new strategy. The firm has decided to refocus on midmarket companies with a marketing message that emphasizes fast, low-cost implementation of a customized CRM solution. As part of its marketing efforts, the company has undertaken the only free software test-drive program that we have encountered. Overall, we believe that Pivotal will need to more clearly articulate the direction of its strategy to customers, employees, and partners.

Product

Pivotal's primary focus has always been a sales force automation (SFA) system, which remains at the core of the company's application suite. In developing its core product, eRelationship, Pivotal identified a number of key success factors, including a low-cost, packaged solution that offers a full range of eCRM functionality, is easily customizable, and is maintained on industry-standard software. To ensure that Pivotal can offer a scalable enterprise-class demand chain solution, the company has invested in re-architecting its software to operate on a common platform. In early 2000, Pivotal introduced ePower, a common framework for all of its applications that enables XML-based communications. We believe that Pivotal has developed a strong core SFA product with a number of extensions that increase the CRM functionality (such as partner relationship management, CRM analytics, and e-selling).

Critics have highlighted the company's sole dependence on the Microsoft platform as one of its primary weaknesses. On August 14, 2001, the company officially announced an Oracle-based edition of its eRelationship software that supports Oracle's 8*i* database. We believe Pivotal also needs to focus its development team on its partner relationship management product, PartnerHub, and a more robust reporting engine than the Crystal Reports engine that comes standard with eRelationship. We would also like to see Pivotal replace its current CRM analytics module, which is provided on an OEM basis by E.piphany, and replace it with an internally developed product or the purchase of an analytics engine.

Culture

The rapid growth and the challenges Pivotal has experienced in the past several years have resulted in a change in the firm's corporate culture. Prior to its rapid growth and reorganization, the company was a tight-knit group of professionals that were extremely passionate about their product. We believe that the challenges of the past year have left the company in transition.

Future

In our opinion, Pivotal will survive the current shakeout in the CRM market and will continue to play a role as a vendor to midmarket enterprises. The official announcement by Microsoft that it would enter the CRM market with a solution for small to medium-sized businesses is expected to have a knock-on effect on Pivotal along with other midmarket CRM vendors. Pivotal's management team has made some initial steps in beginning to turn the company around by reducing its operating cost base and hiring new sales staff. We believe, however, that there is still a significant amount of work ahead in terms of clarifying the company's market position (for example, pricing and product portfolio) and rebuilding its sales and consulting organization across North America after the recent rounds of restructuring.

Overall, we believe that Pivotal is working on a turnaround, and retooling its sales force is a key step in this effort. We maintain our view that it will be several quarters before Pivotal's new sales force begins to perform at full capacity. Despite the challenges outlined above, we believe that midmarket customers seeking an SFA solution that has the ability to expand into other CRM functions should add Pivotal to their list of vendors to evaluate.

Up and Coming

These are companies that I can't ignore because they truly have something to offer. They just haven't reached the exalted Sandbox Playmate status yet. I have no doubts that they will get there someday. Chordiant belongs with the others that follow, but I've covered them sufficiently throughout the book. But don't forget them.

Blue Martini

Blue Martini released its Blue Martini 5 suite in March 2002, at the time that several of the other major vendors were releasing their own new suites. This is a company that is on the radar and below the radar constantly. When their name comes up, good things are said. But the "when" is "not frequently enough." Ask about a major player in the CRM world and you don't hear Blue Martini's name. But ask about a company that can do the job well, and you do hear it.

With the release of Blue Martini 5, they have added serious B2B features. They include stronger lead management, a request for quote

(RFQ) feature, the ability to issue and track return material authorizations (RMA), and invoice presentment; in other words, adding strong back-office and procurement functions to their CRM suite. They have account management features with a Web interface now, which did not exist in prior versions. They are aiming squarely at self-service, a smart move in this day of customer interaction. They have even added, wisely, an IBM edition of this release called Blue Martini 5 – IBM Edition, which comes bundled with IBM's WebSphere Application Server and MQ Series. It works on the IBM AIX operating system.

There are four applications that make up their suite: Marketing, Commerce, Channels, and Service. Blue Martini Marketing is strong in email management and direct mail campaigns. Blue Martini Commerce is the self-service and mobile environment for the suite. Blue Martini Channels is the partner self-service portals, and Blue Martini Service is the call center interfaces. This company has huge strength in the manufacturing world. They have the opportunity to gain strength elsewhere. They are a bit pricey, starting at $85,000 per CPU, but given how many people can use a server-based product, this might not be so bad.

Talisma

This company is energetic. They provide an excellent set of products that run the multifunction gamut. Their hardcore CRM products are focused on the classic gang of three: sales, marketing, and services. They are best known for Talisma Contact Center. They have a terrific set of customer histories in the call center province. They are smart enough to focus attention on usability, developing an interface that not only integrates with Outlook but even looks like Outlook. Talisma has paid attention to providing useful functionality, rather than all the functionality your budget can eat. All these characteristics add up to a company to pay attention to.

They come from, what else, email management. Never forgetting these roots, they now have contact centers based in India as an outsourced service offering—a little different from a typical CRM vendor. These contact centers offer email management, reactive and proactive chat, Web support, and phone support for a company at every level. That means technical support for the client's products, customer support to handle complaints, prospector support to tie incoming communications to the inside sales team, and engineering support for internal IT systems.

This is a fast growing company with 20 to 25 percent growth over the past six quarters. Not bad given the declining revenues of most of their competition. They certainly are a company that should be watched.

Microsoft

I don't really have to say much about Microsoft. I've covered their entry into CRM in this book already, and, if their history means something, they will become in a few years, wherever they enter CRM, if not the 800-pound gorilla, one with a weight of 795 pounds. Or 9,000 pounds. It could be either, but probably not much less. Just think of this: According to Microsoft insiders, they have 198,000,000 registered users of Outlook. They have $39 billion in cash. I don't need to say anything else.

15

CRM Service Offerings: There Really Is Value to You and Yours

The toughest thing in the world occurs after you've bought CRM software. You have to implement it. Well, actually, *you* don't have to implement it. In fact, you don't want to implement it. You have to find some company that will do it for you. If you do attempt to implement it yourself, with rare exceptions, you'll have wasted a lot of money on software and you can actually harm your company more than help it. The question is, who should do it?

It's great to have CRM software and the hardware that is used to carry it. However, it's estimated that the cost of installing and configuring CRM software to enterprise specifications is two to three times the cost of the software itself, at least. That's why the choices for how the software is implemented aren't as easy as they seem at first. Will a professional services company do it? Will the vendor do it with their professional services division? Will internal MIS staff do it? Should you outsource it to an application service provider (ASP) and then let them run it for you? If a professional services company does it, will it be large or small? Not only are all of these issues you must consider, but often choices made can mean dramatic things to a career—whether it's promotion or termination. Many a job has been lost due to cost overruns because of choosing the wrong implementation partner or the idea that to "save money," implementation can be done internally. These are momentous decisions.

Several years ago, I was involved in a bid with Lotus Development Corporation for a Lotus Notes implementation. A government agency issued the request for proposal (RFP). The only competition was a company, the incumbent, that specialized in a groupware product that was not much like Lotus Notes, but which had workflow capabilities. It was called Viewstar. Within the specific agency, there were proponents of Notes and proponents of Viewstar. The internal battle that went on was so ugly that there were threats of termination, threats of quitting, backstabbing, mysterious internal leaks that were designed to hurt some of the agency personnel, and external resources brought in beyond the scope of the RFP to champion one or the other. Ultimately, the budget was cut and no one got anything, but the internecine war was horrible to behold. People still lost jobs and quit over this issue, despite the fact that nothing happened. All due to which software was going to be used! Unfortunately, I've run into this situation more than once over my career. Think about that in a larger context. How important in life is the choice of software at a workplace, really? Yet, this was a deadly serious struggle. That's how important these choices can be on the service side, as well, because services are even more costly than software. There is also a lot more that can go wrong with the wrong choice. Human foibles are a much larger category than software bugs.

The need for CRM services is increasing with implementations of CRM software that can be long and costly, as I've outlined throughout this book—between $1 million and $5 million. In terms of cost benefits, however, they are well worth it. Customers are fully aware of these benefits and are rapidly moving toward purchasing and implementing CRM. The projected proof positive is that IDC is anticipating a $125.2 billion market by 2004. Yet, the availability of CRM-skilled personnel is low despite major investments by dozens of companies in developing those skills. Even with the recession of 2001–2002, CRM-skilled consultants aren't exactly flooding the market. The conundrum is that very large services companies, such as the Big 5 consulting firms, IBM, and EDS, poured millions into creating CRM practices to handle the CRM work—and they did it at similar levels and speeds to the ERP implementation practices they all created in the 1990s to install and customize SAP or PeopleSoft or Oracle applications. Yet, business has slowed and they are carrying some heavy hitters with major CRM skills on their benches. Yet they can't afford to let them go, because CRM has been somewhat recession resistant and continues to be a projected growth area. So there is a lot of overhead and few skills on the market.

There is one other factor. The trend du jour is to implement CRM in a pain-curing, rather than enterprise-wide, package. That means shorter, smaller, and less costly implementations, calling for smaller and more specialized teams. But none of this is really the customer's problem. It actually puts the customer in a good position. If you are considering implementing CRM in some way, remember that the service provider you choose is likely to have a bench that is eating up capital, not creating it, with the talent to handle what you need. Bargain hard. There are plenty of service providers out there.

The Choices

If your company decided to go with a CRM package, what kind of service provider would it be? Vendor? Large consulting services company? Smaller implementation partner? ASP? Let's check it out.

The Vendor

The vendor seems to be a logical choice. After all, who knows the software better than the software provider? However, you have to keep in mind that often, product companies don't want to be anything but product companies. Their professional services department is a courtesy to those customers who want the comfort of extremely knowledgeable engineers. These companies often look at the engineers and their professional services departments as marketing overhead. However, there are a number of vendors who have fully staffed professional services organizations that are as good as any consulting services organization. They are companies such as Oracle, PeopleSoft, SAP, and Siebel.

Many other vendors depend on partner programs to give the customer qualified, certified partners who can do implementations. Companies like this include SalesLogix, whose business partner (implementation partner) programs are strict so that certification is something a partner earns. Their largest partner is (as of 2002) e-Partners. There are some questions you should ask a vendor and criteria you should examine to determine if their professional services organization is just a marketing courtesy, an umbrella "shell" for outside contractors brought in, or a legitimate, going concern. The umbrella shell is often a reality. I know this well because staff members from the last three companies I've been associated with have often been used on vendor-supported projects to fill in for vendor personnel. Live Wire made millions of dollars doing this sort of staff augmentation. Normally, the way this works with a vendor is that staff augmentation divisions of companies like Live Wire will fill some of the technical or functional roles during the lifespan of a project, but the vendor does the project management.

Some of the questions you should ask are:

What is the size of the professional services group? This gives you an idea of what investment the company has made in services.

Carrying a bench (a nonworking group of consultants) is an expensive proposition.

What are the utilization rates of the services group? This will give you an idea of how frequently the services are used and what your chances are of getting a capable team from the vendor when the time comes.

Can I get customer references from the vendor for similar-sized projects? It is not worth your time to get references for much larger or much smaller projects since the scope makes a huge difference in how the implementation is handled.

What percentage of the projects is handled by partners and what percentage by the vendor company? This is important because the partners aren't under the project control of the vendors except officially. The reality is, however, no matter how much contractual control a vendor has with its partners, the partners' employees don't feel particularly loyal to the project or the vendor, and only somewhat loyal to their company interests.

What's it going to cost me? Very often the cost of vendor professional services is high because you are getting "at-the-source resources" that can be counted on to know what they are doing. Even those coming from partners are screened prior to their joining the team. Superior product knowledge advantages can be obtained elsewhere, especially with the larger professional services organizations (such as KPMG). Lower cost and increased customer flexibility can be attained through the smaller vendors. Additionally, often, the vendor professional services group can be intransigent about pricing, refusing to budge. I know at least two of the big four vendors are that way regularly, though not universally.

The Small CRM Services Company

The small CRM services company is a vastly different animal from the vendor. The small services company can be defined as a company in the $3 million to $75 million range, though this is a subjective definition. I remember SAP identifying companies in the SMB market with a revenue range between $200 million and $1 billion. I wish my company were that tiny! Normally, the small or medium-sized CRM company is either a totally dedicated CRM company (at the lower end of the revenue spectrum) or has a strong CRM practice of perhaps between 15 and 50 people. By no means does it have the resources the large systems integrators do or have expertise in the large enterprise market. It is often focused on the SMB market (see Chapter 13) for its implementations. Many of the small companies even specialize in small market companies. They are expert in CRM software such as SalesLogix or Onyx, which are aimed at the less-than-2,500-seat implementations, while perhaps the larger institutions focus on Siebel and Oracle CRM. However, as we saw in Chapter 13, even the larger consulting companies are aiming at the SMBs and implementing SalesLogix and its competitors. Smaller companies also may specialize in niche market segments such as enterprise marketing automation or are even product specific with practices that implement applications such as analytics powerhouse SAS.

The advantages of smaller companies tend to be straightforward: price and knowledge of the market they are part of. Small companies understand the problems and culture of the small market. Ayer, Massachusetts-based Live Wire, Inc., a small market SalesLogix Technology Partner and PeopleSoft partner that specializes in both CRM and back-office e-commerce services, is typical of an excellent small services provider. Live Wire provides CRM SMB implementation services at under-market pricing—either fixed price or time and materials. What they also do, unlike most of the larger enterprises, is provide staff augmentation services. If you are doing an internal implementation using your own staff, Live Wire provides individuals who fill the skills holes you have. This is strictly at time and materials pricing.

So, what does time and materials or fixed pricing mean? These are pricing scenarios used routinely in the CRM services industry, specifically, and e-commerce services world, generally. Time and materials is the combination of an hourly rate that includes the labor costs of individual consultants and expense costs. The expense costs can be built directly into the hourly rate, but just as frequently, they are billed separately. There is no great advantage to the customer with time and materials pricing unless the services vendor finishes the project under the projected time of completion. The biggest customer advantage is the use of an iterative methodology by many of the companies that use time and materials pricing. The customer is involved in each stage of the project and can suggest changes in the application or project routinely and see them implemented in each stage. Each deliverable is reviewed by the customer. The services provider doesn't mind, because the charges are by the hour, so changes are accounted for by simply being billed as additional hours. Typically, Live Wire will charge rates ranging from $90 per hour per person to roughly $150 per hour per person, depending on the skills necessary. These rates are considerably lower than the larger professional services firms or the vendor rates, which range from $125 to $300 per hour, again, depending on the skills acquired.

Fixed price and/or fixed term pricing is much more advantageous to the customer. If the cost of the project exceeds the specified price or the specified time, the services provider eats the continued cost. The advantage to the customer is obvious. The customer can manage his budget prior to the implementation and the risk lies with the services provider. The services provider's advantage is finishing ahead of schedule, which still nets them the fixed amount, increasing their margins. The processes and methodology for a fixed price implementation are far stricter than time- and materials-based projects. Normally, prior to the signing of the fixed price contract with the services company, there is a clear-cut statement of work (SOW) that outlines specifically what is to be done for the fixed price. There is also an agreed-upon written step-by-step change management process that details what the costs and caveats are for changes in the SOW. (See Chapter 4 for change management strategy.) This is a critical difference between the relatively footloose time and materials contract and the very strict fixed price contract. The risks for the services provider are much higher for fixed price. Time and materials shifts the burden to the customer. At one level or another, it's all a crapshoot. Even with the burden on the services provider, the customer could be paying a lot more if the project is done under the proposed timeframe. Additionally, the services provider, always aware of their risk, has built that risk into the cost, so it isn't such an unqualified great deal for fixed price. *Caveat emptor.*

Staff Augmentation

Staff augmentation is a tricky part of the CRM and e-services landscape, because when it is stripped to its essence, it's the sale of the labor power of a body. Because the number of small enterprises focused on staff augmentation is huge, it is a minefield. Yet it is an explosive industry that has engendered some multibillion-dollar enterprises in IT staff placement alone, as with Maxim Group (a subsidiary of the much larger temporary agency Aerotech). However, most staff augmentation companies are very small, even as small as one-person operations. In this case, size really doesn't matter, but quality does.

If you do a lot of your own CRM work and have not farmed it to an ASP, at some point you will need a skill you don't have and don't want to hire for due to the short-term timeframe you need it for. For example, you may need a functional expert in campaign management who is working with you on your Unica implementation. Possibly you will need an Oracle database administrator (DBA) to work with you on the backend for your Siebel implementation. This is where companies such as Live Wire can help. They provide you with temporary (three months and up) labor for a time and materials price. But don't fool around here. Normally, the labor you need is a critical short-term need, so the quality of the individual is crucial. Because there are thousands of companies that do this staff augmentation work and a lot of them are not as reliable or don't have the quality of Live Wire, you should be taking certain precautions and asking certain questions of the small companies, especially if they are not being recommended to you by a friend or business acquaintance.

Here is the information you need to find or know:

How many actual employees does the company have? How many technical consultants? Often, particularly in staff augmentation, the consultants who will end up on your project are either independent contractors (called "1099s" after their IRS status) who have been interviewed by the staff augmentation company, or consultants who come from other vendors and are being passed through. The best of these companies have hired their own technical consultants who they carry on the bench. Press this question pretty far, because often the lower end of the staff augmentation business—the appropriately maligned "body shops"—will hire consultants as full-time employees for the length of a contract, basically to increase margins and to be able to say they are employees. In truth, they are independent contractors who are being given a W-2 status (again, an IRS designation). This is an important distinction because staff augmentation companies have no control over 1099s or other vendors' consultants. There are project accountability issues that can come up, such as tardiness, communication problems, or poor development work. The vendor that doesn't truly employ these contractors can't control them either, so they have their hands tied when it comes to resolution of these issues. I've seen it time and time again in the industry—contractors who don't show up the first day of work because they took a different contracting job and forgot to let you know. These issues will come up. You will have to make sure the path to accountability of your vendor/partner is pristine and sharp at the edges.

What kind of margin is the vendor getting? The vendor doesn't have to reveal this information and is not likely to. Optimally, it would pay for you to strike a deal with the vendor where you pay them a fully loaded rate (as is often the case in government contracting). This means the vendor's total costs—overhead, administration, cost of the consultant, and so on, plus an agreed-upon margin. Typical margins that are considered reasonable in a normal time and materials deal are 30 to 45 percent over the cost of the consultant. This means overhead and everything else is included in that number. Beyond 50 percent is genuine gouging, except in unusual circumstances, none of which occur to me now. Don't expect to get the margin information unless you have a very close partnership with the vendor or are doing substantial volume with them. It may be worth a shot in asking about it, though, if you feel comfortable.

What kind of experience has the vendor's consultant(s) had in doing the specific job? Keep in mind, this is staff augmentation we are talking about here, not project work. *The vendor's experience is less important than the experience of the individual who is going to be your resource.* Since, presumably, you are project-managing this one, the vendor's project management experience is not critical. What is critical is that there is a qualified resource being placed on your job. Don't forget to ask this one.

Who are some of the vendor's clients? This is not the simple question it seems. There are a lot of fly-by-night outfits in the small CRM services world that do staff augmentation. They are characterized by not having any true end clients. What they do is provide contractors to vendors who have end clients. They tend to be middlemen—in other words, body shops. They never know the end client's representatives at all. Their contractor is running through another vendor. Or two. Or three. That puts all accountability on something akin to the level of the sixth degree of Kevin Bacon: distant, indeed, almost nonexistent. The better vendors that do staff augmentation have sales forces that go to end clients that do business with them. For example, Live Wire has 25 to 30 end clients it does business with. Many of them have been clients for the life of Live Wire (four years). They trust us. We trust them. Rush jobs are done on a handshake, without protracted contract negotiations. This is CRM at the functional level: true interaction and trust between the customer/client and the vendor. That is the advantage of the end client model. So you should be asking the question and getting references. The body shop will often use the end client's name though it isn't their client. Thus, the references become *very* important.

With all this precaution, why even use the small CRM services company for staff augmentation? First, most large CRM services companies don't do staff augmentation, though large companies who are IT generalists, like Maxim, do. Second, small company overhead and administrative costs are lower. Small companies are more nimble, and they have a more intense desire to establish themselves. Thus, the small company will provide you with excellent prices for qualified individuals and still be happy with their margins. Ultimately, you're responsible for your own project. Being under budget and on time is a good thing. Small companies can either do it for you or aid you in the process. If you find a good small staff augmentation company or project-ready company (such as Acuent of New Jersey or ApexIT of Minneapolis), you've found a gem.

What About the Big 5?

CRM practices are popular in the larger consulting services companies. The commitment of the giants range from dozens to thousands of consultants dedicated to various CRM services. Often these are product-specific services ranging, for example, from Siebel and SalesLogix to the more specialized E.piphany and Pivotal product lines. Additionally, there are vendor-neutral consulting services or multiproduct consulting services that the larger CRM service companies provide.

Who are these giants? They are the Big 5: Deloitte Consulting, KPMG Consulting, Accenture, PricewaterhouseCoopers, and Arthur Andersen. They are systems integrators such as Cap Gemini (which bought the consulting services unit of Ernst & Young), IBM Global Services, CSC, and Unisys. They are spin-offs of the Big 5, such as EYT, who broke free of Ernst & Young in 2000, setting up a consulting services business, an ASP, and a hardware/software reselling business. All in all, though, they are characterized by hundreds of millions or billions of dollars of revenue, thousands of technology consultants, an end-to-end service offering, and premier expertise at a premium price. Some of them, for reasons revealed in Chapter 16, are superb. Some aren't. If you want specific good companies, check out Chapter 16, where I identify, for reasons explained there, the best integrators.

Since the big guys are pricier, why would a company want to go with them? It'll cost more without a doubt and perhaps even take longer.

Besides, they might be using some of the personnel from the smaller CRM companies and just passing them through.

There are several good reasons. Table 15-1 outlines the strengths and weaknesses of each type of company.

Table 15-1: The Pluses and Minuses of Small and Large CRM Consulting Services Companies

Small Consulting Company	Large Consulting Company
Pricing is considerably cheaper.	Pricing is expensive.
Staff augmentation services readily available.	Staff augmentation rarely available.
Hungrier for business—more flexible terms, willing to negotiate to win the business.	Fixed pricing schedules, set methodologies, often inflexible in terms, though attempting to be more nimble in the twenty-first century.
Post-implementation maintenance not usually part of the plan.	Post-implementation maintenance more likely than in small company.
Specifically vendor/partner-focused or niche-market focused. Strategic consulting not usually a service offered.	End-to-end services including vendor-neutral strategic consulting, reducing the need for multiple companies.
Significant problems handling midstream personnel changes, if they occur.	Very large services organizations that can handle midstream personnel changes.
Generally fewer and smaller implementation experiences.	Solid implementation experience that leads to a consistent methodology, often reducing implementation times (in its best moments) and stabilizing change management processes.
Size works well for the midmarket and small market companies, due to the experience of being one.	Best suited for large enterprises or the upper end of the CRM midmarket, which, according to definition, could amount to a $1 billion revenue company.
Best on time and materials projects. Fixed price projects are not the forte of the small company, though this should not be construed as a blanket statement.	Can do fixed price, fixed term contracts very well, with statements of work that can be exceptionally detailed and parameters that are well defined.
Project management skills are limited for the smaller companies in this range.	Varied, but potentially excellent project management skills.
Will partner to do the job, if necessary.	Will partner to do the job, if necessary.

As you can see, the larger companies have experience and depth on their side. You pay for it, but it is in your interest to do so if you are a large enterprise or a large midmarket company. If you are small or on the lesser-sized end of the midmarket, it might pay for you to consider a smaller company.

A lot of the same questions you put to the small company apply to the larger consultancy. There are a few more you have to decide upon as well:

How is the project management going to be handled? This is almost a matter of preference on your part. The largest consultancies will bring their project managers with them on the project, especially if it's a fixed price. Their project manager will see to it that the project is completed in a timely fashion, because if it isn't, the consultancy eats the remainder of the cost, which is devoutly *not* to be wished by the consultancy. The good project manager is a specialist in three things: relationships with the customer, bringing fixed price projects in at budget or under, and—related to the other two—change management. This means you should interview the project manager to see whether you're going to get along with him or her as you move forward through the project. One thing is definite: There are going to be very rocky periods where you will not be happy with something going on. The project manager becomes the pivotal individual in these situations, so you'd better be sure that this PM is your person of choice before anything gets started.

What about the statement of work and the change management process? This has been the doom of many a project. I participated in an implementation of a large ERP package at a fairly small agency that had a clearly defined statement of work, but an undefined change management process. My company had submitted a fixed price bid to the client. The vendor was doing the project management, due to unusual terms in the vendor contract, though my company did the actual project. The project manager committed to a midstream (in the middle of the statement of work deliverables) product upgrade for free to the customer, without our direct knowledge or participation in the change and commitment process. The change screwed up the completion of the project and cost my company nearly a six-figure amount because there was no clear change management process that said midstream upgrades, well outside the scope of the statement of work, are an additional cost that will affect the time. Consequently, there was a considerable amount of acrimony, though we, in good faith to the customer, did the midstream upgrade. The project finished roughly two months behind schedule, since the upgrade was not a small task. While this may seem to be a benefit to you as a customer—after all, a free upgrade—this is actually a major problem because of the friction and delays in getting up and running. So query the consultancy representatives on how they handle change management. It may save you a fortune later.

Who makes up the proposed project team? Often, the larger consultancies will take advantage of the smaller consultancies' willingness to do staff augmentation work and will augment their project teams with small company consultants or independent contractors. This isn't necessarily bad, if the technical and social skills of the contractor or small company consultants are good. It's just better to know up front and make your decisions with full knowledge. After all, this is likely to be an expensive and long-term vendor, especially as CRM goes from competitive advantage to business necessity.

Are there partners involved? If there is an RFP issued by the soliciting company, the response will often include a partner or two because they can round out the holes in the necessary skill sets. Having partners is not a bad thing, but it is an additional factor for you to consider, since the partner's company comes into the mix for compatibility.

None of these questions are overkill for the small consultancy doing staff augmentation or a smaller CRM implementation or the large consultancy doing a major project. Keep in mind that your decision making can literally mean your promotion or your dismissal. It can mean the difference between a successful, productive company and a counterproductive collapse. ERP failures are notorious, with hundreds of millions of dollars lost in failed implementations. All of a sudden, these questions seem important, don't they?

The Application Service Provider (ASP)

A year and a half ago, the ASPs merited an entire chapter in this book. It was a high-flying market and something that people were interested in intensely. But, sadly, the ASP model hasn't succeeded very well, and ASPs have gone as cold as they were once hot. However, there are several, such as Surebridge, which have succeeded in this market, and the ASP model is a viable alternative, with a great deal of care applied. It has a present and a future, despite its rocky past.

Put simply, an ASP is a company that hosts a software application and rents it out for a monthly fee. The basic value proposition of an

ASP is twofold: firstly, to outsource the headaches and expenses associated with managing a business application, thereby allowing its customers to free up resources for more strategic initiatives; secondly, to enable its customers to conserve capital by paying a monthly service fee instead of having to make the large up-front expenditures required to bring enterprise business applications on line. The economies of scale that an ASP can leverage for their customers are dramatic. Most companies simply can't afford to implement the levels of redundancy, reliability, and security. By using an ASP, even the smallest businesses can gain access to leading business applications and what are often world-class information system infrastructures.

Like any important decision, choosing whether to use ASPs for your business starts by taking a high-level overview of their advantages and disadvantages. The value proposition of an ASP is targeted mostly toward small to midsize companies. ASPs give your business access to leading business applications, implemented rapidly and painlessly, deployed on what is likely to be a world-class infrastructure, supported by a fully staffed, remote IT department, all for one fixed monthly fee. That sounds like a dream come true for smaller businesses, and it could be. But life is a series of tradeoffs, and ASPs are no exception. Following are the basic advantages and disadvantages that need to be contemplated before deciding to use an ASP.

Advantages

Why should you support an ASP with your hard-earned dollars? Here are some compelling reasons to do so:

Rapid implementation ASPs implement the same products on the same platform over and over again. This enables them to become extremely proficient at this task, even to the point of being able to automate the most repetitive parts of the process. Because the implementations all happen within the ASP's data center, certain application components can be predeployed and/or shared among multiple applications, to further reduce the human effort and total time required for the implementation.

Lower cost of entry and ownership ASPs rent applications for a monthly fee. This enables their customers to defer the large capital expenditures traditionally required to bring applications on line. Because ASPs are able to leverage tremendous economies of scale by centralizing and sharing resources such as network connectivity, hardware, software, facilities, and human resources, they are able to pass additional savings on to customers and still maintain substantial profit margins.

Reduced people headaches Let's face it, good people are difficult to find, difficult to recruit, and even more difficult to retain. This has always been true, but never as prominent a problem as in today's IT job market. ASPs directly address this business pain point by effectively outsourcing their customer's IT department, or at least the part of the IT department required to manage each respective application.

Availability Most ASPs advertise 24/7/365 uptime for their customer's applications. To put it another way, "online all the time." This is typically backed up by a service level agreement (SLA), which essentially guarantees that your systems stay up and running or you start getting portions of your money back. This is an especially significant guarantee for mission-critical applications. Try convincing an internal IT staff to start paying their salaries back if the systems they manage experience downtime!

Scalability The very nature of the ASP business requires that they use high-performance, scalable technologies. Leading ASPs have invested millions of dollars to develop a scalable infrastructure because they must be ready to accommodate the needs of the new economy's companies. Because it is already in place, all customers small and large get to enjoy the same world-class infrastructure.

Disadvantages

Why shouldn't you support an ASP with your hard-earned dollars? Reasons here are compelling, too:

Limited choices ASPs typically provide a very limited number of brands when it comes to applications. They are forced to do this if they are going to be able to produce repeatable, scalable results. For example, Surebridge keeps its offering focused on PeopleSoft CRM, so if a customer wants another brand they have to find another ASP, which can be difficult in 2002, due to the large number of ASP failures. Because most ASPs are completely reliant on the marketing efforts of the actual software vendors to drive brand loyalty, they are likely to host only the products with greatest market share. These products are not always the best solution for a customer's business problem—just the safest bet for the ASP.

Integration with other applications Because ASP applications are hosted outside the enterprise, integration with other enterprise apps becomes challenging. Even though actual data connectivity between the enterprise and the ASP can be reasonably robust, the fact that the applications (and the experts who manage them) are not part of the enterprise's core IT function makes integration efforts more complex.

Security For all practical purposes, data held at an ASP is very safe—arguably safer than data held within an enterprise because ASPs must go to extreme measures to protect information in a multi-tenant environment. However, discomfort still exists with many CIOs and IT managers because not only their jobs, but the viability of their company depends on the safety of enterprise data. Simply stated, no matter how you slice it, if the data is located off-site as it is with an ASP, it is outside their direct sphere of control.

Connectivity If an application is operating within the enterprise, it would take a LAN failure to break connectivity to the application. LAN technology is very stable, and in the event a problem does occur, it can be fixed directly by the enterprise. When using an ASP, there are several more variables introduced into the communication loop, including telecom companies. And everyone knows that if there is a problem with a telecom company, you are 100 percent at their mercy and the fix will not be quick!

In summary, for most small to medium-sized businesses, the advantages of an ASP can outweigh the disadvantages—sometimes. ASPs outsource the "low value" work, allowing smaller companies to focus their limited resources on more strategic initiatives that create competitive advantage and drive revenue. For larger enterprises, the use of ASPs is likely to be very limited.

The choices for service provider are extensive. Vendor, consulting services, outsourcing, ASP, small firm, or large firm—each has merits, each its own disadvantages. Find the appropriate provider for your particular company. Hopefully, this chapter can help you do that. In the next chapter, I'll give you my choices for the best of breed in each service provider category so that not only can you make a good choice on the type of company, but also the choice of which specific companies might be a good fit.

16

The CRM Service Providers: They Play in the Sandbox, Too

One truism for the world of information technology is, where there are software applications, there are service providers. Not only are there service providers, but probably about five gazillion service providers for each piece of significant software. Unfortunately, many of those providers aren't that great at what they do. Pretenders abound in the service provider industry—body shops that just push people without regard to talent or skills. So-called integrators who do a poor job cheaply are easily available, too. When choosing a service provider, you have to be even more careful than when selecting a vendor. Especially since services—including implementation and maintenance, or strategic consulting services—are often between double and triple the price of the actual software applications you've just bought for ungodly amounts of dollars.

What makes this even scarier is that the good and bad providers are nonexistent in the eyes of the CRM beholders. A survey on CRM brand leadership was released in December 2001 by the Information Technology Services Marketing Association (ITSMA). The results were amazing and a bit disheartening. Nearly 50 percent of the respondents surveyed could not even name a single CRM service provider. The ones mentioned by the other 50 percent were Accenture, IBM Global Services, and Siebel (as a service provider!), only one of which is among the five key players I mention in this chapter. The respondents were executives using or planning on using CRM.

Part of what I intend to do in this chapter is to begin to rectify this appalling lack of visibility. From now on, I am going to be identifying the good CRM service providers according to the set of criteria I outline in the following pages. Next time ITSMA does its branding survey, hopefully, the respondents won't think branding is just for cattle.

CRM = Very Personal Interactions and Technology

CRM is the most intensely personal of all the so-called technology-related systems because it involves human interactions on the front end continuously, and it has a definitive metric that, minimally, is different things to different people. The metric is often nearly intangible. It is "customer satisfaction." There are ways of quantifying this, but what a company defines as "satisfaction" is as personal as the culture of the company and as individual as the particular single customer. This is why personalization remains so high on the list of things to do in CRM. What also remains high on that list is a personal corporate culture and vision that are coherent with what the ideals of a CRM company should be.

The key concept here is cultural alignment, which in this particular instance means "practice what you preach." If the culture of the particular service provider is not particularly CRM-friendly and they are selling some part of CRM, when problems arise, they won't be solved. Why? Because the service provider won't care once the sale is made. There are unfortunately so many service providers in this category that the notion of service becomes a joke. They probably should be called sale providers. That said, there are also thousands of very good service providers who do care and are true to their genre.

Criteria for Selection of the Other Playmates

In this chapter, I present the service providers that I consider the best. My criteria for liking or disliking a vendor or service provider include the following:

Corporate culture How well does the service provider interact with their customers? How well do they treat their employees? Are their employees compensated for making sure their customers are happy? What is their customer retention rate like? Their employee turnover rate? What do their employees say about the company? What kind of density of long-term employees does the company have? How do they treat employees in adverse circumstances? What is the evidence of their general ethics and business approach? What kind of vision does senior management have for the company and the CRM practice? How does the culture encourage customer participation? What do customers say about their relationship to the company?

CRM leadership Does the service provider have good people at the CRM helm? "Good" here means that the leadership encourages other leaders from the ranks, rewards innovation, and allows risk. It also means that not only do they align the vision of the CRM practice with the corporate vision, but also with the more universal vision of the ideal that CRM can provide. It doesn't mean perfection or idealism—just that the fundamental principles of the practice are coherent with CRM in principle. The respect of their peers, their competitors, the CRM practice staff, and of others in the CRM world is also an important part of this criterion.

Strategy What is their high-level strategy for the coming years? Is it coherent with the trends in the marketplace? How does it compare to the other service providers' strategies?

Approach How do they approach a potential engagement? What do they do to win that engagement? How flexible are they? Are they humble or arrogant? While the latter sounds strange, it is an important differentiator, since there are many arrogant players in this otherwise customer-friendly market. What is their methodology? Are there differentiators in their approach?

Offering What is the depth and breadth of their offering? Are there any differentiators here? Do they ever do work that may not be profitable for them but is good for the customer? In other words, for reasons that would make sense, are they willing to be flexible in their offering? What kind of verticals do they represent? More importantly, what kind of subject matter expertise is onboard for those verticals?

Partners This is less who they partner with and more how well they partner. Are they a partner-focused company? Do they actually work with their partners and return value? What do their partners say about them?

Quality of their work Customer satisfaction raises its head here: if customers I've spoken with informally but systematically over the past year or so are happy. Most of the customers I would categorize as satisfied are happy because the provider did something like come in under budget or in a shorter time than expected, had fabulous follow-up, the metrics identified in the planning phase were met, or there was some other quantifiable reason to be happy. The customer was happy because the service provider did something that satisfied some need determined by the customer's culture, vision, mission, and behavior.

This is not the complete list of criteria, but should give you a sense of my direction. A complete list is available if you email me at either of the email addresses in the introduction.

I've chosen five firms as the most important service providers. They are given the most coverage in this chapter. Additionally, I'm naming other firms that are solid, good firms, but not as substantial in size or scope. There are some that are representative of a certain genre. However, the five I name are the most significant CRM service providers with the widest scope and geographic reach.

Most CRM services companies offer pretty much the same types of services. They are almost all implementation specialists, strategic experts, outsourcers, or consultants. They compete with each other for your dollars, and their categorical offerings are not that different, really. The criteria that I used to make my choices are those differentiators that should be considerations, which go along with price and commitment. But even on the issues of price, the impact of corporate philosophy can't be discounted. There are service providers who don't negotiate price, and there are service providers who do.

How does your company choose a CRM service provider? Do you only consider the price, the offering, the functionality to be provided, and the response to the proposal on paper? Or do you also want to meet the principals involved in person, so that you have confidence in them and their ability to execute on the paper commitments? Ultimately, it is who you trust that tips the scales when all things are otherwise equal.

The following are my choices for the service providers I trust, given everything I've learned about them from my reading, interacting directly with them, speaking with their partners and clients over time, and soliciting opinions from other CRM industry leaders. They all have successful track records, a few failures, appealing cultures, thorough offerings, well-defined vision, strategy and direction, and are, for the most part, what they say they are. They are hype minimalists, though they market like everyone else. On the more general side, each of them is also a useful representative of the "Light Speed CRM best of class." I'm not saying any of these companies or people are perfect. They don't have the biggest CRM practices by comparison to some of their competitors. They don't even necessarily have the strongest traction in their specific domains. They are being recommended because they meet the criteria I used to pick the best. There are others to choose from which might be better for you than these. But generally, I don't think so.

Integrators

These are the group of companies that fit the "XXL" size in offering and staff. The integrators are those companies who can provide enterprise-wide IT services from the back to the front office. They normally shy away from outsourcing due to the hardware and maintenance sides, which they don't ordinarily want to do. This isn't to say they never do it, but they focus on strategy through implementation, integration, and upgrade. They have highly professional services organizations, often numbering in the thousands, that are part of the CRM practice. They often have very strong vertical practices that crisscross with the CRM practice so that subject matter expertise is always available in the designated domain. For example, KPMG Consulting has a media and entertainment practice that handles Oracle, PeopleSoft, and other enterprise applications, in both the back and front office. Integrators have carefully chosen vendor partnerships that are appropriate to their CRM strategy. They tend to the larger CRM vendors such as Siebel because of the size of the engagements they've sold. Their general advantages and disadvantages are discussed in Chapter 15.

KPMG Consulting (www.kpmgconsulting.com)

Imagine a company that was in the CRM business before CRM existed as such. That is KPMG Consulting. They have been doing this since 1989 and doing it extraordinarily well. If you look at the cover of *Darwin* magazine's March 2002 issue, you will see an article highlighted called "Boise Beats the Odds," about the Boise Cascade Office Products CRM project (One Boise), a highly successful CRM project and a Gartner Excellence Award winner in 2001. One of the Boise Cascade project benefits: a cost savings of $3.5 million per year. KPMG Consulting did this.

This is no surprise, really. They are one of the few CRM service providers that actually practice what they preach, which is particularly noticeable in the world of the Big 5 consulting firms. I've worked with many of the Big 5 and their Big 6 and Big 8 pre-mergers predecessors.

Several of them I will never work with again because of their corporate culture, which says to make partner, you must take advantage of everything and everyone you can, including your customers, external partners, fellow employees, and so on. Revenue counts. Being honorable counts only if it gets you somewhere. This is the culture of the shark's world. While there are many good people at those companies, these cultures are driven purely by revenue numbers and have no heart. This would be considered an understatement by many. Sadly, this is the ethical composition of several of the Big 5. Need I say "Enron"? If you are going to sell CRM, your corporate cultural personality matters. I can unequivocally say that, while KPMG Consulting demands revenue success, they don't forget the prime directive—both ethically and for business reasons, it is essential to work well with partners and customers. For simple human reasons, your employees matter. KPMG Consulting holds to very high standards.

KPMG Consulting did over $500 million in CRM revenue alone in 2001, nearly 17 percent of their global revenue. They have a CRM practice with a staff of around 1,500, but they draw on the cross-practice expertise of many other groups within the company, based on the expertise the client needs. They serve 72 of the Fortune 100, and 318 of the Fortune 1000. Their clients remain loyal enough to them to show revenue increases from existing clients of 33 percent in a year. They had a 100 percent retention rate of their top 50 customers and a 96 percent retention rate of their top 150 clients. That means that KPMG Consulting not only has the metrics for customer lifetime value down pat, they also have an understanding of the real value of a customer. Good show.

Vision, Strategy, and Direction

KPMG Consulting's vision, strategy, and direction are guided by Bruce Culbert, senior vice-president and CRM Global Practice Leader. Mr. Culbert, a former IBM Global Services vice-president of ebusiness, encapsulates their vision, strategy, and direction in what KPMG Consulting calls Enterprise Value Creation (EVC). "It requires a relentless commitment to knowing the customer, creating value for that customer, while flawlessly delivering results quickly and incrementally driven by ROI," says Mr. Culbert. While that standard of perfection is ordinarily only achieved in the world of marketing, KPMG Consulting uses the EVC framework to get as close to that as they can.

Lots of companies have "value frameworks." This one is different. EVC is the actual integration of demand chain and supply chain management.

It is a set of tools, insights, best practices, methodologies, and techniques that combines with well-researched company-specific analysis. What makes this framework particularly effective is that KPMG Consulting merged their CRM and supply chain management (SCM) practices so that the framework and the practice were entirely convergent. The investment into this framework is ongoing and dense. Detailed research on 11,000 companies and 27 different market segments goes on around the clock. Additionally, because the CRM practice has been around for 13 years as of 2002, there is a big knowledge base and multiple tools for determining value prior to a CRM project. There are ROI scorecards, business case tools, you name it. It takes into account the necessary changes to the corporate culture that CRM demands for its business success. EVC provides KPMG Consulting's frame for direction and strategy, and is itself defined by the CRM practice's vision.

Using EVC means beginning an engagement by developing a Value Impact Analysis and doing what KPMG Consulting calls Value Chain Blueprinting. These are long-term strategies for both business revenue and shareholder value. This is then applied to a templated Value Realization Roadmap that segments the overall strategy into six-month (or less) phases. Each phase has attached metrics and tracks back to the plan's ROI through the use of the CRM Scorecard. The result is incremental deliverables within the context of long-term strategy so that the ultimate win isn't obscured. When successful, these small wins lead to the big Kahuna. Stockholders and stakeholders can see victories, which makes them a lot happier.

Approach and Offering

EVC drives the actual CRM solutions offering of KPMG Consulting, called Connect to Customer. The purpose of Connect to Customer is to solve problems and drive revenue by creating what KPMG Consulting calls Relationship Equity—valuable, personalized customer experiences that become revenue and profit via "improved" customer behavior.

EVC-driven solutions are offered by KPMG Consulting in the following segments:

- CRM Strategy
- SFA
- PRM or Channel Management
- EMA

▶ Call Center/CIC

▶ Customer Care and Billing

These are classic CRM divisions; very clean, traditional offerings. There is absolutely no doubt about what they are. But the offering goes deeper. What you will see with all of the five providers I discuss in this chapter is that they have strong vertical specialties. Look at them carefully. They will matter in your selection of a provider. When you are in the midst of your provider selection, ask about the subject matter expertise that they actually have onboard in those verticals. This can make or break the success of your implementation. KPMG Consulting shows well in their verticals because they provide industry-specific assets developed with their experience in each of the verticals. Table 16-1 outlines examples of these assets.

Table 16-1: Examples of KPMG Consulting's Industry-Specific Assets

Vertical	Industry-Specific Assets
Insurance	Claims solutions models; GLB/Privacy Response (Gramm-Leach-Bliley Act 1999 privacy response standard)
Banking	Wealth management ; financial advisor managed services; GLB/Privacy Response
Retail	E-Channel (storefronts); wireless; point of sale solution
High Tech	Configurators
Public Sector	Homeland security; service to the citizen

Other verticals they specialize in include:

▶ Utilities

▶ Process and discrete manufacturing

▶ Healthcare

▶ Services

▶ Transportation

▶ Education

▶ Telecommunications

▶ Pharmaceuticals

Even with this large and yet distinct, highly specialized set of offerings, delivering on the offering is the real objective, despite the exciting choice at the smorgasbord. This means that KPMG Consulting has to execute. Successful delivery by KPMG Consulting standards involves client acceptance, which means the users are going to use it and the senior management is happy about that. In turn, the CFO is happy because the project was on time and on budget, and the ROI scorecard benchmarks have been met. KPMG Consulting can leave the engagement happy that the knowledge has become part of the customer's brains and databases. This then means customer satisfaction and 96 percent top-150 customer retention rates.

CRM Partners

KPMG Consulting has one of the more complex alliance structures of my top five, probably only outdone by IBM Global Services. They have four alliance levels (Strategic, Preferred, Emerging, and Complementary) and three by type (Software, Hardware, and Strategy). The category criteria are determined by size of the partner, revenue share, revenue impact projected by KPMG Consulting, mutual resource commitments, mindshare, and repeatable successes. Table 16-2 outlines the 2002 selected alliances.

Table 16-2: The KPMG Consulting Partner Matrix

Category	Software Partner	Hardware Partner	Strategy Partner
Strategic	Siebel, Oracle CRM, PeopleSoft CRM, SAP CRM		
Preferred	KANA, E.piphany, Amdocs Clarify (informal)		
Emerging	Comergent, Port, Interwoven, Vignette, Selectica		Peppers & Rogers Center for Data Insight (informal)
Complementary	Microsoft	Cisco, Hewlett-Packard, Compaq	

What makes this partner grid interesting is that KPMG Consulting manages to perform well with all of it. They are a Gold Star Distinction Siebel Partner with a 2001 growth rate of 300 percent in their Siebel business; they are Oracle CRM's number 1 partner; same for KANA; same for E.piphany. That is quite the partner-centric track record.

Culture

By 2004, KPMG Consulting has to change its name and return the KPMG name to the original accounting firm. In the course of that hunt for a name (anyone out there have suggestions?), the firm that KPMG Consulting hired to find the brand did a survey of customers and others on brand attributes. Paraphrased, the question asked was, "What characteristics do you associate with KPMG Consulting?" What came back was indicative of the rather different corporate culture of this Big 5 firm. Overwhelmingly, customers said that they were "good people" who "cared about the customers" and were "a pleasure to work with."

Bruce Culbert is a good representative of his company in that regard. He gets it right when he says, "While we have business goals that have to be delivered, I'm dealing every day with real people who have real lives. I can't ever take that for granted." He doesn't, and that reflects in the quality of their CRM practice. Those high customer retention rates come from somewhere.

They have a significant amount of their former clients as employees, which tells you something about their customer satisfaction levels and their commitments to it.

I've had many years of experience working with KPMG Consulting in many venues. They have always been highly professional, responsive, not at all concerned with status, driven by their objectives, yet mindful of who they are dealing with. One personal experience is reflective of this.

I wrote a book on PeopleSoft several years back that needed a lot of technical input. I was working with several of the Big 5 on business projects, not related to CRM, that gave me input. I put the word out to my Big 5 partners that I needed help on the book. The only ones who responded were KPMG Consulting, and they responded far beyond what the benefit to them might have been. They set up a team of people coordinated by a marketing manager who gave me eight chapters in a timely manner so that the book could meet publication dates. There was some direct business benefit to them, but not nearly to the level they responded. They told me that I and the company I was working for during that time were good partners and they simply wanted to help by way of thanks. That's what I call a corporate culture. The same efforts, both larger and smaller, are replicated throughout this fine company. Even ex-employees I spoke with for this book over the last year or so had nothing but good to say. I only hope that this is the way I'm remembered. This company sure is.

KPMG Consulting: Summary

As of 2002, KPMG Consulting's CRM practice is now in the highest position of the upper-right quadrant of the Gartner Group's Magic Quadrant. That says volumes, according to Gartner's criteria. My criteria would have them in my upper-right quadrant if I had such a thing. Their culture, quality, and strength speak volumes.

Deloitte Consulting (www.dc.com)

Deloitte Consulting is a member in good standing in the consulting world. Partner to many and a highly respected, honorable institution, it is one of the premier CRM service providers in the world with 34 member practices, which is their proper way of saying practices in 34 locations globally. They serve their clientele well.

Vision, Strategy, and Direction

This service provider shows its strong financial roots in its vision, straight from the CRM practice's mouth:

> We believe the only CRM projects worth doing are the ones that directly create shareholder value. Our focus is to be the best CRM consulting firm in the world at working with clients to create shareholder value.

True to this perspective, they hire staff to that end, invest toward that end, and develop their culture toward that end. They make sure their goals are aligned with the creation of shareholder value. This is a capable, serious business approach.

Their strategy is defined by looking at how to increase revenue, given realistic factors. For example, the economy is sluggish. Therefore, cost reduction is something that companies are looking at carefully. The business case for cost reduction is easier to build than revenue enhancement, but (and this is where Deloitte Consulting differentiates itself) "reducing costs will not create a sustainable competitive advantage in the long run." They also understand that in sluggish economic periods, customer retention and revenue expansion into existing customer segments is where a company is best served. So they are able to maintain a long-term outlook while dealing with real life as it is at the given moment. This gives them a no-nonsense direction. "CRM has moved from a panacea for increasing revenue, to more targeted solutions for solving various business issues," says Steve Pratt, managing partner in charge of global CRM for Deloitte Consulting.

Approach and Offering

The DC offering in 2002 is broad and yet remains highly focused. They are aiming at investing in a number of vertical markets, including automotive, high tech manufacturing, and life sciences—the latter unique to my knowledge. They are creating a wireless industry solution.

Deloitte Consulting has a powerful set of tools that it developed to make sure there is actual shareholder value realized in a proposed project. They aren't kidding in how seriously they take this concept! They run what they call a Value Audit prior to undertaking any project to make sure there is significant value to be returned to the customer. If deficiencies show up, they are able to fix them in advance of beginning the actual project execution.

Like any other company, their partnerships have a strong impact on their package selection process. Their tendency is to recommend the partner's packaged applications, when appropriate. Keep in mind, though, that these partners are not chosen either lightly or randomly. They are value-based choices. Given the Deloitte approach to things, the CRM partners they choose are the appropriate matches. Additionally, they will go outside the partner box, if they feel it is the right thing to do for a client.

They then develop a CRM roadmap that is individualized for each client. For example, it might contain the pieces outlined in Table 16-3. They then use a number of well-established best practices and tools that have been developed to execute that roadmap. They include planning tools that can do CRM diagnostics or ROI estimation. They provide program management and industry-specific directions and maps. They have ongoing knowledge sharing and knowledge transfer as part of their methodology throughout the actual delivery of the CRM system. They handle change management and all facets of strategic and business process transformation. They will implement all the necessary technologies—including new applications, integration with legacy and third-party systems, and data warehousing and data consolidation. If it is to be a Web-architected solution, they will make sure that the Web infrastructure is in place and the appropriate wrappers are available for use of that architecture. Throughout and even more intensely in the final phases of their CRM plan, Deloitte Consulting works with the customer to internally and externally brand and market the system, so that user acceptance is high both from employees and customers.

Table 16-3: A Good Example of Deloitte Consulting's CRM Roadmap

Business Objectives	CRM Strategy	Project Plan	Business Benefits	Business Case/ Risk Analysis
Increase EBITDA	Single view of the customer	Detailed plan for design, implementation, change management, and deployment	Measurable service-level targets and operations metrics: EBITDA margin; customer satisfaction; operational cost; ARPU	Prioritized list of initiatives
Increase revenue	Segmented customer base	Cost projections for infrastructure, operations, and services	Enhanced brand	Detailed plan for design, implementation, change management, and deployment
Increase market share	Standardized customer experience	Project organization, staffing, and governance plan	Streamlined sales/marketing/ delivery processes	Cost projections for infrastructure, operations, and services
Increase subscriber growth	Personalized offers			

CRM Partners

Deloitte Consulting has a wide variety CRM and CRM-related partners. Among them:

- ▶ PeopleSoft
- ▶ SAP
- ▶ Oracle
- ▶ E.piphany
- ▶ Siebel
- ▶ Broadvision
- ▶ Vignette
- ▶ Roundarch
- ▶ IBM
- ▶ Mastek

Culture

The best description of their culture comes from Deloitte Consulting itself: "collegial." Not too formal, not too casual, highly professional. They are an award-winning company with an employee turnover rate 5 percent lower than their direct competitors. They have been one of *Fortune* magazine's "100 Best Companies to Work For" for four consecutive years. They have been officially recognized as one of the best companies for working mothers for seven consecutive years. They have won *Workforce* magazine's Optimas award as a great place to work. They are considered one of the best places to work in England (*Sunday Times* award) and Australia.

That's a lot of accolades. Why the great recognition? What kind of culture do they have that makes this happen? It is a Big 5 culture, which implies "blue blood," but their employees are anything but. They are rewarded for customer satisfaction and meritorious service. They are a consciously diverse culture that is not only ethnically diverse, but aimed at hiring, as they put it, "nice people." They are heavily focused on the business side of CRM and making sure that the value propositions that CRM provides are clearly understood. To that end, they have written a very informative and entertaining book on CRM called *How to Eat the CRM Elephant*. It is a genuinely good, simple look at CRM. They have distributed more than 25,000 copies (as of early 2002) in multiple languages. If you are interested in a copy of the book, please email me at either pgreenberg@live-wire.net or paul-greenberg3@comcast.net. I'll do what I can to secure you a copy. It is worth it.

Deloitte Consulting: Summary

Deloitte Consulting has been a significant achiever in their ability to execute their plan, the completeness of their vision, and their capacity to fulfill that vision, according to the Gartner Group. With the tools, methodology, and strategy that they can provide to clients, in combination with their collegial, diverse, and friendly culture, this is one of the best places to go when CRM is on your plate.

Outsourcers

These are companies that often began their lives as government contractors or as hardware providers and then built a substantial services organization around their hardware and software reselling business. As the years went on, they saw the profitability and value in selling services and began developing either professional services organizations or acquiring companies with specialties in services in particular domains. They never lost their hardware roots, even when services became dominant.

Having this matrix of hardware/software/services makes these kinds of companies perfect for outsourcing. They are able to handle portions of the business that a company would rather not handle. For example, Unisys is a $6 billion company that makes more than 70 percent of its revenue through services. They provide the hardware, software, and services for processing all 250 million tax returns every year. Isn't that amazing? What kind of information technology power must it take to do that? The IRS doesn't handle the processing; they handle customer service, attention to individual returns, auditing, and so on. But the basics—including input, recognition that the return has arrived, and routing the return to wherever it is supposed to go—are outsourced to and handled by Unisys processing centers. Now let's take a look at my three outsourcers.

CSC (www.csc.com)

The consulting arm of CSC is quite the player in the CRM world. As of 2002, the CSC partner and managing director of the North American CRM Practice, Steve Olyha, built and continues to build a well-directed CRM practice with a laser-like vision and approach to the marketplace.

CSC began its life in 1959 with a small contract from Honeywell to develop a business language compiler. Five years later they were a $4 million company and the first software company to be listed on a major stock exchange. They began to focus on the services side even then, moving into federal services, working to provide software, services, and hardware to the federal government, which was a wise decision.

By the 1990s, they moved into the outsourcing market, helped along by a $3 billion contract from General Dynamics. Now CSC is an outsourcing giant and is one of the Fortune 500, with deep tentacles in the government and commercial markets, with vertical specialties in financial services, healthcare, chemicals, consumer goods, and services. All that translates to a 2001 number of $11.3 billion and 68,000 employees—a very good translation, I must say.

Vision, Strategy, and Direction

CSC's CRM vision is consistent with their overall corporate vision and direction. According to Steve Olyha, they provide "a complete end-to-end solution in the CRM marketplace, utilizing a specific and finite set of strategic partners." This tightly knit statement is pretty much typical of their view of the CRM world. They have a strong market-segment-specific strategy that doesn't vary much. That way they can concentrate on providing the best possible services with a strong subject matter expertise. They not only concentrate on verticals, but segments within those vertical markets. For example, they don't concentrate on all facets of healthcare, but the medical device manufacturers of healthcare and pharmaceuticals. That's getting specific. But they go even further. Their CRM strategy is to work within their verticals to solve specific business problems. For example, working with their clients in the consumer packaged goods industry, they deal with inefficiencies to the tune of $73 billion in the handling of trade promotion management. The identification of that problem led CSC to invest in and develop an SFA solution around trade funds management, using Siebel as the front-office technology solution to support redesigned processes that deliver productivity savings. They can now go to clients with a highly developed subject matter expertise in this particular field—a rare subject matter expertise, yet one that is necessary to solve an immensely costly problem. The specific purpose of the solution is to dramatically increase the productivity of the 15 to 18 percent of the gross revenue that is typically spent by a consumer packaged goods company on trade promotion. The business case for this solution is so highly evolved that they can project a solid business proposition for cost savings of around $12 million in a billion-dollar company in the first year of its implementation. The solution itself includes trade promotion strategies, process and organization redesign, and technology selection and implementation.

Approach and Offering

The laser focus on vision, strategy, and partnerships is carried to their approach and offering. They provide CRM services to the above-mentioned consumer packaged goods industry, automotive, medical device manufacturing, and pharmaceutical companies in the healthcare vertical and have strong offerings in the financial services sector, particularly in banking. For the sales force automation side of financial services, they use Siebel. For call centers, they use KANA. End of story. It is a continuation of that incredibly powerful focus on a few markets within markets.

CSC is acutely aware that to succeed with their offering they have to make sure there is an alignment of interest between CSC and their strategic partners in the technology space. They see three facets to that alignment:

Executive level alignment Senior management must be in agreement with CSC on everything ranging from strategy to approach. They have to be comfortable with the time and effort that is required for the relationship, and willing to make the appropriate investments. They have to be comfortable with the cultural alignment between the two organizations. They have to be comfortable with the teams that are doing the work. So far, this isn't a new idea or anything different.

Joint development activities This one is different. In order for a joint relationship to have competitive differentiation, which drives win rates and margin, partners must be willing to invest in creating market-segment-specific solutions (for example, the Consumer Goods trade promotion solution or the development of the new "311" solution for state and local governments with PeopleSoft). It is critical that this joint development also drive the speed of implementation and the garnering of business results more quickly than trying to build a new solution multiple times across multiple segments every time an engagement is won.

Regional relationships Another differentiator. CSC places a strong premium on having regional relationships in the territory of their vendor partners. For example, if they are focusing on the public sector with PeopleSoft as the partner, they are going to know the regional staff of PeopleSoft in that geography. No matter who you know at the national level, they aren't going to help you with a problem in the region. If CSC is working with a customer on a PeopleSoft implementation in Atlanta, Georgia, they will know the PeopleSoft Southeast organization, not Craig Conway, president and CEO of PeopleSoft.

CSC's win rate is high because they ask the questions that are germane to a good business case. They find the potential business value, develop an ROI model, and then build that business case. But embedded in that process is one other question. They ask (seriously), "Who will lose their job if this doesn't work?" A rarely asked question, it identifies the politics of the customer and how the firing line is set up. Politics should always be a concern for a vendor or service provider. If it isn't, then they aren't concerned with how your company works. CSC is.

CRM Partners

These are the current primary CRM partners, though as of spring 2002, there was some dancing going on with a couple of other CRM vendors.

- ► Siebel

- ► KANA

- ► PeopleSoft

- ► SAP

Culture

They are very proud of their corporate culture and they have the right to be. In a segment of the IT world that has 25 to 40 percent personnel turnover as a regular feature (consulting services, not CRM), CSC's CRM practice has a less than 5 percent annualized turnover! That is comparable to what I said about SAS in Chapter 8—a remarkable achievement that is almost mind-boggling and is consistent, not just a one-time event. Five percent is almost beyond comprehension in a world of customer loyalty mavens who are emphatically not employee-loyal.

How do they do that? They took a unique approach to building the CRM practice. They found many of their folks outside the consulting world. Says Mr. Olyha:

> Consultants are not ordinarily great people managers. We needed to copy a culture of success in a people environment, a real operating environment.

This meant not only recruiting from beyond the consulting pale, but also, once recruited, paying attention to those they did employ.

Simple things such as extreme attention to performance reviews were implemented to make sure that the employees realized they would be rewarded for improvements and good execution, rather than ignored. Town hall meetings to discuss innovations or air grievances or to just get together for a good old-fashioned blab session were not only encouraged, but scheduled and carried out by management.

It also meant paying attention to each individual. I think we can all recall a personal kindness or two done by an employer, which was unexpected. It remains with you. Sending flowers for a triumphant or grief-stricken occasion is something easy to do, but not done enough in the IT world. CSC does it.

The business benefit of this type of culture is enormous. As with SAS, the training costs are lower because CSC is not constantly training new employees. But there is much more to it. This is a true case of how the culture can affect the client side.

Adds Mr. Olyha:

> When I'm with a client, my likeability meter goes on and I carry it in front of my heart all the time. When it boils down to it, the clients make the decisions on two criteria. Can you do the work and do I want to work with you? That's about it.

When you buy the application (or the services), you buy the vendor (and its culture). CSC is a good purchase.

CSC: Summary

CSC has a powerful vertical strategy for CRM. If you are one of their verticals and have any interest in CRM, they are a clear winner in the categories. If you are not particularly in their targeted domains, but are looking at outsourcing some of your CRM applications, talk to them anyway. If you are simply looking at how to go about it, all with CRM, try to persuade them to talk to you. They have a lot to say and a lot to give.

Unisys (www.unisys.com)

A few years ago, if you thought of Unisys, you would have thought, "Government contractor; hardware; big." A few years ago, you would have been right. You're still right, but now you can add services, e-business, and CRM to your initial thoughts. Seventy-four percent of their business is services now. They are a strapping $6 billion–plus company and a rising star in the CRM world. Their clients range widely across the government and commercial sectors. As of 2002, they are something very good to be associated with.

Vision, Strategy, and Direction

The Unisys vision and strategy is, on the surface, strikingly similar to some of the other service providers discussed here. It closely ties their CRM solutions offerings to vertical expertise. But it diverges dramatically when you look a bit further. They interpret this vertical vision and strategy as building solutions on top of what they are already doing— in other words, approaching their installed base with CRM solutions.

For some companies, this could be a dangerous road because their installed base just isn't enough. Remember that word "big"? With Unisys, this is a stroke of real intelligence. Let's just take a look at what they are already doing in more than 100 countries:

- They handle 200 airlines, including 18 of the top 25 airlines.

- Their clients include 85 percent of traditional cargo carriers. Unisys provides 36 percent of air freight waybill processing worldwide.

- Customers include 41 of the top 50 world banks.

- Fifty percent of the world's insurers are customers.

- Unisys processes 50 percent of the world's checks.

- Nine of the top ten telecommunications companies are clients, and Unisys handles 18 percent of world voice messaging and 30 billion voice/data messages a year.

- Unisys processes 250 million income tax returns a year.

- They have 1,500 federal, state, and local government agencies as clients.

- They service more than 200 newspapers in 18 countries.

That ought to keep them busy for a while! Obviously, working with just their installed base is something that any company could envy.

They already have great vertical strengths in financial services, communications, and commercial media such as publishing, transportation, and the public sector. In each sector, Unisys can provide a multiplicity of channels that can be used to deliver their CRM implementations, ranging from traditional client-run production environments to ASP-like environments, to full-blown outsourcing. Not only do they have solutions, but they have the hardware, software, and services to provide a full service end-to-end direction and maintenance over a lifetime.

Approach and Offering

The profound commitment to knowledge internally leads to some very innovative approaches to CRM by Unisys. One of the singular practices that seems exclusive to Unisys takes place in the planning stages of CRM. It is an executive level "scenario building" workshop. It is a fascinating meta-approach that has harvested excellent results.

Where it differs from traditional approaches to strategic visioning is in its use of modeling and trends that doesn't rely solely on deductive analysis of past trends for the interpretation. The idea is not to come up with forecasts on how CRM will affect something, but to determine how CRM will need to be positioned or approached considering specific "shaping factors" that are influenced by world events, global business, and societal patterns. In short, it's an inductive process that allows for the development of contextual business models where CRM can be applied. For example, how would CRM apply to the airlines industry and how could it be leveraged to deal with the likely irritation of customers who are slowed by increased security in the wake of the September 11 terrorist attacks? When a specific scenario emerges and opportunities for the use of CRM get identified, then the session moves to the next step that includes facilitating the discussion on how the client organization is positioned to address the scenario. The CRM strategic plan and the implementation plan follow, should the executive participants decide to move to match their organizational vision to the scenario they created. These scenario-building sessions are dynamic and are facilitated by a specialized team of Unisys personnel, led by Michael Chuchmuch, Global Director of Strategic Planning and the associate dean of the Unisys Corporate University. A session in early 2002 in Australia comprised of about 25 senior management members from Australian companies came to the conclusion, despite the disparate industries represented, that while working on their customer service initiatives, they weren't getting true customer input. None of them had realized this until the session. This process is dynamic, interactive, and based on creative transactions among the participants. It leads to CRM contracts for Unisys and solves problems. This is true win/win.

Unisys has developed an interesting twist on a strategic approach. Once the scenario building has been completed and there is a potential customer for their CRM work, they do a large amount of what I would call parallel planning, working on both a long-term strategy and a short-term pain cure as they move through their examination of the customer's capabilities.

Everything begins with interactive sessions and education on CRM involving senior management and other stakeholders. When Unisys is satisfied that these have served their purpose, they begin a value assessment.

They call their approach to this value assessment Customer Value Management (CVM). One of the early steps in their approach is to determine what Unisys calls the "differentiators," those wants and needs that, if understood and fulfilled, would make the customer happy and accomplish customer objectives and goals. These are derived from the likely actual users of the system, not just the senior management or internal decision makers. For example, they might talk to call center operatives or marketing and sales professionals about what they would need. Once that is done, Unisys begins reviews of the operational performance of customer segments, related services, and the profitability of those services. Then they define needed enterprise capabilities (processes) and required enablers (technology, organization, and investments) to meet the customer's desired outcomes.

This is a very complex process because there is a weighting of interactions going on throughout the process. Dick Frederickson, the Unisys CRM Managing Principal, identified it well as working with a "combination of perception and classic customer segmentation" to "find those high value moments of truth," that is, the most important and sustaining interactions. To get to that point, there is an intense due diligence built into the CVM process, because the customer must understand the difference between perception and reality at the company. If they don't, there will be a rough disconnect at some point later in the process.

Once that is all done, there can be a strongly directed scoping of the project. Typically, customers want to deploy things because they can, not because they should. The CVM process provides the introduction of structure and thus, allows the scoping to be more accurate. The scoping process is the first step in the definition of a CRM strategy for the client company. It asks, "Are there broken things that can be fixed through a low-risk deployment while the larger enterprise strategy is being defined, implemented, continuously assessed, and redefined?" The easiest and lowest risk effort is a solution for those points of pain. The way that Unisys incorporates this interesting hybrid perspective is by moving to solve problems that can be quick fixes—cured in 60 days. So there are tactical solutions being implemented and confidence being built while the enterprise-wide strategy is being executed. For example, in one case while Unisys was beginning an enterprise-wide call center CRM project, they found there was a big capacity overload issue at the customer. They decided to implement a Workforce Management solution as an interim solution while the bigger picture was being painted. The interim solution dealt with the pain domain, but stayed within the confines of the overall strategic plan.

CRM Partners

Their current partner list is select, small, and aimed at call center and customer interaction center (CIC) work. If you look at the above list of their clients, it becomes apparent why that is the case.

▶ Siebel

- ▶ Avaya

- ▶ Cisco

- ▶ Genesys

- ▶ I3 (Interactive Intelligence, Inc.) (Note: This company is also CIC-focused through their interaction management applications.)

They also work with PeopleSoft, Oracle, and SAP on a case-by-case basis.

Culture

Unisys has a fascinating corporate culture. Apparently, 87 percent of their employees agree with me here, since they responded positively to an internal survey done by Unisys on that culture. To Unisys's credit, they are taking the complaints of the other 13 percent to heart and working to solve those issues.

What makes Unisys so interesting? They are the single most knowledge-focused corporate culture I've run across in a long time. They are adamantly committed to the consistent upgrading and training of their consultants employed by their Global Industries services arm. The CRM practice falls under this services arm. All Global Industries consultants worldwide are required to take specific courses that are identified on a professional learning path developed and managed through Unisys Corporate University. The equivalent of the director of global training at the time of publication is the previously-mentioned associate dean Michael Chuchmuch. The idea of the Unisys Corporate University is to provide the education that leads to what is hoped to be exceptional individual professional skills, both hard (technical and functional) and soft (communication and problem solving). The continuous education process and cultural encouragement to take courses offered—and even to mandate courses—is a pre-eminent thrust throughout the Global Industries services division. The idea of this whole endeavor is to provide the employee consultants with the freedom to succeed or fail and the tools to increase the chances of success. As Dick Frederickson says, "There is a noose a week offered. Each person has the freedom to weave it into baskets or to hang themselves." Good corporate education means basket weaving is a popular pastime at Unisys.

Unisys: Summary

Unisys is one of the fastest growing CRM service providers. Their access to such an incredible installed base makes their strategy work, where in most other companies this would be a nearly guaranteed failure. Their commitment to education is something that places them apart from other service providers. They have a smart, high caliber, very creative approach to CRM. They'll be busy with their customers for a long time to come.

IBM Global Services (www-1.ibm.com/services)

IBM Global Services (IGS) is probably the largest CRM service provider in the world. I say this without knowing their or anyone's exact numbers, since most companies are reluctant to offer them. But their sheer size and scope reflects their access to CRM resources that exceeds any other company I've run across. Not only do they have a CRM practice that numbers in the thousands, they are doing the largest global Siebel rollout in history as of the writing of this book. They do everything in a big way and provide what is the widest venue of any of the five selected providers in this chapter.

They are so substantial they have go-to-market teams within the CRM practice that are structured by sector and industry. They can draw easily on the cross-industry expertise that exists inside of IBM for each industry and, even with this general sweep, are able to craft a customized solution for an individual company. They are one of the world's most visible service providers and one of the most recognized.

Vision, Strategy, and Direction

IBM Global Service's vice-president of Sell & Support Solutions, Business Innovation Services, Peggy Kennelly, said it well: "It has been a challenging market for the past year, which has changed the way that clients buy. They are less interested in long multiyear engagements. They are looking for those longer engagements in bite-sized chunks so that they can justify the cost." This view goes against the ideal CRM company sales scenario, but is indicative of how realistically IGS looks at their current go-to-market strategy. They are interested in developing the end-to-end strategy and executing that strategy in manageable segments. For example, the ideal IBM Global Services engagement would step the client through the following phases:

1. Management consulting to identify key CRM challenges

2. Business process examination and possibly some re-engineering, if necessary

3. CRM strategy based on specific customer touch points.

4. Implementation strategy

5. ROI business case analysis to justify the CRM strategy

This would then be drilled down to the departmental or divisional levels. After this plan was fleshed out, operational processes (sales force automation, marketing automation, call center transactions) would be examined, and specific plans would be developed for the implementation of each of these business operations. Additionally, in parallel with this would be the evolution and development of plans for customer analysis and the creation of centralized customer data repositories that could get as specific as the collection of data from UPC codes in a store.

When these phases are complete and executed, the next phase in the IBM ideal strategic engagement would be application maintenance, which could mean hosting, outsourcing, straightforward tuning, and upgrading as the needs arose.

Where IBM Global Services then flexes serious muscle is what goes with all this strategic planning and execution. IBM can provide *everything*, including the hardware, all the software, the knowledge transfer and e-learning associated with it, and even the financing! They can actually finance the customer's CRM project. They are entirely self-sufficient. This makes them very important to the current CRM landscape while the economy recovers. Their vision of end-to-end CRM is actually realizable at a level that most other companies won't even attempt to imagine.

Approach and Offering

IGS starts its approach and offering from a dedicated group of subject matter experts (SMEs) for every industry. These subject matter experts identify the key pressure points in each industry. They call these key pressure points "industry big plays." For each of these industry big plays they provide a solution theme that focuses on a major pain point within that industry.

To highlight this, let's look at examples of three sectors:

Distribution (retail) Obviously the retail world needs to woo its individual customers. To do this, personalization is their big play. The theme that IGS has is "extreme customer personalization." They use this theme to both sell into the retail distributors and to provide these specific customized services. This is determined by their SMEs and their customers.

Financial services As pointed out in Chapter 8, much of the financial services market is aimed at preventing the reduction of the financial service company's customer base, which not only means customers leaving the firm, but also customers not diminishing their dollars invested with the instruments of the financial services company. One of the big plays in this sector is something IGS thematically calls "wealth management" and utilizes market data business intelligence to help maximize customer investments. That means analytics play a big part in the design of choices that suit individual customers.

Industrial (automotive) In the automotive industry, "customer care, everywhere" is the theme for IBM Global Services. This includes whatever is wrapped around the car when it is driven off the lot or breaks down. For example, Ford has its Total Care service—a national service that provides a loaner when needed. Ford will come and get you if your car breaks down anywhere in the country. IBM Global Services has a strong focus on this wrapper.

The primary driver of all these big plays is the end customer.

The other aspect of IBM's approach is to focus on consistency across touch points when the implementations are complete. For example, say I contact the Marriott Hotels to take care of a Marriott rewards certificate via the Web and there is a problem. When I call a customer service representative (CSR), what that CSR gets is all the same data related to my customer records that are available from my Internet rewards registration. And the consistency works both ways. My customer experience is the same whether I do it via email, the Web, or the phone. What the Web tells me is what the email tells me is what the CSR tells me.

IGS uses a well-defined methodology for this. They are champions of the use of reusable assets, some of which are available to be licensed and others that are for internal use on implementations only. They call their methodology, what else, the "Global Services Methodology." It is work-product based. There are specific customized paths to take for various types of CRM implementations. There are industry templates that are CRM-enabled. There are customized components, such as particular definitions of call center business processes, that are used to define the approach to a Customer Contact Technology (CCT) implementation.

When IGS embarks on the engagement with the client, they follow steps that have evolved over a long period of time. They have a project launch, develop a project plan, identify the costs, and develop a means of tracking the project. That work product includes what they called in consulting shorthand "org. change management." This is IBM Global Services telling the clients that for a CRM project to succeed, cultural change really needs to be planned for and then carried out. Often, the client will not agree to that part of a plan because of the incremental added cost of having an organizational change management expert on the team. Cost notwithstanding, I think this or not planning for cultural change is unwise, since the cultural change implied in a CRM implementation is the key factor in its success or failure later.

CRM Partners

IGS's partnerships in full would force me to write a second volume to this second edition. A slight exaggeration, but there are partnerships that go to specific vendors based on specific industry or even corporate solutions. For example, one area IGS specializes in is the consumer packaged goods industry, so they have partnered with the German company CAS to handle software solutions for trade promotion management.

Table 16-4 shows examples of the breadth of their partnerships. It is by no means complete and is not reflective of the hundreds of partners they have.

Table 16-4: A Small Representative Example of IBM Global Services CRM Partnerships

General	Customer Contact	Enterprise Customer Solutions
Siebel, PeopleSoft, SAP, J.D. Edwards, KANA, Onyx	Avaya, Genesys, Nortel, Cisco	SAS Institute

Again, the size of this group of relationships is mind-boggling. However, IBM has managed their partners well and has well-designed strategic relationships. Their key public CRM relationship has been Siebel.

Culture

The IBM culture is exemplified by the incredible number of 20- and 30-year veterans of the company who are still there. Loyalty is an actual commitment at IBM, unlike at most of their industry brethren. The culture of IBM Global Services (IBM as a whole, really) is characterized by its emphasis on respect, teaming, and loyalty. They believe in both internal and external commitment. There are multiple awards for employees who succeed at customer satisfaction. It extends throughout the job descriptions. They have a lower than industry average employee turnover rate. I've heard this refrain from key players in CRM there more than once: "I'm a long time IBMer because of the culture."

While you can find violations of these cultural principles at any company, my many years of experience with IBM Global Services and its predecessors show me that they take it seriously. One adverse example will explain how it works. Several years ago, IBM changed their pension plan completely. The result of the change was the most damaging to the 20- and 30-year veterans of the company. The outcry from these long-standing loyal employees was loud. IBM listened and straightened out the problem. The plan was changed, and the 20- and 30-year vets' pensions were protected. This is not typical of corporate giants. If you work for one, you are normally at a disadvantage. Not here. IBM listened and continues to listen. That's why their stock price seems almost impervious to the roller coaster marketplace. Successful employees mean a good company with good performance. IBM Global Services' culture creates that performance.

IBM Global Services: Summary

IBM Global Services is one of the most recognized performers in the CRM market and certainly one of the most successful. They can provide it all. They can even pay for their own implementations, in a manner of speaking, through their financing options, a great asset in a shaky economy. Their personnel are highly qualified, their partnerships extensive, and their practice expertise deep.

Application Service Providers

In 2001, the ASP market proved to be a poor investment, primarily because of concerns that existed over security and infrastructure. Needless to say, with the heightened concern over security post-September 11, this just sealed the fate of many ASPs. But a few survived and even did pretty well, because they were able to break the mold of doubt that covered this particular market. I'm going to highlight one of the rare success stories briefly here, because it shows where an ASP can provide a viable alternative, especially in the SMB marketplace.

Surebridge (www.surebridge.com)

Founded by Pradeep Khurana in 1997, this well-funded ASP provides far more than just CRM hosted services. They cover both the back and front office and even a little on the side. They can handle SalesLogix for the SMBs and Siebel for the ASP-level larger customers in the CRM world, and while they are focused on PeopleSoft ERP primarily, they have the potential to handle the PeopleSoft CRM 8.0 applications also. Vignette, Great Plains, Solomon, Microsoft, Ariba, and Cognos fill out their application services. In other words, they have chosen a well-rounded application set to cover a full-service enterprise. While weighted toward the SMB market, they are not exclusively there (Siebel, PeopleSoft, and Ariba). Their track record is quite good. Even in the horribly down economy of 2001, they secured $15 million in funding from their partners—an incredible feat given the lack of any real IT investment that year. This reflects solid proof of service and a sound value proposition.

Management Consulting Firms

The management consulting firms that specialize in CRM are legion. However, only a few really stand out. What these firms normally do is customer strategies that span enterprises in many industries. What makes them different from an integrator is that they don't do implementations of vendor-specific software applications. They are strategists and campaign planners, and they are CRM's real-world-based academics, doing some of the most significant customer research found in the industry. They are the kings and queens of what are often invaluable case studies. What they are not is vendor-focused in any way. Even though some of them do look at package selection, this is not their strength.

My real concern about this genre is its legions of pretenders. There are an incredible number of firms that claim to be customer strategists that simply aren't. To that end, I'm highlighting what I consider to be the best and also the paradigm of the genre. You can use the Peppers and Rogers Group approach as a template for selection for a customer strategist. (Of course, your best bet is to use Peppers and Rogers Group.)

There are others that are worthy of their designation, of course, such as the Seybold Group, run by Customer.com author and strategist Patricia Seybold, with the significant help of Ronnie Marshak (see Chapter 1 for their take on CRM). There are also management consulting firms that have CRM practices that handle some of the duties of these firms, such as McKinsey Consulting. But the McKinseys are more diversified in their general practices than the companies I'm describing here. CRM strategy is not the only thing they do.

Peppers and Rogers Group (www.1to1.com)

Founded by Martha Rogers and Don Peppers, this company is the grand-parent of one-to-one customer relationships. They invented the term in 1993 with their groundbreaking book, *The One to One Future*. Over the nine ensuing years, they have written another four bestsellers, developed a thriving CRM management consulting services company with international scope, developed a magazine worth reading (*1to1 Magazine*), and a website worth joining. They have an engaging corporate style and a highly professional, friendly corporate culture. The advice that you engage them to give you consists of good, useful strategies, because common sense is not always obvious.

Their array of service offerings is extensive, ranging from strategic services to training and even CRM executive search for marketing and sales professionals. They have divided their services into four broad groups: Business Strategy, Process Design, Momentum Building, and Thought Leadership. Here is a brief list of just some of the services in each area of expertise they offer:

Business Strategy Customer-based strategies, business case development, ROI forecasts, metrics

Process Design Data strategies, customer valuation, marketing communications alignment, privacy strategies

Momentum Building Implementation assessment, momentum-building road map, technology tool optimization, change management, executive search

Thought Leadership Keynote presentations, visioning sessions, capability building

There's nothing bad to say about these folks. They are the crème de la crème of the CRM management consulting world.

CRM Consultancies and Consultants

Individual consultants and small companies, some of them with perhaps 10 to 12 employees, flourish in the CRM bazaar. For the most part, they are very intelligent, pleasant, and accomplished CRM consultants. However, this group can be dangerous. It is subject to the egos of the individuals that it consists of. Be careful who you choose here. Keep in mind, these are going to be the most reasonably priced and can provide superb services, so a look at them is worth it. But there is more risk associated with this reward. When they are strong, their strength can be in specialties such as PRM (Bob Thompson) or an excellent sense of CRM strategy (Dick Lee). Some of them carry substantial influence in the CRM world. I'm only mentioning these two here, but there are dozens of other excellent small and independent CRM consultants and consultancies out there. These two stand out and each is a specialist in CRM, though they have overlapping strengths. For others, feel free to email me at either paul-greenberg3@comcast.net or pgreenberg@live-wire.net.

Bob Thompson, Front Line Solutions (www.crmguru.com; www.frontlinehq.com)

Bob Thompson is the guru of partner relationship management and the most vendor-savvy professional in that realm anywhere. He is a very smart man who, as you may remember, runs the very popular CRMGuru website. He travels the world lecturing and speaking on PRM and has been in the forefront of its evangelists and facilitators.

Mr. Thompson has a strong service offering, with industry briefings and workshops, retainer-based or custom consulting and advisory services, custom publishing (executive-level white papers and other documents that are commissioned by a client), seminars and forums, and research in the CRM world. One interesting thing about Front Line Solutions is that they will do consulting for vendors, not just end-users, and that makes them unusual.

Dick Lee, High-Yield Marketing (www.h-ym.com)

Long known as an outspoken advocate of CRM integrity, Dick Lee, a frequent collaborator with Bob Thompson, has a powerful, very user-focused perspective on CRM. He and I do the *CRM* magazine "Reality Check" column on alternate months, and, believe me, this guy is the epitome of reality check for CRM. He grounds the customer and the industry with cogent strategic thinking and a no-nonsense approach. His company, High-Yield Marketing, in alliance with implementation partner Caribou Lake, provides end-to-end CRM consulting services. That includes strategy, business process re-engineering, systems development, and implementation.

Midsize/Small Integrators and Others

There is a definite advantage to the midsize and small integrators. Most of this advantage is something you read about in the last chapter. What I am going to do here is simply list a few that you should pay attention to when it comes to CRM implementations. These are firms ranging from $3 million to perhaps $100 million in revenues who simply know how to either do the implementations or staff the projects and actually practice CRM. For the most part, they don't focus on strategic planning, but they do provide exceptionally good implementation services. Don't discount them all on the issue of strategic planning, though; they can provide the services. Just make sure that you grill them hard about that. It is easy to talk a good game about strategic planning. It's much more difficult to actually do it.

Midsized: Braun Consulting (www.braunconsult.com)

This is a very classy Chicago-based full-service company that does end-to-end CRM consulting. They are considerably smaller than a KPMG or a Deloitte Consulting, but are a scaled down version of the good Big 5 integrators. Braun Consulting was founded in 1993 and has grown to roughly a $75 million CRM services provider. They specialize in Siebel and Clarify and have a wide variety of clients in vertical industries such as media and telecommunications, healthcare and pharmaceuticals, consumer goods, manufacturing, and financial services. They are experts in CRM process, implementation, and integration. Note that they are on the vendor-specific list that follows. Twice. Not bad.

Small: Live Wire, Inc. (www.live-wire.net)

This is the company I'm executive vice-president of, so, needless to say, I can highly recommend its CRM services for both strategic consulting or staff augmentation. We are not project focused, though. We can support a CRM project, design a vendor-neutral strategy, or help you select the appropriate vendor.

The Rest of the List

This list is focused on some of the application-specific implementation specialists who partner with some of the major CRM vendors. There are handfuls that could fill each slot, but I'm putting in companies that I can vouch for or that have been recommended to me by a vendor, customer, or vendor-neutral consultant—not necessarily the only recommendations, but a representative example, highly thought of. Do they make mistakes? Sure. But they operate with integrity and acumen and have the elasticity of the smaller integrator.

Vendor-Specific

Here they are by vendor, with the location of their corporate head-quarters, though many of them have multiple offices. What is characteristic of all of these companies is that they are midsized or small, and all are good at what they do according to somebody other than themselves. If there is a key vendor missing, it is only due to no information available either from my own experience, other sources, or the vendor. If you have a question on a vendor not here, email me and I'll find out for you.

SIEBEL

Experio Solutions, Dallas, Texas (www.experio.com)
Revere Group, Deerfield, Illinois (www.reveregroup.com)

PEOPLESOFT

Acuent, Parsippany, New Jersey (www.acuent.com)
Apex IT Solutions, Bloomington, Minnesota (www.apexit.com)

ORACLE CRM

Experio Solutions, Dallas, Texas (www.experio.com)

CLARIFY

Braun Consulting, Chicago, Illinois (www.braunconsult.com)
Experio Solutions, Dallas, Texas (www.experio.com)

E.PIPHANY

i-Loft, San Francisco, California (www.i-loft.com)
Wheelhouse, Boston, Massachusetts (www.wheelhouse.com)

SALESLOGIX

Customer FX Corporation, St. Paul, Minnesota (www.customerfx.com)
ePartners Corporation, Dallas, Texas (www.epartnersolutions.com)
THG Sales Automation, Wilmington, Massachusetts (www.thg.com)

UNICA

Braun Consulting, Chicago, Illinois (www.braunconsult.com)
Quaero, Charlotte, North Carolina (www.quaero.com)

SAS

Data Miners, Somerville, Massachusetts (www.data-miners.com)
Elder Research, Falls Church, Virginia (www.datamininglab.com)

CHANNELWAVE

Kanda Software, Concord, Massachusetts (www.kandasoft.com)
Seurat, Charlotte, North Carolina (www.seurat.com)

Analysts

This is both the most influential and the most maligned of all the "other" groups that are mentioned in this chapter. Their power to make or break vendors and service providers is huge. Their judgment is well accepted, though it can be suspect too, depending on the firm. There are analysts who retain an independence of thought and spirit that is entirely commendable. There are a few (not mentioned here) that are doing what someone pays them to do when it comes to an assessment. They are feared, loved, and reviled simultaneously.

What I find interesting is that when dealing with them as individuals, analysts are sometimes quite extraordinary people with great character, and that makes me more comfortable. After all, when you see the analysts' ranking of software, vendors, or service providers, or you see top-20 lists of this or that CRM company, ultimately, no matter what criteria were used to get to those designations, it is a subjective look at those companies. In other words, the criteria chosen to make the determination were chosen by people who had some sort of bias. Editorial decisions govern everything. However, when those editorial decisions are made by people with impeccable character and a clear understanding of what the CRM world looks like, it makes me rest easier. It makes me trust the answers I'm hearing—although it's still a good idea to assess them critically.

The Gartner Group is by far the most important of the analyst powerhouses in the CRM world. I know they have some folks of real integrity there. Also, they provide the rankings and analysis that carry that make-or-break weight I mentioned earlier. There are others, such as META Group, which can be said to have given the first official definition of CRM, and there is some sentiment out there for Forrester Research. Additionally, there are smaller analyst organizations with sharp individuals or solid knowledge, such as the Hewson Group, or a unique but valuable approach to CRM, such as Knowledge Capital Group (KCG). However, Gartner ranks first in the Greenberg Analyst Standings for 2002.

The Gartner Group (www.gartner.com)

Gartner is easily the most influential analyst organization in the CRM world. Most vendors and service providers would do virtually anything (within bounds, of course) to be in the upper-right corner of Gartner's Magic Quadrant. It is perhaps the equivalent of the Academy Award of CRM, but with even more influence over the next contract. To be placed in that corner means that customers will be busting down your doors. While that might be an exaggeration, the reality is that customers do pay close attention to these ratings. The Magic Quadrant is set as a closed box, but along two axes. The vertical axis is titled "Ability to Execute," the horizontal axis is titled "Completeness of Vision." The upper-left box is "Challengers." The lower-left box is labeled "Niche Players." The lower-right box is called "Visionaries," and the coveted upper-right position is called "Leaders." The placement of companies is done in a sort of Cartesian scatter chart with the placement of corporate dots with the name of the appropriate companies next to them. For example, in late 2001, Gartner issued the Relationship Optimization Magic Quadrant. What Gartner calls relationship optimization, I call EMA (see Chapter 7). The companies they place in this quadrant are Unica, E.piphany, NCR, and Protagona. Here's an excerpt of what The Gartner Group says in their public report on this sector, issued October 2001:

> **The Leaders Quadrant:** Despite the current leadership, a plausible scenario exists for any of the leading players to stumble in this market. Despite a growing list of Oracle implementations, NCR is still widely perceived to be wedded to Teradata, a position it must avoid to retain its leadership position. E.piphany's financial performance remains a source of concern—the days of enterprises being able to lose millions of dollars each quarter and retain the confidence of customers and investors is gone. Unless E.piphany can begin to show some "light at the end of the tunnel," prospective clients are likely to lose faith. Unica's relationship with PeopleSoft will bring it more leads, but its ability to manage its pipeline through to successful deployment will be a critical challenge to ensuring the continued satisfaction of their customer base. Protagona is newly

promoted to the leadership segment, but it has to continue to prove it can grow a consistently profitable business by executing well in a wide variety of deals, not just the high-end ones.

In other words, there are caveats and concerns, but they still qualify them as leaders in this industry because they understand the industry's evolution. They make some observations on the industry and its future in general, but you get the idea. This is backed by solid research, customer references, vendor studies, and face-to-face discussions and meetings.

Between the Magic Quadrant and their more in-depth reports and studies, there are no analysts in their class. They carry so much power, it is important to be seen at Gartner conferences.

The one thing I do find odd about Gartner is that their customer service line seems designed to keep people out, rather than let people in to talk. They are afraid of their analysts giving free advice inadvertently, perhaps? I don't really know. I know that on the occasions I call, which are rare, I find it impossible to talk to anyone at all without being virtually patted down and told politely I can't talk to them unless I am a customer, which certainly doesn't incline me to be a customer. Luckily, their website is considerably friendlier, with information and short reports available to the surfer for free, clearly designed to whet the appetite. A kind of schizophrenia between the personal interaction and the website.

That said, there still is no company like Gartner out there with the clout or the depth. I will disagree with them on some of their opinions and even on some of their methodology to the extent I know it, but I respect them a great deal and so should you.

The META Group (www.metagroup.com)

This bunch is an impact player. They don't carry the clout or long-term strategic power of Gartner, but their declarations are met with gravity, and what they say has an incredible level of stickiness. For example, they defined CRM as divided into three parts (see Chapter 1 for details): operational, collaborative, analytic. This definition stuck and has been CRM's definition ever since, right or wrong. They came out with the figures that said 55 to 75 percent of all CRM implementations fail. Those are the numbers quoted everywhere. No one remembers what justification the META Group may have given for those figures. Everyone attaches their own meaning to those figures. But those figures are the biblical references for the CRM industry pundits, writers, and researchers. That's what I mean about the META Group being an impact player. Pay attention to them. They are attention-grabbers.

17

Implementing CRM: Easy as 1, 2, 3, 4, 5, 6, and so on

Once the stakeholders are convinced, the budget is set, the software is chosen, and the integrator/implementation partner is hired, then comes the work. The software must be implemented. This is not a simple matter. Implementation doesn't just mean installing the software and hoping it runs well. It means understanding how the software must conform to the business model and the style of the company. Implementation is always required, regardless of how big or little it is. Very rarely does SalesLogix or a PeopleSoft CRM work right out of the box. If it does, it is more of a miracle than by design and means the likely canonization of your IT director for this nearly celestial choice of CRM application.

The Caveats of Implementation

There is no such thing as an easy implementation. Even installing Microsoft Word or Excel can be problematic on a network for multiple users. CRM is a very complex implementation involving multiple elements and, frequently, back-office integration. It could involve commingling with multiple software packages that are already installed in the corporate system. Issues such as scalability—whether the software can handle the amount of use and number of users it is going to get—are paramount even prior to the selection of the software. Some CRM applications are focused on the smaller and medium-sized companies, others on the Fortune 1000–sized enterprises. Large companies with multiple locations have a different set of problems from small companies with a single location and multiple users. Because each company has a different process and culture, each company will have a unique set of implementation issues to solve—technical, functional, and cultural. Even a perfect technical installation and carefree customization can fail if you have snippy employees who don't take to the system.

You have to plan to resolve all of these issues for an implementation to be successful. You thought getting management buy-in was tough? Wait until you find the salesperson with 25 years of experience continuing to do it "the way he does it," when you ask him to do it another way. Good luck.

The Implementation

If you'd prefer to skip this chapter, do so at your own risk. If you attempt to implement a CRM package without knowing how implementations work and the likely problems you will face throughout the project, you could be in for a fall—and a big one. Even job termination. The statement of work and the change management processes have to be clear prior to even starting the *installation*. Forget about planning it in the course of customization. Figure it this way. The industry rule of thumb is that the implementation services will cost you at least double to triple the price of the software itself. Something that costly needs your attention. For this chapter, I'm going to use the example of a typical midsize implementation, based on the methodology often used by SalesLogix for their installs. There is some variance from their strict mode, but their implementation methodology is a classic example of a thorough approach, so it serves as a useful model for this chapter. Implementations on a larger scale are not covered here—they are more complex in scope and methodology. They have a different set of problems and often a larger team. For example, you'll notice in this chapter that I don't identify a program manager—just two project managers. The program manager is often necessary as the person who tracks the cost, schedule, performance, and risk factors involved in the project. In smaller projects, this isn't really a necessary position. A senior project manager can do it. Another example: It isn't necessarily wise to have a formal steering committee in a small project. However, in a large implementation, such as a PeopleSoft implementation or Siebel implementation, it is often entirely necessary to have a formal steering committee that consists of the stakeholders, program manager, project managers, and so on, who would review the project as it moves through the implementation stages. It is far more complex and beyond the scope of this chapter to look at a Fortune 1000 CRM implementation. If you are interested in a larger implementation, please feel free to contact me (see the Introduction for contact information) and I will refer you to the experts.

Pre-Implementation

The time frame on this one varies from several weeks to several months according to the depth of preliminary work your company needs to do. For example, in this time frame, the decision is made to go with a CRM implementation. The criteria are those questions the CRM software functionality needs to answer and those corporate weaknesses the software and processes need to address. (See Chapters 4 and 5 for some of these questions.) Additionally, this is the phase where the stakeholders at the executive level and (if you wisely choose to include the users) the user level are identified and engaged.

This also is the phase where software selection occurs. If you've read Chapter 4 on CRM strategy, you know you've come to this phase after a long process where multiple other criteria are defined and decisions have been made. Picking the software is nearly an endgame, pre-implementation step. The market is spitting out new CRM choices every day. They can get confusing. If your selection criteria are sharp and if you have some reference (such as this book) to help you identify the established vendors—or if sexy and new is more your speed, the cutting-edge vendors—your path will be considerably easier. The road less traveled can still be the road identified by the markers. Some of the criteria for the selection (beyond the few mentioned in Chapter 4) are:

- ▶ Scalability of software
- ▶ Toolset flexibility for customization
- ▶ Stability of the existing CRM application code
- ▶ Compatibility of the CRM application with legacy systems and Internet systems
- ▶ Level of technical support available during and after the implementation
- ▶ Upgrade support
- ▶ Availability of additional modules such as EMA complementing SFA (marketing module complementing a sales module)

Pay attention to the criteria. Projects fail, and they fail quite often and easily. We know the analysts' numbers are a 55 to 75 percent rate of CRM project failure. Take it further. The average loss in a typical enterprise-wide

IT project is $4.2 million, according to Effy Oz, an associate professor of management at Penn State, quoted in the October 31, 2000, issue of *Computerworld*. There have been projects that have been monumental disasters. For example, one manufacturer spent $112 million on an ERP implementation that failed. What would happen to your job if that were your recommendation? Don't underestimate the selection criteria for both the software and the implementation services. As an executive or someone with authority on this software selection, your and the other corporate stakeholders' acceptance of "buck-stops-here" responsibility must happen. You define the criteria and then choose the software. Accept the consequences of what you define and choose. In other words, there's a hell of a lot at stake here and no company can afford the price of failure. There is no room to be in what Bruce Webster of PricewaterhouseCoopers calls "the thermocline of truth." A thermocline is the area between the hot- and cold-water bands in a lake. In the IT world, it is the area between the corporate executives who think the project is going great and the underlings on the project teams who know the project is failing.

The Kickoff Meeting

Once software selection is made, you move on to the kickoff meeting. This meeting is where it all gets real. This is where the implementation partner—be it the vendor, a large or small consulting services firm, or a systems integrator who is doing more than just the implementation—meets with the customer to figure out the customer's needs. This meeting, which should take one or two days, is where the customer and the partner decide which responsibilities are assigned to whom. The team members meet each other and the chemistry for the implementation is established. Be wary if you notice friction right away, because ordinarily there is a honeymoon period before problems set in. Early friction can be a harbinger of bad things to come.

What should a typical vendor or partner like SalesLogix (or other midmarket CRM application) team look like?

Project manager (PM) The project manager is responsible for all aspects of the implementation, including cost control, quality and testing, and customer satisfaction. Since the PM may be managing several projects simultaneously, the time that he is on the site is not usually 40 hours a week. Don't expect that. Be grateful, too, because he tends to have the highest billing rate of any of the staff members on the project. If there is a problem, the PM is the person you'll speak with and expect to work out the solution. The project manager is the one with the connections back at the vendor company headquarters and his own company's HQ, if he represents a consulting services partner or a systems integrator. If there are changes to the statement of work (SOW), it is the project manager who must work out the details with the customer. There should be a change management process in place that is approved by both the customer and the implementation services company.

Implementation leader Sometimes this person is called the technical lead. He is responsible for technical aspects, directs the system engineers, and is usually dedicated to only one project at a time. He tends to be onsite full time until the end of the project. His strength is a combination of people skills and technical knowledge. Often, he is a CRM architect who takes a hands-on role in the project. He assists in preparing the statement of work with the project manager. However, he does not resolve the problems of the project. That is for the project manager. The technical lead is normally focused on strictly technical issues and not as involved in customer relationships.

Systems engineer(s) Sometimes they go by their particular titles— Java developer or functional sales specialist or whatever the company that employs them wants to call them. Their primary role is to do the coding. Period. They are onsite at all times, unless there is work to do at home. In many implementations, technical and functional expertise is necessary to do the work. CRM implementations are complex. For example, to work with the SalesLogix Architect tool, it's important for the systems engineer to know how corporate sales processes tend to function. They don't necessarily have to know how the particular company's specific processes work, just how the sales workflow functions.

Okay, that's the implementation partner's team. It's now time for introductions and assignments for the customer's team. Yes, you do have to have a team. The team does not consist of the stakeholders. They are "merely" responsible for the project so that there is smooth sailing among the executives and collaboration with the users. Remember, if there are to be cost overruns, it's probably a good idea to have the CFO on your side. Then again, hopefully, there won't be cost overruns. Also, remember that the users are going to be using the CRM applications, so their participation in a review of functionality is very important to the success of the implementation.

You need a team that will be working hand in hand with the implementation partner for a number of reasons. First and foremost, your team is the one with the knowledge of how the company works and is expected to impart that knowledge. Second, your team needs to know how the application you are implementing works. When the implementation is done, the partner will probably not want to hang around and maintain things for you, unless you acquire their company to do that. Therefore, people have to learn how the applications work at the technical level. People on your team.

Who's on this all-important customer team?

Project manager This PM owns the project from the customer's point of view. That means the PM is the liaison to the partner's PM and is also the one who sees to it that the statement of work developed by the partner PM is adhered to. This project manager filters any suggested changes in the SOW prior to a discussion on changes with the partner PM. This PM also is the one who approves (with stakeholder acquiescence) the pricing for the changes. (No, changes are not free.) This is a very political position since he represents the Olympian-level hopes and dreams of the stakeholders and is the direct liaison to the vendor PM. He is also the individual who will take the fall at the company if the implementation fails, and get few of the kudos if it succeeds. Sad, but true.

Systems or business analysts These employees are the functional experts. They provide input on business processes and flow that are enterprise-specific. In the ideal world, they will be assigned full time to the project and not leave it until it is complete. That happens sometimes. The rest of the time, they are onsite when they can be, which doesn't necessarily dovetail with when they *should* be. That can create serious headaches, if not major problems for the implementation's completion in a timely fashion. Here is where some variance might also be the case. This is the typical midmarket implementation as represented by SalesLogix. However, if you are doing a PeopleSoft CRM project with a Fortune 500 company, there may be some differences in the way the project is staffed. For example, there would also be functional expertise on the implementation partner's team in the guise of "business analysts." This would not mitigate the need for the enterprise-process specialists. It is just that the larger CRM packages have enormous specialized functionality best understood by a functional specialist who has background in the area and who also knows the product being implemented.

IT staff These are the administrators of the system, the people who are maintaining and setting up the network and its software. They have to see that there is no significant downtime or problems during the implementation period. Actually, they have to do this all the time. Because a good deal of the effort during an implementation is working the bugs out of it, the stress on the system can be great. The administrators, who have enough stress in their lives as it is, are under greater pressure during this critical period.

Integration expert This person guides the integration of the CRM system with other information systems. This person is very specialized. Who she is is entirely dependent on what the other information systems are. For example, someone who is integrating midmarket PeopleSoft 8.0 with SalesLogix is going to be someone who knows how to make the hooks, find the APIs, write the scripts, and whatever is necessary to make this work. This person is going to be different from the one who is integrating SalesLogix with Unica Affinium 4.0 so that the SFA package talks to the EMA package. Integration, covered in Chapter 12, is extremely complex, now that the prevailing wisdom is apparently moving back to best of breed, rather than one big package that does it all. Companies in CRM or ERP and the like who are trying to be "all things to all people" are having more difficulty than the "one size fits one" schema.

Heads of nontechnical departments They provide input and approval on aspects affecting their departments. Don't kid yourself here—these folks are important to the implementation beyond what may seem to be their official standing. They can make you or break you. They can make the implementation succeed if the partner implementation team members understand that they are nontechnical, which means patience and explanations are necessary. They can make it fail if the non-techies think they *are* technical (which happens pretty frequently) and want to tell the technical groups their job, or they can make it fail if they have insufficient information about what is going on. This usually leads to misunderstandings and wrong decisions. These people make up a very important group of team members.

Now both teams are established, and the kickoff meeting is underway. What are the expectations that have to be resolved? It's important to concur on what the system is functionally and technically going to do. For example, both teams must agree that it will allow forecasting in the sales pipeline that can be managed against the steps of the sales process. It also means agreeing that it will run under Windows 2000 or XP Professional when the company upgrades in 2003—or that it won't run under Windows 2000 or XP Professional when the company upgrades. As long as the agreement is there, either answer is fine.

There also has to be an understanding of what the software can and cannot do. During implementations that are going south, the refrain, "I thought the software could do that," is often heard. Not good. Prior to the project ever beginning, it is important to frame the limitations of the software, whether you are the partner or the customer. That way, expectations have boundaries and excess isn't expected. In fact, this should be done during the sales cycle, but salespeople are often afraid that they will lose the sale if they don't sell the software's wizardry. Sadly, they are ordinarily right. It would be far better if the limitations of the software are identified prior to the implementation and, after the needed functionality is defined, then the limitations can be refined. But life is not like that.

The final task of the kickoff meeting is to create the initial timeline so that each deliverable is scheduled for some date. SalesLogix PMs call it the "need-by" date.

If the meeting was successful, there will be signoffs on what the system can and can't do and what the expectations are for each person. The signoffs can be formal or informal, depending on the relationship between the two parties and their preferences. I would suggest formal. There should be excitement and everyone should be ready to go.

Requirements Gathering

The next phase, requirements gathering, should take about two to three days for a SalesLogix-sized midmarket implementation. The length of the requirements gathering phase can markedly change if the scope of the project is significantly bigger. There can be a quantitative reason: There are a lot more people to interview. It can be a qualitative reason: The complexity of the project means the requirements phase is more complicated. Regardless, this is the phase where meetings happen with the stakeholders, users, other corporate decision makers, and the IT staff. In other words, all those who are going to use the system must be involved. This could be five people, fifteen people, or twenty-five people. The in-between number tends to be midmarket-sized implementations. This requires that departments cooperate, since the CRM implementation is going to affect the interactions of every appropriate department in the company. Marketing, sales, finance, and so on all have a direct need to have input in the teams during the requirements gathering phase. There are a number of actions necessary during this procedure.

Legacy systems need to be analyzed. This is both a technical and a functional issue. This is where there is analysis of the enterprise's sales methodology and the business rules that define the company. This is also the time for some corporate soul-searching. How successful has the sales methodology been? What can be changed? A good requirements analysis will bring out some of these issues and some of the answers, though certainly not all of them. In fact, much had probably been discussed in the early pre-implementation stages prior to package selection. Even so, requirements gathering can bring even more business issues to the public eye. Ultimately, whatever the customer wants to carry forward will be architected into the CRM system. Most CRM packages are fairly flexible in their toolsets, allowing for wholesale or small changes to the business rules that govern the customer's corporate life. One of the major complaints about earlier ERP packages was the inflexibility of the embedded business rules. If you wanted ERP, you did business their way. When the ERP packages were built using object-oriented methodologies and languages (SAP R/3 4.0, for example), the ability to alter the best practices and business rules implanted in the application became a simpler matter. CRM packages have all learned from the mistakes of ERP past.

Once the requirements for the front-office practices are gathered, the next step is the identification of the inputs and outputs. This is the way the users will interact with the system. Some of the questions to be answered in this phase include:

▶ Which screens will be needed to input data?

▶ How will information be retrieved from the system?

▶ How will the customer want to work with the system?

▶ How many users must the system accommodate and how will they connect to it (LAN, individual remote users, remote offices, Web)?

While these questions are being answered, there is a lot of other work to do. For example, what would be the system's optimal functionality if everyone had their wishes granted? The difficulty of this part, though necessary, is twofold. First, the users, unacquainted with what the system can technically do and not do, often ask for functionality that is impossible. Bringing them in at the stakeholder level early on can mitigate this somewhat. Additionally, a briefing on the basics of the CRM application prior to the requirements gathering is often useful in narrowing the field of dreams, especially for those users not involved in the original stakeholding meetings or vendor selection teams. As the project proceeds, the functionality list narrows significantly. Obviously, the plan is to include as much as possible to keep the customer happy, but the technical boundaries and the interactions of the proposed functionality have a lot to do with the ultimate restrictions on what gets implemented.

There is a lot more to be done, with the identification of what data must be imported to the system and what must be exported. Both the one-time efforts that must occur and the ones that will be recurring throughout the life of the system, such as financial data gathered from invoiced sales and the like, must be considered.

To make the requirements gathering go smoothly, it is important to obtain all information possible about the existing system and thus provide a foundation to see how the legacy system and the CRM implementation will fit. This means a look at the legacy system's functionality and how that will conform to the CRM functionality, the usage level, the scalability of the CRM system, and the workflow of the system.

To get this information, nondisclosure agreements and all other necessary paperwork need to be signed during this phase. The nondisclosure agreement states that neither the implementation partner nor the customer will disclose each other's information given during the course of this project to anyone outside those identified as the ones who "need to know." This agreement is binding for the life of the project and usually a term of one year after that and, on occasion, longer than that. That way, both the partner and the customer can get the data and confidential information necessary to start the project work, including the system detail from the customer and other information from the vendor or partner.

Prototyping and Detailed Proposal Generation

This next phase is where the actual hands-on work begins—with a prototype. The purpose of the prototype is to develop some of the key functionality for the customer to examine before the rollout. By doing it in a prototype, the amount of difficulty in the achievement of the functionality and the issues it brings up are all on the table before a complete implementation to all users is done. For example, if the customer wants to be able to click a button in SalesLogix that would populate a custom reporting system, it can be examined in minute detail. This confirms that it can be done or not.

The same goes for the creation of mock screens. With the creation of the screens, the workflow can be demonstrated ("click this button and this happens, taking you to here…."). This allows the user to participate at each step of the workflow and prototype development. In most circles, the methodology that gives the users the maximum participation and input on deliverables as they are delivered is called the "iterative" method. The idea is that the users are involved in all iterations of the application. The result is happy customers because they not only verified the workflow and, often, the look and feel of the screens, but they are also giving input to the team at all times, hopefully with a clear understanding of the scope of the statement of work. The prototype can clarify the customer needs by visualization. When the customer sees the process work or the workflow and agrees to what he or she sees, the development team and the customer team are of like mind, making the project work go that much more smoothly. The prototype can be demonstrated to varying departments, each with their own agendas and ways of viewing data, and can be worked by the development team, even if the data presentation from department to department is conflicting. This process generally takes about two weeks.

Not all customization requires prototyping. On occasion, the requirements are clear and the processes already work well or are embedded in the out-of-the-box version of the software. Also on occasion, tornadoes are known to have lifted cows 350 feet in the air and put them gently back on the ground unscathed.

Once the prototype is done and demonstrated, and the proposed changes to the workflow and functions are acceptable to both the customer and the development team, a formal project proposal that states the deliverables, timelines, and final costs is written for the client. This document can run as small as perhaps ten pages or as large (in the SalesLogix SMB domain) as fifty pages. In the larger PeopleSoft world, these proposals can be one hundred pages long or more.

These midmarket CRM projects are often divided into four phases:

Phase I: Sales module customizations The product catalogs, the sales process embedding, the account and contact databases, and the sales pipeline management criteria, among other things, are developed.

Phase II: Marketing module customizations These are no different in technical process from sales module customizations. They are merely different in what needs to be customized.

Phase III: Integration with external applications This is where there are possible difficulties. The "as is" review is often done in the beginning of the requirements gathering. This is an analysis of the existing information technology infrastructure and the network functionality. This work identifies the integration points between the legacy systems, the CRM application, and the possible installation and customization of other new non-CRM applications and systems. This is always done after the customizations of Phases I and II and a third intermediate phase of other CRM modules if need be (for example, PRM customization—see Chapter 9).

Phase IV: Reporting integration Oddly, this apparently innocuous phase is one of the most important points in the process. Reporting is a vital function, especially for businesses that are scattered beyond one office. The customization of those reports and their generation are critical to corporate success. There are often problems when information isn't appropriately structured or appropriately routed—problems that are life threatening to the corporation. By making sure the appropriate templates are created and the right reports are autorouted to the right recipients, the danger of incorrect decision making is reduced dramatically.

Development of Customizations

Once there are the appropriate signoffs on the formal and final proposal document, the next phase is development of customizations. The time length of the customizations varies widely, with five to seven weeks being typical, and depends on a substantial number of factors:

- ▶ The size of the project.
- ▶ The complexity of:
  - ▶ The interfaces
  - ▶ The workflow
  - ▶ The functions
- ▶ The availability of employees/users to work with the team to improve the customizations at a given iteration.

▶ Technical problems unrelated to the implementation that affect it. These can be resolved by creating an independent environment for development, testing, and eventually production.

▶ Midstream workflow and rules changes for the customization, necessitated by changing corporate business processes. This is something that can be managed, but will affect the timetable and the price.

These are a few of the many reasons the project can exceed its five- to seven-week anticipated timeline.

The elasticity of the application is very important in the ease of creation of the customized application. SalesLogix, for example, has an open architecture, a large third-party integration base, and a very flexible toolset, making the customizations fairly easy. Other products in the same broad CRM category or in the more specialized subcategories such as EMA or PRM may not have the easily usable toolset or may have a proprietary architecture, making the application customization very difficult.

The next step is to assign tasks to developers. These developers may not be, for example, SalesLogix toolset specialists. Rather, they may be Oracle database administrators, PeopleSoft CRM 8.0 or even Vantive integration specialists, Java developers—whatever is needed to ensure the project's success.

An effective implementation partner will then set up a development environment that mirrors the customer site as closely as possible. Needless to say, an exact mirror isn't possible. There are differences that will have to exist, simply because the machines used are not identical. What can be done is a database that is the same as the customer's and a system that is about the same as the customer's. So a copy of the customer's sales/accounts database—for example, in a Microsoft SQL Server 7.0 environment with 25 users—can be reproduced. This means that success in this environment will mean likely success in this system. The processes initiated in the customization phase will be known to work on the customer's system, simply because they are working on a mockup of the customer's system.

The project manager is responsible for a project plan at this phase also. The plan is a checklist of what developers and what team members are assigned to what tasks. Based on the successful checking-off of these tasks, status reports on the state of deliverables can be given to the customer in agreed-upon time frames. Depending on the formalities of the project, status reports can be phone calls or formally written documents with the specific successes (and caveats and failures).

Throughout this customization period, the development team is demonstrating the functionality to the customer and soliciting customer response. *It is important that the customer is engaged at all times in the project.* Involving the customer manages "scope creep"—a scary term for a project potentially inching out of control. With a clear statement of work, strong change management procedures, and the constant education of the customer, scope creep likelihood is reduced significantly. There is simply no way that changes to the original, agreed-upon statement of work won't occur. So the change management process (see Chapter 4 for more on change management) is there to both control costs and time loss. It can satisfy the customer without succumbing to the client feature-lust that is often the case when the client realizes how much more powerful and interesting the application is than they expected. This is a consistent trend in almost every project ever done. If you are the customer, take one piece of advice. More stuff costs more money and loses time. Be sure the features you want are for the benefit of the corporate CRM and its users, not just fun for you alone. That said, the consulting services company or implementation partner will attempt to accommodate you with what you want. If they work well, they will tell you the truth about incorporating a Web connection to the Starbucks delivery unit, rather than the sales forecasting tool. With this level of communication and control, even the project time can potentially be reduced and everyone is happy.

If there are changes to be made, several things must be done. As mentioned earlier, a clear-cut change management process has to be in place so that both the contractors and the customer can accept the changes. The change management document should include the understanding that changes to the statement of work in function or scope will incur extra costs, will increase the delivery time and due date of the total implementation, and that there is no liability to the implementation partner for changes. It also must include a workflow that identifies who the authority is that can sign off on the changes and thus add the changes to the budget.

One very valuable implementation lesson is to "routinize" it as much as possible. In the customization phase, writing data import routines using the CRM toolkit can save days of effort and manual entry. The time saved is inestimable and critical.

Finally, the data routines are written, the screens developed, and the other customizations are completed. The final part of this phase is development team testing—making sure the basic system works. If that is a go and signed off on, you're ready to move on to the next phase.

Power User Beta Test and Data Import

This is where the star users (usually called "power users" since they are among the nontechnical people who "get it") get to play. They get involved in finding the systemic discrepancies that crop up when the customizations are moving to completion and the data migration is being prepared. *The more experienced the users are in this phase, the better.* This is not a case of too many cooks spoiling the broth, but of a need for two, three, or many Emeril Lagasses. By involving power users, verification and acceptance of the system are ensured.

The first major step in this two- to five-day process is to create a testing environment at the site. There are often dangers that seem to be inherent in this. What if the testing environment crashes the system? Usually, the customer in progress purchases a server that can be isolated from the important operational systems and can work side by side with the legacy system, but not as part of it. Very often, systems with the most extensive customizations exhibit the fewest problems in beta testing because they have been checked so extensively during development. To get to this exalted state, however, there has to be a close working relationship between the development team, the internal implementation team, and the IT staff (which may overlap with the internal implementation team to some extent). Meetings with the IT team focus on how to implement and support the system. With some implementation methodologies (such as SalesLogix), this is the beginning of knowledge transfer, with the customer IT staff performing a beta implementation. The success or failure, and strengths and shortcomings of the IT team's beta attempt determine what kinds of backup resources are necessary, what kind of procedural automation is still needed, and what kind of training will be paramount when the time comes for the vendor/consulting services company to leave the premises.

Once the beta installation is complete and analyzed, then comes a very tough part: the test data import. Before the system goes live, there has to be a full-scale test run. The run will identify the usability and accuracy of the data. *This must be done with the full participation of the customer.* The customer must verify the integrity of the data transfer. This is a sensitive part of the implementation.

It is now time to gather last-minute usability requests. The good thing about beta testers is that they often have recommendations for improvement that go beyond simply finding bugs.

Now comes the final part before actual rollout. There is a consistency check for everything ranging from look and feel of the screens to spelling. Rollout is prepared as the system moves from beta to production. But as the departments gear up to roll out, there is one more phase.

Training

Training time depends on the number of users and available facilities for training, and typically runs about two days. There are four parts to training:

Basic training   There are no pushups in this training. This is the plain vanilla training for users on the application. Normally, this is run by the vendor. There are two ways to do it, depending on which is the most cost effective. You could send your users to Scottsdale, Arizona, for example, to get training at SalesLogix headquarters. That means you'd pay the cost of the training plus the cost of hotel, food, airfare (unless you're in the training facility's location), and other incidentals. You could also have a trainer come to your facility, often the cheaper alternative if you have a significant number of users. However, be smart and have the training worked out and put into the original contract and statement of work. This can be a surprisingly costly part of the implementation.

Customization training   This is done by the now-trained employees who have been engaged in the project, though it doesn't have to be. The reason it is best done by the internal project team is their familiarity with the system to begin with. The internal project team cost is what it has taken to get them up to speed on the basic CRM system training and their ordinary labor costs. One other plus with the internal staff is that they have had the benefit of ongoing knowledge transfer throughout the implementation process. Knowledge transfer, for those of you never involved in IT "techspeak," is the continuous education on what has been learned from the vendor/integrator and taught to the customer team who will be using the knowledge in an ongoing fashion. It is ordinarily built into the proposals, contracts, and statements of work that are the basis for the implementation. It is very important that the knowledge transfer is an intentional written part of the statement of work.

Documentation   Another vital part of the process. The vendor or consulting company's implementation team has full responsibility to provide documentation on the customized system to see that future use is ensured. Often, as part of a team, CRM vendor companies or integrators will provide documentation experts (who can be doing something else on the team as well) who know how to piece together useful documentation. Bad writing is endemic to the IT world and making sure that a bad writer isn't writing the documentation is something that, while sounding funny, is deadly serious. Take a tip here and look at some disclosable past documentation written by the person or people who are going to be writing your documentation. Have the documentation deliverables sketched out in detail in the statement of work.

Additional training Some companies recommend additional training. Two highly recommended courses are train the trainer and an integrator course.

> **Train the trainer** As the name implies, whomever you send to this course will be the one who will train the users on your staff. This is a major time and money saver.

> **Integrator course** This course teaches your IT staff how to make their own customizations to SalesLogix or to the other vendors who have such a course.

Rollout and System Hand-off

This is it—the final phase. This is the time when the production environment has to be installed at the site. The production environment is the one your company is going to use.

The final phase is both a delicate and huge task. If anything goes wrong—and there is always ample opportunity for that to happen—it could mean disaster. The legacy system has to be shut down. The data migration has to convert all data into the format of the SalesLogix or PeopleSoft or Siebel databases, which could be Oracle, MS SQL Server 7.0, DB2, Interbase, or any number of other formats. When this is done and acceptable, the new system is powered up.

Normally, this process takes one or two days, and usually occurs on a weekend so there is no (or at least, minimal) disruption of the actual workweek. If it extends beyond the weekend or can't be done on the weekend, alternate arrangements are planned and executed so that the disruption remains minimal. One to two days is midmarket data size. Large implementations of a PeopleSoft CRM Fortune 1000–sized operation could take a week or more. Tools to do nothing more than data mapping and migration in a large environment in a few days are so important, that companies think nothing of spending often tens or even hundreds of thousands of dollars for this tool and will throw it away when it gets the data migration completed.

The other significant part of the rollout is remote user and satellite office preparation. This differs according to different software and methodologies. For the sake of consistency, I've been following a mid-market SalesLogix implementation. Please be aware, though, that variances in both methodology and preparation are related to the individual company and, very often, to the scale of the project.

Each remote user is given a copy of the general database installed on their desktop or laptop. Each of them will be customizing it as they move through a given day. Initially, all users are guided through the use of the system by trained implementation personnel who, if physically possible, will walk around and work with each person in the hands-on use of the system, answer any questions, and increase the overall comfort level in using the system.

This is now a production environment, which, no matter how good the effort has been, is different from the beta environment. That means a developer stays onsite to deal with unexpected problems. Often, the initial problem is not part of the CRM system, but rather is the interaction between the system and the network. One place that normally has some problems—though they are mostly mechanical—is data synchronization with remote users. The sync-up doesn't always run smoothly in the first few moments of the production environment. But when products have good data synchronization engines, these problems get solved very quickly.

Finally, the rollout is complete and the installation/implementation team goes away. What's next?

Ongoing Support, System Optimization, and Follow-up

This is all optional, of course. There are a substantial number of companies who opt to not follow through on support after the rollout. As I've pointed out elsewhere, one of the disadvantages of small companies doing the implementation is their limited ability to provide post-implementation maintenance and support. In any case, the level of service needs to be there, and it is wise to arrange for post-implementation support. Incurring cost is better than incurring systemic failure simply because you did something wrong and didn't know what you did.

The implementation partner has some liability here, too. What that liability is needs to be part of the contract before the implementation ever starts. Finger-pointing never solves problems and, besides, it's impolite.

Presuming who is responsible for what in the post-implementation era has been decided, the implementation partner must be ready to provide the customer with rapidly turned-around support. The support has to be there until the client can swim. Even then, it is good CRM to contact the customer to make sure they are happy and functioning. Occasional onsite assessments should be done after the customer has been habitually ensconced in whatever procedures they have changed and are now using for the system. This lets the implementation partner assess whether the customer is getting maximum benefit from the system.

A Couple of Good Cautions

Make sure you keep your databases from growing too large for the power of your equipment. This can happen if you do too much data importing. Prepare in advance for growth by having more machine power than you need.

When there is an update available, work with the implementation partner to ensure that the customizations aren't overwritten with the update's installation. That is something that could easily happen if you aren't careful.

The End?

It is never the end when you've installed a CRM system. Maintenance is ongoing, but that's because a successful implementation means that happy sales and marketing staff, executives, analysts, and anyone else who has a stake in how customers relate to your business are using the system productively.

18

The Future's Not Hard to See, but Hard to Call

Someday, it's not going to be called CRM anymore. There is an increasingly blurry line spreading between the front and the back office, between the views at the touch points, between the supply and the demand chain, and in the definition of what constitutes a customer. This is being translated into practical action by companies around the globe. The corporate ecosystem is evolving to dominance in the coming years. But don't be afraid. This isn't a giant pod with a single mind. This is a fully integrated set of business processes that makes life potentially so much easier, if we work to let it do that.

Corporate Ecosystem

As noted in Chapter 1, the definition of the customer has been dramatically transformed as the interdependencies of the suppliers, the clients, the partners, and the employees became manifest. The Internet provided the glue for the transformation as the number of users of Internet services doubled and doubled and doubled again in three years. As noted, there are 155 million Internet users in the United States alone. China now has 30 million Web surfers. Malta has an Internet presence. There is no country in the world immune to the Internet entirely. It has become an instantaneous communications channel that provides unprecedented access to information and to services. Think of KANA's model, mentioned in Chapter 14. When you are dealing with the Internet there could theoretically be millions of concurrent users somewhere. Obviously there are limitations imposed by current generations of hardware and software, but the theoretical possibility exists like never before.

Even more than that, the need for the supply and demand chains to be intertwined is greater than ever and more of a reality. In fact, KPMG Consulting merged its SCM and CRM practices because of the obvious recognition of this fact. For example, for a customer to be satisfied with a product order status there has to be instant inventory knowledge wherever the customer service representative is, so that the CSR can help the customer with that order. This could mean a CSR at a desk in a customer interaction center, an email in response to a query, or an inventory check via a Compaq IPAQ 3850 driven wirelessly, hopefully someday by Bluetooth. Order management is now part of this customer-centric picture. But that means logistics and delivery become part of the painting, too. Logistics relationship management (LRM) is being posited by CRMDaily.com. as yet another practice area. Let's face it, if the product is in inventory and the delivery of that product is late to the customer, they aren't going to be very happy.

The corporate ecosystem that this implies is a fact of life, and the response to that ecosystem is the CRM of the future. This is a customer-centric ecosystem. The end-user is the customer, whether an individual customer in a B2C environment or a business in the B2B environment.

Customer-Centric Convergence

This ecosystem is driving convergence. What have historically been disparate systems such as CRM, SCM, or ERP are now being integrated into a single system where a CRM is now, as SAP puts it, "just an on-ramp."

The future of CRM is a part of this trend to convergence. This convergence is not the marketing trick that some companies use to make their products "bigger than CRM." This is a DNA-level convergence where the processes are integrated, the information technology architecture is uniform, and interactions and results are real time. Additionally, the standards are no longer proprietary but open, allowing any application to speak to any other application. In fact, this goes further—not just application to application, but corporation to corporation.

This convergence has been a while in coming, but it has arrived and is currently anthropologically Cro-Magnon.

On the macro-level of this Cro-Magnon–era evolution are the so-called enterprise applications that are being provided by PeopleSoft, SAP, and Oracle. They are the full-service suites that integrate all the customer-facing and back-office functionality so that the source of the information used to provide a customer history or current interactive customer behavior is entirely transparent to the requestor of the information. Over the past several years, these three companies in particular have become the bellwethers of the capacity to "extend the thought across the entire enterprise." The more integrated the applications, the more open the standards due to Internet architectures and XML-compliance, among other facets.

On the micro-level, Oracle's release of the Oracle Collections, strongly tied to Oracle Accounts Receivable, is a kind of ironic reflection of this convergence. The irony is that collections normally doesn't qualify as part of anyone's CRM suite, since customer satisfaction is hardly the purpose of collections. But, rather than a typical back-office application that simply runs the collections process blandly, this application also manages the customer interactions so that individual collections strategies can be charted according to the reasons for non-payment and the history of the customer for payments. In an article on Destination CRM, Sharon Ward, vice-president of enterprise applications for the Hurwitz Group, said, "Oracle is making another significant advancement in integrating CRM and ERP processes." Convergence inside a single application.

Open standards are beginning to tie these convergent processes together. SAP's Drag and Relate technology, purchased from Top Tier, provides a brilliant way of visualizing the integration of the back and front offices. It doesn't matter what vendors provided the applications that you see through the Web portal you've entered. You can drop data from one onto the others, see the results instantly, and have the data updated throughout all the sources it was drawn from. This is true convergence at the browser—conversations between applications, so to speak.

How about conversations between companies that are more complex than just the differences in the use of the same systems? Multi-enterprise interactions that share data sources and data results are now possible. One way that this can be done is through what Scribe Software calls Demand Chain Management. CRM systems at company A can speak to ERP systems at company B if that's what needs to be done. Think about the implications of this for what is now PRM. Partners, systems integrators, vendors, and value-added resellers can exchange data at the meta- and micro-levels, with consistent updating of the data as it changes, through synchronization. This can be done without portals using this method so even client/server technology can provide the conversations.

So what are we seeing here? Integrated processes that can transparently provide, exhibit, and receive data from each other, within or outside a company. All of it is accessible to anyone permitted to see it, from an employee of one of the companies to the end-user customer viewing the data on the Web and watching it change due to his or her activity.

How are the conversations between applications and companies in this customer-centric convergence going to be carried out? Keep reading.

Web Services

What are Web services? Are they Internet architectures? Are they message brokers? Do they involve transactional standards? Are they programming or descriptive languages? Yes, yes, yes, and yes.

Web services are the lower- and higher-level protocols and descriptors that allow disparate applications to talk to each other at the transactional level. The most commonly known Web service is XML (Extensible Markup Language). XML is an open industry standard managed by the World Wide Web Consortium. It enables developers to describe data that is being exchanged between multiple devices, applications, or websites. The format and style are not integrated with the data specifically, so it can be used in multiple ways by XML-compliant sites, applications, or even smart devices. Most of the CRM applications that we have spoken of in this chapter are already XML-compliant. That is often the foundation for their ability to talk to each other and their open standard claim.

To make the transmission of XML effective, there is increasing support being built into CRM applications for the Simple Object Access Protocol (SOAP). There are variations, but it is ultimately a standard for sending an XML-formatted message from SOAP-enabled device to SOAP-enabled device.

There are many other Web services that are being adapted for CRM applications. Among them are Universal Description, Discovery, and Integration (UDDI); Web Services Description Language (WSDL); and for lower-level conversations between applications and Java clients, the Java Connectivity Architecture (JCA). As of 2002, with the widespread adoption of XML, SOAP is the increasingly popular next Web service being supported by the major CRM applications.

Despite their value, there are still some hurdles in their adoption. Security is perhaps the major concern, since breaching these still somewhat primitive protocols and standards can be done easily. There is a need to improve the authentication model so that it is obvious that what was sent is what was received. The current standard is HTTP, and replacing it is in active discussion.

Microsoft .NET is another set of Web services that provide the capability for customers to interact with multiple resources. How many of you reading this book have a Microsoft Passport for the use of Instant Messenger or MSN.com or a host of other services? The Hailstorm platform is the foundation for the integration of chat and IM services or other .NET capabilities with CRM applications or any other application. Java 2 Enterprise Edition (J2EE) compliant APIs and their mobility are another framework for interoperability.

But what the rapid adoption of Web services portends is a further step in the creation of this corporate ecosystem. The standards for communication and messaging become common, and that levels the playing field for interactions and transactions taking place at the lower and higher levels on the Web and between applications. The interoperability of processes becomes a given, not an exciting miracle.

Mobility Is Moving Fast

Once the processes are integrated and the standards and protocols set, the next step is the portability of all of this. Actually, this is the most established piece of the convergence puzzle. All the major CRM vendors have mobile applications for their sales and services modules. Siebel and PeopleSoft are particularly well heeled in this domain. Portability is still not a fait accompli, but carrying the global enterprise in your pocket is not that far from a reality now. It will get its final stamp if 2.5G and 3G systems and the incredible bandwidth they provide ever get past the politics that govern their adoption. The weakness now for mobility is bandwidth and insufficiently powerful hardware, but the stakes have been driven into the ground solidly.

The Real Time Paradigm

With portability comes speed. How does this global spiderweb of cross-devices, cross-functions, interoperable systems, and applications come up with answers in real time? If I'm dealing with a PeopleSoft application in Singapore, and drawing customer data from an SAP BW data store in London, and monitoring customer behavior online in New York, how am I going to provide those customers with what they need from those remarkably diverse sources? We've already seen the possibilities with the E.piphany ActivePath guided navigation and Real Time technology. Their Real Time engine is the current paradigm for a technology that can learn how to respond to you as a "real virtual salesperson."

The Customer Ecosystem in Action

Think about what I've said here. You are an end-user on a website that you are viewing via your HP Jornada 565 to order a specific set of tools necessary to your small business. Those tools are produced in Taiwan and stored in warehouses in London and Cleveland. One tool is in London, but everything else is in Cleveland. The website informs you of this, with a precise delivery time for both the Cleveland tools and the London tool. You are asked by the website if the delivery times are okay. You say yes to Cleveland and no to London. A series of questions pops up onscreen to help you ascertain a possible substitute or set of substitutes. You answer the questions, and a second later there are two options. Option 1 is a brand new set of other tools that also do what you want—all in Cleveland, but 10 percent more expensive. Option 2 is ordering a similar tool that is in Cleveland at roughly the same cost as the London tool, but with a shorter shipping time if you expedite delivery, which adds cost to the total and takes it beyond the London cost. You reject both. A third option then pops up based on your rejection, identifying another company that can sell you the original set of tools you want and has them at a site in Reno, Nevada, and can ship the same day if you pay today. You pay, they ship, and you get it in the exact time that they claimed you would.

This is the customer-centric convergence. This is what it is like to live in a corporate ecosystem, which I will now rename a customer ecosystem because of its revolution around the customer. Imagine the different systems that came into play here. CRM helps you decide how to make your purchase. ERP handles the payment for the tools. SCM investigates a multi-enterprise inventory that is warehoused around the world and does so almost instantaneously. Analytics decides what might be acceptable choices in real time so you don't have to wait on an email or a live representative to take care of this problem. The analytics are self-learning. They come up with the alternative from another company in this ecosystem as a third choice after you reject the first two. The sale is made. You are happy because you get what you want, due to sophisticated transportation management systems that helped plan the timely delivery routes to keep you satisfied. If for some reason your payment is rejected, you can bet Oracle Collections will be on your case!

This is the way that business will be done in the near future, given current market trends and the way that CRM will be going. Being excited about this customer-centric convergence means it isn't part of your mainstream existence yet. When it is, the business paradigm will have been transported to a new level. If you've adopted CRM now or are thinking of it, chances are that you'll have been on the very exciting ride to the effectively ordinary. That's the way I like it. No trouble, just happy customers.

Wild? Fanciful? Not at all. All the technologies described in this chapter already exist with CRM and enterprise applications. This book gave you CRM's map of the present and its promise of the future. What you decide to do with that information helps make that future.

APPENDIX

Customer Lifetime Value

For the business leader who has recently become a stakeholder in a CRM implementation, determining customer lifetime value (CLV) is essential. With companies discovering automated customer service and with customer acquisition and retention a contemporary mantra, having a means to benchmark the value of a customer or customers is a tremendous tool in determining what level of priority to give a customer. Despite the fact that we'd all like to give all customers equal time and treatment, since customers are not political candidates and companies are ordinarily not TV networks, equal time and treatment is not usually part of the deal.

Mei Lin Fung is a managing director of eFrontier Ventures and a pioneer in CRM. She worked with Tom Siebel at Oracle several years ago, when the first CRM systems were being developed and was directly involved in their development. Ms. Fung has become a recognized expert on both customer lifetime value and the "math" of marketing. Her CLV primer, reprinted here with her permission, provides you with a benchmark for determining customer life cycle value. Use it in good (corporate) health.

Customer Value Model, a Primer

Can Customer Retention Be Converted to Financial Value?

The following are useful definitions and explanations:

- ▶ Net present value: Valuing cash flow over time in today's dollars.

- ▶ Expected value: Probability of event × outcome of event.

- ▶ Measuring the expected financial benefits from retention and referrals provides for sustained investment in customer care. Moves beyond good will and lip service.

▶ Quantifying the expected results provides metrics for measuring the impact of customer care programs and actions. Turns data into knowledge that can be acted upon.

Simple Example 1: Calculate the Expected Revenue from a New Customer

Let's look at the two-year history of revenue from customers as shown in Table B-1. Suppose we find that 60 percent of customers come back and make a purchase the next year, while 40 percent of new customers never return. On average, how much revenue do you get from 1,000 new customers over two years?

Table B-1: Example of Expected Revenue Calculations for New Customers

	Year 1	Year 2
New customers	1,000	
Expected number of customers = 1,000 × retention rate of 60%		600
Average size of sale for each customer	$1,000	$1,000
Revenue	$1,000,000	$600,000
Expected revenue from 1,000 new customers, cumulative	$1,000,000	$1,600,000
Average revenue from each of the 1,000 initial customers = expected revenue by Year 2 divided by 1,000 = $1.6M/1,000 or		$1,600

Simple Example 2: Measure the Financial Profit from Increasing Customer Retention

The customer value model can be used to value customer retention. Customer lifetime value is defined as the profit you earn from a customer over their lifetime. This is the net present value (NPV) of the expected value of the profits you earn on sales from that customer in each of the years the customer remains a purchaser. Assume each customer delivers $1,000 in profit to you each year that they are a customer. We'll use expected value to project the expected profit from a new customer in Table B-2.

Table B-2: Example of Expected Profit Derived from Customer Retention

Customer retention rate	50%	
NPV discount rate	25%	
	Year 1	Year 2
New customers	1,000	

Table B-2: Example of Expected Profit Derived from Customer Retention (cont.)

Customer retention rate	**50%**	
NPV discount rate	**25%**	
	Year 1	**Year 2**
Expected number of customers = 1,000 × retention rate of 50%		500
Average profit from each customer	$1,000	$1,000
Profit	$1,000,000	$500,000
Discount rate 25%. Factor	100%	80%
NPV profit	$1,000,000	$400,000
Expected profit from 1,000 new customers, cumulative	$1,000,000	$1,400,000
Average profit over 2 years from each of the 1,000 initial customers = expected profit by Year 2 divided by 1,000 = $1.4M/1,000 or		$1,400

Customer care activities can change the retention rate and satisfaction. If improved customer care increases retention rate, profits will go up. If activities decrease retention rate, profits go down. Use the model shown in Table B-2 to determine the break-even point of customer care costs compared to increase in revenues due to loyal customers.

Balancing Responsiveness and Profits: Customer Value Model Case Study

As we consider the technology available for handling email, return on investment (ROI) is always an issue. The business process within which we consider such an investment is not fixed. We can decide to invest in technology that supports a business process that offers varying degrees of responsiveness to customer email. In Table B-3, we look at four examples of that process.

Table B-3: Example of Cases Addressing the Email Avalanche of 5,000 Emails per Day Received by ACME Company

	Case 1	Case 2	Case 3	Case 4
Automated		100%	95%	90%
Personal handling	100%	5%	10%	
Retention rate	50%	50%	40%	60%
Escalation	5% 1-800	8% 1-800	6% 1-800	4% 1-800

Table B-3: Example of Cases Addressing the Email Avalanche of 5,000 Emails per Day Received by ACME Company (cont.)

	Case 1	Case 2	Case 3	Case 4
Email handling	Handled individually	Fully automated	Partly automated	Part of integrated customer response
Response time	Received after 2–3 days delay on average	Less thorough but immediate	Equally thorough as Case 1; 1 day delay	More responsive, with timely personal touch; 1 day delay
Customer email process		Minimal customer research performed prior to design	Greater investment in design	Greatest investment in design
Ongoing research				Design improvements
Net result: customer lifetime value	−$104	−$100	−$3	$32

Net Result: Customer Lifetime Value

Table B-4 details how the results were obtained, invoking expected value and net present value. If you have questions, email Mei Lin Fung at mlf@resourceful.com.

Table B-4: Detailed Breakdown of CLV Derivation (Reprinted with permission of Mei Lin Fung.)

	Case 1	Case 2	Case 3	Case 4
Number of emails per day	5,000	5,000	5,000	5,000
Time frame	2 to 3 days	Immediate	Average 1 day	Average 1 day
Receipt confirmation	No	Yes	Yes	Yes
Customer email process	None	Self-service	Forms-based	Forms-based
Call center integrated email program	No	No	No	Yes
Response center business analysis investment	$—	$200,000	$100,000	$200,000
Response center technology cost	$—	$200,000	$100,000	$200,000
Relationship enhancement program	$—	$—	$—	$100,000
Response center human involvement	100%	0%	5%	20%

Table B-4: Detailed Breakdown of CLV Derivation (Reprinted with permission of Mei Lin Fung.) (cont.)

	Case 1	Case 2	Case 3	Case 4
Number of emails handled per rep per day	120	None	100	50
Number of emails requiring rep involvement	5,000	0	250	1,000
Number of reps required	41.7	n/a	2.5	20.0
Assume annual cost per rep, fully loaded	$50,000	n/a	$55,000	$60,000
Cost per rep per day	$200	n/a	$220	$240
Cost per email handled by a rep	$1.67	$—	$2.20	$4.80
People cost per day	$8,333	$—	$550	$4,800
Assume transactions that convert to 1-800 escalations	5%	8%	6%	4%
Number of 1-800 escalations per day	250	400	300	200
Assume cost per 1-800 escalation resolution	$25.00	$25.00	$25.00	$15.00*
Total costs in a year (Assume 250 working days)				
Required investment in email program	$—	$400,000	$200,000	$500,000
Email response rep cost per year	$2,083,333	$—	$137,500	$1,200,000
Cost of 1-800 transactions (escalated resolution)	$1,562,500	$2,500,000	$1,875,000	$750,000
Total costs	$3,645,833	$2,900,000	$2,212,500	$2,450,000
Total emails in a year	1,250,000	1,250,000	1,250,000	1,250,000
Prospects and others; breakout 80%	1,000,000	1,000,000	1,000,000	1,000,000
Customers; breakout 20% (Assume each customer sends emails/year: 25)	250,000	250,000	250,000	250,000
Number of Year 1 customers	10,000	10,000	10,000	10,000
Assume profit per customer/year (excluding above costs) Revenue less COGs and selling costs	$200	$150	$175	$200

Table B-4: Detailed Breakdown of CLV Derivation (Reprinted with permission of Mei Lin Fung.) (cont.)

	Case 1	Case 2	Case 3	Case 4
Number of customers Year 1	10,000	10,000	10,000	10,000
Assume customer retention in Year 2	60%	50%	40%	60%
Number of customers Year 2	6,000	5,000	4,000	6,000
Profits from customers in Year 1	$2,000,000	$1,500,000	$1,750,000	$2,000,000
Profits from customers in Year 2	$1,200,000	$750,000	$700,000	$1,200,000
NPV profits from customers in Year 2 (25% discount rate)	$960,000	$600,000	$560,000	$960,000
Gross profit from 10,000 Year 1 customers	$2,960,000	$2,100,000	$2,310,000	$2,960,000
Less cost of email handling Year 1	$(3,645,833)	$(2,900,000)	$(2,212,500)	$(2,450,000)
Less NPV cost of email, 1-800 handling Year 2 *for retained customers only (25% discount rate)*	$(350,000)	$(200,000)	$(128,800)	$(187,200)
Net profit from Year 1 customers over two years; *average expected value per Year 1 customer*	$(1,035,833)	$(1,000,000)	$(31,300)	$322,800
Customer value over two years	$(104)	$(100)	$(3)	$32

Index